A

TREATISE

ON

THE LAW OF COPYRIGHT

IN

BOOKS, DRAMATIC AND MUSICAL COMPOSITIONS, LETTERS AND OTHER MANUSCRIPTS, ENGRAVINGS AND SCULPTURE,

AS ENACTED AND ADMINISTERED IN

ENGLAND AND AMERICA;

WITH SOME

NOTICES OF THE HISTORY OF LITERARY PROPERTY.

By GEORGE TICKNOR CURTIS,

COUNSELLOR AT LAW.

THE LAWBOOK EXCHANGE, LTD.

Clark, New Jersey

2005

ISBN 1-58477-565-3

The quality of this reprint is equivalent to the quality of the original work.
The irregular pagination is reproduced as it was found in the original work.

Printed in the United States of America on acid-free paper

THE LAWBOOK EXCHANGE, LTD.
33 Terminal Avenue
Clark, New Jersey 07066-1321

Please see our website for a selection of our other publications and fine facsimile reprints of classic works of legal history:
www.lawbookexchange.com

Library of Congress Cataloging-in-Publication Data

Curtis, George Ticknor, 1812-1894.
A treatise on the law of copyright in books, dramatic and musical compositions, letters and other manuscripts, engravings and sculpture: as enacted and administered by England and America: with some notices of the history of literary property / by George Ticknor Curtis.
p. cm.
Originally published: Boston: C. C. Little and J. Brown, 1847.
Includes bibliographical references and index.
ISBN 1-58477-565-3 (cloth: alk. paper)
1. Copyright—United States. 2. Copyright—England. I. Title.

KF2994.C82004
346.7304'82—dc22 2004058201

A TREATISE

ON

THE LAW OF COPYRIGHT

IN

BOOKS, DRAMATIC AND MUSICAL COMPOSITIONS, LETTERS AND OTHER MANUSCRIPTS, ENGRAVINGS AND SCULPTURE,

AS ENACTED AND ADMINISTERED IN

ENGLAND AND AMERICA;

WITH SOME

NOTICES OF THE HISTORY OF LITERARY PROPERTY.

By GEORGE TICKNOR CURTIS,

COUNSELLOR AT LAW.

BOSTON:

CHARLES C. LITTLE AND JAMES BROWN.

LONDON:

A. MAXWELL AND SON,

33 BELL YARD, LINCOLN'S INN.

MDCCCXLVII.

BOSTON:
PRINTED BY FREEMAN AND BOLLES,
DEVONSHIRE STREET.

PREFACE.

It was originally my intention to have treated the kindred subjects of Copyrights and Patents for Useful Inventions, in the same work. But after having made some progress in both of these topics, the fact that very different classes of persons, out of the legal profession, are interested in the two subjects, has led me to publish this portion of my labors, as a distinct treatise. It will be followed, I hope, by a work on the law of Patents.

It will be seen that in discussing the various questions involved in this branch of the subject, I have not hesitated to express my own opinion, where the doctrine of decided cases seemed to me to be objectionable. Writers of treatises, in the manner of the English bar, generally content themselves with a dry abstract of the decisions, showing barely what the law is. This is well, as far as it goes. It is not the province of any writer to make the law, and he must certainly state the law as it is, if he means to have his book respectable and respected. But while his text should exhibit clearly the actual state of the law, he should never forget that he is dealing with principles; that it is his task, to exhibit the doctrine of the law, which is its life; and that unless he does this, his work, however accurately he may have strung the cases together, will be a mere collection of husks, the shell without the germinating principle that lies wrapt in the meat. If, then, he essays the task of eliminating the principle of a rule or a decision, tracing it in all its bearings and following it by the thread of analogy into other systems of jurisprudence, in order to ascertain whether it be really part of the general science, and not a local idea, he cannot avoid the expression of his own opinion, to some extent. The study of the law is the pursuit of truth; and he who undertakes to express and embody such truth, must occasionally express his own convictions.

His allegiance to the science which he serves, requires him to examine critically every recorded precedent, and to dissent, if dissent be needful; not as if he were ambitious to be regarded as an authority; but in the way of suggesting to those whose high function it is to revise and declare the law, the means of arriving at more correct results.

With this view, I have introduced into this work a discussion on the general doctrine of the English cases in relation to abridgments, which I consider contrary to principle. Should my observations induce any tribunal to reëxamine that doctrine, they will not have been published in vain.

It did not fall within the scope of this work, to discuss the reasonableness and justice of an international copyright. As between England and the United States I do not see how there can well be two opinions upon the desirableness of such an arrangement. The injustice of the present state of things to authors, especially in my own profession, is palpable and flagrant. The materials for an argument upon this question, which will be incapable of being answered, are fast accumulating, in the numerous proofs of mutual advantages obtained by those publishers in both countries, who have effected arrangements for the exchange and sale of their respective publications. These arrangements, however, rest upon no other security than the courtesy of "the trade," and can never effectually answer the purpose of a law securing the profits on American books in England and on English books in the United States. But this is not the place to enter upon the discussion of this interesting topic. I can only express the hope of seeing the argument at no distant day presented by some one, who will do justice to its great importance. But I could not dismiss this work from my hands, without avowing myself an advocate of an international copyright, both upon grounds of general policy, and of justice to authors.

Boston, October, 1847.

INDEX OF CASES CITED.

LAW OF COPYRIGHT.

INTRODUCTION.

THEORY OF THE RIGHTS OF AUTHORS.

Before we enter upon the field of municipal jurisprudence, it may be well to pass through the more enlarged region of natural law.[1] Literary Property has always asserted claims to a foundation in the principles of general right; and the nature and extent of those claims constitute an important subject of inquiry, whenever the interests of this property

[1] It is somewhat embarrassing, as all students of the Law of Nature know, to use terms accurately descriptive of that code which deals with the general rights of mankind, as held by the publicists of Christendom. The phrase, Natural Law, to an unaccustomed ear, would import simply that body of rules which, by the aid of reason, we deduce from the light of Nature, and which defines only the rights which Nature bestows. But as it has been long used to describe not only the naked rights of man in the natural state, but also the *status* of mankind after those rights have been to some extent modified by the conditions of civilized society, I have followed the example which I cannot control. Grotius, Puffendorff, Burlamaqui, and other writers, have fixed the sense in which the term Natural Law is most frequently used; and in this sense, it describes the natural rights of man after he has entered society, though many of them originate before society is formed.

are drawn into controversy, through any defect of positive law. The present inquiry therefore is, whether the right, to which jurists have given the name of Literary Property, has any foundation in the principles of that code of general law, which defines and establishes other kinds of property.

It is, of course, impossible to look to the mere light of nature for a solution of this question, or to find it in any speculations upon the condition of man in that imaginary state, which has been called the state of nature. Perhaps it would not be a violent supposition, to imagine a rude literature of poems or traditions, preserved and orally transmitted, before society, properly so called, has commenced. But, aside from the fact that the merely natural rights of man could confer no exclusive possession of ideas and sentiments thus uttered, it is to be observed, that the act of committing ideas to any corporeal substance, by means of signs, and the multiplication and delivery of copies, thus produced, for a valuable consideration, are things that can only take place after society is formed and an advanced stage of civilization has been reached. The art of printing, as well as every other systematic art of exhibiting ideas to the eye by means of characters, in any form and on any substance, is the creature of society; and when we add to the exercise of such an art the exchange of what is thus created for any other valuable commodity, or for the common representatives of value, we have reached an artificial and refined condition of mankind, in which the mere light of nature will no longer guide us. We must have recourse to those general principles of justice and right, which mankind are supposed to have brought originally from the state of nature, but by which they have agreed to be bound in a state of civilization, where they have become modified, enlarged, and strengthened.

It is very important to keep this distinction in view, because those who have maintained that literary property has no foundation but in the municipal code, have drawn most of their arguments against it from the naked law of nature, without perceiving, or without choosing to perceive, that it may derive its existence from those broad and comprehensive principles, which govern the relations of man in society, and which, although they have originated in the merely natural rights of man, extend their foundations to the support of his social condition.

It should be observed, also, that it is not at all necessary, in this inquiry, to enter into elaborate disquisitions upon the origin of property, or even to select from the various theories which different jurists or ethical writers have propounded concerning it. These theories are of no greater use, on this occasion, than to illustrate the important and admitted doctrines, on which the existence of property actually depends in civilized society. The primal origin of property opens a wide field of speculation, in which men of consummate and equal genius and learning have pursued different paths, and no theory has been constructed which meets with universal acceptance. But all the speculations of philosophers, from the time of Aristotle to the present age, have sprung from and again conducted to one fact — the existence of property itself; and while its existence has been variously accounted for, the different explanations of its origin have all tended to show, that there are certain great characteristics which mankind have universally attributed to the right thus found to exist, and certain great principles of justice by which they have found that it must be regulated. To these principles and characteristics we must look for a test, in order to answer the question — most material in the present discussion — What constitutes property ? Having satisfied ourselves on this head, we shall be able to say whether any supposed subject of the right possesses the general attributes of property, and whether it is agreeable to justice and fitness that it should be so recognized.

It is very generally conceded, that property, under the modifications and conditions with which we now have it, supposes the consent of mankind, and that those modifications and conditions do not spring from individual will alone.[1] It follows, therefore, that the

[1] Grotius, Droit de La Guerre, &c. liv. 2, ch. 2, § 10, tom. 1, (ed. Basle, 1746.) Rutherforth's Institutes, B. 1, c. 3. The consent of mankind does not indeed establish the principles on which property depends. Men cannot abolish those principles, and consequently they cannot abolish property, strictly and entirely. The Creator has made man a social being, and has made it necessary, for the development of his faculties and to accomplish the ends of his being, that he should

essential qualities of property must be those conditions which mankind have generally agreed in attributing to it.

1. First, then, the definition of property, on which mankind are agreed, is, that it embraces what is not common to the whole race, but belongs to a less number than the whole human family, whether one or more individuals. In a community of goods, among the whole race, or a nation, or a smaller collection of individuals, the right to use is in each individual, in the place of property ; but property in the goods continues, and this property itself is in the whole body. As soon, however, as property with reference to individuals is established, something more than the right to use follows. An exclusive title, which embraces the right to use and the right to exclude all others both from use and possession, and the right to transmit both use and possession to others, constitutes property, in the sense in which all mankind are agreed, implying the total separation of the object itself from a community of goods.

2. In the second place, all property possesses two uses, or qualities. First, it implies the right of pos-

live in some form of society. Some form of property is essential to the existence of society ; and through this chain of reasoning, property is to be traced, as to one of its main supports, to the will of the Creator. In addition to this, he has implanted in the human breast certain principles of justice which will not permit the violation of the essential rights of property, and has thus fortified its existence by the operations of conscience. At the same time, the general consent of mankind is rightly supposed to indicate the main qualities of property, because it actually exists according to the modifications and conditions which that consent has established.

session and use; which constitutes a part of the ownership, or appropriation of the individual. This right of possession and use is full and exclusive. The object may be enjoyed by the individual in any mode consistent with the general welfare; a limitation which does not arise from any inherent defect in the right itself, but is imposed upon it from without. Secondly, property implies the faculty of transmission, by exchange, or sale, or gift. Transmission, if unrestrained, carries with it the full and exclusive right of possession and use of the original owner, indefinitely, so that the object remains forever separated from a community of goods. But, as the original owner may grant the whole unrestricted right of possession and use, so it follows that he may grant a less right than he himself enjoyed, by restricting or qualifying the use. He may thus specify the uses for which he does or does not grant the possession, and may annex various conditions upon which the possession shall be held. The observance of these conditions is to be enforced by the same principles of justice which govern the whole title of the original owner. If he has granted only a part of his right, and the other part is usurped, the same principle of justice is violated, as when his whole right is usurped without his having granted any part of it.

3. In the third place, property may be in everything capable of these uses. Whatever admits of occupancy and of the transmission of occupancy may

be the subject of property. Whatever, on the contrary, does not admit of occupancy, and is not capable of being transferred with an exclusive title to others, cannot be the subject of property. Thus, light and air cannot of themselves be appropriated by individuals to the exclusion of the rest of mankind, because they cannot be included within limits and held and possessed in severalty. Each human being may use all of them that he requires for his own purposes, without exhausting the common stock, which is inexhaustible. In like manner, no man can sell or transfer to another the air or the light, because he cannot first obtain the exclusive occupancy thereof. One may sell or transfer peculiar advantages or positions for the enjoyment of all that portion of the air or the light, which one or more human beings can draw from the common stock, in actual use. But this creates no opportunity to occupy the great body of the air or the light, which are in themselves incapable of being held within limits or boundaries, or parcelled out into different proprietaries.

The same is true of the ocean. The great reasons why the ocean cannot be the subject of property form one of the most interesting topics in the law of nations, into which it would be too great a digression to enter here. It is sufficient to note the illustrations which they present of the qualities which belong to the subjects of property. The ocean cannot be occupied ; for although astronomers and geographers have traced imaginary circles of latitude and longitude, which theoretically divide its surface, nothing like actual occupation by boundaries or barriers has ever been attempted or can ever be possible. No part of the ocean can be taken and held in severalty, because no part of it can be designated as under occupation, by any limits or marks capable of being fixed upon its surface. Every nation and every individual may use it, as occasion requires, and such use in no degree diminishes or restrains the use of it by others, since the same waves will successively and forever transport the fleets of the whole world. Accordingly, there is no evidence that mankind have at any period entertained the intention of making the ocean the subject of property. It has ever been left as the common highway of nations, in and upon which the rights of all mankind, from the necessity of the case, are perfectly equal.[1]

On the other hand, the surface of the earth, and everything upon or beneath it, and everything upon or beneath the surface of the water, capable of being reduced into exclusive possession, may be the subject of property; and the exclusive possession carries with it the faculty of transmitting the whole of the same right, or a part of it, and of dictating in what manner and under what restrictions the subject of the right shall be used. In a refined state of civilization, these subordinate rights become themselves objects of distinct consideration, and are

[1] Grotius Droit de la Guerre, &c. Liv. 2, ch. 2, § 3. Azuni, Droit Mar. De l'Europe, tom. 1, ch. 1, § 5, 25.

made capable of distinct enjoyment, defined by positive rules, or defended by the general principles of justice. The right to pass over the soil, or to gather a definite portion of the fruit that grows upon it, may be severed from the ownership of the soil itself; and the grant of these subordinate rights does not necessarily suppose a grant of the proprietorship of the soil, or of any other of the rights of the original proprietor. The use of an animal, for a fixed period or in a certain manner, may be separated from the ownership of the animal, and a contract for the one does not imply a contract for the other.

We are to inquire, then, whether the claim of authors to the exclusive multiplication and sale of copies of their own literary productions can be brought within the fair scope of these principles. In determining this question, it is obviously necessary to define the right claimed, and to ascertain its essential character.

The right claimed by an author, after publication, is not to the exclusive possession or appropriation, intellectually, of the ideas and sentiments which he originates and puts upon paper. In the first place, such an appropriation becomes impossible, as soon as he imparts to others the means of an intellectual perception of his ideas; and in the next place, it is inconsistent with the very objects for which he publishes to others the conceptions of his own mind. Such an appropriation is impossible, because if I am permitted to read the ideas and sentiments which another has written, they become part of my intellectual possessions, as far as I can retain them in my memory, and no rule can be established which would deprive me of the opportunity to use them for my own enjoyment, or to impart a knowledge of them by speech to others. Such an appropriation by the author is also inconsistent with one of his objects in publishing his thoughts ; which is to impart his own thoughts to others, to induce others to make them part of their intellectual possessions, and thus to influence, refine, or instruct his fellow-men, to gain their admiration, excite their pity, or influence their conduct. The painter, who spreads upon canvass the immortal conceptions of genius, does not ordinarily intend to be the sole beholder of the images which he thus creates. The grandeur and loveliness, to which he has given outward form, he places before the eyes of others, in order, expressly, that they may fully appropriate into their own intellectual perceptions the ideas which he has embodied. In like manner, the author who writes and publishes, writes and publishes that he may be read — that other men may absorb into their own intellectual natures the thoughts which have had their birth in his reason or imagination, making them part and parcel of their own minds.

But it does not follow, because this is one of the objects of the painter or the author, in the exercise of their respective arts, that there may not be another purpose collateral to this, and in all respects consistent with it. It may be the purpose of both the painter and the poet, while they delight or instruct mankind, to receive a direct compensation for the pleasure or instruction which they impart ; and the question is, whether there is any right, by the exercise of which they can make this purpose effectual ; or, in other terms, whether there is anything to which the compensation can be made to attach.

The right to multiply copies of what is written or printed, and to take therefor whatever other possession mankind are willing to give in exchange, constitutes the whole claim of literary property. This claim leaves wholly undisturbed the opportunity of every reader to make an intellectual appropriation of the ideas suggested to him by the characters which he purchases ; it goes no farther than to assert an exclusive right to the profits which may be derived from the production of successive copies of the characters which, in a particular combination, represent a set of intellectual ideas. This right is to be derived, if at all, from the original, exclusive invention and possession by the author of the ideas themselves, and of the combination of characters which exhibits those ideas. If this right can be distinctly traced to original possession and invention, and if the exercise of the right involves the general attributes which belong to property, there is no reason why it should not be placed among the rights of property.

The author of every original literary composition

creates both the ideas and the particular combination of characters which represents those ideas upon paper. He is therefore an inventor, in two senses; and he has the exclusive possession, before publication, of his invention. Every one may use the elemental characters of which the original author makes use, in other combinations, but if any one uses them in the same precise combination, he exhibits necessarily the ideas of the original author. The two subjects of the invention are therefore inseparably interwoven, and when we contemplate them in their blended condition upon the written or printed page, they present to the mind the idea of one creation or invention only. Considered, however, with reference to its component parts, this invention consists of distinct creations, the ideas themselves and the combination of characters which exhibits those ideas to the eye. Both are new, both have never existed before, and both are capable of being retained in the exclusive possession of the original inventor.

The author, then, has in his possession a valuable invention, which he may withhold or impart to others at his pleasure. His dominion over his written composition is perfect, since it is founded both in occupancy or possession, and in invention or creation. No title can be more complete than this.

From this full and complete title flows the right to annex conditions to the transfer of such a written composition, when the author chooses to impart the possession of it to others. It cannot be doubted that this right is inherent in every possession vested in an individual by the rules of natural or positive law. It enables the owner of a literary composition to declare the purposes for which he grants it to others, in the same manner as it enables the owner of a piece of merchandise to declare that he grants the full property, or only a qualified use thereof, when he gives the possession of it to another. In both cases, the principles of justice require that this right of the original owner should be respected in the same manner as his original possession; for if it would be a violation of justice to deprive him of all his rights, when he has reserved them all, it is equally so to deprive him of a part of them, which he reserved, when he granted another part.

The right of literary property commences, therefore, from a full and exclusive intellectual possession of his ideas, by the author, coupled with the physical possession of the combination of characters representing those ideas, which he has traced upon paper or other material. As soon as publication takes place, it is no longer his object or intention to retain to himself the intellectual appropriation and enjoyment of the ideas themselves. What he does seek to reserve is, the exclusive multiplication of copies of that particular combination of characters, which exhibits to the eye of another the ideas that he intends shall be received. His power to do this depends upon his exclusive title to his invention, and upon the fact that each copy constitutes a valuable commodity, which he can exchange for other possessions.

The author's exclusive title is not only theoretically perfect, but it is practically acknowledged by mankind, since in every civilized society men are willing to give him valuable possessions in exchange for the opportunity to read what he has written. This opportunity men will purchase, if they cannot have it without purchase. It is in the power of the author to say, that they must purchase it, because he is the absolute owner of the copy which they desire to peruse. In the contract of sale which thus takes place, the owner of the literary composition may, of course, annex to the transfer any conditions that he pleases; and the question therefore next arises, whether he does not tacitly annex the condition, that other copies shall not be multiplied from the copy that he sells, and whether the purchaser does not take the copy burthened with this restriction.

The fair construction of a contract of sale requires, that the implied rights, which are supposed to be conferred by the seller upon the purchaser, should be determined by the apparent objects of the sale, and the price paid for the thing, when there are no express stipulations made. The delivery of a piece of merchandise for a price ordinarily held to be the measure of value for all the rights in it enjoyed by the owner, implies that the full right of property passes, including the right to use the thing in every form of which it is capable. But if A. is found to have in his possession a chattel formerly known to belong to B., and the consideration paid by A. is sufficient only to cover the value of the possession for a restricted use, and is far less than the full value of the entire and absolute dominion over the chattel, a fair presumption arises in natural equity, that the parties contemplated in the transaction the sale and purchase of a right to use the chattel for a limited purpose.

When the purchaser of a single copy of a book pays for it whatever may be the current price set by the author, if he can, by the rules of natural law, be supposed to acquire thereby all the uses of which the copy is capable, including the faculty of indefinite multiplication, he purchases for a grossly inadequate consideration what is perhaps a mine of wealth. The profits which may be derived from the indefinite multiplication of copies justly belong to some one. The author has created the opportunity of reaping them, and is the sole owner of the original copy from which all others must be taken. This opportunity or faculty of receiving what the public will certainly and freely give, in exchange for copies of a literary production, is therefore a franchise to which no one can show so good a title as the author, who has created it. To hold that he intends to sell it, when he parts with a single copy of his composition for a price implying, if it implies anything, a reservation of it, is wholly inconsistent with the rules of natural justice.[1]

But there is still another proof that the author reserves to himself the sole right of multiplying copies of his works, when he exposes single copies to sale. The object and purpose of publication are to put into the hands of the purchaser of a copy the means of becoming acquainted with the author's thoughts. What proof is there that the author contemplates anything more? If it is supposed that he intends to forego the profits which may be derived from his work, then the consequence also follows that he intends to abandon to others the reproduction of copies, without exercising any care for his own reputation, or any supervision over the manner in which the copies shall be reproduced. If this last supposition prevails, then the author himself defeats the object of publication, since he cannot make it certain to the reader or himself, that his thoughts will continue to be accurately represented. But the interests of the author are far too great to admit of any mere hypothesis as to his intentions, inconsistent with those interests. If he has not expressly or by necessary implication granted or abandoned his

[1] Puffendorff states succinctly the rule of natural equity concerning the equality of contracts. "Since contracts are necessary for my obtaining those things which I had no right to claim; and since it is presumed that a man gives nothing gratis, which he parts with upon contract; we cannot therefore think that any one designs to give away, by contract, more than he supposes he receives; and consequently a contract can give a right to another man's goods no further than as they are equivalent to something which that other man receives." Puffendorf's Law of Nature, &c. by Barbeyrac. B. v. ch. iii. § 1.

rights, it must be presumed that he has reserved them to himself, since it is not ordinarily consistent with human motives, for men to throw away vast interests, which touch both their fortunes and their fame.

That there is no such presumption against the author's reservation, is proved by the practice and consent of mankind. Every civilized nation, of any literary rank, has some law recognizing the property of authors in their works.[1] This universal legislation is founded in a conviction that such property exists in natural justice ; for although the protection thus afforded by positive law is generally temporary, and embodies, as I shall hereafter suggest, a compromise between the strict rights of the author and the demands of society, yet it proves the existence of those rights, by undertaking to reconcile them with the wants and interests of the public at large. There is no other hypothesis to account for the careful legislation of so many countries.

Such being the nature of the author's claim, and such the right upon the exercise of which it depends, it is in the nature of property, because there is in possession an invention capable of being made a source of profit, and which will certainly produce profit to the proprietor, if society does not permit

[1] For a view of the legislation of different countries, on the rights of authors, see the work of M. Charles Renouard, Traité des Droits D'Auteurs, Paris, 1838, t. 1. He gives the legislation of England, France, the United States of America, Holland and Belgium, the different States of Germany, Denmark, Russia, the Kingdom of the two Sicilies, and Sardinia.

others to avail themselves of it without returning any compensation. As soon as the law declares that the profits arising from the multiplied copies of this invention shall not be taken by any one but the author, such profits immediately flow from the use of the invention ; and before the enactments of positive law have so declared, the law of nature makes it clear, that these profits belong to him who has created and holds the invention, and who can withhold it from others, until by some pact or convention, express or implied, he has secured the compensation which he sees fit to demand.

It is not unworthy of remark, also, that public policy requires a recognition of the natural rights of authors, as the basis of legislation. It does so, because the highest policy of society is justice. There is, in the requirements of national character, the same high necessity for honesty and good faith, that lies with the whole weight of moral obligation upon the individual. Society cannot afford to be unjust. Its prosperity is the aggregate prosperity of its members. Its character, its peace and dignity, the amount of happiness which it may attain, or be the instrument of attaining to its members, depend directly upon the harmony that reigns through its internal relations, and upon the degree to which it has enforced the observance of justice and respect for the great maxims in which the essence of justice is enshrined. When society ceases to be just, it ceases to be safe. No infraction of a public principle ever takes place, without being followed by retributive social evils. When, by a total neglect of the natural rights of authors, injustice is done to a class of conspicuous and important benefactors of their race, the violation of principle becomes the more glaring, and the injury to the moral sense of society more striking, from the species of ingratitude involved in the neglect. There is scarcely any civilized people, who would not be shocked by a proposal to withdraw all protection from the interests of literary property.

Public policy also requires a careful protection of the rights of authors, because literature flourishes most when it reaps the rewards consequent upon such protection. There can be no doubt that the body of literature, now extant in the English language, owes a vast deal to the acknowledgment of these rights, imperfect as it has sometimes been. Although no legislative protection existed before the reign of Queen Anne, there was a protection founded in an acknowledged common law right, and the practice of printers and booksellers, which may be traced as far back as the reign of Queen Elizabeth. The existing literature of England, of a date subsequent to that time, and the whole of that of America, have been produced under the stimulus afforded by a greater or less degree of security to the pecuniary interests of authors. It is not easy to say, with certainty, that any portion of this literature would not have been produced, if an author's exclusive right to the proceeds of publication had never been admitted; nor is it easy to find many works, now classical in the language, or of an important character, which we know certainly were written without any view to profit, whether large or small. What we know certainly, is, that from Shakspeare to our own day, everything has been written under some state of the law, admitting an author's right, and that very few great authors have avoided or neglected all recompense for their writings, while the vast majority have written for money as well as fame.[1]

But it is not solely for the encouragement of genius in its transcendent displays, that it concerns the interests of society to protect the rights of authors. The great classes of compilers and scholars, whose works embody the learning of a country or an age — embracing the historian, the lexicographer, the critic and the commentator; the whole body of scientific writers, from the author of a mechanism of the heavens to the author of the last shilling arithmetic; the various grades of writers in every department, from the higher votaries of letters to the day-laborers in the vineyard of knowledge, are all necessary to the formation of a national literature and the development of a general culture. All require that the fruits of their labor, like the fruits of other men's labor, should be under the protection of the law;

[1] There is very little reason to doubt, that the right of authors was practically acknowledged as a common law right, in the reign of Elizabeth. (See post, ch. 2.)

for like other men, they labor for subsistence and the comforts of life, and it is only when these are secured to them, that they can be expected with certainty to labor at all. Glory may be the reward of genius in solitary and irregular cases ; but no man ever wrote a spelling-book or compiled an almanac for that unsubstantial and thankless commodity.

It remains to answer certain objections. In the first place, it may be asked, if the rights of authors are so clearly founded in natural justice, how is it that the law of nations, which recognizes and respects most of the rights of property, has not recognized the property of authors in their works, but has allowed them to be treated, in a foreign country, as if they were *publici juris ?*

The law of nations is an admirable system of rules and principles, tending, more or less directly at different periods, to perfection, but not entirely complete, at present. It has long been accustomed to regard the title of movable property as sacred, wherever found ; so that the real owner may pursue and reclaim it in any country with which his own is at peace. Even in the tumult of war, it exerts a searching and efficient energy, regulated by the maxims of a broad jurisprudence, to distinguish between neutral and belligerent interests ; in order that nothing but the strict rights of warfare shall be allowed to divest the ownership of property. But the law of nations has not always been so careful ; the time has been, when the goods of the merchant, cast by tempestuous weather upon a foreign shore, have been accounted the lawful prey of any occupant. It is manifest, therefore, that the law of nations is a progressive system. The fact, that its principles have never been applied to a certain case, does not disprove the existence of principles, which might be made to regulate it.

At present, however, these principles have not been applied to the rights which we are now considering. The actual law of nations knows no exclusive right of an author to the proceeds of his work, except that which is enforced by the municipal law of his own country, which can operate nowhere but in its own jurisdiction. As soon as a copy of a book is landed in any foreign country, all complaint of its republication is, in the absence of a treaty, fruitless, because no means of redress exist, except under the law of the author's own country. It becomes public property, not because the justice of the case is changed, by the passage across a sea or a boundary, but because there are no means of enforcing the private right. The law of nations, being in great part a body of customary rules, depends upon the practice of nations; and what has not been practised, cannot be affirmed to be part of that law. But the real equity of the case, founded in the principles which govern other rights, requires that the author's interest in his book should be respected throughout the globe, as much as the interest of a merchant in a bale of goods. The natural justice of the case, therefore, has between some nations led to treaty stipulations, by which alone the *casus omissus* of the public law can be supplied; and the example of those nations, which have thus supplied the omission, shows what consistency with the principles of justice requires.

In the next place, it may be asked, how the actual legislation of most countries, limiting the duration of an author's right, is to be reconciled with the theory which gives him, if it gives anything, a perpetuity? If the theory, which founds an author's exclusive right to the proceeds of his work in natural justice, be correct, it certainly involves as a consequence the perpetual duration of the right. The legislation of England and America, and of many other countries, has practically abridged the author's property, and reduced it to a term of years. Does it follow that society, in this course of legislation, is unjust?

The actual legislation on this subject should be regarded as a compromise. The claim of authors, resulting from the principles of natural right, involves the perpetual duration of the property. But in order that such property should be of any value, it is necessary that society should interfere actively for its protection. It can interfere by the enactment of penalties, which, in order to be effectual, must be severe; or it can interfere by prohibition, which is a stern and summary exercise of power. Society will not ordinarily be willing to apply such remedies in favor of an exclusive right, any farther than it finds such a course beneficial to its own interests, in the broadest sense of the term. A perpetuity in literary property involves some inconveniences, which may come to be serious; one of which is, that the text of an author, after two or three generations, if the property be retained so long by his descendants, belongs to so many claimants, that disputes must arise as to the right to publish, which are very likely to prevent publication altogether.[1] This would be a great misfortune to society; and it is to guard against this and other inconveniences, that society may fairly require, as the price of its active protection by stringent enactments, that the author and his representatives should surrender a part of their full right re-

[1] The Emperor Napoleon is reported to have stated this objection to a perpetuity, in council, with his characteristic practical wisdom, as follows: "Napoleon dit que la perpétuité de la propriété dans les familles des auteurs aurait des inconvéniens. Une propriété littéraire est une propriété incorporelle qui, se trouvant dans la suite des temps et par le cours des successions divisée entre une multitude d'individus, finirait, en quelque sorte, par ne plus exister pour personne; car, comment un grand nombre de propriétaires, souvent éloignés les uns des autres, et qui, après quelques générations, se connaissent à peine, pourraient-ils s'entendre et contribuer pour réimprimer l'ouvrage de leur auteur commun? Cependant, s'ils n'y parviennent pas, et qu'eux seuls aient le droit de le publier, les meilleurs livres disparaîtront insensiblement de la circulation.

"Il y aurait un autre inconvénient non moins grave. Le progrès des lumières serait arrêté, puisqu'il ne serait plus permis ni de commenter, ni d'annoter les ouvrages; les gloses, les notes, les commentaires ne pourraient être séparés d'un texte qu'on n'aurait pas la liberté d'imprimer.

"D'ailleurs, un ouvrage a produit à l'auteur et à ses héritiers tout le bénéfice qu'ils pouvent naturellement en attendre, lorsque le premier a eu le droit exclusif de le vendre pendant tout sa vie, et les autres pendant les dix ans qui suivent sa mort.

"Cependant si l'on veut favoriser davantage encore la veuve et les héritiers, qu'on porte leur propriété à vingt ans." LOCRÉ, *Legislation Civile de la France*, t. ix. pp. 17, 18, 19. Renouard, Droits D'Auteurs, tom. 1, p. 387.

garded as a right according to the general principles of natural justice.

The great problem in legislation is to determine the point where this surrender ought to be made. It is a mixed question of policy and justice, with regard to which no positive rule can be laid down. The experience of nearly all nations, however, has shown that the interests of literature, as well as the dictates of natural justice, require that the children of an author should be secured in the enjoyment of the right, for some period after his capacity to provide for them has ceased.[1]

[1] In England, as the law now stands, a copyright lasts during the author's life, and for seven years after his decease; or for forty-two years, in case the life is terminated before thirty-seven years from the day of first publication, (5 & 6 Vict. c. 45, § 3.) In France, the property in a work is secured to the author for his life, to his widow for her life, in case the marriage contract endows her with it, and, after their death, to the children for twenty years. In Holland and Belgium, the duration of a copyright is to the author for his life, and to his heirs and representatives for twenty years after his death. In Prussia, copyright lasts for the author's life, and his heirs have a term of thirty years from his decease. In Russia, it is for the author's life, and for twenty-five years to the heirs. In Austria, the rights of authors do not descend to their heirs. In Denmark, Norway, Sweden, and Spain, copyright is perpetual. Godson on Patents and Copyright, pp. 319, 320. Renouard, Droits D'Auteurs, tom. 1, p. 226, et seq. In the United States, it is for twenty-eight years, with a right of renewal by the widow or children for fourteen years more. Act 3d Feb. 1831, §§ 1, 2.

CHAPTER I.

HISTORY OF LITERARY PROPERTY.

THE object of the present chapter is to state succinctly the history of Literary Property, in the jurisprudence of England and America, from the earliest recognition of such property to its modern condition. Our attention is, of course, first to be directed to its origin in England, as a right of property under the law of England. The foundation of the right in the law of general justice applicable to all property, has been already considered.

The term, "copy of a book," has been used for ages in England, to signify the sole right of printing, publishing and selling a written composition.[1] The question whether, at the common law, the author of such a composition formerly had a perpetual right of property in his work, has been attended with some difficulty; but whoever, at the present time, carefully considers the various authorities bearing

[1] Millar *v.* Taylor, 4 Burr. Rep. 2311. "I use the word 'copy,' said Lord Mansfield in this case, 'in the *technical sense* in which that name or term has been used for ages, to signify an *incorporeal right* to the *sole* printing and publishing of somewhat intellectual, communited by letters."

upon the question, and the manner in which it came finally to be settled against the perpetual right of property, can have little doubt that such a right once existed in England. If this be true, it follows that subsequent legislation, so far as it abridged this right of property, took away what once belonged to authors by the common law of England.

Until the year 1640, the crown exercised an unlimited authority over the press, which was enforced by the summary powers of search, confiscation, and imprisonment, given to the stationers' company, and by the then supreme jurisdiction of the star-chamber. These are undoubtedly lights to which we should not turn for safe guidance upon any question of a public nature, or to ascertain the modern rights of the subject against the crown. But it cannot escape the attention of any one, accustomed to investigate a question of private law, that if, in the period of the most arbitrary features that have at any time existed in the English constitution — features, of which it has now so divested itself that we are accustomed to speak of them as utterly repugnant to the true principles of the constitution — a matter of private right was held, respected, contemplated and even enforced, through that very jurisdiction now discarded and justly reprobated, such a right must have historical evidence in its favor of grave and striking character. Whatever in the law of England concerning justice between man and man, has lived through those periods of the constitution when arbitrary power and prerogative most flourished, when the crown exercised powers founded in scarcely any discretion but that of policy and of the exigencies of state, must, in the eye of juridical history, be deemed of great value. If it happens, as is really the case with regard to the present subject, that the private right, thus recognized and assumed to exist by the supreme power in the state, was one that in no way conflicted with the supposed rights or actual policy of the crown, and if the crown itself asserted and enforced rights of its own of a similar character and depending upon similar principles, the testimony in favor of the doctrine upon which the right is founded is as clear and unexceptionable, as the nature of such an historical inquiry can admit.

As early as the year 1556, decrees and ordinances of the star-chamber regulated the manner of printing and the number of presses throughout the kingdom, and prohibited all printing against the force and meaning of any of the statutes or *laws* of the realm, or of any injunction, *letters-patent*, or ordinances set forth or to be set forth by the grant, commission, or authority of the crown.[1] The rights of owners of copies were not here expressly recognized, as they afterwards were, except so far as they are implied in the prohibition against violating letters patent.[2]

[1] 4 Burr. R. 2312.

[2] It will be seen hereafter, that the letters patent here referred to were not grants to authors, of property in their own works, but grants of the right to print books the sole printing of which belonged to the crown, either by naked prerogative, or by the title of property. Upon which of these two titles the right

By another decree of the star-chamber, of the 23d of June, 1585,[1] every book was required to be licensed; and any one was forbidden to print "against the form or meaning of any restraint contained in any statute or laws of the realm, or the true intent and meaning of any *letters-patent*, commissions or prohibitions under the great seal, or contrary to any allowed *ordinance* set down for the good government of the stationers' company." That this decree was intended to recognize and did recognize some rights of literary property, of some kind, is manifest from what took place in the next reign. In the 21st of James I. a proclamation of the 25th September, 1623, recited the above decree of the 28th of Elizabeth, and declared that the same had been evaded, amongst other ways, "by printing beyond seas such allowed books, works or writings as have been imprinted within the realm by such to whom the sole printing thereof by letters patent, or lawful ordinance or authority, doth appertain;" and then the proclamation enforced the decree referred to.[2]

Now, that the crown did not interfere in this manner simply for the purpose of restraining the press, or of asserting its own rights, is manifest from both the decree and the proclamation. Private rights and private property are protected in both. The kinds of private property thus protected must have included more than the rights derived by grant from the

of the crown is supposed to depend, will also be stated.

[1] 28 Eliz. See 4 Burr. R. 2312.
[2] 4 Burr. 2312.

crown, because the words of the decree and the proclamation embrace other rights of "sole printing," as well as rights which depended on letters-patent. Books, of which the copyright was recognized by ordinance of the stationers' company, were included, and there is a fair implication that books otherwise appertaining to their owners by the "laws" of the realm were also included, and the sole right of printing such books depended on the property of the author, and not on grant from the crown. But even in cases of letters-patent, the argument which deduces the right from property in the crown, is, as we shall see, far stronger than any other view of it that can be taken.

There was another decree of the star-chamber, of the 11th July, 1637, which should here be cited, and by which "no person was to print or import (printed abroad) any book or copy which the company of stationers, or *any other person* hath or shall, by any letters-patent, order or entrance in their register-book, *or otherwise*, have the right, privilege, authority, or allowance solely to print." [1]

There are one or two remarks now to be made with reference to the whole period from 1556 to 1640, at which time the star-chamber was abolished. The judicial proceedings of that tribunal are supposen to be chiefly lost or destroyed, and prosecutions for printing or pirating another man's copy, or other-

[1] 4 Burr. 2312.

wise printing unlawfully, cannot now be found. But it is obvious that no man could print another man's copy, because he could not obtain a license so to do, for two reasons. In the first place, the literature of England was not then so extensive, that the officers of the crown, whose duty it was to license publications, would not, generally, know to whom the copyright of any work belonged, which any applicant might find it worth while to reprint. There was, therefore, little danger that licenses would be incautiously granted. In the second place, the decree of 28th Elizabeth prohibited all printing "contrary to any allowed ordinance set down for the good government of the stationers' company." Now, although we know of no ordinance or by-law of the company relative to copies, until after the year 1640, yet from 1558 to 1582 there are, it is said, entries in the records of the company which show that copies were entered *as property*, and that pirating was punished.[1] This shows the contemporary opinion as to this species of property, and renders it highly probable that no license could have been obtained for printing another man's copy, because it would have been asking for an authority to do what was then held to be immoral, dishonest, and unjust. It is a just inference, that what was so held by the stationers' com-

[1] 4 Burr. 2313. In 1583, two printers, Wolf, and Ward, insisted upon a right of printing all books, even where there were copyrights existing. Stowe, 223, tit. Stationers' Company. But commissioners, appointed by the crown, willed them to desist. See Wedderburn's Argument in Tonson *v.* Collins, 1 W. Black. R. 304.

pany, in that age a recipient of royal favor and of extraordinary powers from the crown, would have been so held by the crown itself.[1]

In 1640, the star-chamber was abolished, and all regulations of the press and decrees against printing, as well as all the charter powers given to the stationers' company, were abolished. But the licentiousness that ensued led the two houses of parliament to pass a new ordinance, which prohibited printing unless the book had been first *licensed* and entered in the register of the stationers' company; and it also prohibited printing without consent of the owner, or importing (if printed abroad,) upon pain of forfeiting the same *to the owner or owners* of the copies of the said books, &c.[2]

There could be no owners of copies in England at the time when this ordinance took effect, except those who held the right to print certain books by letters-patent, or those whose title was that of authors or proprietors at common law. It is not very probable that the parliament of that day passed this part of the ordinance for the purpose of protecting grants of the crown; and as to all other books, the whole foundation of literary property, if it depended upon former decrees of the star-chamber or proceedings of the stationers' company, had been swept

[1] It would seem, therefore, that down to the year 1640, (as has been well remarked by Willes, J. in Millar *v.* Taylor,) "copies were protected and secured from piracy by a much speedier and more effectual remedy than actions at law or bills in equity."

[2] Passed in 1643. 4 Burr. 2314. 4 Black. Com. 152, note.

away. But these decrees and proceedings were not the sources of the right of property; they were merely protective in their character; and it can therefore admit of little doubt, that the understanding of the parliament was, that the property existed at common law, in the "owners" whom they chose to protect, otherwise this provision in their ordinance could only have contemplated "owners" by letters-patent.[1]

There is, however, a contemporary testimony, which places this matter in a very clear light. In November, 1644, Milton published his great tract for the liberty of unlicensed printing, against this ordinance, addressed to the parliament by whom it had been passed. His vigorous and manly denunciation was directed solely against the system of licensing. He expressly excepts from his censure that part of the ordinance which was designed for the protection of the rights of property in authors, and distinctly affirms that one of the "glossing colours" used, to make the ordinance pass, was "the just retaining of each man his several copy, which God forbid should be gainsaid."[2]

[1] Selden sat in the parliament which passed this ordinance.

[2] Milton's "Speech for the Liberty of Unlicensed Printing, to the parliament of England." He had previously said, "For that part which preserves justly *every man's copy to himself*, or provides for the poor, I touch not; only wish they be not made pretences to abuse and persecute honest and painful men, *who offend not in either of these particulars.* But that other clause of licensing books, which we thought had died with his brother quadragesimal and matrimonial when the prelates expired.—I shall now attend with such a homily, as shall lay before ye," &c. . . .

The testimony of Milton must be allowed to have some weight upon this question. He knew the state of the literature of England, if any man knew it, and he cannot be supposed to have thus recorded the general recognition of the rights of authors, and to have thus expressly admitted what the ordinance was intended, by the provision in question, to protect, without knowing of what he affirmed.[1] Many of the arguments used by him against the licensing system also show, incidentally, that the ordinance, when it spoke of "owners," must have contemplated proprietors of books, of which the public might demand successive editions; for his arguments show — as indeed, we know without resorting to them, —

[1] Milton spoke upon this occasion in the name and at the solicitation of the scholars of England. "I might say, if without envy, that he whom an honest quæstorship had endeared to the Sicilians, was not more by them importuned against Verres, than the favorable opinion I had among many who honor ye, and are known and respected by ye, *loaded me with entreaties and persuasions*, that I would not despair to lay together that which just reason should bring into my mind, toward the removal of an undeserved thraldom upon learning. That this is not, therefore, the disburdening of a particular fancy, but the common grievance of all those who had prepared their minds and studies above the vulgar pitch to advance truth in others, and from others to entertain it, thus much may satisfy. *And in their name* I shall, for neither friend nor foe, conceal what the general murmur is." Lord Mansfield has said, that "the single opinion of Milton, speaking after much consideration to what had been the general consent of the kingdom for ages, is stronger than any inferences that can be drawn from gathering acorns or seizing on a vacant piece of ground." 4 Burr. 2399. It is curious that, in nearly a century after Milton's opinion was thus recorded, his own Paradise Lost, in the hands of the assigns to whom the sum of £5 had passed it from him and his heirs forever, was to come before the chancellor of England, to claim successfully for its *then owners* their right in their "several copy." But his great authority does not seem to have been alluded to upon that occasion. Tonson *v.* Walker, before Lord Hardwicke, in 1739. Cited 4 Burr. 2325, and 3 Swanst. 673.

that such books were then proportionally not more rare in the literature of England than they now are.[1]

In 1649, the long parliament made an ordinance, which forbids printing any book legally granted, or any book entered, without consent of the *owner*, upon pain of forfeiture, &c.

In 1662, the licensing act of 13 and 14 Car. II. was passed, prohibiting the printing of any book unless first licensed and entered in the register of the stationers' company, and prohibiting also the printing without consent of the *owner*, upon pain of forfeiting the book and 6*s*. 8*d*. for each copy, half to the king, half to the owner ; to be sued for by the owner in six months.

It is remarkable that there had been thus far no legislation in England, which grants, creates, or establishes the property of an author in his own works. The liberty of publishing, and sometimes the presses which he should employ, had been subjected to

[1] "And what if the author shall be one so copious of fancy, as to have many things well worth the adding come into his mind after licensing, while the book is yet under the press, which not seldom happens to the best and diligentest writers ; and that perhaps a dozen times in one book . . . . . Nay, which is more lamentable, if the work of any deceased author, though never so famous in his lifetime, and even to this day, comes to their hands for licence to be printed, or reprinted, if there be found in his book one sentence of a venturous edge, uttered in the height of zeal, (and who knows whether it might not be the dictate of a divine spirit?) yet not suiting with every low decrepit humour of their own, though it were Knox himself, the reformer of a kingdom, that spake it, they will not pardon him their dash ; the sense of that great man shall to all posterity be lost, for the fearfulness, or the presumptuous rashness of a perfunctory licenser. And to what an author this violence hath been lately done, and in what book of greatest consequence to be faithfully published, I could now instance, but shall forbear to a more convenient season."

regulation and control; but from the introduction of printing to the fourteenth year of the reign of Charles II. it had been assumed that the author of a book has a property in his copy, and successive parliaments had provided for his protection as an "owner," without undertaking to confer that character upon him. The state of the literature of England in 1662 will show that when parliament provided for the protection of "owners," they could not have intended merely the royal patentees, passing by the whole existing body of literature then known by every intelligent Englishman, at least by name. The legislators of that day may also be presumed at least to have known that there were living authors then writing and publishing, not without fame and honor in the land.

The licensing act of Charles II. was continued by several acts of parliament, but expired on the 9th of May, 1679.[1] In 1681, all legislative protection having ceased, the stationers' company adopted an ordinance or by-law, which recites that several members of the company have *great part of their estates in copies*; that by ancient usage of the company, when any book or copy is duly entered in their register to any member, such person hath always been reputed and taken to be proprietor of such book or copy, and ought to have the sole printing thereof. The

[1] In this year, an action on the case was brought in the king's bench, for printing the Pilgrim's Progress, of which the plaintiff alleged himself to be the true proprietor. Ponder *v.* Bradyl, Lilly's Entries, 67. But it does not appear whether the action was proceeded in.

ordinance then further recites that this privilege and interest had *of late* been often violated and abused ; and then it provides a penalty against such violation by any member or members of the company, where the copy had been duly entered in their register. The true view of this ordinance would seem to be, that the members of the stationers' company, finding their estates in copies, which belonged to them by the common law, no longer under the protection of the licensing act, the repeal of which had incidentally withdrawn the protection that had always been inserted in it, though it had necessarily no connection with the system of licensing, undertook to provide for the failure of legislation, as far as they could, by an ordinance applicable of course to their own members only. The ordinance is not to be cited as any other proof of what the common law right was, than as it shows, in connection with other historical proofs, how it was then supposed to be. Now I do not understand this ordinance to rest the exclusive right upon entry in the register book, or upon their usage to respect each other's rights as derived merely from entry. It declares, as a separate and distinct inducement, that "several members of this company have great part of their *estates in copies*." By "estates" must have been meant their capital ; and "copies" they must have intended to use in the ancient technical sense of the sole right to print particular books. This right existed, if at all, by the law of England, and not by the usage of the stationers' company, whose members could have individually no different rights of property from all the rest of the king's subjects. If a member of the stationers' company held a "copy," any other man in England, not a member of that corporation, could also hold a "copy." But as a further inducement to the provision of a penalty upon their own members against violating the rights of another member, they recited the ancient usage of the company to respect these rights when brought to the notice of the company, by entry in their register. It was much the same as if an association of persons were to agree that any one of their number should pay a penalty for violating the acknowledged rights of property of any other person in the association, provided such rights were duly entered in their common records. It would not be an attempt to create the right; but it would justly be regarded as an acknowledgment of the existence of such a right.

The licensing act of Charles II. was revived in the 1st of James II. c. 7, and continued by 4 W. & M. c. 24, and finally expired in 1694. In this last year, the stationers' company, apparently with the same view of supplying, as far as related to themselves, the failure of legislative protection, passed a similar ordinance, or by-law, in a slightly different and stronger phraseology. The same observations apply to this ordinance as to that of 1681.[1]

[1] The two ordinances are recited at large in the special verdict found in Millar *v.* Taylor, 4 Burr. R. 2303.

Having now brought the history of private copyright down to the Revolution of 1688, it is necessary here to turn back to survey a collateral and important branch of the subject, the prerogative copies.

From the first introduction of printing, it was considered to be a matter of state. The reasons upon which it was so regarded were various. It was held to be a matter of a public nature ; that it was a new art introduced by the king, and therefore he had a prerogative right to prescribe the persons who should exercise it ; and that the unrestrained liberty of printing was dangerous. These reasons were from time to time advanced as the foundation for that control exercised over the press from its first introduction to the year 1688.[1] But there were also certain other special reasons assigned for the exclusive right claimed by the crown in certain publications, and granted to individuals by letters-patent, which have been justly supposed to proceed upon the notion of property. At the same time it must be admitted, that with the idea of property was also advanced the claim of naked prerogative, resting upon reasons of state ; and it is not very easy to distinguish, upon the earlier authorities, what the precise grounds were, on which the courts intended to rest the title to the various prerogative copies. In the main, however, this class of cases undoubtedly does show that the crown sometimes claimed a property in copies

[1] Bacon's Abridgment, tit. Prerogative, F. 5. Carter, 90. 3 Mod. 75. Skin. 234. Vern. 275.

entirely analogous to that belonging to private individuals.

The works that have been at different times claimed as belonging to the crown, are all law books, including the Reports and the Statutes, Almanacs, the Latin Grammar, the Book of Common Prayer, and the English translation of the Bible. The earliest case, of which we have any distinct account, was between a Colonel Atkyns and certain members of the stationers' company, in the 18th Charles II. Atkyns, as the law-patentee, claimed the right to print all law books; the defendants had printed Rolle's Abridgment. A bill was brought for an injunction, which the lord chancellor granted against all the members of the stationers' company. An appeal was taken to the house of lords, and it was there argued upon the footing of the king's property in law books, because he pays the judges who pronounced the law; and the decree of the lords, affirming the decree below, has always been cited as a recognition of the copyright in the king, though of course the claim, in its full extent, has been since exploded.[1]

The next case was that of Roper *v.* Streater, in the 22d – 24th Charles II. Roper bought of the executors of Mr. Justice Croke the third part of his Reports. Streater was law-patentee, and printed these Reports "over Roper," who brought an action of debt against him on the licensing act of 13th and 14th Charles II. Streater pleaded the king's grant,

[1] Carter, 89. Bacon's Abridg. Prerogative, F. 5. 4 Burr. 2315.

and the demurrer therefore presented the question between the crown and a purchaser of the author. In short, the question was, whether the king or the plaintiff was the "owner" of these Reports, in the sense of the statute. In the king's bench, judgment was for the plaintiff and against the king's patent; the court considering the plaintiff as owner of the copy at common law by purchase of the executors of the author.[1] This judgment was reversed in the house of lords, upon the ground that the king was the owner of the copy, and therefore that the executors of the author could convey nothing.[2]

The case of the Stationers' Company *v.* Seymour, in the 29th Charles II. was a question between certain grantees of the crown and certain other persons who had printed Gadsbury's Almanac. The court put their decision, in part, upon the fact, that an almanac has no certain author, and that the property of such books is in the king. The defendants claimed to have added "prognostications" to the old almanac; but the court said "these additions did not alter the case, no more than if a man should claim a property in *another man's copy*, by reason of some inconsiderable additions of his own."[3] The reason was also assigned that the defendant's almanac was the same as that printed before the book of

[1] Skinner, 234. 1 Mod. 257. Bac. Abr. Prerog. F. 5. 4 Burr. 2316.

[2] Ibid. It seems, however, that reasons of state were also assigned. See Bacon, ut sup. and the report in Skinner, 234.

[3] 1 Mod. 256. Bacon's Abridg. Prerog. F. 5. 4 Burr. 2317.

common prayer, which regulates the feasts of the church, and therefore it trenched upon that part of the prerogative which concerns the government of the church.[1]

There was also a case of the Stationers' Company *v.* Parker, in 1 Jac. 2. It does not appear what the book in controversy was, but the question was between concurrent patentees, and whether the plaintiff's patent excluded the defendant's.[2] Holt, arguing for the defendant, agreed that the king had power to grant the printing of books concerning law or religion, and admitted it to be an interest, but not a sole interest. The court inclined for the defendant, but reserved the question for advisement.[3]

There is no case in the books concerning the Latin Grammar, but the right of the king was grounded on the allegation, that he paid for compiling and publishing it.[4] Nor is there any reported case prior to the Revolution concerning the Bible, but that was vested in part upon the ground that the king paid the translators; and with regard to the Year Books, it was said, that the crown was at the expense of taking the notes.[5] The further history of the pre-

[1] 1 Mod. 256. Bacon's Abridg. Prerog. F. 5. 4 Burr. 2317.

[2] The work was undoubtedly a law book.

[3] Stationers' Co. *v.* Parker, Skinner, 233.

[4] 4 Burr. 2329. This notion is now of course abandoned.

[5] 4 Burr. 2329, 2401. Blackstone says, that the exclusive right of printing the translation of the Bible is founded upon these two principles, combined, viz. 1. That the king is the supreme head of the church; and 2. That it was translated at the expense of the crown. 2 Black. Com. 410.

rogative copies will be pursued in their connection with the general course of the subject.[1]

The cases which have now been cited, have been considered by very great authorities as proofs that the right of the crown, in certain copies, was regarded as a right of property of the same kind as that of authors.[2] But if they do not show, that the right of the crown was a right of property merely, and if the high notions of prerogative entertained at the time entered into these decisions and affected them with reasons of religion or state, as is quite probable, then there is an argument to be drawn from them of great weight in favor of the existence of a common law right of property in authors, as a right understood at the times when these decisions were made. These cases were decided before the Revolution, at which it seems obviously proper to pause as at a stage in the inquiry. Notions of power and prerogative were then held and acted upon, such as could not be breathed at the present day in Westminster Hall, and the press had long been under the almost absolute control of the crown. Yet, in such a period, it was felt to be necessary to argue in support of the

[1] See post, ch. 2.

[2] Per Lord Mansfield Ch. J. and Willes, J. in Millar *v.* Taylor, 4 Burr. 2317, 2401. Lord Mansfield's remarks upon these cases are very cogent. He considered that "*crown copies* are, as in the case of an author, civil property; which is deduced, as in the case of an author, from the king's right of original publication. The kind of property in the crown, or a patentee from the crown, is just the same; incorporeal, incapable of violation but by a civil injury, and only to be vindicated by the same remedy, as an action upon the case, or a bill in equity." Yates J. in the same case, who dissented, held, that the crown copies were founded on reasons of state or religion.

right of the crown by analogy to the right of the subject; and the courts not only recognized the analogy, but wherever the particular publication afforded the least color for the claim as a claim of property, they always took care to rest the king's copy upon the same grounds that would have established the right in a private person. Fictions were resorted to, as in the case of the Latin Grammar, in order that the right of the king might stand upon property. All this shows that there existed at that time a right of property in copies, growing out of authorship, so well settled, so universally received and acted upon, and so thoroughly established in the notions of the profession and the public, that the crown was forced to borrow the aid of its analogies, and to claim upon the same title, as that which protected a sermon or a poem.

The proprietors of copies applied to parliament in 1709, for an act more effectually to secure their property forever, by what they thought a more adequate remedy than any that had then been used. It seems, that no one had then supposed that a bill would lie for an injunction and relief in equity.[1] But the common law remedy of an action was understood, though it was justly regarded as totally inadequate, both because of the difficulty of proving all the actual damages, and because "the defendant was always a pauper."[2] The petitioners therefore prayed, that CON-

[1] Millar *v.* Taylor, 4 Burr. 2317, 2405. Vern. 220, 275.

[2] So assigned in the petition of the booksellers. 4 Burr. 2318. Al-

FISCATION *of the counterfeit copies* might be made one of the penalties. This led to the Statute 8 Anne, c. 19, passed in 1709.[1]

The preamble of this act is worthy of attention. It is as follows: "Whereas printers, booksellers, and other persons have of late frequently taken the liberty of printing, reprinting, and publishing, or causing to be printed, reprinted and published books and other writings without the consent of the authors or proprietors of such books and writings to their very great detriment, and too often to the ruin of them and their families; for preventing therefore such practices for the future, and for the encouragement of learned men to compose and write useful books; be it enacted,"[2] &c. The first section of the act then provides, that after the 10th of April, 1710, the authors of books already printed, who have not transferred their rights, and the booksellers, &c. who have purchased copies, shall have the sole right of printing them for the term of twenty-one years; and the authors of books already composed and not printed, or thereafter to be composed, and their assigns, shall have the sole right of printing the same for fourteen years; with a penalty and forfeiture for printing without consent of the proprietor.[3] The

though there was no precedent of a common law action tried, yet that it was universally held that an action at common law would lie is apparent from this petition.

[1] See Appendix, p. I.

[2] The title of the act is, "An Act for the encouragement of learning, by vesting the copies of printed books in the authors or purchasers of such copies, during the times therein mentioned."

[3] 8 Anne, c. 19.

second section declares that the books, the property of which is intended to be "secured" by this act are such as shall, before publication, have been entered at Stationers' Hall.

It is now necessary to trace the history of the subject in the courts, after the passage of this act, until the year 1769; in order to see whether this statute was considered as the source of literary property, or whether in fact literary property was held to depend upon principles of the common law known and received before and independent of the statute.

There are two classes of cases, within the period now under consideration, both of which have proceeded upon the author's right of property independent of the statute. The first class is that of books or other writings after publication; the second class embraces manuscripts before publication.

1. The question as to the common law right, with reference to old copies, after publication, could only arise after the full term of the act of Anne had passed, that is, at the end of twenty-one years from the tenth of April, 1710, or after the tenth of April, 1731. From this time until the case of Tonson *v.* Collins, in the king's bench in 1761, the court of chancery exercised a jurisdiction by injunction, in which the antecedent right of property must have been the right to which the court granted its protection.

The first case was one before Sir Joseph Jekyll, as master of the rolls, in 1735, in which he granted an injunction against printing the *Whole Duty of Man.*

This book first appeared in 1657, and the statutory term had passed. The right of the plaintiff therefore could only have been the general right of property.[1] In the same year also, (1735) Lord Talbot granted an injunction against printing Pope's and Swift's Miscellanies, many of which were originally published before the statute.[2]

In 1736, Sir Joseph Jekyll granted a third injunction against printing Nelson's Festivals and Fasts, a book first published in 1703.[3]

In 1739, Lord Hardwicke granted a fourth injunction against printing Milton's Paradise Lost, the title to which the plaintiffs derived under an assignment made by the poet in 1667.[4]

In 1751, Milton's poem again came before Lord Hardwicke, in an application for an injunction to restrain the defendant's printing an edition of the poem with the notes of Dr. Newton and other commentators, all of which belonged to the plaintiffs. The bill derived a title to the poem by the author's assignment in 1667, to the life by Fenton, published in 1727, to Bentley's Notes, published in 1732, and to Dr. Newton's Notes, published in 1749. The defendants put in an answer immediately, and set up

[1] Eyre *v.* Walker, cited 4 Burr. 2325; 3 Swanst. 673. Sir Joseph Jekyll sat in parliament when the act of Anne was passed.

[2] Motte *v.* Falkner, cited in Millar *v.* Taylor, 4 Burr. 2325, and in Tonson *v.* Walker, 3 Swanst. 673. Lord Mansfield, (1 W. Blackst. 331) said that this case was argued on the objection that the statute term had expired.

[3] Walthoe *v.* Walker, cited *ut supra.*

[4] Tonson *v.* Walker, cited, *ut supra.* At the date of this injunction, the term of twenty-one years secured by the statute to old copies, had been exhausted for eight years.

notes of their own, of which it appeared there were twenty-eight; while the notes of the other commentators belonging to the plaintiffs, and included in the defendant's edition, numbered fifteen hundred. Lord Hardwicke gave judgment in 1752, and held that the plaintiff's *notes* were within the protection of the statute; and as to the *poem*, although he said that the general question had never been determined and there was a doubt, yet he granted an injunction until the hearing against printing the poem, the life, and all the notes that had been combined by Dr. Newton.[1] When the authority of this case came to be afterwards considered in the king's bench, in the time of Lord Mansfield, his lordship, and the rest of the judges who concurred with him, had no doubt as to the real opinion of Lord Hardwicke, and they attributed his suggestion of a doubt to his great decency and prudence in not acting decisively upon a question of law, on which a doubt had been raised, and which had not been settled in a court of common law since the statute.[2]

[1] Tonson *v.* Walker, 3 Swanst. 673.

[2] Millar *v.* Taylor, 4 Burr. 2327, 2403, 2404. There is very little reason to doubt what Lord Hardwicke's opinion was, if the report of what fell from him, (in the case of Tonson *v.* Walker, in 3 Swanst.) be correct, and there is good reason to believe it to be so. He granted the injunction as to the *poem* until the matter could be considered at the hearing, because there was a "probability of right in the plaintiffs;" and he then went on to say that in the cases of crown copies the general argument had been, that the books were made at the expense of the crown, and therefore the property is in the crown; and that these cases are used as tending to prove a general right in the author. (3 Swanst. 680.) Willes, J. in Millar *v.* Taylor, quoted Lord Hardwicke as saying, "these arguments being allowed to support that right [of the crown] *infer* such a *property existing*." (4 Burr. 2327.) Lord Mansfield added, "I heard

All these injunctions were submitted to; and Lord Mansfield said of them, that, although they were not granted upon a final hearing, yet he looked upon them as equal to any final decree, "for the judicial opinions of the great men who granted these injunctions, in cases clearly not within the statute, uncontradicted by any book, judgment, or saying, must weigh in any question of law; much more, in a question of mere theory and speculation as to what is agreeable or repugnant to *natural principles*." [1]

2. The cases of injunctions against printing surreptitiously from unpublished manuscripts proceeded upon the admitted doctrine that every author has a property in his own writings before publication; and it is difficult to say, that the argument, which proves a property before publication, does not equally prove a property in the same writing after publication.[2] But without considering at present the ques-

Lord Hardwicke say what Mr. Justice Willes has quoted, as to these arguments from property in support of the *king's* right necessarily inferring an *author's*." (4 Burr. 2403.) He also pointed out, that at the time when Lord Hardwicke used this argument, the question was depending in the king's bench in a case sent there by him for determination. This was the case of Baskett *v.* The University of Cambridge, (1 Black. R. 105,) sent from the court of chancery in 1743; but it lay dormant for many years, and the judges' certificate was not granted until 1758. It was a question between rival patentees of the crown, with regard to printing acts of parliament, &c. The court of king's bench held that the right was concurrent in the plaintiff and the university, *exclusive of all other persons.* The case is a full authority for the position that the *king's copy* continues after publication, at common law; and we have seen that the great effort always was to make the king's copy depend upon property like that of the subject. See Lord Mansfield's remarks in 4 Burr. 2401, 2404. See also Baskett *v.* Cuningham, 1 Black. R. 370; 2 Eden, 137.

[1] 4 Burr. 2399.

[2] Lord Mansfield rejected the idea of any distinction. See 4 Burr. 2397.

tion, whether publication is a dedication or abandonment to the public of an author's property in his own work, it is important here to state historically the jurisdiction that was exercised in the period now under consideration, with regard to manuscripts.

In 1732, Sir Joseph Jekyll, on a bill filed by the son of Mr. Webb, a conveyancer, granted an injunction against a person who was intending, without authority, to print the draughts left by Mr. Webb in manuscript.[1] The injunction was acquiesced in.

In 1741, in Forrester *v.* Waller, there was another injunction granted against printing the plaintiff's notes, obtained surreptitiously, without his consent.[2]

In the same year, also, in the case of Pope *v.* Curll, known to literary history, Lord Hardwicke granted an injunction against printing Pope's Letters to Swift.[3] The injunction was submitted to.

[1] Webb *v.* Rose, cited 4 Burr. 2330. 2 Bro. P. C. 138.

[2] Forrester *v.* Waller, cited ut supra.

[3] 2 Atk. 342. Dr. Johnson believed this case to have been got up by Pope himself, in order to create for himself an opportunity to publish his letters as if in self-defence. "One of the passages of Pope's life, which seems to deserve some inquiry, was a publication of letters between him and many of his friends, which falling into the hands of Curll, a rapacious bookseller, of no good fame, were by him printed and sold. This volume, containing some letters from noblemen, Pope incited a prosecution against him in the house of lords for a breach of privilege, and attended himself to stimulate the resentment of his friends. Curll appeared at the bar, and, knowing himself in no great danger, spoke of Pope with very little reverence: 'He has,' said Curll, 'a knack at versifying, but in prose I think myself a match for him.' When the orders of the house were examined, none of them appeared to have been infringed; Curll went away triumphant, and Pope was left to seek some other remedy.

"Curll's account was, that one evening a man in a clergyman's gown, but with a lawyer's band, brought and offered for sale a number of printed volumes, which he found to be Pope's Epistolary Correspondence; that he asked no name and was told none, but gave the

In 1755, in the case of Manley *v.* Owen, a bill was filed by some printers, who had bought of the lord-mayor the copy of the Sessions paper of trials, to enjoin the defendants from printing it. The injunction was granted, upon the ground that the property passed by the lord-mayor's grant to the plaintiffs.[1] This injunction was acquiesced in.

In 1758, the Duke of Queensborough, as the representative of Edward, Earl of Clarendon,[2] filed a bill to restrain the defendants from printing, publishing, or disposing of Lord Clarendon's History of the reign of Charles the Second. The bill stated, that Henry, late Earl of Clarendon,[3] was at his death possessed of a manuscript copy of this history, in the handwriting of Edward, Earl of Clarendon, to the

price demanded, and thought himself authorized to use his purchase to his own advantage.

"That Curll gave a true account of the transaction, it is reasonable to believe, because no falsehood was ever detected; and when, some years afterwards, I mentioned it to Lintot, the son of Bernard, he declared his opinion to be, that Pope knew better than anybody else how Curll obtained the copies, because another parcel was at the same time sent to himself, for which no price had ever been demanded, as he made known his resolution not to pay a porter, and consequently not to deal with a nameless agent.

"Such care had been taken to make them public, that they were sent at once to two booksellers; to Curll, who was likely to seize them as a prey; and to Lintot, who might be expected to give Pope information of the seeming injury. Lintot, I believe, did nothing; and Curll did what was expected. That to make them public was the only reason, may be reasonably supposed, because the numbers, offered to sale by the private messengers, showed that the hope of gain could not have been the motive of the impression.

"It seems that Pope, being desirous of printing his letters, and not knowing how to do, without imputation of vanity, what has in this country been done very rarely, contrived an appearance of compulsion, that, when he could complain that his letters were surreptitiously published, he might decently and defensively publish them himself." — *Johnson's Life of Pope.*

[1] Manley *v.* Owen, cited 4 Burr. 2329, 2404.

[2] Edward, first Earl of Clarendon, the lord chancellor.

[3] Henry, second Earl of Clarendon, son of the lord chancellor.

sole property whereof the plaintiff, as administrator to the late earl, became entitled. The defendant, Shebbeare, by his answer, stated, that the defendant, Gwynne, from whom he received the manuscript copy, told him that Henry, Earl of Clarendon, thirty-three years before, delivered to his (Gwynne's) father the original manuscript of the history, that he might take a copy of it, and make use of the copy as he should think fit; and that a copy was accordingly taken. The court was of opinion, that it was not to be presumed that when Lord Clarendon, the son, gave the elder Gwynne a copy of his father's manuscript, he intended that he should have the right to print it; that Mr. Gwynne might make every use of it, except that.[1] The injunction was granted, and was acquiesced under; and Shebbeare afterwards recovered against Gwynne, before Lord Mansfield, large damages, for representing that he had a right to print.[2]

Thus stood the law of England upon this subject until the year 1761, when the action of Tonson *v.* Collins, upon the copyright of the Spectator, was brought in the court of king's bench. The plaintiffs were the representatives and assigns of Jacob Tonson, who purchased the work of Mr. Addison and Sir R. Steele, in 1712. Of course, this copy was not within the statute of Anne, the term of protection

[1] Duke of Queensbury *v.* Shebbeare, 2 Eden's Ch. R. 329, cited 4 Burr. R. 2330, 2397.

[2] 4 Burr. 2330, 2397.

given by that act having long passed before the commencement of the action. The case was twice solemnly argued in the king's bench, and was then, by direction of Lord Mansfield, adjourned into the exchequer chamber, to be argued before all the twelve judges.[1] This reference was not made from any difference of opinion or difficulty among the judges of the king's bench; but they suspected collusion, and thinking that there might be no writ of error brought, they chose to take the opinion of all the judges. The court were afterwards clearly informed that it was a case of collusion between the parties, though it had been argued *bona fide* by the counsel, and the case therefore fell to the ground.[2]

In this manner passed away the first opportunity for the establishment, in a court of law, of a doctrine of the highest interest and importance to letters and literary men. But few years, however, could elapse before the question must have been again presented, in a serious contest between parties litigating actual interests. The literature of England embraced so many standard works in the latter part of the last century, out of which the question must necessarily arise whether all the rights of the author or his assigns were lost at the expiration of the period of protection fixed by the statute of Anne, that it is remarkable that the decision was deferred to so late a period as the year 1769. It was reserved for the

[1] Tonson *v.* Collins, 1 W. Black. R. 301, 321, 345.

[2] See 4 Burr. 2400, statement of Lord Mansfield.

most celebrated work of the poet Thomson, to present the case upon which the doctrine of perpetual property was to be adjudged in the court of king's bench, before it was finally overthrown in another cause, which went to the house of lords from the court of chancery.

"The Seasons, by James Thomson," was first published by him, for his own use and benefit as proprietor, at several times between the beginning of the year 1727 and the end of the year 1729. In the latter year he sold the work to Andrew Millar, who entered it at stationers' hall, and continued to publish it down to the time of the poet's death, which occurred in August, 1748, and from thence until the year 1763, when Robert Taylor put forth an edition of the poem, without the license or consent of Millar. The term of years secured by the statute of Anne had expired; and the action brought by Millar in the king's bench, in 1766, proceeded upon the claim of a perpetual property at common law in the author and his assigns.[1]

The special verdict in this case found that before the reign of Queen Anne, it was usual to purchase from authors the perpetual copyright of their books, and to assign the same from hand to hand for valuable considerations, and to make the same the subject of family settlements, &c. The verdict also found the by-laws of the stationers' company, passed in 1681 and in 1694, which have already been cited.[2]

[1] Millar *v.* Taylor, 4 Burr. 2303.

[2] Ante, pp. 36, 37.

The cause was twice argued before a full bench, Lord Mansfield presiding, and judgment was finally rendered for the plaintiff in 1769, Yates, J. dissenting.[1]

The great men concerned in this cause, the ability with which it was argued, and the deliberation attending the decision, must forever give it a high value in the estimation of every lawyer. It was argued and adjudged with consummate learning and ability; Lord Mansfield's judgment was worthy of his great name, and he was assisted by two of his brethren in a manner that reflects upon them and him the highest honor. A writ of error was afterwards brought, but it was never prosecuted; and the lords commissioners, after Trinity term, 1770, granted an injunction.

In estimating this celebrated decision, it is necessary for the historical inquirer to notice by what

[1] The first argument was by Mr. Dunning for the plaintiff, and Mr. Thurlow for the defendant; the second by Mr. Blackstone for the plaintiff, and Mr. Murphy for the defendant. The judges concurring in the judgment were Lord Mansfield, C. J., Willes J. and Aston J.; Yates J. dissented. — The case first arose in the court of chancery, and was sent to the king's bench for a decision of the general question of property, at the time when the case of Tonson *v.* Collins hung in that court under an *appearance* of doubt. In the court of chancery, in July, 1765, in the case of Millar *v.* Donaldson, reported 2 Eden's Ch. R. 327, Lord Chancellor Northington dissolved an injunction that had been obtained, because the general question had never been determined, and directed an action at law to try the right. In consequence of this, the question was afterwards brought forward in the shape of a special verdict, as it now appears in Millar *v.* Taylor, 4 Burr. Lord Mansfield in this case took notice of the circumstances under which the case had been sent before him, and said that "there never had been a doubt in the court of chancery, until a doubt was raised there from decency, upon a *supposed* doubt in this court in the case of Tonson *v.* Collins." 4 Burr. 2400.

standard the right of the plaintiff, as a right at common law, was tried. Printing was introduced into England within the time of legal memory, that is, since the reign of Richard II. It was therefore out of the question to found the right of perpetual literary property upon immemorial usage or precedent. But a right may exist at the common law of England upon principles of natural justice, moral fitness, and public convenience ; which, when applied to a new subject, make common law without a precedent ; and if the alleged right has been received by usage, it is still stronger. The argument therefore divided itself into two great branches. Under the first head, the inquiry was directed to the legislative and the judicial, as well as the common opinion of the country, to ascertain whether this right had been generally received and treated as a right of property ; and, under the second head, the justice, fitness, and convenience of the doctrine furnished the grounds on which the adjudication was in part rested.[1]

[1] M. Renouard has put the question, with great pertinency, "What were the provisions of the common law in England, before the statute of Anne? Had the author any right of copy? Has the statute of Anne given a right which the common law did not confer, or has it on the contrary restrained a right which the common law did confer?" — (*Traité des Droits D'Auteurs, Par Augustin-Charles Renouard, Conseiller a La Cour de Cassation.* Paris, 1838, tom. 1, p. 233.) It is difficult to escape from the answer that must be given to these questions, after a survey of the historical part of the argument. An author in England either had some right to enjoy the profits of his publication, before the statute, or he had none. If he had any right at all, it is difficult to see what restrained it to a right short of a perpetuity. I have never met with the argument which denies the existence of all right whatever, except that which goes the length of inferring an abandonment or surrender to the public by the act of publication.

One great struggle in this, and the preceding case of Tonson *v.* Collins was, to show that by the act of publication, the author abandoned or surrendered any right of property which he might have had in his ideas, or in the form in which they were expressed. But this was answered conclusively by the court. From the doctrine, that the author had by the common law of England, as had always been admitted, a property before publication, the court declared that there could be no just distinction founded on the mere fact of publication. If the property exists, while the work is still in manuscript, before publication, there is nothing in the mere act of publication which shows an intention to abandon or give away that property. If the author does not mean to abandon or give it away, then the question resolves itself into this, whether it is agreeable to natural principles, moral justice and fitness, to allow him the copy after publication, as well as before ? Of this question, said Lord Mansfield, " the general consent of the kingdom for ages is on the affirmative side ;" and he, as well as the judges who concurred with him, deduced that consent from the whole judicial and legislative opinion that had preceded the statute.

Having thus deduced the right of literary property, the question remained to be disposed of, whether the statute of Anne had abridged it, so that the owner could claim only the exclusive right for a term of years. Upon this question, the court held, that the statute had not taken away the property of authors at common law; but was merely intended to give, for a term of years, a more efficient protection, where the entry and the other provisions of the act should have been complied with.[1]

But this decision was not long acquiesced in.

A cause had been for some time pending in the court of chancery, in which a Mr. Becket complained of a publication by the Messrs. Donaldson of a book belonging to him. After the decision in Millar *v.* Taylor, Lord Chancellor Apsley granted an injunction, as of course, in favor of Mr. Becket, pursuant to the decision of the general question in the court of king's bench, and an appeal from this decree was taken to the house of lords.[2] This appeal came on to be heard in 1774, and was argued by Thurlow, attorney-general, and Sir John Dalrymple against the right at common law, and by Wedderburn, solicitor-general, and Dunning, in favor of it. The judges were ordered to deliver their opinions. Ten of the judges were of opinion that at common law an

[1] Yates, J. dissented upon this question also.

[2] Apsley is the proper title of this chancellor to the year 1775, though he was afterwards Lord Bathurst, and is called by the latter title by Lord Campbell, through the whole of his chancellorship. I have followed the reporters, but he is usually styled Lord Bathurst in modern times. He professed to have made this decree as of course, because the point had been so decided in the king's bench, (17 Parl. Hist. 1001.) If he had said he had followed *Lord Mansfield*, he would probably have given a reason of great significance with him. Lord Campbell represents him as a weak person, accustomed to lean upon the chief justice. But when he came to speak to this question in the house of lords, he seems to have emancipated himself from the authority of Lord Mansfield, and declaring himself impartial, went the other way, (17 Parl. Hist. 1001.) See his Life, in Lord Campbell's Chancellors, vol. v. pp. 432-472.

author of any book or literary composition had the sole right of first printing and publishing the same for sale, and might bring an action against any person who printed, published and sold the same without his consent; and one judge was of the contrary opinion. Three judges were of opinion that the law took away the right after publication, so that any person could, without leave of the author, print and publish a book which the author had once published; and eight were of the contrary opinion.

Six judges were of opinion that the statute of Anne took away the action at common law, and that an author had no remedy except upon the foundation of that statute; and five were of the contrary opinion.

Seven judges were of opinion that the author of any book or literary composition, and his assigns, had the sole right of printing and publishing the same, in perpetuity, by the common law; and four were of the contrary opinion.

Six judges were of opinion that this right in perpetuity is impeached, restrained and taken away by the statute of Anne; and five were of opinion that it is not.[1]

Lord Mansfield, being a peer, did not deliver any opinion; but it was notorious, that he adhered to the judgment which he had delivered on all these questions;[2] and thus, of the twelve judges, the great

[1] 17 Parl. Hist. 971 et seq.; 4 Burr. R. 2408, et seq.

[2] Sir James Burrow says it was notorious that Lord Mansfield ad-

weight of authority and numbers was in favor of the perpetuity at common law; and upon the question, whether such right was taken away by the statute, the judges were equally divided.[1]

In this posture of the case, Lord Camden came forward to move the judgment of their lordships, and delivered an elaborate argument against the common law right of property, which turned the scale. His speech was able and ingenious, but sarcastic, sophistical, and not altogether fair towards the other side of the question. It was chiefly devoted to answering the judgment of Lord Mansfield in Millar *v.* Taylor.[2]

hered to his opinion; but it being very unusual (from reasons of delicacy) for a peer to support his own judgment, he did not speak. 4 Burr. 2417. He was afterwards much blamed in the house of commons for not speaking. This was on the occasion of an application by the booksellers for an extension of the term of copyright, they having, as it was shown, laid out great sums, on the authority of the decision in the king's bench. It was even said, that had Lord Mansfield defended his judgment, in the house of lords, the then pending bill would never have been brought in. 17 Parl. Hist. 1090.

[1] The leading argument, adverse to the right of perpetuity, among the judges, was that delivered by De Grey, Lord Ch. Justice of the common pleas. He thus disposes of the question as to the effect of publication: "But it is said, that the sale of a printed copy is a qualified or conditional sale, and that the purchaser may make all the uses he pleases of his work, except that one of reprinting it; but where is the evidence of this extraordinary bargain? or where the analogy of law to support the supposition. In all other cases of purchase, payment transfers the whole and absolute property to the buyer; there is no instance where a legal right is otherwise transferred by sale, an example of such a speculative right remaining in the seller. It is a new and metaphysical refinement upon the law; and laws, like some manufactures, may be drawn so fine as at last to lose their strength with their solidity." 17 Parl. Hist. 990.

[2] As an American, I am bound to hold the memory of Lord Camden, the statesman, in the highest honor. But to a lawyer, the cause of truth, in all that concerns the science of human rights, is cosmopolitan. It is impossible to read this speech of Lord Camden's, with the book of history open before us, without perceiving that there were secret causes of bias operating upon his judgment. He spoke sincerely, without doubt. He was too great and too

The passage of declamation in which he argued that glory and not profit is or should be the reward of men of letters, has been often quoted, and is now the most familiar portion of the speech. He declared that there was no foundation for literary property in the common law, and none in the principles of sound policy, or good sense. He denounced the perpetuity contended for, as odious and selfish, deserving of reprobation, and likely to become intolerable.[1] He

good a man, not to say too great a lawyer, to have purposely misled the judicial action of the house of lords. But it cannot be doubted, that he was predisposed to encounters with Lord Mansfield; and, that his opinions were thus influenced by a rivalry in which he was prone to indulge, is but too apparent in the speech itself. It is, without direct allusion, a running answer to Lord Mansfield's judgment in Millar *v.* Taylor. He handles the same topics, follows in the same track, and turns or seeks to turn the positions of the illustrious chief of the king's bench and of his associates who agreed with him. The truth is, these great men for a long time time contended for the supremacy as law lords in the upper house. It appears that when Lord Camden first entered that assembly, "Lord Mansfield instinctively dreaded a contest for the supremacy which he had enjoyed there since the death of Lord Hardwicke;" (Lord Campbell's Lives of the Chancellors, V. 252,) and although when he and Lord Camden sat together at the hearing of appeals, they conducted with great decorum, and rarely differed in opinion, when settling together the law in the last resort, there were other occasions when they attacked each other in debate so sharply as almost to render it necessary for the house to interfere. In one scene, which occurred about four years before the discussion of the question of literary property, they had a personal controversy of a very disagreeable character, in which Lord Camden seems to have triumphed by the exhibition of more nerve than belonged to "the silver-tongued Murray." (Campbell, ut sup. p. 295.) Alas, that history should be obliged to chronicle the foibles of the great, who demand and receive the reverence of posterity.

[1] "If, then, there be no foundation of right for this perpetuity by the positive laws of the land, it will I believe find as little claim to encouragement upon public principles of sound policy, or good sense. If there be anything in the world common to all mankind, science and learning are in their nature *publici juris*, and they ought to be as free and general as air or water. They forget their Creator, as well as their fellow creatures, who wish to monopolize his noblest gifts and greatest benefits. Why did we enter into society at all, but to enlighten one another's minds, and improve our faculties, for the common welfare of the species? Those great

was answered, it is said, very ingeniously, by Lord Littleton, a lay peer, who spoke in favor of au-

men, those favored mortals, those sublime spirits, who share that ray of divinity which we call genius, are intrusted by Providence with the delegated power of imparting to their fellow-creatures that instruction which heaven meant for universal benefit; they must not be niggards to the world, or hoard up for themselves the common stock. We know what was the punishment of him who hid his talent, and Providence has taken care that there shall not be wanting the noblest motives and incentives for men of genius to communicate to the world those truths and discoveries which are nothing if uncommunicated. Knowledge has no value or use for the solitary owner: to be enjoyed it must be communicated. 'Scire tuum nihil est, nisi te scire hoc sciat alter.' Glory is the reward of science, and those who deserve it, scorn all meaner views: I speak not of the scribblers for bread, who tease the press with their wretched productions; fourteen years is too long a privilege for their perishable trash. It was not for gain, that Bacon, Newton, Milton, Locke, instructed and delighted the world; it would be unworthy such men to traffic with a dirty bookseller for so much a sheet of a letter press. When the bookseller offered Milton five pound for his Paradise Lost, he did not reject it, and commit his poem to the flames, nor did he accept the miserable pittance as the reward of his labor; he knew that the real price of his work was immortality, and that posterity would pay it. Some authors are as careless about profit as others are rapacious of it; and what a situation would the public be in with regard to literature, if there were no means of compelling a second impression of a useful work to be put forth, or wait till a wife or children are to be provided for by the sale of an edition? All our learning will be locked up in the hands of the Tonsons and the Lintons of the age, who will set what price upon it their avarice chooses to demand, till the public become as much their slaves, as their own hackney compilers are." 17 Parl. Hist. 999, 1000.

As Lord Camden cites the example of Milton, to show that he placed no value upon the right of property in his great poem, it may be well to repeat the authentic facts concerning the sale of that copyright. Milton sold his copy to Samuel Simmons in 1667, for an immediate payment of five pounds. But the agreement entitled him to a conditional payment of five pounds more when thirteen hundred copies should be sold of the first edition; of the like sum after the same number of the second edition; and of another five pounds after the same sale of the third edition. The number of each edition was not to exceed fifteen hundred copies. In two years, the sale gave the poet a right to his second payment, for which he signed a receipt on the 26th of April, 1669. The second edition was not printed till 1674, and Milton did not live to receive the payment stipulated for this impression. The third edition was published in 1678; and his widow, to whom the copy was then to devolve, agreed with Simmons, the printer, to receive eight pounds for her right, according to her receipt, dated December 21, 1680; and she gave him a general release, dated April 29, 1681. Simmons sold the thors.[1] Their lordships divided, twenty-two for reversing the decree, and eleven for confirming it. Thus the right of authors in their publications, as a right at the common law of England, affirmed by a majority of the judges to have previously existed, was lost forever.

Lord Camden's argument, on this occasion, went the length of maintaining that publication is an abandonment to the public of all the author's previous right over his own productions. Admitting that every man has a right to his thoughts while they continue his, he contends that they become *publici juris*, as soon as he has published them; that the common law had never recognized ideas as subjects of property, and had never declared whether

right to Brabason Aylmer, a bookseller, for twenty-five pounds, and Aylmer sold it to Jacob Tonson, one moiety in August, 1683, and the other moiety in March, 1690, at a price considerably advanced. (Todd's Life of Milton, 193–195, Lond. 1826.) It thus appears that the poet was very careful to assert his full right of property, as he and others understood it at the time, and to make it available to his family. The amount which he chose to receive, compared with the real value of the poem, or measured by a modern standard, seems very trifling. But as such rights were estimated then, and considering that the poem gained slowly upon the attention of his own age, it was not a grossly inadequate price. When it had been published fourteen years and upwards, the copyright *between one bookseller and another*, brought only twenty-five pounds. Yet its value could not have been affected by any apprehension, at the time of this sale, that it was not protected by the common law. Such a notion had not then arisen; and long after, viz. in 1739, Lord Hardwicke protected by injunction the title of Tonson, derived under the assignment made by the poet in 1667. (Ante, p. 47,) Doubtless Milton did not write his great poem for money; but we have seen that he supposed the right of exclusive property in authors was acknowledged by the law of his country, and he took pains practically to assert the right in his own case. It seems to me by no means a wild conjecture, that he did this for the sake of example, as well as in order to preserve his reputation, by keeping the control of the text of his poem.

[1] Thomas, second Lord Littleton.

they were descendable, transferable or assignable. "When published," he asks, "can the purchaser lend his book to his friend? Can he let it out for hire as the circulating libraries do? Can he enter it as common stock in a literary club, as is done in the country? May he transcribe it for charity? Then what part of the work is exempt from this desultory claim? Does it lie in the sentiments, the language and style, or the paper? If in the sentiments or language, no one can translate or abridge them. Locke's Essay might, perhaps, be put into other expressions, or newly methodized, and all the original system and ideas be retained. These questions show how the argument counteracts itself, how the subject of it shifts, and becomes public in one sense, and private in another; and they are all new to the common law, which leaves us perfectly in the dark about their solution."[1]

[1] 17 Parl. Hist. 998. "And how are the judges," he continues, "without a rule or guide, to determine them when they arise, whose books and studies afford no more light upon the subject than the common understandings of the parties themselves? What diversity of judgments! what confusion in opinion must they fall into! without a trace or line of law to direct their determination! What a code of law yet remains for their ingenuity to furnish, and could they all agree in it, it would not be law at last, but legislation.

"But it is said that it would be contrary to the ideas of private justice, moral fitness, and public convenience, not to adopt this new system. But who has a right to decide these new cases, if there is no other rule to measure by but moral fitness and equitable right? Not the judges of the common law, I am sure. Their business is to tell the suitor how the law stands, not how it ought to be; otherwise each judge would have a distinct tribunal in his own breast, the decisions of which would be irregular and uncertain, and various, as the minds and tempers of mankind. As it is, we find they do not always agree: but what would it be, where the rule of right would always be the private opinion of the judge, as to the moral fitness and convenience of the claim? Caprice,

He denied also that there is any implied contract between the person who sells and the person who buys a printed copy, which he called a "flimsy supposition, as unmeaning in itself, as it is void of a legal foundation."[1]

It can scarcely be necessary, at the present day, to make any answer to some of these arguments. It is sufficient to observe that the whole bench of judges, with one exception, held that at common law an exclusive right to publish the contents of a manuscript resided in the author, and that nine of them, (including Lord Mansfield,) did not consider that publication made the literary composition *publici juris.* No one supposed then, and it has not since been contended, that the common law recognized ideas as the subject of property, in the sense which Lord Camden attributes to his opponents. No English jurist, then or since, ever supposed that the pur-

self-interest, vanity, would by turns hold the scale of justice, and the law of property be indeed most vague and arbitrary. That excellent judge, Lord Chief Justice Lee, used always to ask the counsel, after his argument was over, 'Have you any case?' I hope judges will always copy the example, and never pretend to decide upon a claim of property, without attending to the old black letter of our law, without founding their judgment upon some solid written authority, preserved in their books, or in judicial records. In this case I know there is none such to be produced." 17 Parl. Hist. 998, 999.

[1] Ibid. p. 1000. It had for ages been admitted that the proprietor of a manuscript had the sole right to publish it, and the judges had, almost unanimously, just declared this to be common law. Repeated injunctions had been granted, to restrain the publication of manuscripts without authority. Did they proceed upon anything but an implied contract on the part of the person into whose possession the manuscripts had come, not to do more than the purpose warranted for which they had come into his hands? And was this contract a "flimsy supposition?"

chaser of a printed copy of a book could not lend it, or let it out for hire to a reader, or even transcribe it for charity, without violating the alleged exclusive right of the author. The exclusive privilege of the author consists in the sole right to print a written composition and to take the profits of the sale of printed copies. In this sense, the law of England undeniably recognized a species of property in ideas, for it absolutely prohibited the printing of a written composition, still in manuscript, without the consent of the author or proprietor. Yet in the case of manuscripts, the same argument could be urged, from possession of the copy, as from possession of the copy of a printed book. If the common law recognized this incorporeal right, in the one case, it needed no other element of property to recognize it in the other. The only remaining question, after publication, is, whether the sale of a printed copy carries with it a license of publication, when the loan of a manuscript, or its delivery for a specific purpose, carries no such license, according to the common law.

The decision in the house of lords was immediately followed by an application to parliament, on behalf of the booksellers of London, representing that large sums had been invested in the purchase of ancient copyrights, not protected by the statute of Queen Anne, upon the generally prevalent opinion that that statute did not interfere with the common law right ; that by the late decision of the house of lords, such common law right of authors and their assigns had been declared to have no existence, whereby the petitioners would be very great sufferers, through their former involuntary misapprehension of the law; and praying for relief in the premises. Evidence was thereupon taken before a committee of the house of commons, and a bill was brought in, to vest the copies of old books, not protected by the act of Anne, in the purchasers of such copies from authors or their assigns, for a limited time.[1] Counsel were heard at the bar for and against the bill, and a long and angry debate ensued upon the question of its passage. After a struggle at every stage of its progress, the bill finally passed the commons, on the 26th of May, 1774, by a vote of 40 to 22,[2] but was afterwards thrown out in the lords, chiefly through the exertions of Lord Camden.

In this posture of things, the universities applied to parliament, and succeeded in obtaining in 1775 an act, which enabled the two universities in England,

[1] The evidence showed that a great amount of money had been invested in such old copies.

[2] 17 Parl. Hist. 1077—1110. The whole discussion, both on the part of the counsel and the members opposed to the bill, was marked by a spirit of acrimony quite unworthy of the occasion. The appeals to prejudice against the booksellers, as a class of monopolists, were of the coarsest character. The principal persons who supported the bill were Mr. Fielde, Col. Onslow, and Mr. Burke, the latter taking that enlarged and liberal view of it consonant to his elevated character. The interests arrayed against it were the country and the Scotch booksellers; but letters were produced by several members from Mr. Hume, Dr. Hurd, Dr. Robertson, Dr. Beattie, and other writers of established reputation, containing the warmest wishes for the petitioners, lamenting the late decision in the house of lords, as fatal to literature, and expressing the hope that the booksellers might get speedy relief. Mr. Charles James Fox was among the opponents of the bill. *Ibid.*

the four universities in Scotland, and the several colleges of Eton, Westminster and Winchester, to hold in perpetuity their copyright in books given or bequeathed to them for the advancement of useful learning and other purposes of education.[1]

A quarter of a century later, the statutory term of copyright for authors in general was extended to twenty-eight years, in case the author should be living at the expiration of the first fourteen years.[2]

Subsequently, a further change was introduced, by which, instead of copyright for fourteen years and contingently for fourteen more, authors were to have a term of twenty-eight years, and also for the residue of their lives if living at the expiration of that term.[3]

The next important step was the passage of an act, 3 Will. IV. c. 15, giving to the authors of dramatic compositions the sole right of representing their plays or causing them to be represented in the British dominions.[4]

This was followed by the international copyright act, 1 and 2 Vict. c. 59, passed 31st July, 1838, giving a copyright in England to foreign authors whose governments shall have engaged to give the same privilege to British authors.[5]

[1] 15 Geo. 3, c. 53. See Appendix, p. 18.

[2] 41 Geo. 3, c. 107. See Appendix, p. 29.

[3] 54 Geo. 3, c. 156. Appendix, p. 38.

[4] See Appendix, p. 51.

[5] Ibid. p. 57.

Finally, by the 5 and 6 Vict. c. 45, passed 1st July, 1842, the former laws relating to literary copyright were revised, the term extended to the natural life of the author and for seven years after his death, or to forty-two years from the first publication; and many other important changes were introduced.

Upon a review of the history of the rights of authors in England, it must be admitted that they have long had to struggle against a great weight of prejudice and illiberality in the legislature. Every important concession that has been gained for them has been won as a trophy from a well fought field.[1]

[1] To Mr. Serjeant Talfourd belongs the chief honor of the last and greatest of these achievements. It was mainly through his exertions that the act 5 & 6 Vict. was passed. But it required repeated efforts to accomplish his purpose. In 1837, he addressed himself to the task in the following manly and generous strain of eloquence: "Although I see no reason why authors should not be restored to that inheritance which, under the name of protection and encouragement, has been taken from them, I feel that the subject has so long been treated as matter of compromise between those who deny that the creations of the inventive faculty, or the achievements of the reason, are the subjects of property at all, and those who think the property should last as long as the works which contain truth and beauty live, that I propose still to treat it on the principle of compromise, and to rest satisfied with a fairer adjustment of the difference than the last act of parliament affords. I shall propose — subject to modification when the details of the measure shall be discussed — that the term of property in all works of learning, genius, and art, to be produced hereafter, or in which the statutable copyright now subsists, shall be extended to sixty years, to be computed from the death of the author; which will at least enable him, while providing for the instruction and the delight of distant ages, to contemplate that he shall leave in his works themselves some legacy to those for whom a nearer, if not a higher duty, requires him to provide, and which shall make "death less terrible." When the opponents of literary property speak of glory as the reward of genius, they make an ungenerous use of the very nobleness of its impulses, and show how little they have profited by its high example. When Milton, in poverty and in blindness, fed the flame of his divine enthusiasm by the assurance of a duration coequal with his language, I believe with Lord Camden that no thought crossed him of the

That a period of nearly a century and a half should have passed away, after the propriety of legislative

wealth which might be amassed by the sale of his poem; but surely some shadow would have been cast upon "the clear dream and solemn vision" of his future glories, had he foreseen that, while booksellers were striving to rival each other in the magnificence of their editions, or their adaptation to the convenience of various classes of his admirers, his only surviving descendant — a woman — should be rescued from abject want only by the charity of Garrick, who, at the solicitation of Dr. Johnson, gave her a benefit at the theatre which had appropriated to itself all that could be represented of Comus. The liberality of genius is surely ill urged as an excuse for our ungrateful denial of its rights. The late Mr. Coleridge gave an example not merely of its liberality, but of its profuseness; while he sought not even to appropriate to his fame the vast intellectual treasures which he had derived from boundless research, and colored by a glorious imagination; while he scattered abroad the seeds of beauty and of wisdom to take root in congenial minds, and was content to witness their fruits in the productions of those who heard him. But ought we, therefore, the less to deplore, now when the music of his divine philosophy is forever hushed, that the earlier portion of those works on which he stamped his own impress — all which he desired of the world that it should recognize as his — is published for the gain of others than his children — that his death is illustrated by the forfeiture of their birthright? What justice is there in this? Do we reward our heroes thus? Did we tell our Marlboroughs, our Nelsons, our Wellingtons, that glory was their reward, that they fought for posterity, and that posterity would pay them? We leave them to no such cold and uncertain requital; we do not even leave them merely to enjoy the spoils of their victories, which we deny to the author; we concentrate a nation's honest feeling of gratitude and pride into the form of an endowment, and teach other ages what we thought, and what they ought to think, of their deeds, by the substantial memorials of our praise. Were our Shakspeare and Milton less the ornaments of their country, less the benefactors of mankind? Would the example be less inspiring if we permitted them to enjoy the spoils of their peaceful victories — if we allowed to their descendants, not the tax assessed by present gratitude, and charged on the future, but the mere amount which that future would be delighted to pay — extending as the circle of their glory expands, and rendered only by those who individually reap the benefits, and are contented at once to enjoy and to reward its author?

"But I do not press these considerations to the full extent; the past is beyond our power, and I only ask for the present a brief reversion in the future. 'Riches fineless' created by the mighty dead are already ours. It is in truth the greatness of the blessings which the world inherits from genius that dazzles the mind on this question; and the habit of repaying its bounty by words, that confuses us and indisposes us to justice. It is because the spoils of time are freely and irrevocably ours — because the forms of antique beauty wear for us the bloom of an imperishable youth —

protection had been admitted, before the enactment in England of the first law that does nearly adequate

because the elder literature of our own country is a free mine of wealth to the bookseller and of delight to ourselves, that we are unable to understand the claim of our contemporaries to a beneficial interest in their works. Because genius by a genial necessity communicates so much, we cannot conceive it as retaining anything for its possessor. There is a sense, indeed, in which the poets 'on earth have made us heirs of truth and pure delight in heavenly lays;' and it is because of the greatness of this very boon — because their thoughts become our thoughts, and their phrases unconsciously enrich our daily language — because their works, harmonious by the law of their own nature, suggest to us the rules of composition by which their imitators should be guided — because to them we can resort, and 'in our golden urns draw light,' that we cannot fancy them apart from ourselves, or admit that they have any property except in our praise. And our gratitude is shown not only in leaving their descendants without portion in the pecuniary benefits derived from their works, but in permitting their fame to be frittered away in abridgments, and polluted by base intermixtures, and denying to their children even the cold privilege of watching over and protecting it!

"There is something, sir, peculiarly unjust in bounding the term of an author's property by his natural life, if he should survive so short a period as twenty-eight years. It denies to age and experience the probable reward it permits to youth — to youth, sufficiently full of hope and joy, to slight its promises. It gives a bounty to haste, and informs the laborious student, who would wear away his strength to complete some work which 'the world will not willingly let die,' that the more of his life he devotes to its perfection, the more limited shall be his interest in its fruits. It stops the progress of remuneration at the moment it is most needed, and when the benignity of nature would extract from her last calamity a means of support and comfort to survivors. At the season when the author's name is invested with the solemn interest of mortality — when his eccentricities or frailties excite a smile or a sneer no longer — when the last seal is set upon his earthly course, and his works assume their place among the classics of his country, your law declares that his works shall become your property, and you requite him by seizing the patrimony of his children. We blame the errors and excesses of genius, and we leave them — justly leave them — for the most part, to the consequences of their strangely-blended nature. But if genius, in assertion of its diviner alliances, produces large returns when the earthly course of its frail possessor is past, why is the public to insult his descendants with their alms and their pity? What right have we to moralize over the excesses of a Burns, and insult his memory by charitable honors, while we are taking the benefit of his premature death, in the expiration of his copyright and the vaunted cheapness of his works? Or, to advert to a case in which the highest intellectual powers were associated with the noblest moral excellence, what right have we to take credit to ourselves justice to authors, is indeed surprising. Addison is said to have been concerned in procuring the act of

for a paltry and ineffectual subscription to rescue Abbotsford for the family of its great author (Abbotsford, his romance in stone and mortar, but not more individually *his* than those hundred fabrics, not made with hands, which he has raised, and peopled for the delight of mankind,) while we insist on appropriating now the profits of his earlier poems, and anticipate the time when, in a few years, his novels will be ours without rent-charge to enjoy — and any one's to copy, to emasculate, and to garble ? This is the case of one whom kings and people delighted to honor. But look on another picture — that of a man of genius and integrity, who has received all the insult and injury from his contemporaries, and obtains nothing from posterity but a name. Look at Daniel De Foe; recollect him pilloried, bankrupt, wearing away his life to pay his creditors in full, and dying in the struggle! — and his works live, imitated, corrupted, yet casting off the stains, not by protection of law, but by their own pure essence. Had every school-boy, whose young imagination has been prompted by his great work, and whose heart has learned to throb in the strange yet familiar solitude he created, given even the halfpenny of the statute of Anne, there would have been no want of a provision for his children, no need of a subscription for a statue to his memory!

"The term allowed by the existing law is curiously adapted to encourage the lightest works, and to leave the noblest unprotected. Its little span is ample for authors who seek only to amuse; who, 'to beguile the time, look like the time;' who lend to frivolity or corruption 'lighter wings to fly;' who sparkle, blaze, and expire. These may delight for a season — glisten as the fire-flies on the heaving sea of public opinion — the airy proofs of the intellectual activity of the age; — yet surely it is not just to legislate for those alone, and deny all reward to that literature which aspires to endure. Let us suppose an author, of true original genius, disgusted with the inane phraseology which had usurped the place of poetry, and devoting himself from youth to its service; disdaining the gauds which attract the careless, and unskilled in the moving accidents of fortune — not seeking his triumph in the tempest of the passions, but in the serenity which lies above them, — whose works shall be scoffed at — whose name made a by-word — and yet who shall persevere in his high and holy course, gradually impressing thoughtful minds with the sense of truth made visible in the severest forms of beauty, until he shall create the taste by which he shall be appreciated — influence, one after another, the master-spirits of his age — be felt pervading every part of the national literature, softening, raising, and enriching it; and when at last he shall find his confidence in his own aspirations justified, and the name which once was the scorn admitted to be the glory of his age — he shall look forward to the close of his earthly career, as the event that shall consecrate his fame and deprive his children of the opening harvest he is beginning to reap. As soon as his copyright becomes valuable, it is gone! This is no imaginary case — I refer to one who 'in this setting

Anne to be passed. From his time to the present reign, authors, as a class, seem to have had little influence in parliament.[1] Upon nearly all occasions, when their claims have been brought to the attention of the legislature, they have been so much entangled with the interests of booksellers and publishers, in whose hands the great mass of literary property, existing at the time, has generally been found, that they have had to encounter all the national prejudice against monopolies. Gradually, however, the true merits of the question have worked themselves free from irrelevant issues, and the present reign has become distinguished by a measure, of which it was well said, in advance, by a venerable poet and peti

part of time' has opened a vein of the deepest sentiment and thought before unknown — who has supplied the noblest antidote to the freezing effects of the scientific spirit of the age — who, while he has detected that poetry which is the essence of the greatest things, has cast a glory around the lowliest conditions of humanity, and traced out the subtle links by which they are connected with the highest — of one whose name will now find an echo, not only in the heart of the secluded student, but in that of the busiest of those who are fevered by political controversy — of William Wordsworth. Ought we not to requite such a poet, while yet we may, for the injustice of our boyhood! For those works which are now insensibly quoted by our most popular writers, the spirit of which now mingles with our intellectual atmosphere, he probably has not received through the long life he has devoted to his art, until lately, as much as the same labor, with moderate talent, might justly produce in a single year. Shall the law, whose term has been amply sufficient to his scorners, now afford him no protection, because he has outlasted their scoffs — because his fame has been fostered amidst the storms, and is now the growth of years?" (Three Speeches delivered in the house of commons in favor of a measure for an extension of Copyright. By T. N. Talfourd, Serjeant-at-Law. London. 1840.) In 1838 and 1839 he made similar efforts, and the measure was finally carried in 1842.

[1] The petitions of the authors of England to the house of commons, in favor of Mr. Serjeant Talfourd's bill, form a body of interesting documents, to be found in the tract from which the above extract is taken.

tioner, "that in this, as in all other cases, justice is capable of working out its own expediency."[1]

In America, since the adoption of the constitution of the United States, the protection of literary property depends upon the laws passed by congress pursuant to the power granted in that instrument. Whether there was any common law right of authors, in published works, in any of the states of this Union, before the adoption of the constitution, is a question not free from difficulty.

The fundamental principle of American law, in relation to common law rights, is, that the colonists brought with them into each colony all the body of the common law of England which was applicable to their situation, or, as it is sometimes said, which was suited to their circumstances and condition.[2] The existence of a common law right of authors, in any one of the American colonies, depends, of course, upon its existence in England, when the colony was

[1] Mr. Wordsworth.

[2] 1 Story's Commentaries on the Constitution, 137–140. Vanness *v.* Packard, 2 Peters S. C. R. 144. Wheaton *v.* Peters, 8 Ib. 591. Parsons, C. J. in Commonwealth *v.* Knowlton, 2 Mass. R 534, stated the doctrine thus: "Our ancestors, when they came into this new world, claimed the common law as their birthright, and brought it with them, except such parts as were judged inapplicable to their new state and condition."

settled, and also upon the fact of its having been brought by the colonists, as part of the body of the common law, not unsuited to their circumstances and condition. That this was the case, seems to have been denied by a majority of the supreme court of the United States, the question having arisen, whether there was any copyright at common law, in relation to printed books, in the state of Pennsylvania.[1]

We have seen, if the historical account given in the foregoing pages be correct, that the position cannot be maintained, that there existed in England no common law right of authors, previous to the settlement of the American colonies. It is clear, that there was such a thing as literary property in England, before the reign of Queen Anne; and it is equally clear that in the years 1769 and 1774, in the cases of Millar *v.* Taylor, and Donaldson *v.* Becket, this property was ascertained and declared to have been a right at common law, and consequently it must have existed ever since the introduction of printing into England. The last of these cases, if the answers of the judges are the proper *criteria* of the decision, decides only that the common law right had been taken away by the statute of Anne.

[1] Wheaton *v.* Peters, 8 Peters S. C. R. 591. The opinion of the court was delivered by Mr. Justice McLean. Mr. Justice Thompson and Mr. Justice Baldwin dissented, the former in an able and instructive opinion, in which he reviewed the authorities showing that the common law right existed in England prior to the statute of Anne, and affirmed that this right formed part of the common law of Pennsylvania.

How far this portion of the common law was part of the common law of any American colony, depends not upon the fact of the colonists having or not having had occasion to claim and act upon it, on their arrival, but upon the fact of there being or not being anything in their situation, during their early colonial history, so inconsistent with it, as to preclude the idea of its having been brought by them along with the rest of the body of the common law. The presumption is, that the whole of the common law, as it then existed, not inapplicable to the state and condition of the colonists, was brought by them from England. If there were any books published, in any of the colonies, at any time before they legislated on the subject, as there certainly were in many of them, there was nothing in their circumstances and situation unsuited to such a right, or inconsistent with its being claimed and recognized as part of the common law. There were objects to which the right could a tach, and any author could claim it as a right at the common law of England. Undoubtedly, the right lay dormant in all the colonies for a long period of time; and afterwards, when books began to be printed, the right was here, as in England, tacitly assumed and acted upon. There is some evidence, however, that it had been regarded as a common law right in several of the states, before the adoption of the constitution of the United States.[1]

[1] So far as the decision in Wheaton *v.* Peters negatives the adoption of the common law right of authors in the colony of Pennsylvania, I do

In March, 1783, the legislature of Massachusetts passed "an act for the purpose of securing to authors the exclusive right and benefit of publishing their literary productions, for twenty-one years." This act was preceded by the following remarkable preamble: "Whereas the improvement of knowledge, the progress of civilization, the public weal of the community, and the advancement of human happiness, greatly depend on the efforts of learned and ingenious persons in the various arts and sciences: As the principal encouragement such persons can have to make great and beneficial exertions of this nature must exist in the legal security of the fruits of their study and industry to themselves; and as such security is one of the natural rights of all men, there being no property more peculiarly a man's own than that which is produced by the labor of his mind: therefore, to encourage learned and ingenious persons to write useful books for the benefit of mankind, Be it enacted," &c.[1]

not feel authorized to criticize it, although I have made some suggestions in the text to show that a different view may be taken of that question. But that part of the decision, which denies the existence of the common law right in England, I must dissent from. The learned judge who pronounced the opinion of the majority, said, "the question was involved in great doubt and perplexity; and a little more than a century ago it was decided by the highest judicial court in England, that the right of authors could not be asserted at common law, but under the statute." (8 Peters, 660.) This is true; but if Donaldson *v.* Becket, the case referred to, decides anything, it is that the common law right existed anterior to the statute of Anne, and was taken away by that statute. Upon the existence of the common law right before the statute, the judges stood seven to four; and if the known opinion of Lord Mansfield is added, eight of the twelve judges affirmed the existence of the right.

[2] 1 Mass. Laws, 94, (edit. 1801.)

This preamble has been justly thought to recognize a right already understood to exist, and it seems manifestly to have been the purpose of the act to provide for the right additional security, and not to create it *de novo*.[1]

Soon after this act was passed, on the 27th May, 1783, a report was made in the old congress by Mr. Madison, on sundry papers and memorials on the subject of literary property, and the following resolution was passed.

"Resolved, That it be recommended to the several states, to *secure* to the authors or publishers of any new books not heretofore printed, being citizens of the United States, and to their executors, administrators and assigns, the copyright of such books for a certain time, not less than fourteen years from the first publication; and to secure to the said authors, if they shall survive the term first mentioned, and to their executors, administrators and assigns, the copyright of such books for another term, or time, not less than fourteen years; such copy or exclusive right of printing, publishing, and vending the same, to be secured to the original authors or publishers,

[1] It expresses more comprehensively than any other piece of legislation in the language, on the same subject, the principles of public policy and private right, on which literary property must always depend. The state of Connecticut had previously, in January, 1783, passed an act with the following preamble: "Whereas it is perfectly agreeable to the principles of natural justice and equity, that every author should be secured in receiving the profits that may arise from the sale of his works; and such security may encourage men of learning and genius to publish their writings, which may do honor to their country and service to mankind." (Cited 8 Peters S. C. R. 683.)

their executors, administrators and assigns, by such laws and such restrictions as to the several states may seem proper." [1]

Pursuant to this recommendation, several states passed laws, with preambles similar to those of the Massachusetts and Connecticut acts, all designed to "*secure*" to authors the profits arising from the sale of their works.[2] This studied phraseology, which had not been employed in the English statutes, evinces some intention to protect and secure a pre-existing right. The necessity for state legislation was soon afterwards superseded by the constitution of the United States, (art. 1, § 8,) which conferred upon congress power "to promote the progress of science and the useful arts, by securing, for limited times, to authors and inventors, the exclusive right to their respective writings and discoveries." As the states could not separately make effectual provision for these objects, the power was wisely granted to the national government.[3]

The first act passed to carry this provision into effect, so far as it related to authors, was the act of May 31st, 1790, chap. xv. entitled "An act for the encouragement of learning, by securing the copies

[1] 8 Cong. Journ. 257. 8 Peters S. C. R. 681.

[2] Cited 8 Peters S. C. R. 683, 684. Authors who aimed at national reputation entered their works in each of the states which had passed such laws. A copy of a popular work published in Massachusetts is before me, which was entered in New York, Pennsylvania and South Carolina, under the respective laws of those states, in the year 1787.

[3] 3 Story's Com. on the Constitution, p. 48, et seq. The Federalist, No. 43.

of maps, charts and books, to the authors and proprietors of such copies, during the times therein mentioned." The Supreme Court of the United States have held that this act, instead of sanctioning an existing perpetual right in an author in his works, created the right secured for a limited time; and that the word *secure*, in the constitution, does not mean the protection of an acknowledged legal right, but is used in reference to a future right to be created.[1]

If this decision is to be understood as declaring that the constitution and the act of 1790 created copyright throughout the United States, it may be readily assented to. We find the states, at the time of the establishment of the constitution, conferring upon the national legislature the power to "secure" the rights of authors and inventors. Each of the states, at that time, possessed the power to secure these rights within its own limits, as part of its sovereignty. But no state legislature could provide securities for the rights of authors which should operate over the whole country, and make a copyright of a book written and published in Massachusetts of equal validity in Pennsylvania. In order, however, to obviate this inconvenience, the state laws, passed before the adoption of the federal constitution, generally contained a proviso, that the benefit of the law was not to extend to authors, in-

[1] Wheaton *v.* Peters, 8 Peters S. C. R. 591.

habitants of, or residing in other states, until such states should have passed similar laws.[1]

These provisions show that the rights of authors in their published works existed by statute, in some of the states, before the constitution of the United States was formed ; and there cannot be much doubt that they also existed, in the older states, at common law. What, then, were the rights of authors, to be "secured," under the power granted to the national legislature ? The object to be gained by this grant of power will aid in determining the meaning of the language employed. The object clearly was to enable the general government to make laws which should secure the proceeds of a book in all the states to an author residing and publishing in any one of the states. The old congress had this object in view, when they recommended to the states to pass laws for this purpose ;[2] and it was distinctly urged, by the advocates for the adoption of the federal constitution, as the main reason for the provision.[3]

It would seem, therefore, that the rights of authors to be "secured" by congress, under this clause of the constitution, were exclusive rights to take the profits of their own publications throughout the United States. In this view, the constitution and the act of 1790 created a right which did not

[1] 1 Mass. Laws, 94, (edit. 1801.) Wheaton *v*. Peters, 8 Peters S. C. R. 681, 662, 683.

[2] Ante, p. 78.

[3] The Federalist, No. 43.

exist before ; and this may account for the use of the word "secure." Whether this power is exclusive, so that the states cannot now legislate for the protection of authors within their own limits, is one of the grave questions of our complex system of government.[1]

The act of 1790 was followed by a supplementary act, passed April 29th, 1802, which extended the benefits of the former statute to engravers.[2]

By an act passed February 3d, 1831, the former laws were consolidated and revised, and this act constitutes the existing copyright law of the United States.[3]

[1] See Story's Com. on the Constitution, § 1149.

[2] See Appendix, 2 U. S. Statutes at large, 171.

[3] See Appendix, 4 U. S. Statutes at large, 436.

CHAPTER II.

OF THE SUBJECTS OF LITERARY PROPERTY, BEFORE AND AFTER PUBLICATION.

In the following chapter, the various subjects of literary property, both before and after publication, will be considered in detail.

I. And first, with regard to that class of writings, to which rights and remedies have been applied, bearing a close analogy to those applicable to copyrights, viz. writings existing in manuscript and unpublished. We have already seen that in general, the author or owner of an unpublished manuscript possesses a property therein, which consists in the right to appropriate it to such uses as he shall please.[1] This is a right at common law, and is of course wholly independent of the statutes which create a property after publication, consisting in the exclusive right to the profits of publication. The existence of such a property has been repeatedly recognized with regard to many sorts of compositions, and it is now perfectly well settled, that the author or proprietor of an unpublished man-

[1] Ante, p. 49–52.

uscript may obtain the interference of a court of equity, to prevent its unauthorized publication.[1]

This right of property rests upon one of the ultimate foundations which sustain property in general; namely, the right which every man has to the exclusive possession and control of the products of his own labor. In the great case of Millar *v.* Taylor, in which the principles on which this right depends were so fully examined, Lord Mansfield declared that the source from which the common law is drawn, in respect of a copy before publication, is this — "Because it is *just*, that an author should reap the pecuniary profits of his own ingenuity and labor. It is *just* that another should not use his name without his consent. It is *fit*, that he should judge when to publish, or whether he ever will publish. It is *fit*, he should not only choose the time, but the manner of publication; how many — what volume — what print. It is *fit*, he should choose to whose care he will trust the accuracy and correctness of the impression; to whose honesty he will confide, not to foist in additions."[2]

[1] Webb *v.* Rose, cited 4 Burr. 2330; 2 Bro. P. C. 138; Forrester *v.* Walker, cited ut supra. Pope *v.* Curl, 2 Atk. 342; Manley *v.* Owen, cited 4 Burr. 2320, 2490. Duke of Queensbury *v.* Shebbeare, 2 Eden's Ch. R. 329; Southey *v.* Sherwood, 2 Meriv. 434; Macklin *v.* Richardson, Amb. 694; Donaldson *v.* Becket, 4 Burr. 2408; Wheaton *v.* Peters, 8 Peters S. C. R. 591, 661; 2 Story's Eq. Jurisp. § 943; Eden on Inj. ch. 13, p. 275, 276.

[2] Millar *v.* Taylor, 4 Burr. 2398. Sir W. D. Evans has intimated strong doubts of the correctness of Lord Mansfield's reasoning in this case on the subject of a property in manuscripts, or what his lordship accurately calls, in technical language, "*copy*, before publication." Lord Mansfield's argument was, that the same principles of justice and fitness, which are the admitted foundation of an author's sole right before publication, apply to his right

The incorporeal right in an unpublished manuscript belongs exclusively to the author, and cannot be seized by creditors, to the effect of entitling them to publish it.[1]

after publication; and that as the common law recognizes and protects the former, it follows that the latter is equally a right at common law, unless the act of publication is to be taken as an abandonment of the right, which he denies. Sir W. D. Evans seems to think that, as the house of lords in Donaldson *v.* Becket, overthrew the decision in Millar *v.* Taylor, and declared that there is no perpetual right at common law in published works, the reasoning of Lord Mansfield on the subject of a copy in manuscripts is also probably overruled. He closes some extended remarks with the following observation: "Lord Mansfield, to support the perpetual right to works published, argues that an unpublished manuscript cannot be distinguished from them; and may not that argument now be applied to the ultimate decision of the house of lords against a perpetual common law right of publications, and extended to manuscripts?" 2 Evans's Statutes, 20, note [14]. See also his edition of Lord Mansfield's decisions, vol. i. p. 386, note (*a*). The learned commentator seems not to have carefully considered the points actually decided in Donaldson *v.* Becket. An analysis of the questions put to the judges, and of their answers, exhibits the force of that decision. Eleven judges attended, and gave their answers. Ten were of opinion that at common law, an author of any literary composition had the sole right of first printing and publishing the same for sale, and might bring an action against any person who printed, published and sold the same without his consent; eight were of opinion that the law did not take away his right, upon his printing and publishing such book or literary composition, and four were of the contrary opinion. Six were of opinion that the author's right of action at common law, after he had published, is taken away by the statute 8 Anne, and that he has no remedy except on the foundation of that statute; while five were of opinion that the statute did not take away the common law right of action. It is manifest, therefore, that this decision confirms, in the most solemn manner, the doctrine of a sole right before publication, as part of the common law; that it negatives the position that publication alone takes away the right, but that it decides, by a bare majority of the judges who spoke, that the sole right at common law to multiply copies, after publication, is taken away by the statute, and depends wholly upon the terms and conditions of the act. See ante, p. 58, 59.

[1] Mr. Bell says, "The right at common law can exist only while the composition remains unpublished. But the property of unpublished literary compositions is not within the reach of creditors, to the effect of entitling them to publish them. No man can be forced, by any operation of the law, to publish his thoughts, even for the benefit of his creditors. And his right of withholding the publication will continue till the very moment his book

This property in copy descends to personal representatives, though neither the author nor his representatives have any manuscript whatever of the work. Thus, the copy of Lord Clarendon's History, at the distance of near a hundred years, was adjudged to his representatives,[1] and Lord Mansfield thought that although the manuscript in the defendant's hands might have been the only copy in existence, they could not print and publish without the plaintiff's consent.[2] In like manner, the son and devisee of Mr. Webb, a convey-

is actually given out to the public. Even the printer of the book will not be entitled to sell it for his payment, although there is not the smallest doubt that he has a complete lien over it till delivery, to prevent the author, or his creditors, from taking advantage of the publication till he shall be paid. When a book is published, the property of it forms a subject which creditors are entitled to attach and sell: and the price unpaid by the bookseller is as completely open to the diligence of creditors, as the price of any other commodity or piece of merchandise." 1 Bell's Com. p. 68.

[1] Duke of Queensbury *v.* Shebbeare, 2 Eden's Ch. R. 329.

[2] 4 Burr. 2397. The facts of the case were these. Henry, the second Earl of Clarendon, son of the lord chancellor and historian, gave to one Gwynne the original MSS. of his father's history, in order that he might take a copy of it, and make use of the copy as he should think fit; and a copy was accordingly taken. The administrator of Lord Clarendon, the son, brought a bill to restrain the publication of this work by Dr. Shebbeare, to whom Gwynne's son had sold or delivered the MSS. The lord keeper, Henley, was of opinion that it was not to be presumed that when Lord Clarendon, the son, gave the elder Gwynne a copy of his father's MSS. he intended he should have the right to print it; that Mr. Gwynne might make every use of it except that. Duke of Queensbury *v.* Shebbeare, 2 Eden's Ch. R. 329. Upon this case Lord Mansfield observes, "Mr. Gwynne was entitled, undoubtedly, to the *paper* of the transcript of Lord Clarendon's history; which gave him the *power* to print and publish it, after the fire at Petersham, which destroyed one original. This might have been the *only* manuscript of it in being. Mr. Gwynne might have thrown it into the fire, had he pleased. But, at the distance of near a hundred years, the copy was adjudged the property of Lord Clarendon's representatives; and Mr. Gwynne's printing and publishing it, without their consent, was adjudged an injury to that property; for which, in different shapes, he paid very dear." 4 Burr. 2397.

ancer, obtained an injunction against his father's clerk, to prevent him from printing his father's manuscript draughts.[1] So also, the assignees of the writings of President Washington, who derived their title through his devisee, obtained an injunction against certain persons who had pirated them from the edition published by them.[2]

Under what circumstances the author or proprietor of a manuscript may be deemed to have authorized its publication, is a question of some nicety as well as importance. Merely parting with the possession of a manuscript, or intrusting the possession to a third person, are acts which do not carry with them proof of an intent to part with the ownership of the intellectual contents. Such acts must be limited, in point of effect, to the purposes, expressed or implied, for which the possession was given.[3] Thus the giving of a manuscript copy of Lord Clarendon's history, to be used as the donee should think fit, was held not to have authorized its publication,[4] and the possession of letters by the person to whom they were addressed, does not take away from the writer the right to object to their publication.[5] So the allowing a manuscript play to be acted will not amount to a license to publish it.[6] And where copies of a piece

[1] Cited in Millar *v.* Taylor, 4 Burr. 2330. See also Thompson *v.* Stanhope, Amb. 739. Earl of Granard *v.* Dunkin, 1 Ball & Beat. 207. Folsom *v.* Marsh, 2 Story's R. 100.

[2] Folsom *v.* Marsh, 2 Story's R. 100, 168.

[3] 2 Story's Eq. Jurisp. § 943.

[4] Duke of Queensbury *v.* Shebbeare, 2 Eden's Ch. R. 329.

[5] Pope *v.* Curll, 2 Atk. 342. Thompson *v.* Stanhope, Amb. 773.

[6] Macklin *v.* Richardson, Ambl. 694.

of music had been distributed in manuscript for a year, by the author, before it was printed, it was held that the copyright was not lost.[1] But Lord Eldon seems to have thought that the circumstances in Mr. Southey's case, where he had left his manuscript a long time in the hands of a publisher, without inquiry, authorized the inference that he had abandoned his own right as author.[2] Perhaps the soundest rule would be, to hold that when express consent is not proved, the negative is implied as a tacit condition.[3] Most of the cases seem to proceed upon this principle,[4] and it was adopted and acted upon by Mr. Justice Story, in relation to the writings of Washington, consisting of his correspondence, addresses, messages and other papers, official and private.[5] The ground was taken in this case that these writings were public in their nature and were intended by the author for public use. But the facts of the case did not show that General Washington intended them as a donation to the public, and the court laid down the principle, that unless there be a most unequivocal dedication of private letters and papers by the author, either to the public or to some private person, the author has a property therein, and the copyright thereof exclusively be-

[1] White *v.* Gerooch, 2 B. & A. 290.

[2] Southey *v.* Sherwood, 2 Meriv. See some observations upon this case, *ante*.

[3] Per Willes J. in Millar *v.* Taylor, 4 Burr. 2330.

[4] Thompson *v.* Stanhope, Amb. 737. Duke of Queensbury *v.* Shebbeare, 2 Eden.

[5] Folsom *v.* Marsh, 2 Story's R. 100, 109.

longs to him.[1] In the United States, manuscripts are now under the protection of the statute of 1831, which gives a remedy, at law and in equity, against any person who shall print or publish, or be about to publish any manuscript whatever without the consent of the author or legal proprietor first obtained, if the author or proprietor be a citizen of or resident in the United States.[2]

II. LETTERS, addressed from one correspondent to another, have formed the subject of special discussion in courts of equity, and the principles on which the respective rights of the parties depend are analogous to those which govern in the case of other

[1] The learned judge said, "In relation to this objection, it is most manifest, that President Washington deemed them his own private property, and bequeathed them to his nephew, the late Mr. Justice Washington, through whom the late Mr. Ch. Justice Marshall and Mr. Sparks acquired an interest therein; and, as appears from the contract between these gentlemen, annexed to the report, the publication of these writings was undertaken by Mr. Sparks, as editor, for their joint benefit; and the work itself has been accomplished at great expense and labor, and after great intellectual efforts, and very patient and comprehensive researches, both at home and abroad. The publication of the defendants, therefore, to some extent, must be injurious to the rights of property of the representatives and assignees of President Washington. Indeed, as we shall presently see, congress have actually purchased these very letters and manuscripts, at a great price, for the benefit of the nation, from their owner and possessor under the will of Mr. Justice Washington, as private and most valuable property. That President Washington, therefore, intended them exclusively for public use, as a donation to the public, or did not esteem them of value as his own private property, appears to me to be a proposition, completely disproved by the evidence. Unless, indeed, there be a most unequivocal dedication of private letters and papers by the author, either to the public, or to some private person, I hold, that the author has a property therein, and that the copyright thereof exclusively belongs to him."

[2] Act of Congress of 3d Feb. 1831, § 9.

manuscript writings. It may be well briefly to review the authorities on this subject, in their historical order.

The first case is that relating to the letters of Pope to Swift. Mr. Pope obtained an injunction against Curll the bookseller, to prevent the vending of a book containing his letters to Swift. The ground was taken, on a motion to dissolve the injunction, that a letter is in the nature of a gift to the receiver. Lord Hardwicke said he was of opinion that it is only a special property in the receiver, possibly the property of the paper may belong to him ; but this does not give a license to any person whatsoever to publish it to the world, for at most the receiver has only a joint property with the writer.[1] The objection was also raised, that the letters were only on familiar subjects, and the book could not properly be called a learned work. But his lordship did not admit the distinction.[2] An injunction was granted against the letters written by Pope, but not against the rest of the book.

The next case related to Lord Chesterfield's letters to his son, containing characters of persons, besides disquisitions on politics, literature and education. The widow of the son, in whose possession the letters remained, restored to Lord Chesterfield some

[1] Pope *v.* Curll, 2 Atk. 342. Mr. Pope had no copies of these letters. See Lord Mansfield's statement, 4 Burr. 2397.

[2] It seems that the book was in print, when the injunction was obtained. Lord Hardwicke held that a book of letters was within the grounds and intention of the act of Anne, as much as any other work.

of the characters, at his request, but kept copies of them; and she also kept the rest of the original letters, which he did not ask for. After Lord Chesterfield's death, she was about to publish the letters, not including the characters, when his executors applied for an injunction. Lord Apsley, C. granted the injunction, upon the ground that the defendant had not obtained the consent of Lord Chesterfield or his executors.[1]

The case of Perceval *v.* Phipps, next in point of time, seems to admit the right of the holder of letters to publish them, where the publication is necessary to the defence of his character against an unjust imputation.[2] The acts of the parties in this case supplied reasons for not restraining the publication.

In Gee *v.* Pritchard, the doctrine of property in the writer, in letters of familiar friendly correspondence, was admitted by Lord Eldon, as well as the qualified property of the receiver; but as the latter had returned the letters to the writer, with the declaration that he did not consider himself entitled to retain them, keeping copies without apprizing her, it was held, under the circumstances, that he had renounced the right of publication, even if he previously had it for purposes of self-vindication.[3]

In explaining the grounds upon which the court acts in these cases, his lordship observed, that the

[1] Thompson *v.* Stanhope, Amb. 737.

[2] Lord and Lady Perceval *v.* Phipps, 2 Ves. & B. 19.

[3] Gee *v.* Pritchard, 2 Swanst. 402, 427.

property is qualified in some respects; that, by sending a letter, the writer has given, for the purpose of reading it, and in some cases of keeping it, a property to the person to whom the letter is addressed; yet, that the gift is so restrained, that, beyond the purposes for which the letter is sent, the property is in the sender. Under such circumstances, it is immaterial whether the intended publication is for the purpose of profit or not. If for profit, the party is then selling; if not for profit, he is then giving that, a portion of which belongs to another. Property, therefore, is the ground of the interference of the court.

From these decisions it is not difficult to extract the general doctrines which govern the interference of courts of equity, in cases of this class. 1. The leading principle is, that the writer of letters has such a qualified property in them, as will intitle him to an injunction to restrain their publication by the party written to, or his assignees or representatives. 2. That this qualified property descends to representatives. 3. That it is a right of property independent of the right to take the profits of publication, and consequently does not depend upon or involve the pecuniary value of the letters proposed to be published. 4. That for the purposes of justice publicly administered, in the ordinary modes of proceeding, or to vindicate his character from an accusation publicly made, the receiver of letters may publish them.[1]

[1] Perceval *v.* Phipps, 2 Ves. & B. 19. Gee *v.* Pritchard, 2 Swanst. 418, 426, 427. Folsom *v.* Marsh, 2 Story's R. 100, 110, 111. 2 Story's Eq. Jurisp. § 948.

But a doubt has been suggested, whether mere private letters, not intended as literary compositions, are entitled to the protection of an injunction in the same manner as compositions of a literary character.[1] This doubt has probably arisen from the habit of not discriminating between the different rights of property which belong to an unpublished manuscript, and those which belong to a published book. The latter, as I have intimated in another connection, is a right to take the profits of publication. The former

[1] By Sir Thomas Plumer, vice-chancellor, in Perceval *v.* Phipps, 2 V. & B., and Mr. Chancellor Walworth, in Brandreth *v.* Lance, 8 Paige's R. 24, 26. In the former case, the vice-chancellor thought that the letters of Pope and of Lord Chesterfield derived their right to protection from their character as literary compositions. But there is no evidence in either case, as reported, to show that either of the writers intended those letters for literary compositions, or wrote them with a view to publication. In Pope *v.* Curll, Lord Hardwicke dealt with the subject, on one point, as a book, because it was already printed by the defendant. See 2 Atk. 342. With regard to Lord Chesterfield's Letters, however elegantly written, the case presents only a domestic correspondence between father and son. They certainly were not written for publication, so far as we can judge from the report in Ambl. 737. In like manner, Mr. Chancellor Walworth (8 Paige, 27,) supposes that Lord Eldon, in Gee *v.* Pritchard, went the length of allowing the remedy for a right of property, where the plaintiff's interest was no other than that of violated feelings. He says, "The complainant's bill was not to prevent the publication of her letters on account of any supposed interest she had in them as literary property, but to restrain the publication of a private correspondence, as a matter of feeling only." 8 Paige, 28. The learned chancellor seems to understand Lord Eldon's use of the term "property" to refer to a subject of pecuniary value; whereas it is clear that his lordship uses it in reference to private correspondence, which has no pecuniary value for purposes of publication, when he speaks of a joint property in the writer and the receiver of a letter. See his observations, cited in the text, *ante*, from 2 Swanst. 415. This is equally manifest from his lordship's remark on the case of Perceval *v.* Phipps, which he did not understand to have denied Lady Perceval's *property* in the letters. See 2 Swanst. 415. So, too, he says that his predecessors did not inquire whether the intention of the writer was or was not directed to publication. Ib. p. 414. Such an intention must be the only sensible test of the literary character of a letter.

is a right to control the act of publication, and to decide whether there shall be any publication at all. It has been called a right of property; an expression perhaps not quite satisfactory, but on the other hand sufficiently descriptive of a right which, however incorporeal, involves many of the essential elements of property, and is at least positive and definite. This expression can leave us in no doubt as to the meaning of the learned judges who have used it, when they have applied it to cases of unpublished manuscripts. They obviously intended to use it in no other sense, than in contradistinction to the mere interests of feeling, and to describe a substantial right or legal interest.[1]

If this be the correct view of the adjudged cases, it follows that there can be no sound distinction between private letters or letters of friendship or business, and letters intended as literary compositions, so far as the remedy afforded to the writer by courts of equity is concerned. In either case, the writer proceeds, when seeking that remedy, upon a right which the courts have recognized as a right of property; though in the case of letters which the writer intended for publication and profit, his right has the other element of an anticipated loss of pecuniary profits. Indeed, there is a moral reason why the rights of property should not be deemed to

[1] Gee *v.* Pritchard, 2 Swanst. 403. Southey *v.* Sherwood, 2 Meriv. 435. Folsom *v.* Marsh, 2 Story's R. 100, 108, 109. Denis *v.* Leclerc, 1 Martin's Louis. R. 297. 2 Story's Eq. Jurisp. § 945, 948 a. Ante, note, p. 93.

exist only when the letters are literary compositions, which has been pointed out by an eminent jurist. "If the mere sending of letters to third persons is not to be deemed, in cases of literary composition, a total abandonment of the right of property therein by the sender; *a fortiori*, the act of sending them cannot be presumed to be an abandonment thereof in cases where the very nature of the letters imports, as matter of business, or friendship, or advice, or family or personal confidence, the implied or necessary intention and duty of privacy and secrecy.[1]

There is another, and, as it seems to me, decisive objection to the supposed distinction between private letters and letters of a literary character. It is impossible to make any such distinction, in point of fact.[2] Literary subjects, elegance and finish of style,

[1] 2 Story's Eq. Jurisp. § 947.

[2] Mr. Godson has divided epistolary writings into three classes: 1. Letters originally intended for the press, constituting a literary work, to which the form of epistolary composition is given as a matter of dress. 2. Letters which have actually passed from one person to another, but which, from the *nature of the subject, and the literary character of the writer*, may be considered, *when a great number of them are collected*, as forming a literary work. 3. Common letters on business, and on every subject that can occur in the intercourse of private life, but which *never could have been intended to be published*, and therefore cannot be considered as *literary compositions, and entitled to protection, on the ground of a copyright existing in them*. As to the latter class, the learned author thinks, that the ground on which courts of equity have interfered to prevent publication, is "not upon copyright, but that the publication is a breach of *contract*, or *confidence*, or when they are to be made a source of *profit*, at the risk of wounding private feelings." Godson on Patents, &c. 327, 328. It will be seen that I have taken a very different view both of the authorities, and of the supposed distinction between different classes of letters. As to the authorities, it is clear that they proceed upon a property in the writer, and upon nothing else, whether the letters are of one class or another. As to the distinction, it may well be asked, what degree of scholarship, what number of letters, and what subject, are to determine whether a man's letters are to be considered as tak-

elaborate and beautiful writing, eloquent description, may all be found in letters of friendship, as much as personal anecdote or topics of domestic interest. What is the friendly correspondence of the learned, but, in a critical sense, literary composition; in which knowledge, taste and eloquence, on subjects of general and literary interest, are so copiously displayed, that the treasures which lie hidden in private repositories doubtless exceed in value and importance all that the world has yet possessed in published epistolary writing? Yet it would be extremely inaccurate to apply to such writings the term literary compositions, in the sense in which alone that term can have any legal acceptation; for in this sense it must mean compositions written with a view to their publication as literary works. If the style or the subject is to be the test of the literary character of a letter, in a court of justice, a vast mass of private correspondence would at once fall under that designation; but if this test is to decide the question of protection from unauthorized publication, a still greater mass of familiar writing, that can exhibit no atoning merits of style or subject to console the feelings wounded by publication, must be left out of the pale of human rights. Fortunately for the peace of mankind, the law establishes no such distinction.[1]

ing the character of a literary work, when they were not written for publication? No such test can be applied.

[1] Mr. Justice Story, in a case from which I have already quoted, thus sums up the doctrine in relation to letters. "There is no small confusion in the books, in reference to the question of copyright in let-

The question is probably disposed of in this country, by the statute which gives a remedy against

ters. Some of the *dicta* seem to suppose, that no copyright can exist, except in letters, which are professedly literary; whilst others again recognize a much more enlarged and liberal doctrine. Without attempting to reconcile, or even to comment upon the language of the authorities on this head, I wish to state what I conceive to be the true doctrine upon the whole subject. In the first place I hold, that the author of any letter or letters, (and his representatives,) whether they are literary compositions, or familiar letters, or letters of business, possess the sole and exclusive copyright therein; and that no persons, neither those to whom they are addressed, nor other persons, have any right or authority to publish the same upon their own account, or for their own benefit. But, consistently with this right, the persons to whom they are addressed may have, nay, must by implication possess the right to publish any letter or letters addressed to them, upon such occasions, as require or justify the publication or public use of them; but this right is strictly limited to such occasions. Thus, a person may justifiably use and publish, in a suit at law or in equity, such letter or letters as are necessary and proper to establish his right to maintain the suit, or defend the same. So, if he be aspersed or misrepresented by the writer, or accused of improper conduct, in a public manner, he may publish such parts of such letter or letters, but no more, as may be necessary to vindicate his character and reputation, or free him from unjust obloquy and reproach. If he attempt to publish such letter or letters on other occasions, not justifiable, a court of equity will prevent the publication by an injunction, as a breach of private confidence or contract, or of the rights of the author; and *a fortiori*, if he attempt to publish them for profit; for then it is not a mere breach of confidence or contract, but it is a violation of the exclusive copyright of the writer. In short, the person to whom letters are addressed has but a limited right, or special property (if I may so call it,) in such letters, as a trustee, or bailee, for particular purposes, either of information or of protection, or of support of his own rights and character. The general property, and the general rights incident to property, belong to the writer, whether the letters are literary compositions, or familiar letters, or details of facts, or letters of business. The general property in the manuscripts remains in the writer and his representatives as well as the general copyright. *A fortiori*, third persons, standing in no privity with either party, are not entitled to publish them, to subserve their own private purposes of interest, or curiosity, or passion. If the case of Perceval *v.* Phipps, (2 Ves. & Beam. 21, 28,) before the then vice-chancellor, (Sir Thomas Plumer,) contains a different doctrine, all I can say is, that I do not accede to its authority; and I fall back upon the more intelligible and reasonable doctrine of Lord Hardwicke, in Pope *v.* Curll, (2 Atk. R. 342,) and Lord Apsley, in the case of Thompson *v.* Stanhope, (Amb. R. 737,) and of Lord-Keeper Henley, in the case of the Duke of Queensbury *v.* Shebbeare, (2 Eden R. 329; 4 Burr. R. 2330,) which Lord Eldon has not scrupled to hold to be binding authorities upon the point in the unauthorized publication of *any manuscript whatever.*[1]

The question has been mooted in this country, whether official letters, addressed to the government by public officers, can be the subject of copyright. In these cases, there seems to be a right on the part of the government to publish or to withhold from publication, from principles of public policy, according to the exigencies of the public service. But this exception in favor of the government, which has been

Gee *v.* Pritchard, (2 Swanst. R. 403, 414, 415, 419, 426, 427.) But I do not understand, that Sir Thomas Plumer did, in Perceval *v.* Phipps, deny the right of property of the writer in his own letters; and so he was understood by Lord Eldon in Gee *v.* Pritchard; who, however, said, that that case admitted of much remark. Indeed, if the doctrine were otherwise, that no person, or his representatives, could have a copyright in his own private or familiar letters, written to friends upon interesting political and other occasions, or containing details of facts and occurrences passing before the writer, it would operate as a great discouragement upon the collection and preservation thereof; and the materials of history would become far more scanty than they otherwise would be. What descendant, or representative of the deceased author, would undertake to publish, at his own risk and expense, any such papers; and what editor would be willing to employ his own learning, and judgment, and researches, in illustrating such works, if, the moment they were successful and possessed the substantial patronage of the public, a rival bookseller might republish them, either in the same or in a cheaper form, and thus either share with him, or take from him the whole profits? It is the supposed exclusive copyright in such writings which now encourages the publication thereof, from time to time, after the author has passed to the grave. To this we owe not merely the publication of the writings of Washington, but of Franklin, and Jay, and Jefferson and Madison, and other distinguished statesmen of our own country. It appears to me, that the copyright act of 1831, (ch. 16, § 9,) fully recognizes the doctrine for which I contend. It gives by implication to the author or legal proprietor of any manuscript whatever, the sole right to print and publish the same, and expressly authorizes the courts of equity of the United States to grant injunctions to restrain the publication thereof, by any person or persons, without his consent." See also 2 Story's Eq. Jurisp. § 947, 948. The same doctrine substantially is held in France. Renouard, tom. ii. p. 294, 295.

[1] Act of Cong. Feb. 3, 1831, § 9.

thought to stand upon principles analogous to those which give a right to private individuals to publish the letters of their agents upon fit and justifiable occasions, is not supposed to make such letters common property, to be published by any person who may see fit, without the sanction of the government, nor to take away the property of the writers or their representatives.[1]

But the occasion, on which this doctrine was alluded to, did not require a direct adjudication of the question whether the despatches of a public officer, addressed to his government, can be the subject of

[1] Folsom *v.* Marsh, 2 Story's R. 100, 113. In this case Mr. Justice Story said, "In respect to official letters addressed to the government, or any of its departments, by public officers, so far as the right of the government extends, from principles of public policy, to withhold them from publication, or to give them publicity, there may be a just ground of distinction. It may be doubtful, whether any public officer is at liberty to publish them, at least in the same age, when secrecy may be required by the public exigencies, without the sanction of the government. On the other hand, from the nature of the public service, or the character of the documents, embracing historical, military, or diplomatic information, it may be the right, and even the duty, of the government, to give them publicity, even against the will of the writers. But this is an exception in favor of the government, and stands upon principles allied to, or nearly similar to, the rights of private individuals, to whom letters are addressed by their agents, to use them and publish them, upon fit and justifiable occasions. But assuming the right of the government to publish such official letters and papers, under its own sanction, and for public purposes, I am not prepared to admit, that any private persons have a right to publish the same letters and papers, without the sanction of the government, for their own private profit and advantage. Recently the Duke of Wellington's despatches have (I believe) been published, by an able editor, with the consent of the noble duke, and under the sanction of the government. It would be a strange thing to say, that a compilation involving so much expense, and so much labor to the editor, in collecting and arranging the materials, might be pirated and republished by another bookseller, perhaps to the ruin of the original publisher and editor. Before my mind arrives at such a conclusion, I must have clear and positive lights to guide my judgment, or to bind me in point of authority."

private copyright.[1] In France, it seems to be considered that official documents are not subjects of the privilege of authors.[2]

III. Lectures. The right of property in lectures, oral and written, has been recognized in England by statute. The 5 and 6 Wm. IV. chap. 65, sec. 1, enacts, that from and after the first day of September, 1835, the author, or his assignee, of lectures to be delivered in any school, seminary, institution, or other place, shall have the sole right to publish them; and the 3d section declares that no person allowed for a certain fee and reward or otherwise to attend and be present at any lecture delivered at any place, shall be deemed and taken to be licensed, or to have leave to print, copy and publish such lectures, only because of having leave to attend them. But the 5th section provides that the operation of the act is to be restricted to lectures, of the delivery of which notice in writing shall have been given to two justices living within five miles of the place of delivery, two days before the delivery thereof. And it is further provided, that the act shall not extend to any lecture or lectures delivered in any university or public school, or college, or on any public foundation, or by any individual, in virtue

[1] The letters and documents of an official character, published by the defendants in this case, were not more than one-fifth part of the whole, and the court did not expressly decide the question concerning them. See 2 Story's R. 114.

[2] See a very able discussion of the question in Renouard, tom. 2, p. 132, et seq.

of or according to any gift, endowment, or foundation. This last provision is not a liberal one. A professor on a foundation has discharged his duty when he has delivered his lecture to his class. The salary has bought of him no service beyond this, whether it is paid by the state, or is the gift of an individual. It certainly has not bought for the public the substance of lectures which may have cost their proprietor the labor of a life. This illiberal exception is unknown on the continent of Europe. In most countries, this kind of public discourse is under the full protection of the law.[1]

In the United States, the right of property in lectures depends upon the general principles of the common law, and the statute which protects the owner of manuscripts.[2]

In relation to a lecture purely oral, of which the speaker has no manuscript, or any other writing which is such in its nature, as that, coupled with what is delivered orally, it may be taken that he has substantially a written composition, the common law has not gone the length of saying that he can, on the footing of property, have a remedy for an unauthorized publication. A written composition has been hitherto held to be the subject of literary property; concerning which the court must be satisfied that the publication complained of is an invasion of a written work, and this can only be done by comparing the composition with the piracy.

[1] Renouard, tom. ii. pp. 144–149. [2] Act of Cong. 3d Feb. 1831, § 9.

But it does not follow that because the information communicated by a lecturer is not committed to writing, but orally delivered, it is therefore within the power of any person who hears it to publish it. When persons are admitted, as pupils or otherwise, to hear public lectures, it is upon the implied confidence and contract that they will not use any means to injure or to take away the exclusive right of the lecturer in his own lectures. The hearer may take notes for purposes of his own information, but he may not publish them for profit.[1]

Accordingly, if a person attending such lectures undertakes to publish them, or furnishes another person with the means of publishing them, a court of equity will restrain such a publication, as a violation of trust and confidence, founded in contract, or implied from circumstances.[2]

Where a lecture has been reduced to writing, either wholly or substantially, the author has a right of property in it as a literary composition, in the same manner as in the case of other manuscripts. The admission of persons to hear such a lecture affords no presumption that the speaker intends to give them a right to publish the information which they may acquire. But when a court of equity is called upon to restrain a publication, on the ground

[1] Abernethy *v.* Hutchinson, 3 Law Journ. 209, 219. 2 Story's Eq. Jurisp. § 949.

[2] 2 Story's Eq. Jurisp. § 949.

that it is a piracy of a composition in writing, the writing must be produced.[1]

The act of congress, 3d February, 1831, § 9, gives an action on the case against any person who shall print or publish any manuscript whatever without the consent of the author or proprietor, and empowers the courts of the United States to grant injunctions according to the principles of equity, to restrain such publication. The remedy thus afforded would, without doubt, extend to the case of any lecture, of which the author could produce notes, showing that he had substantially reduced the same to writing.[2]

IV. Dramatic Compositions, when in manuscript, are protected, like other literary compositions, nor does the author lose the exclusive right of printing and publishing a play, by allowing it to be represented on the stage.[3]

[1] Ibid.

[2] In France, the *cour royale* of Paris had before it, in 1828, the interesting question, whether, when a course of oral lectures is merely the reproduction of a work previously published by the professor, a person who publishes the lectures from notes taken by a stenographer, can be made responsible for a piracy to the publisher of the work thus reproduced. The decision of the question was given in the affirmative. See Renouard, tom. 2, p. 146.

[3] Macklin *v.* Richardson, Amb. 695. The plaintiff, in this case, was the author of a farce called "*Love a la Mode*," consisting of two acts, which was performed, by his permission, several times, at the different theatres, in successive years, but was never printed or published by him. When the farce was over, he used to take the copy away from the prompter; and when it was played at the benefits of particular actors, he made them pay a certain sum for the performance. The defendants, who were proprietors of a magazine, employed a short-hand writer to take down the words of the play at the theatre, and thus published the first act, giving notice that they would publish

Whether the property of an author in a published play includes, at common law, the sole right of representation upon the stage, is a point admitting of some doubt. In an action brought for the penalty under the statute 8 Anne, c. 19, in which the only evidence of publication was by representation of the play in question, Lord Kenyon held that the statute only extends to prohibit the publication of the book itself by any other than the author or his assigns, and that the acting of a play is not a publication.[1] In a subsequent case, where Lord Byron's tragedy of Marino Faliero, altered and abridged for the stage, was performed without the consent of the owner of the copyright, who applied for an injunction, the court of K. B., on a case sent by the Lord Chancellor, certified it as their opinion that an action could not be maintained "for publicly acting and representing the said tragedy, abridged in manner aforesaid."[2]

The consequence of these decisions, in England, was, that while the authors of dramatic and musical compositions, after printing and publishing their works, enjoyed their copyrights, they had no exclusive privilege to the more valuable form of representation or performance. This defect in the law led to the enactment of statutes giving this exclusive

the second act in their next number. Lord Commissioner Smythe, in granting an injunction, negatived the idea that acting a play is a publication of it.

[1] Coleman *v.* Wathen, 5 T. R. 245.

[2] Murray *v.* Elliston, 5 B. & Ald. 657.

right. The 3 Wm. IV. c. 15, sec. 1, gave to the author or his assignee, of any printed and unpublished tragedy, comedy, play, opera, farce, or other dramatic piece or entertainment, the sole right of having it represented in any part of the British dominions; and to the author or his assignee of any such dramatic production which was printed or published after the passing of the act, or ten years before, the sole right of representation, from the time of publication, or of the passing of the act, for a period of twenty-eight years, or, if the author were living at the end of that time, for the remainder of the author's life.[1]

By the 5 and 6 Vict. c. 45, sec. 20, it is enacted that the sole liberty of representing or performing or permitting to be represented or performed, any dramatic piece or musical composition, shall endure, and be the property of the author or his assignee for the same term as is provided in the act for the duration of copyright in books. The same section extends the provisions in the act respecting literary copyright and the registration thereof, to the liberty of representing or performing any dramatic piece or musical composition, except that the first public representation or performance shall be deemed equivalent to the first publication of a book.[2]

V. Books. The term "Book" is made use of

[1] 3 Wm. IV. c. 15, sec. 1. See Appendix.

[2] 5 and 6 Vict. c. 45, s. 20. See Appendix.

in both the English and American statutes, and the question has arisen, whether its construction is to be confined to those forms of publication only which are popularly called books.

The question first arose in England at Nisi Prius upon a song printed on a single sheet of paper, which it was contended could not be within the protection of the act 8 Anne, c. 19, which, in the enacting clause, mentions only "books." Lord Ellenborough was inclined to think that such a publication was not protected by the statute, as the word *book* only means in common acceptation a plurality of sheets, and is decidedly used in this sense in the clause of the statute which speaks of "every sheet or sheets being part of such book or books." He therefore nonsuited the plaintiff, but reserved the point for the opinion of the court. Erskine, at the next term, moved and obtained a rule to show cause why the nonsuit should not be set aside ;[1] but when

[1] Mr. Erskine, on this occasion, argued "that the legislature could never have meant to make the operation of the statute depend upon the type in which any composition is printed, or the form in which it is bound up. This song might easily have been extended over several sheets, and rendered a duodecimo volume. In Bach *v.* Longman, Cowp. 623, it was decided that music is within the act, and musical compositions most generally appear in this fugitive form. [Lord Ellenborough. In the case cited, the musical composition was a *sonata*, and a sonata may be a book.] It never occurred to the lord chancellor who directed the issue, or to Lord Mansfield, or any of the judges who decided the case, that the form of the publication could make any difference, and therefore it is not stated. If a different construction were put upon the act, many productions of the greatest genius, both in prose and verse, would be excluded from its benefits. But, might the papers of the Spectator, or Gray's Elegy in a Country Church Yard, have been pirated as soon as they were published, because they were first given to the world on single sheets? The voluminous ex-

the counsel for the defendant proceeded to show cause, the court directed the matter to be reconsidered by a special verdict, that it might be ascertained whether the piece was a book within the meaning of the legislature. But the cause was not again carried down for trial.[1]

In a subsequent case, upon the same point, Lord Ellenborough reconsidered his former opinion, and it was settled unanimously by the court that it could not depend upon the form of the publication, whether it were entitled to the privileges of the statute or not; that a composition on a single sheet might well be a book within the meaning of the legislature.[2]

tent of a production cannot, in an enlightened country, be the sole title to the guardianship the author receives from the law. Every man knows that the mathematical and astronomical calculations which will enclose the student during a long life in his cabinet, are frequently reduced to the compass of a few lines: and is all this profundity of mental abstraction, on which the security and happiness of the species in every part of the globe depend, to be excluded from the protection of British jurisprudence? But there is nothing in the word *book* to require that it shall consist of several sheets bound in leather, or stitched in a marble cover. *Book* is evidently the Saxon *boc*, and the latter term is from the beech-tree, the rind of which supplied the place of paper to our German ancestors. The Latin word *liber* is of a similar etymology, meaning originally only the bark of a tree. *Book* may therefore be applied to any writing; and it has often been so used in the English language. Sometimes the most humble and familiar illustration is the most fortunate. The *horn book*, so formidable to infant years, consists of one small page protected by an animal preparation, and in this state it has universally received the appellation of a *book*. So in legal proceedings, the copy of the pleadings after issue joined, whether it be long or short, is called the paper *book* or the demurrer *book*. In the court of exchequer, a roll was anciently denominated a *book*, and so continues in some instances to this day. An oath as old as the time of Edward I. runs in this form: "And you shall deliver into the Court of Exchequer a book fairly written," &c. But the book delivered into court in fulfilment of this oath, has always been a roll of parchment." 2 Campb. 28, 29, note.

[1] Hime *v.* Dale, 2 Campb. 27, note.

[2] Clementi *v.* Goulding, 2 Campb. 25, 32; 11 East, 244.

By the 5 and 6 Vict. c. 45, s. 2, the word "book," as used in that act, is to be construed to mean and include every volume, part, or division of a volume, pamphlet, sheet of letter press, sheet of music, map, chart, or plan separately published. It is said, however, to have been held in this country, that a *price-current*, published in a semi-weekly newspaper, is not a *book* within the act of congress, because not a work of science or learning, but of mere industry.[1] This is inconsistent with the previous decisions, and the reason given for it is at variance with all the analogous principles on the subject. Works of industry are as much the subjects of protection as works of genius. Indeed, there can be no line drawn between a production, the fruit of learning, and one the fruit of mere industry. All learning is the accumulation of knowledge gathered by the exercise of industry.[2]

VI. MUSIC was formerly held in England to be within the protection of the act of Anne, it being a *writing*;[3] and now by the statute of 5 and 6 Vict.

[1] Clayton *v.* Stone, cited 2 Kent's Com. 380, note, as decided in the circuit court of the United States, at New York, Dec. 1828. The case is not reported.

[2] I cannot but think that the true reason was that the publication, being in a newspaper, had not been duly entered according to the act of congress.

[3] Bach *v.* Longman, Cowp. 623. In this case Lord Mansfield said, "The words of the act of parliament are very large — *books and other writings*. It is not confined to language or letters. Music is a science: it may be *written*; and the mode of conveying ideas is by signs and marks. If the narrow interpretation contended for in the argument were to hold, it would equally apply to algebra, mathematics, arithmetic, hieroglyphics. All these are conveyed by signs and figures. There is no color for saying that music is not within the act." See also Platt *v.* Button, 19 Ves. 447. Clementi *v.* Walker, 2 B. & C. 861.

c. 45, s. 2, the word "book," in the construction of that act, is to mean and include "every volume, part or division of a volume, pamphlet, sheet of letter-press, sheet of music, map, chart, or plan, separately published."[1] Musical compositions, intended for the stage, fall under the head of dramatic compositions. In the United States, published music is included in the "Act for the encouragement of learning," under the term "musical composition."[2] But we have no statute in this country to secure to the authors of musical compositions the sole right of performance in public.

VII. Periodical Publications. Periodical publications, when the requisites of the statutes have been complied with, of course fall under their protection as books.[3] There is also a particular remedy, through the jurisdiction of courts of equity, by which the property in the good will of a periodical can be protected from invasion. Thus an injunction will be granted against publishing as a continuation or new series of an established periodical, new num-

[1] See Appendix.

[2] Act of congress of 3d Feb, 1831, sec. 1.

[3] In the United States, in order to claim the benefit of the statute, it would be necessary to enter each volume or number of the work. In England, special provision is now made for "encyclopedias, reviews, magazines, periodical works, or other works published in a series of books or parts," by giving the benefits of registration, on entering in the book of registry, 1. *The title of such encyclopedia or periodical.* 2. *The time of the first publication of its first volume, number or part, or of the first number or volume published after the passing of the act.* 3. *The name and place of abode of the proprietor, or of the publisher when the publisher is not the proprietor.* 5 & 6 Vict. chap. 45, § 19. Newspapers are regulated by the act 6 & 7 Wm. IV. ch. 76.

bers, so disguised with contrivances as to the cover, &c., as to induce purchasers to take it for the old work;[1] and against assuming the name of a newspaper for the fraudulent purpose of deceiving the public and supplanting the plaintiff in the good-will of his own newspaper.[2] The jurisdiction in cases of this kind is said, however, not to be founded in the law of copyright, but on the peculiar powers of the court to restrain a defendant from carrying on a trade or from publishing a work under a fraudulent representation that such trade or work is that of the plaintiff.[3]

The rights of the authors of articles and essays, forming parts of periodical publications, have been recently regulated by statute in England. The act 5 & 6 Vict. c. 45, § 18, provides that when a volume, part, essay, article, or portion, written for publication in any encyclopedia, review, magazine, periodical work, or work published in a series of books or parts, or any book whatsoever, shall have been composed for the proprietor of such work, and paid for by him, upon the terms that the copyright therein shall belong to him, he shall enjoy the same rights therein as if he were the actual author, and shall have the same term of copyright therein as is given to the authors of books; except that in the case of essays, articles, or portions forming part of and first

[1] Hogg v. Kirby, 8 Ves. 215.

[2] Bell v. Locke, 8 Paige R. 75.

[3] 8 Ves. 215, note *a*, Sumner's ed. 2 Story's Eq. Jurisp. § 951. Eden on Injunctions (2d Am. edit.) 339, 369, et seq. Curtwell v. Lye, 17 Ves. 335.

published in reviews, magazines, or other periodical works of a like nature, after the term of twenty-eight years from the first publication thereof respectively, the right of publishing the same in a separate form is to revert to the author for the remainder of the term of copyright given by the act; and during the term of twenty-eight years, the proprietor of the work is not at liberty to publish any such essay, article, &c. separately, without the consent of the author or his assigns; but authors who have reserved to themselves the right to publish their articles in a separate form, within the twenty-eight years, are to have the copyright in their compositions when published in a separate form, without prejudice to the right of the proprietor of the work in which they originally appeared.[1]

VIII. Engravings, Maps and Charts. In the United States, engravings, maps and charts are within the protection of the act of 3d February, 1831, which gives the sole right and liberty of printing, reprinting, publishing and vending the same, for a period of twenty-eight years, to any person or persons, a citizen or citizens of the United States, or resident therein, his executors, administrators, or assigns, who shall invent, design, etch, engrave, work, or cause to be engraved, etched, or worked from his own design, any print or engraving, or who shall be the author or authors of any map or chart.

[1] 5 & 6 Vict. c. 45, § 18. See Appendix.

In England, by the 8 George II. c. 13, the property in historical and other prints was vested in engravers, who took from their own designs, for a period of fourteen years.[1] By the 7 George III. c. 38, § 1, the benefit of the former statute was extended to the prints of any portrait, conversation, landscape, or architecture, map, chart, or plan, or any other prints whatsoever, whether taken from the artist's own original designs, or from any picture, drawing, model, or sculpture, either ancient or modern; and the term of enjoying the right was in all cases enlarged to twenty-eight years.[2]

The 17 George III. c. 57, enabled the engravers of prints to recover certain penalties for the violation of their right.[3]

These statutes did not expressly vest the property in prints in the assignees of the artist, as well as in himself. But inasmuch as the 8 George II. c. 13, § 2, enabled any purchaser of a plate from the original proprietors to print and reprint from the same, without incurring the penalties, and the first section of the same act made it necessary, before a print can be copied, to obtain the consent of the proprietor, in writing, signed in the presence of two witnesses; it was held that the assignee of a print may maintain an action against any person who has pirated it.[4]

It seems that the plates, which are introduced to ornament or illustrate a book, are within the protec-

1 See Appendix.

2 Ibid.

3 Ibid.

4 Thompson *v.* Symonds, 5 T. R. 41.

tion of these statutes. In an action on the case, for pirating a book, and certain prints contained in it, in which the plaintiff declared separately for the piracy of his prints on the act 17 George III. c. 57, Lord Ellenborough directed the jury to find separate damages for the letter-press and the prints.[1] It seems, too, that a writer, treating the same subject in original letter-press, cannot copy and use the plates published by a former writer in illustration of that subject.[2]

The property in an engraving may consist in the subject and design, or in the particular print, and not in the subject and design. It is not very easy, however, to define, in general terms, when the property will be in the design and subject, and when in the particular print only; but the distinction may be illustrated by particular cases. Thus, where the subject and design are purely the product of the artist's imagination, his property will consist in both subject and design, and the particular print. His property in the print itself would be violated by a copy or a *fac-simile;* and his property in the subject and design would be violated by an imitation falling short of a *fac-simile*, but in which the alterations should be merely colorable.[3] Thus, where the plaintiff, in a work on the art of fencing, had introduced figures to illustrate the different positions in fencing,

[1] Roworth *v.* Wilkes, 1 Campb. 94.

[2] Wilkins *v.* Aiken, 17 Ves. 422.

[3] A copy is that which comes so near to the original as to give every person seeing it, the idea created by the original. Per Bailey, J. in West *v.* Francis, 5 B. & Ald. 737.

Lord Ellenborough said, that the question was, as to the prints, whether the defendant had copied the main design; and if there was such a similitude and conformity between the prints, that the person who executed the one set must have used the others as a model, he would in that case be a copyist of the main design.[1] But where the engraving is merely a print of a drawing taken from an object in nature, or a work of art, which anybody is at liberty to copy, the property of the artist is merely in his particular print; but to this extent he has a property, which has been held to be clearly within the protection of the statutes. Thus, on an application to Lord Hardwicke, to restrain the defendant from copying and publishing the plates of a work on botany, his lordship said, "the defendant, to make out the case he aims at, must show me that these prints of medicinal plants are in any other book or herbal whatsoever, *in the same manner and form as they are represented here*, for they are represented in all their several gradations—the flower and the flower-cup, the seed-vessel, and the seed."[2] So, where the plaintiff, in a work on the antiquities of Greece, had published prints taken from drawings made by himself, Lord Eldon granted an injunction against a direct copying, applying the doctrine applicable to books, that any

[1] Roworth *v.* Wilkes, 1 Campb. 94.

[2] Blackwell *v.* Harper, 2 Atk. 92. His lordship also said, "I do not think the act [8 Geo. II. c. 13,] confines it merely to invention; as, for instance, an allegorical or fabulous representation; nor to historical only, as the design of a battle, &c., but it means the designing or engraving anything that is already in nature."

one was at liberty to make new original drawings of the subjects, but not to copy the work of another.[1]

But where a work of art is the subject of the engraving, any person has a right to copy it, provided he goes to the original and not to a prior engraving; nor can a prior engraver, by obtaining the permission of the owner of a picture to copy it, acquire any monopoly in the subject, which will prevent a subsequent engraver from copying from the same picture.[2]

There can be no property in an engraving of an obscene, immoral, or libellous nature.[3]

Maps, charts, and plans are included, under the term "book," in all the benefits of the act 5 and 6 Vict. c. 45.[4]

IX. Sculpture. In the United States, the sole right and property of an artist in original sculpture, is protected for seven years, by a law which requires an entry to be made at the Patent Office. This protection extends to any citizen or citizens, alien or aliens, having resided one year in the United States, and taken the oath of his or their intention to become a citizen or citizens.[5] In England, by the 54 George III. c. 56, the sole right and property of every new and original sculpture, model, copy or cast of the human figure, or of any bust, or any part of the human figure, clothed in drapery or otherwise;

[1] Wilkins *v.* Aiken, 17 Ves. 422.

[2] De Berenger *v.* Wheble, 2 Starkie's N. P. C. 548.

[3] Fores *v.* Johnes, 4 Esp. N. P. C. 97. Du Bost *v.* Beresford, 2 Campb. 511.

[4] Sect. 2.

[5] Act of Cong. Aug. 29, 1842, § 3. See Appendix, p. 101.

or of any animal, or of any part of an animal, combined with the human figure or otherwise; or of any subject being matter of invention in sculpture, or of any alto or basso-relievo representing any of the above-mentioned matters; or any cast from nature of the human figure, or part of the human figure, or any subject containing or representing any of the above-mentioned matters and things, whether separate or combined, is vested in the person who shall make them or cause them to be made, for the term of fourteen years from the time of first publication; provided that the proprietor's name, before publication, with the date, be put on such original sculpture, model, copy, or cast, &c.

The sixth section gives an additional term of fourteen years to the person who originally made or caused to be made the sculpture or other matter, if he be living at the end of the first term, and have not divested himself of the copyright by sale or otherwise.[1]

X. Prerogative Copies. The prerogative copyrights of the crown of England constitute a peculiar branch of literary property, which has given rise to much controversy, and is involved in some obscurity. It formerly embraced, in practice, the English Translation of the Bible, the Book of Common Prayer, The Statutes, Almanacs, and the Latin Grammar, of which the exclusive right of printing

[1] See Appendix.

was held to be vested in the king, and was accustomed to be granted by letters-patent. We have seen, in a former chapter of this work, that Lord Mansfield considered this right of the crown to be founded upon property, like the right of a private author or his assigns, and consequently that he held it tenable, in the cases in which the property of the crown could be traced, independent of reasons of state or of naked prerogative.[1] But the subject is attended with great difficulties, growing out of the fact that the right has at various times been exercised as a naked prerogative, and as founded in reasons of state policy, though it seems to be clear that it was also sometimes rested upon property. It is not my purpose to endeavor to decide the very intricate questions arising under this branch of the subject, but simply to state the doctrines which have prevailed in the law of England, with reference to the principal objects to which this right has been supposed to attach.[2]

1. *The English Translation of the Bible.* Sir William Blackstone says, that the claim of the king to the exclusive printing of the English Bible rests upon the two grounds of original purchase, and of his being the head of the church.[3] Lord Mansfield held it to be a mere right of property, the king having bought the translation.[4] The translation which the

[1] Millar *v.* Taylor, 4 Burr. 2401.

[2] For a more full discussion of the prerogative copies, see Godson on Patents, p. 316, 331.

[3] 2 Black. Com. 410.

[4] 4 Burr. 2405. In Baskett *v.* The University of Cambridge, 1 Bl. 105, 113, Yorke, solicitor-general, argued, that the crown has no prerogative at common law over the art of printing, but is merely entitled to some special copyrights,

king was supposed to have bought, or to have had printed at his own expense, was that executed in the reign and under the superintendence of King James I.

The notion of private purchase seems to be now abandoned;[1] but the right itself, whatever it may be founded on, seems to be fully recognized, although it has been the subject of learned doubts, on the part of respectable authorities.[2] In the case of an application made to Lord Eldon, for an injunction against the king's printer in Scotland, who had a patent for the sale of Bibles, to restrain him from printing or selling Bibles in England, the question was between rival patentees. The injunction was granted upon motion, and before the hearing, upon the ground that possession, under color of title, was sufficient for an injunction, until it was proved at law that there was no real title.[3] Subsequently, the converse of this case came before the house of lords, the question being whether the king's printer in Scotland could interdict the sale in Scotland of Bibles imported from England. In this case, the right of the crown to grant a patent for the exclusive

among which he enumerates the translation of the great English Bible under Grafton, performed at the king's expense. Lord Mansfield, who presided, seems to have taken the same view of the king's right, then, and in the subsequent case of Millar *v.* Taylor, where he expressly asserts the king's right by purchase.

[1] Maugham on Literary Property, p. 107. Manners *v.* Blair, 3 Bligh's R. (N. S.) 402, 403.

[2] 2 Evans's Statutes, 17, 18, notes. Maugham, 107, and the remarks of Lord Chancellor Clare, there cited. Lord Gifford's observations, in Manners *v.* Blair, 3 Bligh's R. (N. S.) 391, 398.

[3] Universities of Oxford and Cambridge *v.* Richardson, 6 Ves. 689.

printing of Bibles was elaborately discussed by Lord Chancellor Lyndhurst, in moving the judgment of their lordships. He defined the nature of the right, as flowing from the duty imposed upon the chief executive officer of the government, to superintend the publication of acts of state, and of the works upon which the established doctrines of religion are founded — a duty imposed upon the king, and carrying with it a corresponding prerogative.[1]

[1] Manners *v.* Blair, 3 Bligh's R. (N. S.) 391, 402. In this case, the lord chancellor said, "The principal respondents in this case are the king's printers in Scotland. They hold that office under a patent from the crown. The appellants are members of certain Bible societies in Scotland, and have been in the habit of importing Bibles from England; and the material question to be decided in this case, is whether or not the king's printers in Scotland have, by virtue of their office and their patent, a right to exclude persons from importing Bibles, and the other works which are contained in the patent from England?

"Two important questions were raised in this case. One, which was raised, and which was argued at great length in the court below, and argued very ably at your lordships' bar, was as to the right of the crown to grant a patent, the effect of which shall be, to prevent persons in Scotland from importing Bibles, and other works of the description mentioned in the patent, certain religious works, from England; and the second question turned upon the particular construction of the terms of this patent.

"With respect to the first question, it arose out of the case of Manners and Miller *v.* Blair, which was before your lordships' house two or three sessions ago. When that case came on for argument, and was argued at your lordships' bar, it occurred to the learned lord who then presided here (Lord Gifford), that there was a doubt as to the validity of the patent, and as to the power of the king to grant a patent of that description. I do not mean to suggest that the noble and learned lord expressed any opinion upon that subject, but that he was desirous, before he decided that question, that that point should be argued at your lordships' bar; but which was in fact, never argued in the particular case, because the case in which I am about to propose that your lordships should give judgment, was before the courts below; and being before the courts below, the point was raised before the judges of the court in Scotland, which had not in fact been raised in the case of Manners and Miller *v.* Blair; and that case having come before your lordships upon appeal, it was considered more convenient and proper that the argument, with respect to the validity of the patent, and with respect to the prerogative of the crown,

The effect of these decisions is, that so long as there are separate subsisting patents for England

should be on that particular case, than on the case of Manners and Miller; but your lordships' decision in the one case, will be of course governed by the decision in the other.

"In conducting the argument, with respect to the prerogative of the crown, reference was made, and very properly made, to the cases of prerogative in England. For two hundred years and more, the kings have, in England, granted patents to their printers here, as extensive as the patent we are now considering, and perhaps more extensive, but extensive enough to raise the question we are now considering. In England, the power of the king to grant patents of this description, or to appoint to such an office, has never been seriously questioned. Those patents have from time to time come under the review of our courts, and the judges have been called upon to decide upon them. One case occurred before Sir Joseph Jekyll, so far back as the year 1720, and others at different periods, both in the courts of equity, and also before this house during the last century; and I would state it as a point not admitting now of doubt or controversy, that as far as relates to the office of king's printer in England, the crown has the prerogative to grant a patent as extensive as that we are now considering, — assuming, for the purpose of argument, that the patent is as extensive as it is contended on the part of the respondents to be.

"But although the power of the king and his prerogative in England has never been questioned, it has been rested by judges on different principles. Some judges have been of opinion, that it is to be founded on the circumstance of the translation of the Bible having been actually paid for by King James, and its having become the property of the crown, and therefore it has been referred to a species of copyright. Other judges have referred it to the circumstance of the king of England being the supreme head of the church of England, and that he is vested with the prerogative with reference to that character. Other judges have been of opinion, and I confess, for my own part, I am disposed to accede to that opinion, that it is to be referred to another consideration, namely, to the character of the duty imposed upon the chief executive officer of the government, to superintend the publication of the acts of the legislature, and acts of state of that description, and also of those works, upon which the established doctrines of our religion are founded, — that it is a duty imposed upon the first executive magistrate, carrying with it a corresponding prerogative. That was the opinion of Lord Camden, as expressed in the case of Donaldson *v.* Becket, (4 Burr. 2408.) in most direct and eloquent terms in this house: that was the opinion also expressed by Chief Baron Skinner, in the case of Eyre and Strahan *v.* Carnan; (Court of Excheq. 1781.) and I think that may be collected or inferred to be the opinion of a learned and noble earl, now a member of your lordships' house, from what fell from that noble and learned lord, in the case of the Universities of Oxford and Cambridge *v.* Richardson. (6 Ves. 704, 5.)

"If that be so, if that is the true principle upon which this preroga-

and Scotland, for the printing of Bibles, no other copies can be sold in either country except those

tive is to be rested, it appears to me that all difficulty ceases with respect to the prerogative in Scotland. In Scotland, as well as England, patents of this description have been granted without dispute or contest, for more than two hundred years. These patents have at different periods been made the subject of suits in the courts of Scotland, and particularly in the case of Watson *v.* Baskett, in the year 1716, or the year 1717, which cases came afterwards by appeal to the house of lords. In another case, that of the King's Printers *v.* Bell and Bradfute, this patent came under the consideration of the courts of justice in Scotland; and many other cases may be referred to, for the purpose of establishing the same fact: so that we have in Scotland, as well as England, patents granted successively for a period of more than two hundred years. These patents have been the subjects of suits. These cases have come to your lordships' house; and I do not think, that until the doubt was thrown out by the noble and learned lord to whom I have referred, the late Lord Gifford, the prerogative of the crown of Scotland was ever called in question. Certainly it never did occur to the very able counsel who argued the case of Manners and Miller *v.* Blair, in the court below, seriously to consider or to contest that point.

"In the course of this argument it was assumed, as the basis of a part of an argument, that the prerogative in England depended upon the king's character as supreme head of the church; and it was argued, that that principle did not apply to Scotland, for that although the king was the supreme head of the church in England, he was not the supreme head of the church in Scotland; and therefore the prerogative might well exist in this part of the island, and yet not exist in Scotland. But, I have already stated, that I do not refer the prerogative to the circumstance of the king being, in a spiritual or ecclesiastical sense, the supreme head of the church in England, but to the kingly character — to his being at the head of the church and state, and it being his duty to act as guardian and protector of both, — a character which he has equally in Scotland and England. It is perfectly clear, that it is the duty of the king to act this part, as the guardian of the church in Scotland. That is a principle laid down by the authorities in Scotland as much as in England. By the authority of the statute by which the Reformation was established in Scotland, it is declared to be the duty of the magistrates, and the king as supreme magistrate, to be the protector of the church; and in the act of 1690, by which the Presbyterian church was established, when the Episcopalian church authority was finally put an end to in Scotland, the same principle is laid down and acknowledged. I think, therefore, that this right and prerogative depends upon the king's character as guardian of the church and guardian of the state, to take care that works of this description are published in a correct and authentic form; and that those arguments upon which the authority rests in this country apply also in Scotland.

"But it was said at the bar, that in England, as far as relates to the translation of the Holy Bible, we have the translation recognized by public authority, introduced into the printed by the patentee in that country; and so long as there is a subsisting patent for either country, no

service of the church by public authority; and that the prerogative in England will properly apply to this translation, but that the same principle does not apply in Scotland.

"With respect to the Bible which was translated in the reign of James I., and which indisputably was translated under his sanction, and by virtue of his authority, it does not appear that he contributed anything towards the expense. It does not appear that that translation of the Bible was introduced into the church by the authority of any act of parliament, by the authority of any act of convocation, or by proclamation; but undoubtedly it was introduced under the sanction and authority of the head of the church, under the sanction of the king of that period, — in what precise way does not appear by evidence. It is probable, that after it was completed, and the heads of the church were satisfied with it, it was by the authority of the bishops, in their respective dioceses, introduced into general use throughout the kingdom, possibly without any further act for that purpose. But is there any essential difference between the situation of England and Scotland in this respect? I apprehend clearly none; because the same translation has, if not by the actual authority, at least by the sanction of the general assembly of Scotland, been introduced into their church, and used there for a period I believe of one hundred and fifty years; and I understand that use of it in Scotland is as general, and indeed as exclusive and universal as in England. This translation, therefore, has been sanctioned in the country by the church of that country, and by the proper ecclesiastical authorities; and I apprehend that it stands in the same situation, and is guarded by the same privileges, and is in point of law, unless the general assembly should order otherwise, as compellable to be used in the churches of Scotland as it is in the churches of England. I do not apprehend, therefore, that there is any difficulty in this respect, or that any argument whatever can be founded on the idea, that by some authority in this country that particular translation has been introduced into universal use in our church, and that no corresponding authority exists in Scotland. I have no doubt there is some authority, at least some implied authority, for the introduction of it in England; and I apprehend there is the same implied authority, the same sanction for it by ecclesiastical authorities in Scotland.

"It was in consequence of this circumstance, and some doubts arising out of this particular view of the case, that the noble and learned lord to whom I have referred, was desirous that in this particular view, it should be considered again.

"It appears to me, that as far as relates to the translation of the Holy Scriptures, the case with respect to Scotland is precisely the same as it is with respect to England. But in this patent there are other works noticed. There is the Confession of Faith. I find that the Confession of Faith was ratified by the general assembly, in the year 1649; it is therefore a book adopted by the proper ecclesiastical authority in the country. The larger and the shorter Catechisms were also ratified by the general assembly about that same period: and with respect to the me-other copies can be sold except those printed by the patentee or patentees.

2. *The Book of Common Prayer.* The doctrine with reference to the publication of the Liturgy ot the Church of England, is that the king, as chief executive magistrate and head of the church, has a

trical version of the Psalms, which is also contained in that patent, that was, as I am informed, prepared by the authority of the general assembly, and it is used in the churches by authority of that general assembly. It appears to me, therefore, that these works come within the same principle as the Holy Scriptures, and within the same principle as the Book of Common Prayer in this country.

"A question has been raised with respect to the Book of Common Prayer, which is also contained in this patent; and it is said, that at all events, the king could not in Scotland confer the exclusive right of printing this work on his printer in Scotland. The court below entertained some doubt upon this point, and in this particular stage of the cause, they have excepted the Common Prayer from the operation of their interdict, without, however, pronouncing any decision upon it. At one period episcopacy existed in Scotland. During that time, there is no doubt the king's authority applied to the Book of Common Prayer, as well as to the other works to which I have referred. It is true, that by the act of parliament passed in the year 1690, an alteration was made in this respect. By the effect of that act of parliament in 1690, the presbyterian form of worship became the established form in Scotland, and the church of that persuasion became the established church of Scotland: but, those persons who were members of the church of England, who were in her communion, were still entitled to the protection of the crown; there was nothing in that act of parliament to deprive them of that protection; and if the king possessed the prerogative previous to the passing of the act in 1690, by which he had the exclusive right, by himself or his officers, in Scotland, to publish the Book of Common Prayer, there is nothing in the act of 1690 to deprive him of that prerogative, which he had previously enjoyed.

"It does not appear to me, therefore, in this view of the case, that there is any essential difference between that part of the patent which relates to the Book of Common Prayer, and that which relates to the other works. I think, therefore, that with respect to this question, which was not originally mooted in the court below, namely, the general question of the validity of the patent, which was only afterwards argued in the second case, in consequence of the wish intimated by the noble and learned lord to whom I have adverted, that your lordships will have no difficulty in coming to the opinion, that in Scotland, as in England, the king possesses this prerogative, and that he has a right to confer it upon his printer."

right to the exclusive publication of the books of divine service. In 1781, a bill was filed in the exchequer, to restrain the defendant from printing and publishing a form of prayer, which had been ordered by his majesty to be read in all churches. Lord Ch. Baron Skinner, who delivered the judgment of the court, declared that whatever the origin of this right, this was certain, that it has ever been a trust reposed in the king, as executive magistrate, and the supreme head of the church, to promulgate to the people all those civil and religious ordinances which were to be the rule of their civil and religious obedience.[1] It appears that down to the 34th year of Henry VIII. the mass book and other books of divine service had not been printed in England, but had been brought from other countries, probably from Rome. In that year, however, a patent was granted for the sole printing of such books; but no other instance of the superintending care of the crown in printing books of divine service, occurs, until the first year of Queen Elizabeth, when the exclusive right of printing books of divine service was inserted in the

[1] Eyre *v*. Strahan and Carnan, reported 5 Bacon's Abridg. Prerogative, F. p. 597. Mr. Erskine, in his speech at the bar of the house of commons, in 1788, against the monopoly of almanacs, admitted that the king had the exclusive right to publish religious and civil constitutions; "in a word, to promulgate every ordinance which contains the rules of action by which the subject is to live and to be governed." Erskine's Speeches, vol. I. Sir W. D. Evans argues very strenuously against the existence of the legal right, and thinks that it could not now be agitated, as between the public and a patentee, with any prospect of success. 2 Evans's Stat. pp. 15, 16, 17, notes. But the decision of the house of lords, in Manners *v*. Blair, solemnly affirms the right, although the question was between rival patentees.

same patent with the right of printing the acts of parliament, which had been granted some time before, and from that time they had been regularly granted together, to the time of this decision.[1] The recognition of the whole doctrine of prerogative copies by the house of lords, in 1828, shows that as to books of divine service, it remains the same.[2]

3. *The Statutes.* The exclusive right of printing acts of parliament has been regarded more favorably than the other branches of prerogative copyright. The reasons that have been given for it are, that it is necessary that there should be a responsibility for correct printing, and because copy can only be had from the rolls of parliament, which are within the authority of the crown.[3] Anciently, the king's officers transmitted copies of the ordinances of the state to the sheriffs, who caused them to be publicly read in their county courts. When the demand for authentic copies began to increase, and the introduction of printing facilitated the multiplication of copies, the people were supplied, by the king's command, by his patentee. This, it is said, seemed a very obvious and reasonable extent of that duty which lay upon the crown to furnish the people with the authentic text of their ordinances.[4] In this practice, the claim of right originated, and it was certainly recognized in repeated decisions from the

[1] Ibid.

[2] Manners *v.* Blair, 3 Bligh's R. (N. S.) 394.

[3] Per Lord Clare, in Grierson *v.* Jackson, cited Maugham, p. 104, as reported in Ridgway's R. 304.

[4] Per Lord Ch. B. Skinner, ut supra.

18 Chas. II. to the year 1781.[1] But some of these cases went the length of asserting the sole right of the crown to print the other law books, such as the Reports, the Year Books, and Rolle's Abridgment, and this right was contended for on grounds of property.[2] These notions are now of course exploded, and the right of the patentees of the crown to the sole printing of the statutes, as now recognized in England, must depend upon usage and the force of a decision of the court of king's bench, made in 1758, and upon the recognition of the doctrine of prerogative copies by the house of lords in 1828. The former was a case stated by order of the court of chancery, between the king's printer and the university of Cambridge, both claiming under grants from the crown. The court certified it as their opinion, that the plaintiffs were entitled to the right of printing acts of parliament, and abridgments of acts of parliament, exclusive of all other persons, not authorized to print the same by prior grants from the crown; but that the university of Cambridge is intrusted with a concurrent authority to print acts of parliament and abridgments of acts of parliament, within the university, upon the terms of their pa-

[1] Atkyns's Case, Carter 89. Bacon's Ab. Prerogative, F. 4 Burr. 2315. Roper *v.* Streater, Skin. 234. Stationers' Co. *v.* Parker, Skin. 233. Eyre *v.* Strahan & Carnan, Bac. Ab. Prerog. F. p. 597. Baskett *v.* University of Cambridge, 1 W. Black. R. 105. Baskett *v.* Cunningham, Ib. 370.

[2] Atkyns's Case, Carter 89. Roper *v.* Streater, Skin. 234. Stationers' Co. *v.* Parker, Ib. 233. Vide ante chap. 1, p. 40–44.

tents.[1] This case is open to the same remark that has been made upon Oxford *v.* Richardson, that it does not present the question of the validity of these patents, as between the crown and the public, for direct decision. It does, however, assume the exclusive right to be in the king, and it will require solemn argument and great deliberation, to set it aside. It was subsequently followed in the court of chancery,[2] and to this day constitutes the principal authority upon which applications for relief in that court have been rested. The case in the house of lords has been already cited.[3]

It seems to be agreed, that the privileged copies, both the Bible and the Statutes, may be printed by others than those having the patent right, if accom-

[1] Baskett *v.* The University of Cambridge, 1 W. Black. R. 105, 121. (1758.)

[2] Baskett *v.* Cunningham & others, 1 Black. R. 370, (1762.) The defendant, in conjunction with several booksellers, was publishing in weekly numbers, A Digest of the Statute Law, containing the Statutes at large, with notes from Lord Coke and other writers of the law. He had contracted with Strahan and Woodfall, *the proprietors of the patent for printing law books*, to print this work, and it was printed at their press. Baskett, the king's printer, (whose patent extended to Statutes) filed his bill against the proprietors and the law printers, for an injunction. The Lord Chancellor was of opinion that the work was entirely within the patent of the king's printer, and that the notes were merely collusive. But he would not interfere between the two contending patents, in the summary method of injunction; but left them to adjust their respective rights, at law. He therefore ordered an injunction to issue, to restrain the proprietors from printing at any other than a patent press; which, as Woodfall and Strahan were secretly in league with Baskett, and were at that time jointly concerned in a new edition of the Statutes, was equivalent to a total injunction. — In 1804, a bill filed by the king's printer in Ireland, to establish his right to print and distribute the copies of the statutes for Ireland, and for an account against the king's printer for England, was dismissed, upon the ground that the plaintiff had no equity which the court could administer. Grierson *v.* Eyre, 9 Ves. 341.

[3] Manners *v.* Blair, see ante, p. 119–123.

panied by *bona fide* notes.[1] But with this exception, the sole right to print the Bible and the Statutes, is now held in England to be vested in the two universities of Oxford and Cambridge, concurrently with the king's patentees.[2]

4. *Almanacs.* A patent was granted by James I. for the exclusive printing of almanacs, which were claimed as prerogative copies, upon the following curious reasons : — 1st. Because an almanac has no certain author, and the property of such books is in the king ; 2dly. Because almanacs regulate the feasts of the church.[3] In the 15 George III., upon a case sent from the court of chancery, the court of common pleas, after two arguments, decided that the crown had not a prerogative or power to grant the exclusive printing of almanacs.[4] A bill was then brought into parliament to revest the monopoly in the universities and the stationers' company, and Mr. Erskine was heard at the bar against it, and defeated it.

5. *The Latin Grammar.* The foundation of the claim, in the case of the old Latin Grammar, was the allegation that it was originally composed and published at the king's expense.[5] But the pretension is now considered utterly groundless.[6]

[1] Maugham, p. 106. 2 Evans's Statutes 19, note 11.

[2] Burke on Copyright, p. 5. Lond. 1842. Manners *v.* Blair, 3 Bligh's R. (N. S.)

[3] Stationers' Co. *v.* Seymour, 1 Mod. 256. Bacon's Ab. Prerogative, F. 5. 4 Burr. 2317.

[4] Stationers' Co. *v.* Carnan, 2 W. Black. R. 1004.

[5] 4 Burr. 2329, 2401.

[6] Ib. 2315. 3 P. Williams, 255.

X. Reports of Judicial Proceedings. The house of lords, in England, has for a long time claimed and exercised the right to appoint the publisher of any trial that takes place before it, as an exclusive privilege, and the practice has been to order that the lord chancellor do cause the trial to be published, and that no other person do presume to print or publish the same.[1] The lord chancellor appoints a publisher of the trial, upon this order, and it seems that any one who infringes upon the exclusive privileges thus conferred, may be enjoined by a court of equity.[2] But it does not appear to be held that the order of the house confers anything like literary property; but that it proceeds upon the ground that the house, as a court of justice, exercises of right a superintendence over the publication of its own proceedings, on the principle that such superintendence is necessary for the due and impartial administration of the laws.[3] It is likened to the publication of the statutes by the king's patentee, and the person who is appointed publisher of a trial is said to stand in the same situation as the king's printer.[4]

The courts of law have, in modern times, claimed and exercised the right to restrain the publication of their proceedings, when such publication would be likely to defeat the ends of justice.[5] Formerly it was held to be a contempt of court to publish any

[1] Gurney *v.* Longman, 13 Ves. 493, 506, 507.

[2] Ibid.

[3] Ibid. Godson, p. 340.

[4] Ibid.

[5] The king *v.* Clement, 4 B. & Ald. 218.

reports whatever,[1] but the practical application of this doctrine has been much relaxed. The ancient doctrine was, that the property of all law books is in the king, because he pays the judges who pronounce the law; and in the reign of Charles II. this doctrine was twice affirmed by the house of lords, in relation to Rolle's Abridgment,[2] and Croke's Reports.[3] Soon after the restoration, an act of parliament, founded apparently upon the doctrine of the king's prerogative copy, prohibited the printing of law books without the license of the lord chancellor, the two chief justices and the chief baron; and in consequence of this act, it became the practice to prefix such a license to all reports published after that period, in which it was usual for the rest of the judges to concur, and to add to the *imprimatur* a testimonial of the learning and judgment of the author.[4] The act was renewed from time to time, but finally expired in the reign of King William. But the same form of license continued in use until the judges, as it is said, came to a resolution not to grant them any longer, and from Douglass down to the present day, the Reports have appeared without them.[5] Sir James Burrow offers an apology for publishing his Reports without an *imprimatur*, and says he is aware that it is a contempt of court to publish their proceedings.[6] It

[1] Preface to Sir J. Burrow's Reports.

[2] Carter 89. Bacon's Abridg. Prerog. F. 5. 4 Burr. 2315.

[3] Skinner, 234, 1 Mod. 217. Bacon ut supra. 4 Burr. 2316.

[4] Preface to Douglass's and Burrow's Reports.

[5] Ibid.

[6] Preface, 1 Burrow's R. p. vii.

seems, however, that since the Year Books, no judicial proceedings have been published under authoritative care and inspection, either by the house of lords, or by any court in Westminster Hall, except state trials.[1]

The idea of property in the king, as the chief foundation of the prerogative copies, has been long abandoned, with reference to most of them, and such as still exist are upheld by reasons of convenience and of the relation of the king, as head of the state and the church, to his subjects. The practice of treating the publication of judicial proceedings as a contempt, except in cases where a special order has been made, has fallen into desuetude ; and on the other hand, the courts take no official measures for the publication of their judgments. There is therefore no other right of property acquired by the reporters in the judgments of the courts, than such as is founded on the diligence and skill that may be used in taking notes in court of what may fall from the judges. If the judgments are in some cases furnished to them in manuscript by the court, there seems to be no ground upon which it can be said that the court thereby confers anything like a right of property upon the reporters. The statements of the cases and the arguments of counsel may be the subject of property in the reporter, by reason of his personal skill and diligence in reporting them, which

[1] Ibid.

make them to a certain extent his own compositions. It was apparently upon this ground that the copyrights of the Term Reports and the Reports of Vesey Jr. have both, at different times, been protected by injunction.[1]

In America, the subject of copyright in the reports of the decisions of the Supreme Court of the United States, has undergone very elaborate discussion in that tribunal. By an act of congress, the Supreme Court of the United States is attended by an official reporter, who receives a stated salary from the government, and is required to furnish a certain number of copies of his reports to the department of state for the use of the government. But the court, in the case here alluded to, were unanimously of opinion that the reporter can have no copyright in the written opinions delivered by the court, and that the judges cannot confer upon any reporter any such right.[2] The ground of this decision was, that the opinions of the court, being published under the authority of congress, were not the proper subject of private copyright. But it was not doubted by the

[1] Butterworth *v.* Robinson, 5 Ves. 709. Vesey *v.* Sweet, cited 5 Ves. 709, note 3 (Sumner's Edition.) In Saunders *v.* Smith, 3 Mylne & Cr. 711, it appears that copyrights of the Term Reports and the Reports of East, Taunton, Barnewell & Cresswell, and Bingham, were claimed by the plaintiffs as their property, but the Lord Chancellor assuming but not deciding the legal right, decided the application for an injunction upon evidence of a presumed consent by the plaintiffs. The case is reported as presenting the *quære*, whether it is not piracy to print, at full length, cases contained in the Law Reports, although with the addition of notes, however voluminous. The book complained of was Smith's Leading Cases.

[2] Wheaton *v.* Peters, 8 Peters R. 591, 668.

court that the reporter had a copyright in his own marginal notes, and in the arguments of counsel, as prepared and arranged in his work.[1]

[1] Per Story J. in Gray *v.* Russell, 1 Story's R. 4.

CHAPTER III.

OF THE PERSONS ENTITLED TO THE PROTECTION OF THE STATUTES.

THE author, or his assignee, of any publication entitled to the protection of copyright, may secure the benefits of the law ; but an important question arises, whether the citizenship of the author affects in any way the exercise of this right.

In England, the statute of Anne, while it secured a copyright to authors generally, contained a proviso that nothing therein should be construed to extend to prohibit the importation, or selling of any books in Greek, Latin or any other foreign language, printed beyond the seas. Under this act, it was possible that a Latin book might be written and first published in England, and afterwards republished abroad, and then imported into England. To remedy this defect, the 12 George II. c. 36, prevented the importation into England of books printed in England and reprinted in any other country. These are the only statutes which bear upon the subject of foreign books, prior to the 1 and 2 Vict. c. 59 ; and they left open the questions, whether a foreigner could take a copyright in England of a work which he first publishes there ; whether a British subject could take a copyright of a work which he had bought in manuscript from a foreign author ; and whether a foreign author could take a copyright in England after he had published his work abroad.

Upon the first of these questions, whether an alien friend, by first publishing his work in England, can take a copyright there, a strong opinion in the affirmative has been expressed and acted upon, in equity. Sir L. Shadwell, V. C., in a recent case, said, that if an alien friend wrote a book, whether abroad or in England, and gave the British public the advantage of his industry and knowledge by first publishing the work there, he was, in his opinion, entitled to the protection of the statutes. But as the question was a legal one, he directed an action, which was brought, and the defendant consented to a verdict.[1]

The International Copyright Act, 1 and 2 Vict. c. 59, is silent upon this question, although it declares that foreign authors, who first publish out of her Majesty's dominions, can have no copyright ex-

[1] Bentley *v.* Foster, 10 Sim. 329. In a more recent case, Lord Lyndhurst, C. B., intimated the opinion, that an alien friend, first publishing in England, is entitled to the protection of the statutes. Chappel *v.* Purday, 4 Y. & Coll. 485, 488. It seems also that the case of Bach *v.* Longman, Cowp. 623, was an action brought by a foreigner; and *semble*, that a foreigner who resides and publishes in England, is entitled to copyright like a British subject. D'Almaine *v.* Boosey, 1 Y. & Col. 288, 298. The statutes are consistent with a foreigner bringing a work with him, and publishing or selling it in England. *Per* Ld. Lyndhurst, C. B. in Chappel *v.* Purday, 4 Y. & Col. 485, 490.

cept under its provisions.[1] This omission furnishes a strong presumption that alien friends, who may first publish in England, are understood to be entitled to the protection of the statute.

The second question, whether a British subject, who buys an unpublished work of a foreign author, can make it the subject of copyright in England, has likewise been answered in favor of the right. The English assignee of a foreign musical composer obtained an injunction to protect the work in England. It was held that the plaintiff, being a British subject, could acquire the copyright as well from a foreigner as from an Englishman. The title thus acquired, depends upon the common law right of the assignee of a manuscript.[2]

[1] See Appendix, p. 57.

[2] D'Almaine *v.* Boosey, 1 Y. & Col. 288. Before Lord Lyndhurst, in the Exchequer, in Equity, in 1835. In Chappel *v.* Purday, 4 Y. & Col. 485, 495, his lordship said, "Many points have been introduced into the argument which were not absolutely necessary in the view which I take of this case, but as I have been much pressed for my opinion upon them I cannot let them fall to the ground without observation. A question was made whether the statute of Anne raises any protection for foreigners, and that case of D'Almaine *v.* Boosey was cited to show that I had formed that opinion. Therefore I shall address a few words to that question. The statute of Anne was passed for the protection of British subjects. It does not in terms extend its protection to the publication of foreigners. But take the whole question together, and see whether the same principles do not apply to both cases. I may be allowed, perhaps, to state in the presence of gentlemen who, no doubt attend to matters of literature, that when I came to the profession I took a great interest in the case of Millar *v.* Taylor, and other cases of that sort. In that case Lord Mansfield and two of the judges differed from Mr. Justice Yates, and I own I think that to the material parts of Mr. Justice Yates's argument Lord Mansfield made a successful reply, though unquestionably the arguments of Mr. Justice Yates were very ingenious. Lord Mansfield said, — 'That the reasons for supporting the author's right before publication were equally applicable after publication;' and I think that was a successful reply. That case

But the question, whether a foreigner, who had first published abroad, could, before the act 1 and 2 Vict. c. 59, afterwards obtain a copyright in England, was one of greater difficulty. Whether the act of printing and publishing abroad, made the work at once *publici juris*, or whether there was an interval, in which, by due diligence, the alien author could secure a copyright in England, was a question which had been left undecided, before the passing of the International Copyright Act. It had, however, been held, that where an author first published abroad, and instead of using due diligence, forbore until some other person had published in England, fairly and without blame, but afterwards published in England himself, he could not insist upon his pri-

was disposed of at common law. But the case of Donaldson *v.* Beckett, (4 Burr. 2408,) in which the same question was raised, went to the house of lords. In that case eight of the judges were of opinion, first, that the author had a right at common law to the exclusive publication of his work in the first instance. Lord Mansfield, the ninth judge, gave no opinion. The other judges were of a contrary opinion. Then the second question was, whether, admitting the author had originally a right at common law, he retained the right after publication. Mr. Justice Yates thought he had given it to the public, but eight of the judges were of opinion that he did retainit. That being the case, the law was then settled as regarded the common law right. But then the question was, whether the right of protection given by the common law was not limited by the statute of Anne, and upon that the majority of the judges were of opinion that the statute had put an end to the right which had existed at common law, because it gave the protection for fourteen years, and *no longer*. Now the statute was made for the protection of British subjects; but the same reasons apply to protect a foreigner. We must presume that the foreign law would do the same for him, and, it does. A foreigner, therefore, having a copyright in his own country, might give the same right to a British subject. Therefore, it appears to me that a foreigner who is the author of a work unpublished in France, may communicate his right to a British subject, at least for the period prescribed by the statute of Anne, that is to say, fourteen years."

vilege, and, at a distance of time, stop a publication which had taken place in the interim, and treat the continuation of that publication as a piracy.[1] So too, where the plaintiff had acquired an equitable title to a copyright, so far as related to Great Britain, of a work composed and published in France, and afterwards obtained a legal conveyance, but had in the interim sold several copies to the defendant, who republished it, other copies having been imported by other tradesmen, an injunction was refused.[2] But it is now, by the 1 and 2 Vict. c. 59, § 14, declared, that the author of any book to be after the passing of the act first published out of her Majesty's dominions, or his assigns, shall have no copyright within her Majesty's dominions, otherwise than such (if any) as he may become entitled to under this act, namely, by treaty.[3]

The object of the acts which protect engravings, (8 George II. c. 13; 7 George III. c. 38, and 17 George III. c. 57,) was to protect those works which were designed, engraved, etched, or worked in Great Britain, and not those which were designed, engraved, etched or worked abroad, and only published in

[1] Clementi *v.* Walker, 2 B. & C. 861. See also D'Almaine *v.* Boosey, 1 Y. & Col. 298. Guichard *v.* Mori, 9 Law J. 227.

[2] Chappel *v.* Purday, 4 Y. & Col. 485, 495. Lord Lyndhurst, C. B. said, "This case is not exactly the same as Clementi *v.* Walker. The question is, whether a party, who, before the copyright had been actually parted with to him, (because at that time there was no conveyance,) had permitted the books to be imported here, and sold without interference, is afterwards to be at liberty to come forward, and say, that no party shall do the like again? It is an important question, and I think it is sufficiently doubtful, to prevent my interference by injunction until it is decided."

[3] See Appendix, p. 57.

Great Britain; and therefore prints engraved and struck off abroad and only published in England, are not entitled to protection.[1]

In theatrical and musical compositions the English law secures to the author a double copyright, and each of the rights may be assigned. A published play, or musical composition, when duly entered, is protected like other books; and whether published or unpublished, the author may enjoy the sole right of representation or performance, under the acts 3 Wm. IV. c. 15, and 5 and 6 Vict. c. 45, § 20.[2]

The first of these acts was passed 10th June, 1833, and it provided, among other things, that the author of any tragedy, comedy, play, opera, farce, or any other dramatic piece or entertainment, printed and published within ten years before the passing of the act by the author thereof or his assignee, or which should thereafter be so printed and published, *or the assignee of such author*, should have as his own property the sole liberty of representing, or causing to be represented such production, for a certain term of years.[3] Upon this provision, the question arose, whether the assignee of all the author's right, title, and interest in the copyright of a play, printed within ten years before the passing of the act, where the assignment was also made before the passing of the act, was to be deemed, in the sense of the statute, *the assignee of the author*, so as to be entitled, as

[1] Page *v.* Townsend, 5 Simons, 395.

[2] See Appendix, pp. 51, 75.

[3] Ibid. p. 51.

against the author, to the sole right of representation, as well as to the copyright of publication. The court of king's bench held that such a party was *the assignee of the author*, in the sense of the statute, and by virtue of the act became entitled to the sole right of representation.[1]

To prevent this consequence, the 5 and 6 Vict. c. 45, § 22, enacts, that no assignment of the copyright of a book consisting of or containing a dramatic piece or musical composition, shall convey to the assignee the right of representation or performance, unless an entry of the assignment be made in the registry book, expressing the intention of the parties that such right should pass by the assignment.[2]

By the 8 George II. c. 13, § 1, the property in historical and other prints was vested in engravers, who took from their own designs.[3] By the 7 George III. c. 38, § 1, the benefit of the former act was extended to the prints of any portrait, conversation, landscape or architecture, map, chart or plan, or any other prints whatsoever, whether taken from the artist's own original designs, or from any picture, drawing, model, or sculpture, either ancient or modern.[4]

In prints, therefore, the designs of which are original, (with the exception of maps, charts, or plans,) the property can only be vested in the person who has made the design himself, whether he en-

[1] Cumberland *v.* Planché, 1 Ad. & Ellis, 580.

[2] See Appendix, p. 76.

[3] Ibid. p. 8.

[4] Ibid. p. 15.

graves or causes it to be engraved. A person procuring a drawing to be made, is not entitled to the protection of the statutes.[1]

The manner in which the assignee of a print or engraving, in England, becomes entitled to protection, has been pointed out in a former chapter.[2]

Maps, charts and plans, and musical compositions, are, by the 5 and 6 Vict. c. 45, § 2, placed upon the same footing as "books," and therefore the title derived from authorship in such productions is to be regulated by the same rules as in the case of books.[3]

The protection of sculpture, in England, depends upon the provisions of the 54 George III. c. 56, which vests a copyright in the person who has made or caused to be made the new and original sculpture, model, copy or cast, of the subjects therein recited.[4]

In the United States, there can be no copyright of a book, map, chart, or musical composition, print, cut or engraving, unless the author be a citizen of the United States, or resident therein, at least at the time of publication. Whether it is necessary that the work should have been made or composed in the United States, or while the author was a citizen of, or resident in the country, does not present a question of much doubt. The provisions of the statute are these:

"Any person or persons, *being a citizen or citizens*

[1] Jeffreys *v.* Baldwin, Ambl. 164. Godson on Patents and Copyright, 403–404.

[2] Ante, page 112.

[3] See Appendix, p. 64.

[4] Ibid. p. 38.

of the United States, or resident therein, who shall be the author or authors of any book or books, map, chart, or musical composition, which may be now made or composed, and not printed and published, or shall be hereafter made or composed, or who shall invent, design, etch, engrave, work, or cause to be engraved, etched, or worked from his own design, any print or engraving, and the executors, administrators, or legal assigns *of such person or persons* shall have the sole right and liberty of printing, reprinting, publishing and vending such book or books, &c., in whole or in part, for the term of twenty-eight years from the time of recording the title thereof, in the manner hereinafter directed."[1]

It would seem, upon this statute, that at the time of recording the title, whether by the author or by his assignee, the author must be a citizen of the United States, or resident therein. What constitutes such residence as is here contemplated, may present a question of some difficulty. Does the statute mean that the party shall have come to reside *animo remanendi*, and that if he has so come, he may take a copyright before he can become a citizen of the United States? Or does it mean, that he shall have come, not only with the intention of remaining, but also with the intention of becoming a citizen? Or, again, does it mean that he shall be temporarily resident only, so that he may take a copyright when he has

[1] Act of Congress, Feb. 3, 1831, § 1.

come solely for the purpose of taking it? And in either case, does it mean that he must have resided, while he made or composed his work, or can a resident foreigner publish and take a copyright of a work which he has composed abroad?

The intention of the act seems to have been, that the author should be a citizen of or resident in the United States, when the title is entered, because it is to such citizens or residents alone, or their assignees, that the law grants the exclusive right, which is secured by the entry. If the entry were made by an assignee, before the author had come to reside, such assignee would have the common law title of an unpublished manuscript; and the common law does not inquire whether the title to an unpublished work was derived from a citizen or a foreigner. But the statute has apparently taken away the common law right derivable from a non-resident alien, as soon as the work is published, because it declares, in effect, that the persons entitled to copyright, shall be only such authors as are citizens or residents, and *their* assignees; and if the assignee takes his title before the author has come to reside, he takes from a person who is not within the privilege of the statute, and has nothing to confer.

The kind of residence contemplated by the act can only be gathered from its general scope and policy. The same provision has existed in all the acts of congress for the protection of authors, and the general policy of all these statutes has been the encouragement of native literature. On one side, it may be said that the statute intended to encourage all literature that should be first published in the United States, and that the industry and arts connected with the manufacture of books may also be supposed to be objects of the same policy, so that if a foreigner is actually resident at the time he prints and publishes here a work that has never been printed and published elsewhere, it is immaterial whether he came *animo remanendi aut revertendi*. But suppose he brings the work already printed, but not published; is there anything in the act which declares that the paper and print shall be products of American industry? It is difficult to extract from the act anything like a tariff protection to the mere arts of paper-making and printing. Literary labor and the advancement of the literature of the country, were the great objects of encouragement; and it is by no means clear that all literature, first published in the country, is not included in the scope of this policy. But the question is not free from difficulty, and remains for judicial determination.[1]

With regard to the place where the work may have been composed, the act is wholly silent, and it is obviously immaterial, whether it was written in or

[1] The 8th section of the act declares that nothing in this act contained shall be construed to extend to prohibit the importation or vending, printing or publishing of any map, chart, book, musical composition, print, or engraving, written, composed, or made by any person not being a citizen of the United States, *nor resident within the jurisdiction thereof.*

out of the country, provided the author comes within the description of persons intended by the statute to be benefited. Any other construction would equally deprive citizens of the United States of the benefit of copyright in works written abroad, though first published at home; which clearly could not have been intended.

The person who is to be regarded as the author of a print or engraving, so as to be entitled to copyright, is he who has invented and designed and personally etched, engraved or worked it, or who has caused it to be engraved, etched or worked from his own design. In either case, the design must be the production of the party claiming the copyright; and an important question arises, what constitutes the design of a print, in the sense of the statute?

If the party personally engraves the subject of his conception, then he is both the inventor and designer; since he has not only conceived the subject of the picture, but has represented it in a visible form. But if the engraving is made by another under his direction, it must be made from his "design;" and the question is, whether this term means only the intellectual conception, or work of the imagination, before it is reduced to some visible form, or whether it implies a drawing or other visible representation of the invention, by the hand of its author. Under the act of 29th April, 1802, ch. 36, which contained a similar provision, it was held by Mr. Justice Washington, that the party must not only have invented, but he must have designed or represented the subject in some visible form, from which the engraver who executes it must have taken the picture.[1] The term "design," therefore, means the visible form given to the conception of the mind, and this must be done by the inventor himself.[2]

We have no statute in this country for the protection of prints or engravings of portraits, or other pictures, models, or sculpture, unless the painter or sculptor causes or authorizes the print or engraving to be made. If the painter of a picture procures and authorizes it to be engraved, he is, as to the design, within the statute of 1831, since he is the author of the design thus engraved, and may transfer his copyright in the engraving to an assignee. But the copyright must be founded on the title of the painter as the author of the design.

[1] Binns *v.* Woodruff, 4 Washington's Rep. 48. The act of 1802 was in these words: "Any person being a citizen of the United States, or a resident within the same, who shall invent and design, engrave, etch or work, or from his own works and inventions shall cause to be designed and engraved, etched or worked any historical or other print, shall have the sole right," &c.

[2] Ibid. The American statutes on the subject of engravings, are similar to the 8 George II. c. 13.

CHAPTER IV.

CHARACTER OF THE WORK CLAIMING PROTECTION.

One of the first questions that present themselves, in considering what may be the subject of a valid copyright, is, whether the law undertakes, when asked to extend its protection, to notice the tendency or usefulness of the publication. No discrimination is made by statute, either in England or America, between publications of a good and those of a bad tendency. In both countries, the statutes deal in general terms, with a property in "books." For the protection of this property, various remedies exist, to be administered by the public tribunals; and it is only when the tribunals of justice are appealed to, that the question arises, how far they may, in the exercise of their respective jurisdictions, consider the moral or political tendency of the publication, as an element in determining whether there exists a valid right of property in such publication.

There is doubtless a general right in every political society, to declare upon grounds of public policy in what things it will permit its members to claim and exercise the rights of property, and in what things it will not permit the exercise of those rights to their full extent, even where they seem to spring from the rules of natural right. Thus, a man may be engaged in a manufacture, all the materials of which are justly and truly his own, but if, in the midst of society, the process of such manufacture or the product itself be injurious to the public health or safety, society may and will not only interfere to prevent or regulate the production, but will even destroy the materials, if necessary to the abatement of the nuisance. It will thus greatly abridge and even wholly deny the otherwise perfect rights of property. So that although the protection of property is one of the ends for which political society is instituted, and although the law regards every innocent right of property as eminently sacred, yet there may be cases, in which the title becomes inherently defective, by reason of a necessary principle of public policy, which makes the asserted right inconsistent with the public good.

The true ground, therefore, upon which the refusal to protect a particular publication rests, would seem to be, not that the author or his assignee has not *prima facie* a naked right of property, but that the law will not extend its active protection to that naked right, when it can be enjoyed only for mischievous purposes or with injury to public morals. The rule has sometimes been laid down in terms which deny that there is any property at all in a publication of an immoral or mischievous tendency;[1] and so far as the rule of public policy tends to defeat or impair the beneficial character of the right of property, this mode of enunciating it may be correct. But strictly the *prima facie* right of property is the same in all publications; and the rule of public policy merely withholds that protection to which the publication, but for its character and tendency, would be entitled. This distinction is not unimportant, for it places the burthen of proof upon the party defending the piracy or denying his liability to the author, to show clearly, that notwithstanding the copyright confers a *prima facie* title, yet that the title is, as to remedies, inherently defective, by reason of requirements of public policy. This is where the burthen ought always to be, in cases of a denial of any right of property established or recognized by the law.

In America, there has been no decision involving this question; but the English authorities have established certain general principles, some of which are sound, while others are open to objection.

1. *Works injurious to public morals.* By the law of England, (and the same is of course true in the United States,) when the character of a book is such that the sale of each copy of it is an offence against the law, the first publisher can maintain no action for damages against any person who afterwards pub-

[1] 2 Story's Eq. Jurispr. § 936. Lawrence *v.* Smith, Jacob's R. 472.

lishes it, upon the clear principle that as the first publisher had and could have no right to sell, he cannot sustain any loss by an injury to the sale. This was conclusively settled, in an action brought by the first publisher of a book of a libellous and obscene character, purporting to be a history of the amours of a courtesan, against a subsequent publisher; in which Abbott, Lord Chief Justice, said, "It would be a disgrace to the common law could a doubt be entertained upon the subject."[1]

2. *Works injurious to religion.* With regard to publications supposed to be of this character, the adjudged cases have not proceeded upon very satisfactory doctrines. The general principle upon which they proceed is the same as that which denies protection to a work injurious to public morals.

In 1822, an application was made to Lord Eldon, for an injunction to restrain a piratical edition of Lord Byron's Cain. The injunction was refused, upon the ground of a doubt, whether the poem was not intended to vilify and bring into discredit that portion of scripture history to which it relates. His lordship read the poem, and refused the injunction until the counsel for the plaintiff should show him that an action could be maintained at law.[2] With

[1] Stockdale *v.* Onwhyn, 5 B. & C. 173. 7 D. & R. 625. 2 C. & P. 163. See also Fores *v.* Jones, 4 Esp. N. P. C. 97.

[2] "The jurisdiction of this court, in protecting literary property, is founded on this, that where an action will lie for pirating a work, then the court, attending to the imperfection of that remedy, grants its injunction, because there may be publication after publication which you may never be able to hunt down by proceeding in the other courts.

great submission, I am obliged to differ from the reasoning employed by his lordship in this case.

But where such an action does not lie, I do not apprehend that it is according to the course of the court to grant an injunction to protect the copyright. Now this publication, if it is one intended to vilify and bring into discredit that portion of scripture history to which it relates, is a publication, with reference to which, if the principles on which that case at Warwick (Dr. Priestley's case) was decided, be just principles of law, the party could not recover any damages in respect of a piracy of it. This court has no criminal jurisdiction; it cannot look on anything as an offence; but in those cases it only administers justice for the protection of the civil rights of those who possess them, in consequence of being able to maintain an action. You have alluded to Milton's immortal work; it did happen in the course of last long vacation, I read that work from beginning to end; it is therefore quite fresh in my memory, and it appears to me that the great object of its author was to promote the cause of Christianity; there are, undoubtedly a great many passages in it, of which, if that were not its object, it would be very improper by law to vindicate the publication; but, taking it altogether, it is clear that the object and effect were not to bring into disrepute, but to promote, the reverence of our religion. Now the real question is, looking at the work before me, its preface, the poem, its manner of treating the subject, particularly with reference to the fall and the atonement — whether its intent be as innocent as that of the other with which you have compared it; whether it be to traduce and bring into discredit that portion of sacred history. This question I have no right to try, because it has been settled, after great difference of opinion among the learned, that it is for a jury to determine that point; and where, therefore, a reasonable doubt is entertained as to the character of the work, (and it is impossible for me to say I have not a doubt — I hope it is a reasonable one,) another course must be taken for determining what is its true nature and character.

"There is a great difficulty in these cases, because it appears a strange thing to permit the multiplication of copies, by way of preventing the circulation of a mischievous work, (which I do not presume to determine that this is,) but that I cannot help; and the singularity of the case, in this instance, is more obvious, because here is a defendant who has multiplied his work by piracy, and does not think proper to appear. If the work be of that character which a court of common law would consider criminal, it is pretty clear why he does not appear, because he would come *confitens reus*, and for the same reason the question may, perhaps, not be tried by an action at law; and if it turns out to be the case, I shall be bound to give my own opinion. That opinion I express no further now than to say, that after having read the work, I cannot grant the injunction until you show me that you can maintain an action for it. If you cannot maintain an action, there is no pretence for granting an injunction; if you should not be able to try the question at law with the defendant, I cannot be charged with impropriety if I then give my opinion upon it. "It is true that this

Without entering into the question of criticism raised by comparing the poem with Paradise Lost, — upon which a great critic and poet held a very different opinion from that expressed by Lord Eldon[1] — and admitting that an injunction before a trial at law should not be granted in a palpable case of malicious attack upon the scriptures or the doctrines of revealed religion, it is yet quite too strict to say, that because a poem admits of a suspicion of improper intentions, the author's copyright is not to be protected until he has purged himself of that suspicion. The boldness and license of poetry admit of a latitude which would not be allowed in didactic prose; and where the line is to be drawn closely, the court may not only mistake the tendency and intention of the work, but may, as Lord Eldon did on this occasion, apply its own views of doctrinal subjects to determine the innocence of the author's intention, instead of judging it by that broad, liberal and catholic spirit in which the intent of all poetry is to be judged.[2] If canons of criticism are to be applied in this manner, and a publication, which falls under the

mode of dealing with the work, if it be calculated to produce mischievous effects, opens a door for its wide dissemination; but the duty of stopping the work does not belong to a court of equity, which has no criminal jurisdiction, and cannot punish or check the offence. If the character of the work is such, that the publication of it amounts to a temporal offence, there is another way of proceeding, and the publication of it should be proceeded against directly as an offence; but whether this or any other work should be so dealt with, it would be very improper for me to form or intimate an opinion." (6 Petersdorff Abr. 558-9.)

[1] Sir Walter Scott; Letter to John Murray, Esq. accepting the dedication of Cain. Lockhart's Life of Scott, VI. 424, 2d edition.

[2] See the Letter above cited.

doubts engendered by such criticism, is to be refused protection in the first instance, there can be no safe literary property in the higher works of imagination, which deal with such subjects as man's future destiny or the events of scripture history ; for the refusal of a court of equity to grant an injunction in such cases, would be only a signal to invite more piracies than the courts of law could check. It would be a far more sound rule, to hold that unless a malicious intent or mischievous tendency be apparent on its face, every work is *prima facie* entitled to protection, until the bad intent and tendency are established by those who rely upon them.[1]

In another case, Lord Eldon refused to continue an injunction to restrain a pirated edition of certain lectures delivered by Mr. Lawrence at the college of surgeons, on "Physiology, Zoology and the Natural History of Man." He doubted whether many particular parts of the work did not lead to a disbelief in the immortality of the soul — one of the doctrines of the scriptures.[2] He therefore dissolved the injunction, and left the plaintiff to bring an action at law.[3] In this case, his lordship said that

[1] See Hime *v.* Dale, 2 Campb. 29, note. 11 East, 244, note.

[2] Lawrence *v.* Smith, Jacob's R. 471.

[3] It seems not to have occurred to Lord Eldon — or if it did, he gave no heed to the consideration — that the mere rumor of the dissolution of an injunction upon such doubts as he expressed in this case, would place the author in a most unequal position with a piratical publisher in a court of law, if it should be worth his while to go there ; for both court and jury would know that the plaintiff came before them after he had been turned away from the court of chancery, upon the belief or doubt raised in the mind of the first magistrate in the realm that his book was not entitled to the protection of the law.

"he was bound to look, not only to the tenor, but also *to particular passages unconnected with the general tenor; for if there were any parts of it which denied the truth of scripture*, or which furnished a doubt as to whether a court of law would not decide that they had denied the truth of scripture, he was bound to look at them and decide accordingly."[1]

If this is to be regarded as the statement of a rule by which to determine the validity of a copyright, it is quite unsound. It seems, however, to be only a statement of the rule that should govern a court of equity, in determining whether an injunction shall be granted before the right of property has been established at law. But even in this view, the doctrine is not satisfactory; and in announcing it, Lord Eldon is inconsistent with himself. In the previous case, in refusing an injunction to protect Lord Byron's Cain, he had said of Paradise Lost, that there are undoubtedly a great many passages in it, of which, if the promotion of Christianity were not its object, it would be very improper by law to vindicate the publication; but that, *taking it altogether*, it is clear that the object and effect were not to bring into discredit, but to promote the reverence of our religion.[2] Here, his lordship assumed as the criterion the general tenor of the work; and it is not very apparent why the same rule should not have been applied to Dr. Lawrence's Lectures. In the

[1] Lawrence *v*. Smith, Jacob's R. 471. [2] Murray *v*. Benbow.

one case, the good general object of the work excuses from censure the passages which would be otherwise inexcusable. In the other case, the alleged bad character of certain detached portions, it is said, renders the general tenor of the work wholly immaterial.[1]

3. *Works injurious to the public peace.* The general principle of the law of England on this subject is, that there can be no right of property in publications which tend to disturb the public peace, to be injurious to the good government of the state, or to bring into contempt the administration of justice. This principle has, however, sometimes been applied without due discrimination.

There is a *dictum* of Lord Chief Justice Eyre, reported traditionally, upon which a great deal more has been built than is consistent with principle. Dr. Priestley brought an action against the hundred for damages sustained by him in consequence of the riotous proceedings of a mob at Birmingham; and, among other property alleged to have been destroyed, claimed compensation for the loss of certain unpublished manuscripts, offering to produce booksellers to prove that they would have given considerable sums for them. On behalf of the hundred, it was alleged that the plaintiff *was in the habit of publish-*

[1] We may ask, also, what his lordship means by "parts which deny the truth of scripture"? If an author introduce into his book a passage denying the truth of *any* part of scripture, is his copyright thereby vitiated? Or is it the general truth of scripture, that must not be denied?

ing works injurious to the government of the state; but no evidence was produced to that effect; upon which Lord Chief Justice Eyre is reported to have said, that if any such evidence had been produced, he should have held it fit to be received as against the claim made by the plaintiff.[1] In this case, it is obvious, that Dr. Priestley was seeking damages for the destruction of what might have been the source of pecuniary profit. The dictum of the Lord Chief Justice, therefore, goes only to this, that a work existing in manuscript may be of such a character that the author cannot make lawful profits by its publication, and in this sense it may be said that there can be no property in such a work. But this position was afterwards assumed to justify a very different doctrine, namely, that the author of an unpublished manuscript, of a character not innocent, or doubtful, cannot have the interposition of a court of equity to restrain its publication by a person who is about to publish it against his will; as if the Lord Chief Justice had said, that any one of the mob who might have stolen one of Dr. Priestley's MSS. could have published it, as against the author, and the court of chancery would not have interfered, on account of the character of the work. This doctrine, it will presently be submitted, is untenable, notwithstanding the high authority by which it has been countenanced.

[1] So cited in Walcott *v.* Walker, 7 Ves. 1, and in Southey *v.* Sherwood, 2 Meriv. 437.

In the year 1817, Mr. Southey, the poet, made application to Lord Eldon for an injunction to restrain the publication of a poem called "Wat Tyler," which he had left for a long time in the hands of a bookseller, unpublished. The motion was resisted upon the ground that the work, from its seditious tendency, was of such a nature that there could be no copyright therein. The work had never been printed by Mr. Southey, or by his permission, and his application to the court proceeded upon the right of an author to restrain the publication of his own manuscript. Lord Eldon said, "If this publication is an innocent one, I apprehend that I am authorized, by decided cases, to say that, whether the author did or did not intend to make a profit by its publication, he has a right to an injunction to prevent any other person from publishing it. If, on the other hand, this is not an innocent publication, in such a sense as that, an action would not lie in case of its having been published by the author and subsequently pirated, I apprehend that this court will not grant an injunction."[1]

It may admit of great doubt, whether the law of England recognizes any such distinction as Lord Eldon here seems to suppose. It does undoubtedly say, that in order to obtain an injunction, or to recover damages, to protect a work that has been published by the proprietor, the work itself must be

[1] Southey *v.* Sherwood, 2 Merivale, 435, 437.

innocent; but it may be doubted whether the law carries this distinction into the case of an unpublished work, where the author proceeds merely upon his right to possess and control, to publish or not to publish his own manuscript. Lord Eldon says justly, that "it is to prevent the use of that which is *the exclusive property* of another, that an injunction is granted;" but he seems to overlook the fact that the law recognizes two kinds or degrees of property in a literary work. There is a right of property, which consists in the right to take the profits of a book, when published; and there is also a right to the exclusive possession and control of a manuscript, or the right to publish or to withhold from publication altogether.[1] The first of these rights depends now, in England and in America, upon statute. The other is a right at common law, independent of the property created or recognized by statute. The law of England has never said that an author has no property in his manuscript *qua* manuscript, or in the ideas and sentiments written upon it before publication. If it had, it would only be necessary to steal a manuscript, in order to be able to print it with impunity; and the author could only take the profits, or obtain an injunction, by showing that he himself intended to publish and to take the profits. It has long been settled, however, that the author and proprietor of a manuscript has the sole

[1] See Wheaton *v.* Peters, 8 Peters S. C. R. 591.

dominion over it, and may obtain an injunction to prevent its publication by another; and in no case has it been considered, that his right depends on his intention to publish and to make a profit.[1] But the cases proceed upon the ground of a *right of property;* and what seems to be intended by this is a right to the possession and control of the manuscript, and to publish or to withhold from publication.[2] In the great case of Donaldson *v.* Becket, in the house of lords, in which the perpetual right of authors after publication was held to have been taken away by the act of Anne, eleven of the judges (including those who decided against some of the claims of authors) affirmed the sole right and dominion of an author over his own manuscript, as a right at common law.[3]

[1] Webb *v.* Rose, cited 4 Burr. 2330; 2 Bro. P. C. 138; Forrester *v.* Waller, cited ut supra; Pope *v.* Curll, 2 Atk. 342; Manley *v.* Owen, cited 4 Burr. 2329, 2404; Duke of Queensbury *v.* Shebbeare, 2 Eden's Ch. R. 329, cited 4 Burr. 2330, 2397; Macklin *v.* Richardson, Amb. 694.

[2] The cases of injunctions to restrain the publication of letters proceed upon this ground. None of them proceed upon an intention to publish and to make a profit. Pope *v.* Curll, ut supra. Thompson *v.* Stanhope, Amb. 737. Earl of Granard *v.* Dunkin, 1 Ball & Beat. 207. Perceval *v.* Phipps, 2 Ves. & Bea. 19. Gee *v.* Pritchard, 2 Swanst. 402. Lord Eldon admits the right to control, independent of any intention to publish and take the profits, where the work is innocent. But if it be not innocent, and the author does not intend to publish, his lordship thinks there is no ground for an injunction. But why not, as much as in the case of an innocent work which the author does not intend to publish? In neither case does he rest upon his right to the profits, but upon his right to control his own writings. The question is, does the law, where the work is not innocent, invalidate the author's right over his manuscript, or does it merely say that the *profits* of such a publication are unlawful gains?

[3] Donaldson *v.* Becket, 4 Burr. 2408. 2 Bro. Parl. Cas. 129. The following extracts, purporting to be made in the language of the judges, are given by Mr. Maugham, in his work on The Laws of Literary

When, therefore, an author has not published, or does not intend to publish a work existing in manuscript, but on the contrary desires and intends to withhold it from publication, the question as to its innocence cannot arise, because that question, according to principle and the decisions, affects only so much of his right of property as consists in the right to take the profits of the publication. It is in this sense, that the law declares there can be no property in an immoral, irreligious, or seditious publication; and not that there can be no right to the ex-

Property, without citing the source from which they are taken: —

"Nares, J. It is admitted on all hands that an author has a beneficial interest in his own manuscript.

"Ashurst, J. If a man lends his manuscript to a friend, and his friend prints it, or if he loses it, and the finder prints it, an action would lie.

"Yates, J. Admitted this doctrine.

"Blackstone, J. When a man, by the exertion of his rational powers, has produced an original work, he has clearly a right to dispose of it as he pleases.

"Willes, J. I declare it as my opinion, that an author hath an indisputable power and dominion over his manuscript.

"Aston, J. An author hath a natural right to the produce of his mental labor.

"Perrot, B. An author certainly hath a right to his manuscript; he may line his trunk with it, or he may print it.

"Gould, J. I agree that an author hath a right at common law to his manuscript.

"Smyth, L. C. B. The cases prove, and it is allowed, that literary property *is property* previous to publication.

"De Grey, L. C. J. There can be no doubt that an author has the sole right to dispose of his manuscript as he thinks proper.

"Lord Mansfield. It is just that an author should reap the pecuniary profits of his own ingenuity and labor."

Sir W. D. Evans, in the notes to his edition of the Statutes, vol. ii. p. 20, n. 14, commenting upon the decisions granting injunctions in favor of the *representatives* of the authors of manuscripts, has intimated a doubt whether a mere manuscript presents such a case of property, that an injunction can be founded on it at the suit of an executor. But it is apparent, from the question put to the judges in Donaldson *v.* Becket, 4 Burr. 2408, that they intended to affirm the right of an author over his own manuscript to be a right at common law, without making it necessary for him to rest upon its value as a marketable commodity. See also White *v.* Gerooch, 2 Barn. & Adol. 298. Wheaton *v.* Peters, 8 Peters S. C. R. 591.

clusive possession and control of whatever a man writes, before publication, unless it be innocent.[1]

[1] It would seem, that Lord Eldon's remarks in the case of Southey *v.* Sherwood, must be very imperfectly reported. He is reported to have made the following observations at the time of the hearing: "If this publication is an innocent one, I apprehend that I am authorized, by decided cases, to say that, whether the author did or did not intend to make a profit by its publication, he has a right to an injunction to prevent any other person from publishing it. If, on the other hand, this is not an innocent publication, in such a sense as that an action would not lie in case of its having been published by the author and subsequently pirated, I apprehend that this court will not grant an injunction. The court does not interfere in the way of injunction to punish or to prevent injuries done to the character of individuals; but it leaves the party to his remedy at law. It is to prevent the use of that which is the exclusive property of another, that an injunction is granted. There is, however, a difference between the case of an actual publication by the author, which all the world may pirate, and that of a man who, having composed a work, of which he afterwards repents, wishes to withhold it from the public. I will not say that a principle might not be found which would apply to such a case as that; but then it is necessary to take all the circumstances of the case into consideration. The circumstances of the present case are very extraordinary. I will assume that the work is of such a nature that the sending it forth into the world might have been treated as a criminal act. In that view of the circumstances, I have no jurisdiction to consider its criminality. The work was composed so long ago as the year 1794. The plaintiff's affidavit admits that, in that year, there was a serious intention of publishing it. It was sent by the plaintiff to Mr. Ridgeway, and is supposed to have been delivered by him to Symonds. The affidavit goes on to state that it was afterwards determined not to publish it. I will suppose that it was not thought worth while to publish it, in a pecuniary view. Mr. Ridgeway gives no account how it passed out of his hands; and all that is alleged concerning the subsequent disposal of it is, that Mr. Southey, living in the country, forgot it. If the work be such a one as it has been described to be, it is extraordinary that, with the change alleged to have taken place in Mr. Southey's opinions, there should be nothing stated to account for its having been left by him in Mr. Ridgeway's hands to the present time, but that Mr. Southey forgot it. It is impossible that Mr. Southey could have forgotten it. There must have been some other reason. If a man leaves a book of this description in the hands of a publisher, without assigning any satisfactory reason for doing so, and has not inquired about it during twenty-three years, he surely can have no right to complain of its being published at the end of that period."

It is obvious, that the case for which his lordship would not say, that "a principle might not be found," was the very case before him. Mr. Southey had sworn in his affidavit, that he had forgotten having left the MS. in the hands of

Lord Ellenborough, in the case of Hime *v.* Dale, said, "If the composition appeared, upon the face of

Ridgeway, with whom in fact he had originally deposited it; that he was very desirous it should not be published; and his counsel rested his application upon the right of an author to control his own MSS. Yet his lordship, if correctly reported, not only felt authorized to say, "it is impossible that Mr. Southey could have forgotten it," (there was no counter affidavit); but proceeded afterwards to decide the cause without finding the principle which he intimates might have been found for the case actually made by the application. With regard to his lordship's *dictum*, contained in the last sentence of the passage above cited, it seems scarcely necessary to say, that nothing short of a license, or an assignment of copyright, can deprive an author of the right to complain of the publication of his own MS. Whether the fact of his having left it without inquiry for three-and-twenty years, explained by his affidavit that he had forgotten it, would be presumptive evidence of a license or an assignment, may admit of much doubt. On a subsequent day, his lordship delivered judgment as follows: "I have looked into all the affidavits, and have read the book itself. The bill goes the length of stating, that the work was composed by Mr. Southey in the year 1794; that it is his own production, and that it has been published by the defendants without his sanction or authority; therefore seeking an account of the profits which have arisen from, and an injunction to restrain, the publication. I have examined the cases that I have been able to meet with, containing precedents for injunctions of this nature, and I find that they all proceed upon the ground of a title to the property in the plaintiff. On this head a distinction has been taken, to which a considerable weight of authority attaches, supported, as it is, by the opinion of Lord Chief Justice Eyre, who has expressly laid it down, that a person cannot recover in damages for a work which is in its nature calculated to do injury to the public. Upon the same principle, this court refused an injunction, in the case of Walcot *v.* Walker, inasmuch as he could not have recovered damages in an action. After the fullest consideration, I remain of the same opinion as that which I entertained in deciding the case referred to. It is very true that, in some cases, it may operate so as to multiply copies of mischievous publications by the refusal of the court to interfere by restraining them; but to this my answer is, that sitting here as a judge upon a mere question of property, I have nothing to do with the nature of the property, nor with the conduct of the parties except as it relates to their civil interests; and if the publication be mischievous, either on the part of the author, or of the bookseller, it is not my business to interfere with it. In the case now before the court, the application made by the plaintiff is on the ground only of his civil interest; and this is the proper place for such an application. I shall say nothing as to the nature of the book itself, because the grounds upon which I am about to declare my opinion render it unnecessary that I should do so. [His lordship here recapitulated the circumstances already detailed, of the original intention to publish, the subsequent abandonment of that intention, the it, to be a libel so gross as to affect the public morals, I should advise the jury to give no damages. I know the court of chancery, on such an occasion, would grant no injunction."[1]

4. *Works injurious to private reputation.* The same

length of time during which the plaintiff had suffered the work to remain out of his possession without inquiry, and its recent publication by the defendants.] Taking all these circumstances into my consideration, and after having consulted all the cases which I could find at all regarding the question, — entertaining also the same opinion with Lord Chief Justice Eyre as to the point above noticed, — it appears to me that I cannot grant this injunction until after Mr. Southey shall have established his right to the property by an action."

From this it would seem that his lordship really refused the injunction, partly upon the ground that he was not satisfied that Mr. Southey had not parted with his right, and partly upon the ground that the work was one with which the court could not interfere. Upon both grounds, the decision is very unsatisfactory.

[1] Hime *v.* Dale, 2 Campb. 27, n. This was an action for pirating the words of a song called "*Abraham Newland,*" published on a single sheet of paper. *Garrow*, for the defendant, contended, that the song was of such a description that it could not receive the protection of the law in whatever shape it appeared. It professed to be a panegyric upon money; but was in reality a gross and nefarious libel upon the solemn administration of British justice. The object of this composition was, not to satirize folly, or to raise the smile of innocent mirth, but, being sung in the streets of the capital, to excite the indignation of the people against the sacred ministers of the law, and the awful duties they were appointed to perform. The mischievous tendency of the production would sufficiently appear from the following stanza; after hearing which, the court would say whether the nonsuit ought to be disturbed.

"The world is inclined,
To think Justice blind;
Yet what of all that?
She will blink like a bat
At the sight of friend *Abraham Newland!*
Oh, *Abraham Newland! Magical Abraham Newland!*
Though Justice, 't is known,
Can see through a millstone,
She can't see thro' *Abraham Newland!*"

Lord Ellenborough. "If the composition appeared on the face of it to be a libel so gross as to affect the public morals, I should advise the jury to give no damages. I know the court of chancery on such an occasion would grant no injunction. But I think the present case is not to be considered one of that kind."

Lawrence, J. "The argument used by Mr. Garrow on this fugitive piece as being a libel, would as forcibly apply to *The Beggar's Opera*, where the language and allusions are sufficiently derogatory to the administration of public justice." — It is certainly not easy to see the seditious tendency of the stanza quoted by the learned counsel.

general motives of public policy, which defeat a copyright in a seditious, irreligious, or obscene publication, exclude from protection libels upon private character.

Such works are wholly excluded from the protection of the law. An action cannot be maintained at law for the invasion of that which a man calls his property, but which the policy of the law will not permit him to consider and enjoy as property ; and a court of equity will not grant an injunction where an action could not be maintained at law, even upon a submission in the answer.[1]

The principle of public policy, which thus defeats a copyright through the bad character of the work, has been met with the objection that it only encourages and multiplies the circulation of mischievous works. But to this objection the answer has been made, that so far as the action of courts of equity is concerned, those courts have no criminal jurisdiction ; and as they have only to look at the civil rights of parties, if such rights do not exist by the law of the land, they cannot restrain a publication which one man has as much right to make as another, where neither have any right at

[1] Walcott *v.* Walker, 7 Ves. 1. So upon analogous grounds, where an artist exhibited for money a picture called "Beauty and the Beast," which was a scandalous libel upon a gentleman and his wife, who was the sister of the defendant, and great crowds went daily to see it, till the defendant one morning cut it in pieces ; Lord Ellenborough instructed the jury, in assessing the damages, not to consider the picture as a work of art, but to award the plaintiff merely the value of the canvas and paint which formed its component parts. Du Bost *v.* Beresford, 2 Campb. 511.

all.[1] To this it might be added, that so far as the action of courts of law is concerned, when adjudicating between party and party, the sole inquiry is, does the law permit a copyright in an immoral, irreligious, or seditious publication? If not, then there can be no damages awarded to the proprietor of such a book. The public consequences of the operation of this principle can be remedied by legislation alone.[2]

At the same time, it cannot be denied, that this salutary general principle is subject to great difficulties in the application. Great care should be exercised, not to pronounce any copyright invalid by reason of illegality in the work itself, unless it is a clear case. In equity, the sounder rule would be to refuse no injunction, where the book is not illegal "upon the face of it;" and both in equity and at law, the defendant should not be relieved of the burthen of proof, by any disposition on the part of the court to apply its private opinions, doctrines, or standards, to the publication in question.[3] *Prima*

[1] Lawrence *v.* Smith, Jacobs R. 471. 2 Story's Eq. Jurisp. § 937.

[2] For an interesting discussion on the effects of refusing protection to illegal works, see 6 Petersdorff's Abridg. 560, 561, and an article in the Quarterly Review for April, 1822. This doctrine does not enter into the law of copyright in France. All works are equal before the law, without reference to their character. Renouard, tom. 2, p. 94.

[3] "The soundness of this general principle," says Mr. Justice Story, "can hardly admit of question. The chief embarrassment and difficulty lie in the application of it to particular cases. If a court of equity, under color of its general authority, is to enter upon all the moral, theological, metaphysical and political inquiries, which in the past times have given rise to so many controversies, and in the future may well be supposed to provoke many heated discussions, and if it is to decide dogmatically upon the character and bearing of such discussions,

facie the copyright confers title ; and the burthen is upon the other side to show clearly, that notwithstanding the copy, there is an intrinsic defect in the title.[1]

5. *Works innocent in their contents, but put forth under a false and fraudulent representation as to their authorship.*

It has been recently held in England that there can be no valid and subsisting copyright, in a book which falsely purports to have been written by an author of reputation, and which, under color of such a representation, seeks to impose upon the public. The plaintiff published a book, professing upon its title-page to be a translation from a deceased German author, whose works had been translated and much sought for in England. The preface of this book falsely represented it to be the work of the German author, when in reality it was written and composed wholly by a person employed and paid by the plaintiff for the purpose. The court distinguished this entirely from the cases of works

and the rights of authors, growing out of them ; it is obvious that an absolute power is conferred over the subject of literary property, which may sap the very foundations on which it rests, and retard, if not entirely suppress, the means of arriving at physical as well as at metaphysical truths. Thus, for example, a judge, who should happen to believe, that the immateriality of the soul, as well as its immortality, was a doctrine clearly revealed in the Scriptures (a point upon which very learned and pious minds have been greatly divided,) would deem any work anti-christian, which should profess to deny that point, and would refuse an injunction to protect it. So, a judge who should be a Trinitarian, might most conscientiously decide against granting an injunction in favor of an author, enforcing Unitarian views ; when another judge, of opposite opinions, might not hesitate to grant it." 2 Story's Eq. Jurisp. § 938.

[1] 2 Story Eq. Jurisp. § 936, n. 2.

published under a fictitious authorship, in which there is no intent to deceive or defraud the public; and held, that where a publisher seeks to obtain the money of the public by a pretence that his book was written by a known author, the transaction ranges itself under the head of *crimen falsi*, and that he cannot have a valid and subsisting copyright in his publication, or maintain an action in respect of its infringement.[1]

[1] Wright *v.* Tallis, 1 Manning, Granger & Scott, Com. Bench Rep. 893. In this case, Lord C. J. Tindal said, "The first observation, therefore, that arises, is, that the present case is perfectly distinguishable from those which have been referred to at the bar, of books of amusement or instruction having been published as translations, whilst they have been, in fact, original works; or having been published under an assumed, instead of a true name. Such was the instance given of 'The Castle of Otranto,' professing to be translated from the Italian; and such the case of innumerable works published under assumed names — voyages, travels, biography, works of fiction or romance, and even works of science and instruction; for, in all these instances, the misrepresentation is innocent and harmless. There is not found, in any one of those cases, any serious design on the part of the author to deceive the purchaser, or to make gain and profit from him by the false representation: the purchaser, from anything that appears to the contrary, would have purchased at the same price, if he had known that the name of the author was an assumed, and not a genuine name; or had known that the work was original and not translated. And, indeed, in most of the cases that can be put, the statement is not calculated in its nature to deceive any one, but is seen, upon the very first glance, to be plainly and manifestly fictitious. In those cases therefore, it was perfectly indifferent to the public, whether the representation was true or not; and in all probability, the book would have obtained an equal sale, whether it was a translation or an original, whether the name of the author was assumed or genuine.

"But, in the case before us, no one of these observations will apply. The facts stated in the plea import a serious design on the part of the plaintiff to impose on the credulity of each purchaser by fixing upon the name of an author who (once) had a real existence, and who possessed a large share of weight and estimation in the opinion of the public. The object of the plaintiff is, not merely to conceal the name of the genuine author, and to publish opinions to the world under an innocent disguise; but to deceive the public, in inducing them to believe that the work is the original work of the author whom he names, when he himself knows it not to be so, to obtain from the purchaser a greater price than he would otherwise obtain. The transaction, therefore, ranges itself under the head of *crimen falsi*. The publisher seeks to obtain money under false pretences; and as not only the original act of publishing the work, but the sale of copies to each individual purchaser, falls within the reach of the same objection, we think the plaintiff cannot be considered as having a valid and subsisting copyright in the work, the sale of which produces such consequences, or that he is capable of maintaining an action in respect of its infringement.

"The cases in which a copyright has been held not to subsist where the work is subversive of good order, morality, or religion, do not, indeed, bear directly on the case before us; but they have this analogy with the present inquiry — that they prove that the rule which denies the existence of copyright in those cases, is a rule established for the benefit and protection of the public. And we think the best protection that the law can afford to the public against such a fraud as that laid open by this plea is, to make the practice of it unprofitable to its author."

CHAPTER V.

OF THE ORIGINALITY NECESSARY TO A VALID COPYRIGHT.

THE party who comes into a court of law or equity, seeking protection to a copyright, must be the author of the work, or must derive title from the author. If any part of the book is copied or adopted by the writer from a preëxisting work, of course the title fails *quo ad hoc:* as the writer cannot have been the author of what he has borrowed from another.[1] Hence it may become a grave question, to

[1] The statutes both in England and America make use of the word *Author*, which *ex vi termini* imports originality, to some extent. In France, the law of copyright is founded on the decree of July 19th, 1793, which embraces in its provisions "*les auteurs d'écrits en tout genre.*" Upon this expression, M. Merlin has made the following commentary, which would lose in a translation the fine and clear distinction between the terms "esprit" and "genie."

"Mais il ne faut pas séparer, dans cet article, les mots *écrits en tout genre*, de l'expression *auteurs ;* et la propriété dont cet article déclare que les *écrits en tout genre* sont susceptibles, ne peut évidemment être réclamée que par ceux qui en sont *auteurs*, dans la véritable acception de ce terme.

"Or, le mot *auteurs*, quel sens a-t-il en général? Quel sens a-t-il relativement aux écrits? Quel sens a-t-il dans la loi du 19 juillet 1793?

"En général, le mot *auteur* désigne, suivant la définition qu'en donne le Dictionnaire de l'Academie française, *celui qui est la première cause de la quelque chose;* et il est aussi, suivant la même définition, synonyme d'*inventeur*.

"Appliqué aux écrits, le mot *auteur* se dit (toujours suivant le même Dictionnaire) *de celui qui a composé un livre, qui a fait quelques ouvrages d'esprit en vers ou en prose ;* et il est bien clair qu'en ce sens, le mot *auteur* est opposé à *copiste*.

"Enfin, la loi du 19 juillet 1793 ne permit pas de douter qu'elle n'exclue également les copistes de la dénomination d'auteurs. *Les héritiers de l'auteur d'un ouvrage de* determine in a particular case what is or is not original on the part of the writer; or in other words, whether any part of his work is copied or adopted from that of another.

It is very difficult to lay down any legal definition of originality in a literary composition, that may be resorted to as a universal test. Many intellectual productions present no more difficulty, upon the question of their originality, than some inventions or discoveries. The poems of the great masters in every language, and a vast body of other writings, however freely their authors may have used the thoughts of others, are at once seen to be just as original in a legal as they are in a critical sense. But in every species of composition, in all literatures, there is of necessity a constant reproduction of what is old, mixed with morc or less that is new, peculiar and original. There are also large classes of

littérature ou de gravure, dit-elle, art. 7, *ou* DE TOUTE AUTRE PRODUCTION DE L'ESPRIT OU DU GÉNIE, *qui appartient aux beaux-arts*, *en auront la propriété exclusive pendant dix années*. Ces termes, *ou de toute autre production de l'esprit ou du génie, qui appartient aux beaux-arts*, ne sont ni obscurs ni équivoques. Ils signifient clairement que les productions de l'esprit ou du génie sont de deux sortes; que les unes consistent en ouvrages de littérature; que les autres appartiennent aux beaux-arts; mais que nul ne peut être réputé auteur soit d'un ouvrage de littérature, soit d'un ouvrage d'arts, si ce n'est pas à son esprit ou à son génie qu'en est due la production.

"Donc, les expressions d'*écrits en tout genre*, ne sont employées dans l'art. 1er de la même loi, que pour désigner tous les genres de compositions littéraires.

"Donc, elles n'y désignent pas les écrits qui ne seraient pas des compositions, mais de simples copies.

"Donc, celui qui ne fait que copier une composition littéraire ne peut jamais être réputé auteur de la copie de cette composition, ni par conséquent en avoir la *propriété*, dans le sens attaché à ce mot par la loi du 19 juillet 1793 et par le Code pénal 1810." —Merlin, Répertoire de Jurisprudence, Titre Contrefaçon, § xi.

works, the materials of which are common to all writers, existing in nature, art, science, philology, history, statistics, &c., where there must be considerable resemblances, however independently of each other the different authors may have written. Over this vast field, it is impossible to erect an unvarying general rule, which can be fitted to all cases and capable of determining whether a particular work exhibits the degree of originality necessary to a valid copyright. The laws which protect literary property are designed for every species of composition, from the great productions of genius, that are to delight and instruct mankind for ages, to the most humble compilation that is to teach children the art of numbers for a few years, and then to disappear forever. Hence these laws must be so administered, that every literary laborer shall find in them an adequate protection to whatever he can show to be the product of his own labor. Something he must show to have been produced by himself; whether it be a purely original thought or principle, unpublished before, or a new combination of old thoughts and ideas and sentiments, or a new application or use of known and common materials, or a collection, the result of his industry and skill. In whatever way he claims the exclusive privilege accorded by these laws, he must show something which the law can fix upon as the product of his and not another's labors. But in order that the law should do this ample justice to the great variety of claimants, it is necessary that its rules should be capable of adaptation to the objects of their labor.[1] They must include in their range everything that can be justly claimed as the peculiar product of individual efforts; otherwise they would exclude from the benefits of literary property objects which are as clearly the products of individual labor, as the most original thoughts ever written, namely, new and important combinations and arrangements, or collections of materials known and common to all mankind.

It is therefore of some importance to ascertain, in the first place, what the law does not look to, in applying a test of originality to a literary composition.

1. The mere utility of a book, or its adaptation to the end which it professes to answer — its value in a critical point of view — cannot determine its legal originality. The law takes upon itself none of the functions of the critic, in this sense. It looks only for some substantial product of individual thought or labor, and leaves to public taste or judgment to determine its value, and to bestow its due reward. So that whether a book be more or less useful, more or

[1] "The rule of decision," said Lord Mansfield, in Sayre *v.* Moore, 1 East, 361, 362, note, "is a matter of great consequence to the country. In deciding it we must take care to guard against two extremes equally prejudicial; the one, that men of ability, who have employed their time for the service of the community, may not be deprived of their just merits, and the reward of their ingenuity and labor; the other, that the world may not be deprived of improvements, nor the progress of the arts be retarded. The act that secures copyright to authors guards against the piracy of the words and sentiments; but it does not prohibit writing on the same subject."

less successful, or brilliant, or important, if in a just sense the claimant is the author of that in which he claims an exclusive property, he is entitled to his copyright *valere, quantum valere potest.*[1] It is true, there may be cases, in which the question will arise, whether a subsequent author has made any improvements upon his predecessors ; and in such cases it may become necessary to apply collaterally, as a test of originality, an inquiry into the practical and relative value of his publication. But this will be done, in order to determine whether he has borrowed any, and how great a part of his matter from sources common to all writers — whether he has actually produced anything of his own, and not whether his production is better or worse than the productions of others. If it appears that he has produced anything of his own, not borrowed or adopted from a previous writer, its effect in advancing or retarding the progress of knowledge, or its value in a critical point of view, can have no influence upon his title to a copyright.

2. The law does not require that the subject of a book should be new, or that the materials of which it is composed should be original ; but there may be a valid copyright in the book itself, though the subject and the materials are common to all writers. In all such cases, the true inquiry is, whether the claimant's book contains any substantive product

[1] Emerson *v.* Davies, 3 Story's R. 768.

of his own labor? If so, the law declares it entitled to the protection of a copyright. Thus, if a person collects an account of natural curiosities, or of works of art, or of mere matters of statistical or geographical information, and employs the labor of his mind in giving a description of them, his own description may be the subject of copyright. It is equally competent to any other person to compile and publish a similar work. But it must be made substantially new and original, like the first work, by resort to the original sources, and must not copy or adopt from the other, upon the notion that the subject is common.[1]

There have been several cases, upon works of different kinds, which have recognized and established this principle. One of the earliest of this class of cases is that concerning Road Books or Itineraries.

There was formerly an old work, called Patterson's Road Book, published in England, from 1771 to 1796. In 1797, one Cary was employed by the postmaster-general to make an actual survey of the roads, and the book published by him contained many material corrections of and additions to the last edition of the original work by Patterson. Subsequently, a book was published purporting to be founded on Patterson's, but in reality, as was alleged, copied from the improved work of Cary, with some

[1] Hogg *v.* Kirby, 8 Ves. 215, 221.

colorable alterations. Cary applied to Lord Chancellor Loughborough for an injunction against the latter publication, in 1799; but his lordship refused to make an order, thinking that the two books were very unlike.[1] Two years afterwards, Cary brought an action in the court of king's bench, for piracy, against the publishers of the same or a similar book, which purported to be the twelfth edition of Patterson's, but containing also nine-tenths of Cary's improvements. The defendant's counsel contended that Cary could not be considered as the *author of the book*, within the meaning of the statute, the greater part of it having been published before by another person. Lord Kenyon, C. J., said, "Certainly the plaintiff had no title on which he could found an action to that part of his book which he had taken from Mr. Patterson's; but it is as clear that he had a right to his own additions and abbreviations, many of which were material and valuable; and the defendants are answerable at least for copying those parts in their book. The courts of justice have been long laboring under an error, if an author has no copyright in any part of a work, unless he have an exclusive right to the whole book." [2]

So, in the case of a work called The Court Calen-

[1] Cary *v*. Faden, 5 Ves. 24.

[2] Cary *v*. Longman, 1 East, 358, 360. It is not apparent whether the book complained of in this case was or was not the same as in the case of Cary *v*. Faden (*ante*) before Lord Loughborough. The defendants being different, it is probable that the works were different. But the principle involved was the same, and it is surprising that Lord Loughborough should have summarily disposed of it in the few words reported in 5 Ves. 26.

dar, Lord Eldon held that although the subject was open, no man could on that account be justified in sparing himself the labor and expense of collecting the original information and copying the work previously published by another.[1] So also Lord Erskine C. held, although the East India Calendar could not be a subject of copyright, yet, that if a man from his situation having access to the repositories in the India house, has by considerable expense and labor procured with correctness all the names and appointments on the India establishment, he has a copyright in that individual work.[2]

The same principle was also applied to a work on the Antiquities of Greece, containing prints taken from drawings made by the plaintiff;[3] and in like

[1] Longman *v.* Winchester, 16 Ves. 269. In this case, Lord Eldon said, "I cannot go the length of stating the proposition, that copyright cannot subsist in a work of this description: nor would I disturb the injunction upon that ground without putting them to a trial. Assuming, that there may be a copyright, there is not much difficulty in the rest of the case. Take the instance of a map, describing a particular county; and a map of the same county, afterwards published by another person: if the description is accurate in both, they must be pretty much the same: but it is clear, the latter publisher cannot on that account be justified in sparing himself the labor and expense of actual survey, and copying the map, previously published by another. So as to Patterson's Road Book, it is certainly competent to any other man to publish a book of roads; and if the same skill, intelligence and diligence, are applied in the second instance, the public would receive nearly the same information from both works: but there is no doubt that this court would interpose to prevent a mere re-publication of a work, which the labor and skill of another person had supplied to the world. So in the instance, mentioned by Sir Samuel Romilly, a work, consisting of a selection from various authors, two men perhaps might make the same selection: but that must be by resorting to the original authors, not by taking advantage of the selection already made by another."

[2] Matthewson *v.* Stockdale, 12 Ves. 270.

[3] Wilkins *v.* Aikin, 17 Ves. 422. See also Sayre *v.* Moore, 1 East, 361, note, with reference to charts.

manner, a person may have copyright in mathematical tables actually calculated by himself, although, on a fresh calculation the same tables would result from the same data and the same principles, and although they may have previously been published before his appeared.[1]

3. A book may also be original, in the sense of the law, although the materials of which it is composed, the hints and sources from which its matter was derived, can all be traced out in former works, provided the author has exercised selection, arrangement and combination, and has thereby produced anything new.[2] In a scientific treatise, to be used

Wyatt *v.* Barnard, 3 Ves. & B. 77, with reference to specifications of patents copied from the public office.

[1] Bailey *v.* Taylor, 3 Law Journ. 66.

[2] The following eloquent description of original authorship is from an argument by M. Merlin before the Court of Cassation. "Sans doute, il est des compilations d'ouvrages littéraires qui, par l'immensité des recherches qu'elles supposent, par le discernement et le goût qu'elles exigent, peuvent et doivent passer pour de véritables productions de l'esprit, et qu'il n'est pas plus permis de contrefaire que si elles étaient réellement des compositions originales.

"Par exemple, les *Pandectes* de Pothier ne sont, à peu de chose près, qu'une compilation des Institutes, du Digeste, du Code et des Novelles de Justinien; c'est-à-dire, de recueils qui, depuis plusieurs siècles, sont incontestablement dans le domaine du public.

"Cependant, si Pothier vivait encore, et qu'un imprimeur s'avisât de publier une édition de ses *Pandectes*, sans sa permission, qui est-ce qui oserait contester à Pothier le droit de le poursuivre comme contrefacteur? Qui est-ce qui oserait dire que Pothier, en compilant à sa manière les Institutes, le Digeste, le Code et les Novelles de Justinien, n'a pas fait un ouvrage qu'il n'appartenait qu'à un jurisconsulte du premier ordre d'entreprendre et d'achever? Qui est-ce qui oserait dire qu'un simple copiste eût pu, comme lui, tirer tous les textes du droit romain de l'espèce de chaos dans lequel ils sont dispersés; les ranger dans un vaste cadre où, enchaînés les uns aux autres, ils s'expliquent mutuellement; rapprocher de chaque règle générale toutes les exceptions qui la limitent; placer à côté de la loi ancienne, la loi moderne qui la modifie; et la loi plus moderne encore qui l'abroge; en un mot, substituer l'ordre à la confufor example for purposes of instruction, the author who takes existing materials from sources common to all writers, and arranges and combines them in a form and gives them an application unknown before, is protected in the exclusive enjoyment of what he has thus collected and produced, in that particular form. In like manner, an author who takes, from the hints and suggestions of objects in nature or art, or from the ideas and methods to be found in other books, the materials of a method of illustration, and gives to them a new application, or a new use, or uses them in a new form, produces something which the law recognizes and protects as original. This doctrine has been elaborately expounded, in two modern cases.

Thus, where an editor of a modern edition of Adam's Latin Grammar had made many improvements and additions, and had compiled many new notes to the old work, although the elemental materials of his improvements and additions and the substance of his notes could more or less be traced to other and various sources in other works, yet Mr.

sion, la lumière à l'obscurité, la facilité d'étudier et d'apprendre aux dégoûts et aux épines qui arrêtent, dès leurs premiers pas, tous les aspirants à l'exacte connaissance des lois romaines?

"Compiler de cette manière, ce n'est pas copier, c'est créer; c'est faire ce que ferait un architecte qui, après avoir démoli un édifice gothique, en emploierait tous les matériaux pour élever un superbe palais, un temple majestueux.

"Mais il est aussi des compilations qui se font, comme on le dit vulgairement, *avec des ciseaux*, qui n'exigent qu'un travail de manœuvre, et qui, pour cette raison, ne peuvent pas mériter à leurs artisans le titre d'auteurs." Merlin, Rep. de Jurisp. title Contrefaçon, § xi.

Justice Story held the editor entitled to copyright in the matter of his own edition, because it had never been before collected and embodied in a former single work.[1]

[1] Gray v. Russell, 1 Story's R. 11. In this case the court said, "The argument proceeds mainly upon this ground, that there is nothing substantially new in Mr. Gould's notes to his edition of Adam's Latin Grammar; and that all his notes in substance, and many of them in form, may be found in other works antecedently printed. That is not the true question before the court. The true question is, whether these notes are to be found collected and embodied in any former single work. It is admitted, that they are not so to be found. The most, that is contended for, is, that Mr. Gould has selected his notes from very various authors, who have written at different periods, and that any other person might, by a diligent examination of the same works, have made a similar selection. It is not pretended, that Mr. Cleveland undertook or accomplished such a task by such a selection from the original authors. Indeed, it is too plain for doubt, that he has borrowed the whole of his notes directly from Mr. Gould's work; and so literal has been his transcription, that he has incorporated the very errors thereof.

"Now, certainly, the preparation and collection of these notes from these various sources, must have been a work of no small labor, and intellectual exertion. The plan, the arrangement, and the combination of these notes in the form in which they are collectively exhibited in Gould's Grammar, belong exclusively to this gentleman. He is, then, justly to be deemed the author of them in their actual form and combination, and entitled to a copyright accordingly. If no work could be considered by our law as entitled to the privilege of copyright, which is composed of materials drawn from many different sources, but for the first time brought together in the same plan and arrangement and combination, simply because those materials might be found scattered up and down in a great variety of volumes, perhaps in hundreds, or even thousands of volumes, and might, therefore, have been brought together in the same way and by the same researches of another mind, equally skilful and equally diligent, — then, indeed, it would be difficult to say, that there could be any copyright in most of the scientific and professional treatises of the present day. What would become of the elaborate commentaries of modern scholars upon the classics, which, for the most part, consist of selections from the works and criticisms of various former authors, arranged in a new form, and combined together by new illustrations, intermixed with them? What would become of the modern treatises upon astronomy, mathematics, natural philosophy, and chemistry? What would become of the treatises in our own profession, the materials of which, if the works be of any real value, must essentially depend upon faithful abstracts from the Reports, and from juridical treatises, with illustrations of their bearing. Blackstone's Commentaries is but a compilation of the Laws of England,

So, where the plaintiff, the author of an arithmetic, designed to teach children the elements of that science, claimed a peculiar plan of lessons and method of illustration, as his own invention, and it was alleged by the defendant, and partially proved, that some of the different parts and elements of his plan and method had been in use before, and that the materials of his book were to be found in many different works; the same learned judge held that as the same plan, arrangement, and combination of materials had never been used before for the same or any other purpose, the plaintiff was entitled to a copyright.[1] In this case, the subject of the copyright

drawn from authentic sources, open to the whole profession: and yet it was never dreamed, that it was not a work, which, in the highest sense, might be deemed an original work; since never before were the same materials so admirably combined, and exquisitely wrought out, with a judgment, skill, and taste absolutely unrivalled. Take the case of the work on insurance, written by one of the learned counsel in this cause, and to which the whole profession are so much indebted; it is but a compilation with occasional comments upon all the leading doctrines of that branch of the law, drawn from reported cases, or from former authors; but combined together in a new form, and in a new plan and arrangement; yet I presume, none of us ever doubted, that he was fully entitled to a copyright in the work, as being truly, in a just sense, his own."

[1] Emerson *v.* Davies, 3 Story's R. 768. In this case the court said, "The book of the plaintiff is in my judgment, new and original, in the sense in which these words are to be understood in cases of copyright. The question is not, whethor the materials which are used are entirely new, and have never been used before; or even that they have never been used before for the same purpose. The true question is, whether the same plan, arrangement and combination of materials have been used before for the same purpose or for any other purpose. If they have not, then the plaintiff is entitled to a copyright, although he may have gathered hints for his plan and arrangement, or parts of his plan and arrangement, from existing and known sources. He may have borrowed much of his materials from others, but if they are combined in a different manner from what was in use before, and *a fortiori*, if his plan and arrangement are real improvements upon the existing modes, he is entitled to a copy-right in the book embodying such improvement. (See Lewis *v.* Fullerton, 2 Beav. R.

was not in the subject or in the materials, but in the plan, arrangement, and combination, which were

6.) It is true, that he does not thereby acquire the right to appropriate to himself the materials which were common to all persons before, so as to exclude those persons from a future use of such materials; but then they have no right to use such materials with his improvements superadded, whether they consist in plan, arrangement or illustrations, or combinations; for these are strictly his own. A man who constructs a new machine, is entitled to a patent therefor, if the combination and arrangements thereof are new and his own invention, although he uses old materials and old mechanical apparatus and powers in constructing such machine. He may use wheels, or levers, or screws, or toggle-joints, or cranks, or any other known modes of accomplishing given mechanical ends, if he combines them in a new manner, and thus produces a beneficial result. The steam-engine, the steam-boat, the cut-nail machine, the card machine, are all but new combinations of old materials, old processes, and old mechanical powers and apparatus.

"In truth, in literature, in science and in art, there are, and can be, few, if any, things, which, in an abstract sense, are strictly new and original throughout. Every book in literature, science and art, borrows, and must necessarily borrow, and use much which was well known and used before. No man creates a new language for himself, at least if he be a wise man, in writing a book. He contents himself with the use of language already known and used and understood by others. No man writes exclusively from his own thoughts, unaided and uninstructed by the thoughts of others. The thoughts of every man are, more or less, a combination of what other men have thought and expressed, although they may be modified, exalted, or improved by his own genius or reflection. If no book could be the subject of copyright which was not new and original in the elements of which it is composed, there could be no ground for any copyright in modern times, and we should be obliged to ascend very high, even in antiquity, to find a work entitled to such eminence. Virgil borrowed much from Homer; Bacon drew from earlier as well as contemporary minds; Coke exhausted all the known learning of his profession; and even Shakspeare and Milton, so justly and proudly our boast, as the brightest originals, would be found to have gathered much from the abundant stores of current knowledge and classical studies in their days. What is La Place's great work, but the combination of the processes and discoveries of the great mathematicians before his day, with his own extraordinary genius? What are all modern law books, but new combinations and arrangements of old materials, in which the skill and judgment of the author in the selection and exposition and accurate use of those materials, constitute the basis of his reputation, as well as of his copyright? Blackstone's Commentaries and Kent's Commentaries are but splendid examples of the merit and value of such achievements.

"In truth, every author of a book has a copyright in the plan, arrangement and combination of his materials, and in his mode of illustrating his subject, if it be new and original in its substance. Sir John Leach, original and peculiar. So, also, in the case of a work called "The Topographical Dictionary of England,"

in Barfield *v.* Nicholson, (2 Sim. and Stu. 1, 6,) recognized this doctrine in its fullest extent; and there stated, that a copyright might well be taken where the composition is either new, or there is a new arrangement thereof. Nay, the right to a copyright goes much farther. A man has a right to a copyright in a translation, upon which he has bestowed his time and labor. To be sure, another man has an equal right to translate the original work, and to publish his translation; but then it must be his own translation by his own skill and labor; and not the mere use and publication of the translation already made by another. (Wyatt *v.* Barnard, 3 Ves & Beam. 77.) A man has a right to the copyright of a map of a state or country, which he has surveyed or caused to be compiled from existing materials, at his own expense, or skill, or labor, or money. Another man may publish another map of the same state or country, by using the like means or materials, and the like skill, labor and expense But then he has no right to publish a map taken substantially and designedly from the map of the other person, without any such exercise of skill, or labor, or expense. If he copies substantially from the map of the other, it is downright piracy; although it is plain that both maps must, the more accurate they are, approach nearer in design and execution to each other. (Matthewson *v.* Stockdale, 12 Ves. 270; Wilkins *v.* Aiken, 17 Ves 422.) He, in short, who by his own skill, judgment and labor, writes a new work, and does not merely copy that of another, is entitled to a copyright therein; if the variations are not merely formal and shadowy, from existing works. He, who instructs by a new plan, and arrangement, and combination of old materials, in a book designed for instruction, either of the young, or the old, has a title to a copyright, which cannot be displaced by showing that some part of his plan, or arrangement or combination, has been used before.

"The case of Gray *v.* Russell, (1 Story R. 11,) affords a strong illustration of the doctrine, as that was a case confessedly of a mere improvement of an old work, Adam's Latin Grammar, a subject that had been discussed and treated in many hundred works, and in which little more could be done than to arrange the materials upon a new plan, or in a new combination, with additional illustrations and initial remarks. Yet the Court held it clearly to be the subject of a copyright; and from the doctrine therein stated I feel not the slightest inclination to depart. It was upon the like ground that an action has been held to lie for the recovery of damages for pirating the new corrections and additions to an old work, (the Itinerancy of England.) Upon that occasion, Lord Kenyon said: 'The courts of justice have been long laboring under an error, if an author have no copyright in any part of a book, unless he have an exclusive right to the whole book.' (See also Trusler *v.* Murray, and Tonson *v.* Walker, cited in 1 East, 360, 361, and notes.) Another illustration may be found in the cases of histories and dictionaries, as stated by Lord Mansfield in Sayre *v.* Moore, (1 East R. 361, note.) 'In the first, a man may give a relation of the same facts, consisting partly of compilations and selections from former works, and partly of original compositions,

and in the same order of time; in the latter, an interpretation is given of the identical same words. But he must not servilely copy the words of another on either subject. An author has as much right in his plan, and in his arrangements, and in the combination of his materials, as he has in his thoughts, sentiments, opinions, and in his modes of expressing them. The former as well as the latter may be more useful or less useful than those of another author; but that, although it may diminish or increase the relative values of their works in the market, is no ground to entitle either to appropriate to himself the labor or skill of the other, as embodied in his own work.'

"It is a great mistake to suppose, because all the materials of a work or some parts of its plan and arrangements and modes of illustration, may be found separately, or in a different form, or in a different arrangement, in other distinct works, that therefore, if the plan or arrangement or combination of these materials in another work is new, or for the first time made, the author, or compiler, or framer of it, (call him which you please,) is not entitled to a copyright. The reverse is the truth in law, and, as I think, in common sense also. It is not, for example, in the present case, of any importance that the illustrating of lessons in Arithmetic by attaching unit marks representing the numbers embraced in the example, may be found by dots in Wallis's Opera Mathematica, (p. 28) or in Colburn's Arithmetic in the form of upright linear marks, in a pamphlet detached from the main work. That is not what the plaintiff purports to found his copyright upon. He does not claim the first use or invention of unit marks for the purpose above-mentioned. The use of these is a part of and included in his plan; but it is not the whole of his plan. What he does claim is, 1. The plan of the lessons in his book; 2. The execution of that plan in a certain arrangement of a set of tables in the form of lessons to illustrate those lessons; 3. The gradation of examples to precede each table in such manner as to form with the table a peculiar and symmetrical appearance of each page; 4. The illustration of his lessons by attaching to each example unit marks representing the numbers embraced in the example. It is, therefore, this method of illustration in the aggregate that he claims as his invention, each page constituting of itself a complete lesson; and he alleges that the defendants have adopted the same plan, arrangement, tables, gradation of examples and illustrations by unit marks, in the same page, in imitation of the plaintiff's book, and in infringement of his copyright, and, in confirmation of this statement, he refers to divers pages of his own book in comparison with divers pages of the book of the defendants. Now, I say that it is wholly immaterial whether each of these particulars, the arrangement of the tables and forms of the lessons, the gradation of the examples to precede the tables, the illustration of the examples by unit marks, had each existed in a separate form in different and separate works before the plaintiff's work, if they had never been before united in one combination or in one work, or on obtained for the plaintiffs at their own cost, Lord Langdale, M. R. said, "there is no doubt but that a work of this nature may be the subject of copyright."[1]

In like manner, the Court of Cassation, in France, decided that a *compilation* may be the subject of copyright, under the law of July 19th, 1793.[2] The book was a devotional work, consisting of extracts

one page in the manner in which the plaintiff has united and connected them. No person has a right to borrow the same plan, and arrangement, and illustrations, and servilely to copy them into any other work. The same materials were certainly open to be used by any other author, and he would be at liberty to use unit-marks and gradations of examples and tables and illustrations of the lessons, and to place them in the same page. But he could not be at liberty to transcribe the very lessons and pages and examples and illustrations of the plaintiff, and thus to rob him of the fruits of his industry, his skill, and his expenditures of time and money.

"I have dwelt the more upon this point, because it seems to me that some of the learned witnesses, whose evidence is in the case, have entirely misunderstood the law upon this subject; and some portions of the argument at the bar seem to me to have proceeded upon an equally inadmissible ground, that if none of the materials of the plaintiff's book were new, or invented by him, that new combinations or arrangements, or illustrations of the old materials would not give a title to a copyright. My judgment is far otherwise; and as far as the evidence in this case goes, it is clear to my mind, that the plaintiff has a good copyright in his book; that, taking his plan, arrangements, lessons, examples and illustrations, as a whole, they are not to be found combined in any former work. I must confess that it strikes me that the plaintiff's method is a real and substantial improvement upon all the works which had preceded his, and which have been relied on in the evidence; but whether it be better or worse is not a material inquiry in this case. If worse his work will not be used by the community at large; if better, it is very likely to be so used. But either way, he is entitled to his copyright, *Valere quantum, valere potest.*"

[1] Lewis *v.* Fullerton, 2 Beavan's R. 6. See also Trussler *v.* Murray, 1 East, 363 note. Hogg *v.* Kirby, 8 Ves. 215; 5 Ves. 85, note 3, (Sumner's edition.) It seems that on a change of a description of roads from letter-press to copperplate delineation, the latter form is to be deemed so far original, as to justify the author in doing it after he has sold the copyright in the letter-press. Carnan *v.* Bowles, 5 Ves. 81.

As to new corrections and additions to an old work, see Tonson *v.* Walker, cited 4 Burr. 2325. Tonson *v.* Collins, Bl. R. 321. Motte *v.* Falkner, cited Bl. R. 331. King *v.* Reed, 8 Ves. 223, note.

[2] Cited ante, p. 169.

from the devotional writings of eminent churchmen, arranged in a particular manner with reference to the festivals of the church. The correctional tribunal at Lyons decided that the law of July 19, 1793, extended the privileges of authorship only to those who can strictly be called authors, — to those who could claim the first conception of a work of literature or art — and not to one who had only copied from the works of others. They held that the compiler of this book had only copied passages from the works of others, with slight verbal alterations and additions, and that neither these nor the plan and arrangement of the book gave it the character of a new work, because the greater part of it, which was copied, and was therefore *publici juris*, drew to itself the lesser part, which was really new, and attached to it the same condition of publicity. From this decree the proprietor appealed to the court of cassation; and M. Merlin, arguing against the decree, contended that the law applied not merely to works the fruit of the conceptions of genius, but also to the productions of intelligence;[1] and that the decree confounded a compilation which is the fruit of taste, intelligence, and exquisite and ingenious combination and arrangement, with a compilation which implied nothing but an expenditure of time and research, and an indefatigable patience in copying word

[1] It is very difficult to render into English phrases equally happy and distinct, the expressions "*productions de génie*" and "*productions de l'esprit.*" But the distinction is obvious.

for word. He maintained, that under this decree the Pandects of Pothier would be no subject of property, but would be open to the first occupant.[1]

The court held that the law extends to selections, compilations, and other works of that nature, when they require in their execution, discernment, taste, learning, and intellectual labor; when, in short, instead of being simply copies from one or more other books, they are at the same time the product of conceptions foreign and of conceptions peculiar to the author, in the union of which the matter receives a new form and a new character. The work in question possessed these characteristics, and the decree of the court of first instance was therefore annulled.[2]

4. It is upon principles somewhat analogous, but requiring perhaps a more careful discrimination than they have heretofore received, that translations and abridgments have been said to be original works and subjects of copyright.

Translations are so far original, as the labor spent in the translation may make them, and upon this ground they have been held to be undistinguishable from other works.[3] It is undoubtedly true, that the translation of a work from a foreign tongue incorporates with the original so much new labor, that it may with propriety be treated, for some purposes,

[1] See his eloquent vindication of the *authorship* of Pothier, ante, p. 177.

[2] Merlin, Rep. de Jurisp. tit. Contrefaçon, tom. 3, p. 701–708.

[3] Wyatt *v.* Barnard, 3 Ves. & B. 77. Drury on Injunctions, Part II. ch. 2, § 20, p. 213.

as a new work. It is the policy of the laws which protect copyright to encourage this and every other species of literary labor, as far as may consist with the vested rights of authors. But it may perhaps admit of question, whether it is not necessary, in order that a translator should acquire a new title and a valid copyright in literary matter, originally composed by another, that the original should have been first published in a foreign country. If a British or American author should see fit to publish in his own country an original work in a foreign or a dead language, and should secure the copyright thereof in the manner required by law, can any person translate it, and by such translation acquire the right to publish it in the vernacular tongue? The answer to this question must depend in a good degree upon the effect to be given to the act of translation, as a new labor, taken in connection with the fact that the original author has an undoubted copyright in the matter of the work, as he put it forth. Translation of a work published in a foreign country is the adoption of matter in which no one has an exclusive right in the country where the translation is made, since it is there *publici juris;* and the translator impresses upon that matter so much of a new character by his own labor, that the law treats his translation as a new product, and holds him entitled to a copyright, to protect this new product, as such. At the same time any one else may make a new translation. But where the matter of the work is not *publici juris*, is the new form given to it by translation sufficient to override the exclusive right of the original author in the matter itself? Notwithstanding the general principle of the English law in relation to translations, this question, I apprehend, would be not easy of solution, in the case of a scientific work written, for instance, in Latin, intended for the learned, and intended to convey a new discovery, or other information peculiarly original. It would be urged, in such a case, that the translation had given the work a new dress, in which the matter of it would be brought within the reach of a far greater number of persons; and this, it would be contended, was not only meritorious, but was a result of new labor of a purely intellectual kind. Still, the principle which allows the character of originality to the product of new labor upon old materials, would, in such a case, encounter the exclusive right of the original author in the matter of the work itself. In other analogous cases, this principle is not always of sufficient force to give to the mere labor of preparing a new dress, or a new form, the right to appropriate to itself the original matter of another author. Where the adoption and use of the matter of an original author, whose work is under the protection of copyright, is direct and palpable, and nothing new is added but form or dress, or an immaterial change of arrangement, the law will treat the alteration as merely colorable, and will stamp it with the character of piracy. Whether the change of form, or dress, produced by a close translation, in cases where the original work is under the protection of copyright, can have any greater effect than belongs to a change of form or dress, in other cases, is an interesting question, not determined, as it seems to me, by the general principle of the law of England, which treats translations as original works. This general principle was established only with reference to translations of foreign works, not under the protection of copyright.[1]

The same question might arise, where a treaty, establishing international copyright, subsists between two countries, without express provision being made for the case of translations. The British interna-

[1] The question here considered seems to have actually arisen once in England, but the case was disposed of upon grounds sufficiently absurd, which did not touch the point raised, if the imperfect report of it is correct. A bill was brought for an injunction to stay the printing and publishing a translation of Burnett's *Archæologia Sacra*, suggesting it to be an injury to the executor, in whom the property of the book was vested by 8 Anne, c. 19. It was insisted, for the defendant, that a translation of a book was not within the intent of the act. Lord Chancellor Parker said, that though a translation might not be the same with the reprinting the original, on account that the translator has bestowed his care and pains upon it, and so not within the prohibition of the act, yet this being a book which to his knowledge (having read it in his study) contained strange notions intended by the author to be concealed from the vulgar in the Latin language, in which language it could not do much hurt, the learned being better able to judge of it, he thought it proper to grant an injunction to the printing and publishing it in English; that he looked upon it, that this court has a superintendency over all books, and might, in a summary way, restrain the printing or publishing any that contained reflections on religion or morality. Burnett *v.* Chetwood, 2 Meriv. 441, note. For the talents and acquirements of Lord Ch. Parker, see Lord Campbell's Lives of the Chancellors.

tional copyright act contains a proviso, saving the right to publish and sell translations of any book, the author whereof and his assigns may be entitled to the benefit of the act.[1]

In like manner there is a general doctrine in the English law, that a *bona fide* abridgment of a previous work may be the subject of copyright in the person who makes it, upon the ground that it is a new work. The present chapter is not the appropriate place to consider in what cases an abridgment will constitute a piracy. This question will be discussed at large in a subsequent part of this work. But it is proper here to inquire into the doctrine which declares abridgments to be the subjects of new copyright, and to consider what discriminations ought to be made from the general position which some of the authorities appear to sanction.

The general doctrine is that a *bona fide* abridgment is in the nature of a new and meritorious work. The most elaborate general statement of this doctrine, found in the books, was that made by Lord Chancellor Apsley, assisted by Mr. Justice Blackstone, in a case relating to an abridgment of Hawkesworth's Voyages. His lordship is reported to have said, "that to constitute a true and proper abridgment of a work, the whole must be preserved in its sense; and then the act of abridgment is an act of understanding, employed in carrying a large work

[1] 1 and 2 Vict. c. 59, s. 13. See Appendix.

into a smaller compass, and rendering it less expensive, and more convenient both to the time and use of the reader, which made an abridgment in the nature of a new and a meritorious work." He further stated it as his own and Mr. Justice Blackstone's opinion, "that an abridgment, where the understanding is employed in retrenching unnecessary and uninteresting circumstances, which rather deaden the narration, is not an act of plagiarism upon the original work, nor against any property of the author in it, but an allowable and meritorious work."[1]

Without discussing at present the soundness of this definition of an allowable abridgment, it is sufficient to remark here, that if there are certain classes of works, such as translations, histories, &c. in which, by abridgment, a subsequent writer can acquire a new and independent title upon the footing of a new work, there are also other classes of works, with reference to which the doctrine of abridgment must encounter an exclusive title in the original author, so inseparable from the matter and substance of the work, that it must create the gravest doubts whether

[1] Anon. Lofft's R. 775. The other authorities are Gyles *v.* Wilcox, 2 Atk. 142. Bell *v.* Walker, 1 Brown's Ch. R. 450. Dodsley *v.* Kinnersly, Ambl. 403. Butterworth *v.* Robinson, 5 Ves. 709. In these cases, the general doctrine of a fair *bona fide* abridgment, as constituting a new work, is taken for granted, but no approach is made to a definition of such an abridgment. In Dodsley *v.* Kinnersly, Sir Thomas Clarke, M. R. said, that "no certain line can be drawn to distinguish a fair abridgment, but every case must depend on its own circumstances;" and Mr. Justice Story, in Gray *v.* Russell, 1 Story's R. 11, 19, has made the same suggestion. The authorities will be found collected and examined in the chapter relating to piracy, post.

the pretensions of the subsequent writer can prevail over the rights of the original author.

It has been recently held, that an author has as much right in his plan, and in his arrangement, and in the combination of his materials, as he has in his thoughts, sentiments, opinions, and his modes of expressing them.[1] If this doctrine be correct, it follows that a subsequent author cannot, by abridgment, acquire a new and independent title in the plan, arrangement, and combination of materials, made use of by a former author, who has secured his title in the due course of law. It would seem to be quite as consistent with sound principle, to hold that a mechanician may acquire a new patent by making a reduced copy of an original machine, previously protected by a patent, as to hold that by the mere act of abridgment, a new title can be acquired in the peculiar matter of a book.[2]

[1] Emerson *v.* Davies, 3 Story's R. 768.

[2] For a further discussion of this subject, see post, Chap. IX.

CHAPTER VI.

OF THE STATUTE REQUISITES FOR A VALID COPY-RIGHT.

1. In the United States.
2. In Great Britain.

1. THE act of congress of 3d February, 1831, § 4, requires that a printed copy of the title of any book, or books, map, chart, musical composition, print, cut, or engraving, to be entitled to the benefits of the act, shall, before publication, be deposited in the clerk's office of the district court of the United States for the district where the author or proprietor resides, which title is to be recorded by the clerk, and a certified copy of the title as recorded is to be delivered to the author or proprietor. Within three months from the publication, the author or proprietor is to deliver, or cause to be delivered, a copy of the book, map, &c. to the clerk, which it is made the duty of the clerk to transmit to the secretary of state.[1]

[1] Act of Cong. Feb. 3, 1831, § 4. See Appendix.

The fifth section of the same act makes it necessary to insert in the several copies of each and every edition published during the term secured, on the title-page, or the page immediately following, if it be a book; or if a map, chart, musical composition, print, cut, or engraving, to impress on the face thereof, or if a volume of maps, charts, music, or engraving, upon the title or frontispiece thereof, the words, "Entered according to act of congress, in the year , by A. B., in the clerk's office of the district court of ," (as the case may be.)[1]

These steps are all essential to a perfect title, according to a decision made by the supreme court of the United States, upon the former acts, that of 1790 and that of 1802. Upon those acts, it was held by the court, that although the right was vested, when a copy of the title was deposited with the clerk, and a copy of his record was printed, as the act of 1802 required, yet that the performance of the other conditions was essential to a perfect title.[2]

[1] Sec. 5. See Appendix. The act of 1790, § 3, required the author or proprietor to publish a copy of the record or certificate of entry in one or more newspapers printed in the United States, for the space of four weeks. The act of 1802 required, that the copy of the record, which by the act of 1790 the author or proprietor was required to publish, should also be inserted in the page of the book next to the title. (See Appendix, p. 89.) With the exception of publication in the newspapers, and the time and mode of deposit in the secretary of state's office, the requisites remain the same under the act of 1831, as they stood at the time that act was passed. The act of 1790, § 4, required the author or proprietors, within *six months* of the publication, to deliver or cause to be delivered to the secretary of state, a copy of the book, to be preserved in his office. The act of 1831 directs the copy for this purpose to be deposited with the clerk of the court, within *three months* from the date of publication.

[2] Wheaton *v.* Peters, 8 Peters S. C. R. 591, 663, 665. Upon this point, the court said, "It will be

As the law now stands, there are but three requisites for securing a valid copyright. 1. The deposit of a printed copy of the title, before publication, with

observed, that a right accrues under the act of 1790, from the time a copy of the title of the book is deposited in the clerk's office. But the act of 1802 adds another requisite to the accruing of the right, and that is, that the record made by the clerk shall be published in the page next to the title-page of the book.

"And it is argued with great earnestness and ability, that these are the only requisites to the perfection of the complainant's title. That the requisition of the third section to give public notice in the newspapers, and that contained in the fourth to deposit a copy in the department of state, are acts subsequent to the accruing of the right, and whether they are performed or not, cannot materially affect the title.

"The case is compared to a grant with conditions subsequent, which can never operate as a forfeiture of the title. It is said also that the object of the publication in the newspapers, and the deposit of the copy in the department of state was merely to give notice to the public; and that such acts, not being essential to the title, after so great a lapse of time, may well be presumed. That if neither act had been done, the right of the party having accrued, before either was required to be done, it must remain unshaken.

"This right, as has been shown, does not exist at common law — it originated, if at all, under the acts of congress. No one can deny that when the legislature are about to vest an exclusive right in an author or an inventor, they have the power to prescribe the conditions on which such right shall be enjoyed; and that no one can avail himself of such right who does not substantially comply with the requisitions of the law. This principle is familiar, as it regards patent rights; and it is the same in relation to the copyright of a book. If any difference shall be made, as it respects a strict conformity to the law, it would seem to be more reasonable to make the requirement of the author, rather than the inventor. The papers of the latter are examined in the department of state, and require the sanction of the attorney-general; but the author takes every step on his own responsibility, unchecked by the scrutiny or sanction of any public functionary.

"The acts required to be done by an author, to secure his right, are in the order in which they must naturally transpire. First, the title of the book is to be deposited with the clerk, and the record he makes must be inserted in the first or second page; then the public notice in the newspapers is to be given; and within six months after the publication of the book, a copy must be deposited in the department of state.

"A right undoubtedly accrues on the record being made with the clerk, and the printing of it as required; but what is the nature of that right? Is it perfect? If so, the other two requisites are wholly useless. How can the author be compelled either to give notice in the newspaper, or deposit a copy in the state department. The statute affixes no penalty for a failure to perform either of these acts, and it provides no means by which it may be enforced.

"But we are told they are unimportant acts. If they are indeed the clerk of the district court; 2. Notice to the public, by printing, in the place designated, the fact of the entry, in the form prescribed by the statute;

wholly unimportant, congress acted unwisely in requiring them to be done. But whether they are important or not, is not for the court to determine, but the legislature; and in what light they were considered by the legislature, we can learn only by their official acts.

"Judging then of these acts by this rule, we are not at liberty to say they are unimportant, and may be dispensed with. They are acts which the law requires to be done, and may this court dispense with their performance?

"But the inquiry is made, shall the non-performance of these subsequent conditions operate as a forfeiture of the right?

"The answer is, that this is not a technical grant of precedent and subsequent conditions. All the conditions are important; the law requires them to be performed, and consequently their performance is essential to a perfect title. On the performance of a part of them the right vests; and this was essential to its protection under the statute: but other acts are to be done, unless congress have legislated in vain, to render the right perfect.

"The notice could not be published until after the entry with the clerk, nor could the book be deposited with the secretary of state until it was published. But these are acts not less important than those which are required to be done previously. They form a part of the title, and until they are performed the title is not perfect. The deposit of the book in the department of state, may be important to identify it at any future period, should the copyright be contested, or an unfounded claim of authorship asserted. But, if doubts could be entertained whether the notice and deposit of the book in the state department, were essential to the title, under the act of 1790; on which act my opinion is principally founded, though I consider it in connection with the other act; there is, in the opinion of three of the judges, no ground for doubt under the act of 1802. The latter act declares that every author, &c. before he shall be entitled to the benefit of the former act, shall, 'in addition to the requisitions enjoined in the third and fourth sections of said act, if a book, publish,' &c. — Is not this a clear exposition of the first act? Can an author claim the benefit of the act of 1790, without performing the requisites enjoined in the third and fourth sections of it? If there be any meaning in language, the act of 1802, the three judges think, requires these requisites to be performed 'in addition' to the one required by that act, before an author, &c. 'shall be entitled to the benefit of the first act.'

"The rule by which conditions precedent and subsequent are construed, in a grant, can have no application to the case under consideration, as every requisite, in both acts, is essential to the title.

"A renewal of the term of fourteen years can only be obtained by having the title-page recorded with the clerk, and the record published on the page next to that of the title, and public notice given within six months before the expiration of the first term."

See also Ewer *v.* Cox, 4 Wash. C. C. R. 486.

3. The deposit with the clerk of a copy of the publication, within three months from the date of publication.[1] These acts are also made essential to a perfect title, by the statute itself, which declares that *no person shall be entitled to its benefits*, unless he shall have complied with these directions.[2]

In all cases of renewal of copyright, under the act of the 3d February, 1831, the entry, deposit at the clerk's office, &c., must be made a second time, within six months before the expiration of the first term, and notice thereof must be given, by publishing a copy of the record within two months fıom the date of the renewal, in one or more newspapers published in the United States, for the space of four weeks.[3]

The provisions of law respecting transfers and assignments of copyrights, will be found stated in a subsequent chapter.

It is not essential to the validity of a copyright,

[1] Act of Congress, 3d Feb. 1831, § 4. I do not include, as one of the conditions for a perfect title, the recent enactment, which requires a copy of every work, of which the copyright shall be secured, to be sent to the library of the Smithsonian Institute; but I should not advise the neglect of this requisition, although it is not enforced by any penalty whatsoever. The statute, containing this provision, is in these words:

"And be it further enacted, That the author or proprietor of any book, map, chart, musical composition, print, cut, or engraving, for which a copyright shall be secured under the existing acts of congress, or those which shall hereafter be enacted respecting copyrights, shall, within three months from the publication of said book, map, chart, musical composition, print, cut, or engraving, deliver, or cause to be delivered, one copy of the same to the librarian of the Smithsonian Institution, and one copy to the librarian of Congress Library, for the use of the said libraries." Act of Congress, 10th Aug. 1846, ch. 178, § 10.

[2] Ibid.

[3] Act of Congress, 3d Feb. 1831, § 3.

that the author's name should appear upon the title-page.[1]

2. Registration, under the English law, seems not to be essential to a good title, but merely affects the remedy. By the 5 and 6 Vict. c. 45, § 11, it is enacted, that a book of registry be kept at stationers' hall, wherein may be registered the proprietorship in the copyright of books, and assignments thereof, and in dramatic and musical pieces, whether in manuscript or otherwise, and licenses affecting such copyright; and certified copies of any entry are made *prima facie* proof of the proprietorship or assignment of copyright or license, as therein expressed.[2] The 13th section makes it lawful for the proprietor of a copyright in any "book"[3] published before or after the act, to make entry in the registry book of the stationers' company, of the title of such book, the time of the first publication thereof, the name and place of abode of the publisher, and the name and place of abode of the proprietor of the copyright, or of any portion thereof, according to a form annexed to the act, and it is also made lawful for every such registered proprietor to assign his interest, or any portion of his interest, by making en-

[1] Beckford *v.* Hook, 7 T. R. 620.

[2] Act 5 and 6 Vict. c. 45, § 11.

[3] The word "book," in this act, includes every volume, part, or division of a volume, pamphlet, sheet of letter-press, sheet of music, map, chart, or plan separately published, sec. 2.

try in the book of registry of such assignment, and of the name and place of abode of the assignee, in a form annexed to the act ; and such assignment, so entered, is declared to be, without stamp or duty, of the same force and effect as if made by deed.[1]

The 19th section provides, that the proprietor of the copyright in any encyclopedia, review, magazine, periodical work, or other work published in a series of books or parts, shall be entitled to all the benefits of registration under the act, on entering in the book of registry the title of the work, the time of the first publication of the first volume, number or part, or of the first number or volume first published after the passing of the act, in any such work which shall have been published before the act, and the name and place of abode of the proprietor, and of the publisher, when the publisher is not the proprietor.[2]

The 24th section enacts, that no proprietor of copyright in any book which shall be first published after the passing of the act, shall maintain any action or suit, at law or in equity, or any summary proceeding, in respect of any infringement of such copyright, unless he shall, before commencing such action, suit, or proceeding, have caused an entry to be made in the book of registry of the stationers' company, of such book, pursuant to the act ;[3] provided always,

[1] Act 5 and 6 Vict. c. 45, § 13.

[2] Ibid. § 19.

[3] Formerly, an action for damages could be maintained, although the work had not been entered at stationers' hall; but the penalties given by the 8 Anne, c. 19, could not be recovered. Beckford *v.* Hood, 7 T. R. 620.

that the omission to make such entry shall not affect the copyright in any book, but only the right to sue or proceed in respect of the infringement thereof; provided also, that nothing in the act shall prejudice the remedies which the proprietor of the sole liberty of representing any dramatic piece shall have by virtue of the act 3 Wm. IV. or of this act, although no entry shall be made in the book of registry.[1]

By the 20th section of this act, dramatic and musical compositions are to be registered, by entering the title of the production, the name and abode of the author or composer, the name and abode of the proprietor, and the time and place of the first representation or performance.[2] But the omission to register is not to affect the remedies which the proprietor of the sole liberty of representation has by virtue of this act, or of the 3 Wm. IV. c. 15.[3]

University and Collegiate Copyright.

The acts 15 George III. c. 53, § 1, and 41 George III. c. 107, § 3, secure to the two universities of Oxford and Cambridge and the colleges within them, the four universities in Scotland, Trinity College, Dublin, and the Colleges of Eton, Westminster, and

[1] Act 5 and 6 Vict. c. 45, § 24. The 12th section of this act makes it an indictable misdemeanor, punishable accordingly, for any person wilfully to make, or cause to be made, any false entry, or wilfully to produce, or cause to be tendered in evidence, any paper falsely purporting to be a copy of any entry in the registry book.

[2] Act 5 and 6 Vict. c. 45, § 20.

[3] Ibid. § 24. The term "dramatic piece," in this act, includes every tragedy, comedy, play, opera, farce, or other scenic, musical, or dramatic entertainment. Sect. 2.

Winchester, a copyright in books given or bequeathed to them for the advancement of useful learning or other purposes of education ; and this copyright they hold in perpetuity, unless the bequest is expressly stated to be for a limited term, and if they continue to print at their own presses. But the penalties given by these acts against piracy, cannot be recovered, unless the title to the copy of the book be entered at stationers' hall, within the space of two months after the bequest or gift thereof shall have come to the knowledge of the vice-chancellors, or heads of colleges, or principals, of the said institutions, respectively.[1] If the clerk of the stationers' company neglect or refuse to make the entry and grant a certificate thereof, when required, then the proprietors (notice being first given of such neglect or refusal in the London Gazette,) are to have the like benefit as if the entry and certificate had been made and given, and the clerk is subjected to a penalty.[2]

Prints and engravings are regulated by the acts 8 Geo. II. c. 13, 7 Geo. III. c. 38, and 17 Geo. III. c. 57, the latter being extended to Ireland by the 6 and 7 Wm. IV. c. 59. Registration does not seem to be required ; but the statute 8 Geo. II. c. 13, § 1,

[1] Sawyer *v.* Dicey, 3 Wills. 60.

[2] Acts 15 Geo. III. c. 53, § 5; and 41 Geo. III. c. 107, § 5. The rights of the several universities and colleges mentioned in these acts are saved to them by the 5 and 6 Vict. c. 45, § 27. The universities obtained these rights by special enactment, after the decision of the house of lords, in Donaldson *v.* Becket, had unexpectedly overthrown the doctrine of perpetual copyright at common law.

requires that the day of the first publication shall be truly engraved with the name of the proprietor on each plate, and printed on every copy. The fulfilment of this requisition has been held to be necessary, to enable a party to recover, in case of piracy, the penalties imposed by the statutes. But it was formerly doubted whether an action at law for damages, or a bill in equity for an account and injunction, could not be sustained, without a compliance with these requisitions.[1] But it has since been settled, that no action for the piracy of a print can be maintained, unless the date and name of the proprietor were engraved upon it, according to the act.[2]

Sculpture, which is protected by the act 54 Geo. III. c. 56, (which amended the 33 Geo, III. c. 71,) must have the name of the proprietor, with the date, put upon each original copy or cast.[3]

Delivery of Copies to certain Public Libraries.[4] The

[1] Blackwell *v.* Harper, 2 Atk. 95. Roworth *v.* Wilkes, 1 Camp. 95. Harrison *v.* Hogg, 2 Ves. Jr. 323. Thompson *v.* Symonds, 5 T. R. 41.

[2] Brooks *v.* Cock, 3 Ad. & Ellis, 138.

[3] Act 54 George III. c. 56, § 1. See Appendix.

[4] It has long been a part of the policy of English legislation on the subject of literature, to support certain institutions by compelling a delivery of a certain number of copies of all published works. The first statute containing this requirement, was the 13 and 14 Car. II. c. 33, by which three copies were ordered to be delivered, one for each of the two English universities, and one for the king's library. This was followed by the 8 Anne, c. 19, which extended the number of copies to nine ; one for the King's Library, two for the libraries of Oxford and Cambridge, four for the libraries of the four Scotch universities, one for Sion College in London, and one for the library of the Faculty of Advocates in Edinburgh. The 41 George III. c. 107, gave two more copies, one to Trinity College, and one to the King's Inn, Dublin. The 54 George III. c. 156, substituted the British Museum, in place of the King's Li-

5 and 6 Vict. c. 45, § 6, requires the delivery to the British Museum, of a printed copy of every book published after the passing of the act, together with all maps, prints, or other engravings belonging to it, finished and colored as are the best copies of the work ; also of a printed copy of any second or subsequent edition published with additions or alterations, whether in the letter-press or in the maps, prints, or other engravings, and whether the first edition was published before or after the passing of the act ; and also of a printed copy of any second or subsequent, of which the first or some preceding edition has not been delivered to the Museum. Each of these copies is required to be bound, sewed or stitched together, and to be upon the best paper on which the work is printed ; and the delivery must be made within one calendar month after the book is first published within the bills of mortality, or within three calendar months after it is first published in any other part of the united kingdom, or within

brary. Under these statutes, all books published, whether entered at stationers' hall or not, were demandable, under a penalty. The University of Cambridge *v.* Bryer, 16 East, 317. This legislation has recently been followed in the United States, in the law establishing the Smithsonian Institute, (Act of Congress, Aug. 1846, c. 178,) which directs, without any penalty, a copy of every book, of which the copyright shall be secured, to be sent to the library of that institution. It is to be regretted that this species of tax upon literature should have been introduced into this country. If confined to a single institution, it will never be very seriously felt. But, should the instances be multiplied, the justice and expediency of the measure will require grave consideration. In 1818, evidence was taken before a committee of the house of commons, upon the propriety of this tax. For this evidence and other discussions on the subject see Maugham on Copyright, Appendix, p. 229, et seq.

twelve calendar months after it is first published in any other part of the British dominions.[1] The seventh section of the act prescribes the days on which the delivery is to be made, and directs the person receiving the book to give a receipt for the same in writing.[2]

The eighth section of the same statute requires that a copy of every book, or of any second or subsequent edition containing additions or alterations, together with all maps, and prints belonging to it, published after the passing of the act, on the paper of which the largest number of copies is printed for sale, and in like condition with them, shall, on demand in writing, left at the publisher's abode within twelve months after publication, under the hand of the officer of the stationers' company, or of any person with authority from the Bodleian Library at Oxford, the Public Library at Cambridge, the Library of the Faculty of Advocates at Edinburgh, and the Library of Trinity College, Dublin, be delivered within one month after such demand, to the officer of the stationers' company; which copies the officer is required to receive for the use of the library for which such demand shall have been made, and to give a written receipt therefor.[3] But it is optional with the publisher to deliver the copies at the libraries, instead of at the stationers' company.[4] The penalty for default in delivering copies as required

[1] Act 5 and 6 Vict. c. 45, § 6.
[2] Ibid § 7.
[3] Ibid. § 8.
[4] Ibid. § 9.

by the act, is, besides the value of the book, a sum not exceeding five pounds, to be recovered to the use of the library, by summary conviction before two justices of the peace, or by an action of debt.[1]

[1] Act 5 and 6 Vict. c. 45, § 10.

CHAPTER VII.

DURATION OF COPYRIGHT.

1. Duration of Copyright in England.

1. *Books.*[1] The act 8 Anne, c. 29, (passed April 18th, 1710,) gave the author or proprietor of a book, then already printed, the sole and exclusive right of printing it for twenty years. It also gave to the author and his assignee of a book then already composed, but not published, or of a work that should thereafter be composed and published, the sole liberty to print and reprint it for the term of fourteen years and no longer, to commence from the day of its first publication; with the further provision, that in case the author should be living at the end of the first term of fourteen years, then the sole right of disposing of copies of the work should return to him for another term of fourteen years.[2] In the 54 Geo. III. c. 156, (passed July 20th, 1814,) all the provisions of the former acts were consolidated; con-

[1] For the definition of the statute term "book," see post, p. 207, n. 2.

[2] See Appendix, p. 2. By the 41 Geo. III. c. 167, the law of copyright in Ireland was assimilated to that in Great Britain.

siderable alteration was at the same time made in the law; the term of copyright in the author and his assignee was extended to twenty-eight years absolutely, and for the life of the author; and to benefit the families of those authors who were alive at the time the act was passed, but who might die before the first fourteen years from the day of publication had expired, a further term of fourteen years was given to the personal representatives of such authors, without prejudice to all or any part of the former term.[1]

The 5 and 6 Vict. c. 45, (passed July 1st, 1842,) revised the whole subject. The 3d section of that act provides, "That the copyright in every book,[2] which shall, after the passing of this act, be published in the lifetime of its author, shall endure for the natural life of such author, and for the further term of seven years, commencing at the time of his death, and shall be the property of such author and his assigns; provided always, that if the term of seven years shall expire before the end of forty-two years from the first publication of such book, the copyright shall, in that case, endure for a period of forty-two years; and that the copyright in every book which shall be published after the death of its author, shall

[1] See Appendix, p. 38. For this short analysis of the two acts recited in the text, I am indebted to a little work on Copyright, by Peter Burke, Esq. of the Inner Temple, Barrister at Law, published at London in 1842, 12mo. pp. 64.

[2] By the 2d section, the word "book," in the construction of this act, is declared to include "every volume, part or division of a volume, pamphlet, sheet of letter-press, sheet of music, map, chart, or plan, separately published."

endure for the term of forty-two years from the first publication thereof, and shall be the property of the proprietor of the author's manuscript, from which such book shall be first published, and his assigns."[1]

According, therefore, to the present law of England, the copyright of every book published during the author's lifetime is to last certainly for forty-two years from the date of its first publication; and if the author's life and the seven years after his decease cover a longer period than forty-two years, the copyright may last longer. The copyright of a book published after the author's death will endure for forty-two years from the date of the first publication.

The fourth section of the statute enacts, "That the copyright which at the time of the passing of this act, shall subsist in any book theretofore published (except as hereinafter mentioned,) shall be extended and endure for the full term provided by this act in cases of books thereafter published, and shall be the property of the person who at the time of the passing of this act shall be the proprietor of such copyright; provided always, that in all cases in which such copyright shall belong, in whole or in part, to a publisher, or other person who shall have acquired it for other consideration than that cf natural love and affection, such copyright shall not be extended by this act, but shall endure for the term which shall subsist therein at the time of the passing

[1] See Appendix, p. 66.

of this act, and no longer ; unless the author of such book, if he shall be living, or the personal representative of such author, if he shall be dead, and the proprietor of such copyright shall, before the expiration of such term, consent and agree to accept the benefits of this act in respect to such book, and shall cause a minute of such consent, in the form in that behalf given in the schedule to this act annexed, to be entered in the book of registry hereinafter directed to be kept, in which case such copyrights shall endure for the full term by this act provided, in cases of books to be published after the passing of this act, and shall be the property of such person or persons as in such minute shall be expressed."

Copyrights, therefore, which existed before the passing of this act, and which had not expired, are extended through the natural life of the author, and for seven years after his decease, or for forty-two years certain from the date of first publication. This extended term, however, will not belong to the proprietor who has obtained the assignment for other consideration than that of natural love and affection, unless the extension be agreed on between such proprietor and the author, or his personal representative.

In order to provide against the suppression of books of importance to the public, the fifth section of the statute makes it lawful for the judicial committee of the privy council, on complaint made to them, that the proprietor of the copyright in any book, after the death of its author, has refused to republish, or to allow the republication of the same, and that by reason of such refusal such book may be withheld from the public, to grant a license to such complainant to publish such book, in such manner, and subject to such conditions as they may think fit, and that it shall be lawful for such complainant to publish such book according to such license.[1]

2. *Dramatic and Musical Compositions.* By the law of England, a double copyright may exist in a dramatic or musical composition, viz. the sole right of printing, and the sole right of representation or performance.

The sole right of printing and publishing plays and musical compositions is vested in the authors for the same period of time as is provided in the case of books.[2]

By the 3 Wm. IV. c. 15, § 1, the sole right of representation or performance of plays, composed or to be composed and not printed and published by the author or his assignee, was secured to the author and his assignee, indefinitely; and in the case of plays, printed or published after the passing of the act, (10th June, 1833,) or within ten years before, the sole right of representation or performance was given to the author or his assignee, for a period of twenty-eight years from the time of publication, or of the passing of the act, or, if the author were living at the

[1] Act 5 & 6 Vict. c. 45, § 5.

[2] Ibid. § 2.

end of that period, for the remainder of the author's life.

By the 5 and 6 Vict. c. 45, § 20, the sole liberty of representing or performing, or causing or permitting to be represented or performed, any dramatic piece or musical composition, was made to endure and be the property of the author and his assigns, for the term provided in the same act for the duration of copyright in books, viz. for the author's life, and seven years after his death, or for forty-two years.

The question may arise, under these statutes, whether the author of an unpublished play or musical composition, has the exclusive right of representation or performance forever. The act 3 Wm. IV. c. 15, gave to the author, or his assignee, of an unpublished play, the sole liberty of performing it, without any limitation of time, and when it is considered that by the common law it had previously been settled that representation is not publication, and that consequently, so long as the author keeps his play in manuscript, no one can acquire the right to perform it by printing it surreptitiously from the mouths of the actors, it would seem that this act is merely declaratory of the common law, and intended to confirm a perpetual exclusive right in the case of an unpublished play. But the act 5 and 6 Vict. c. 45, § 20, without noticing the distinction between published and unpublished plays, contained in the former act, recites as follows: "And whereas an act was passed in the third year of the reign of his late Majesty, to amend the law relating to dramatic literary property, *and it is expedient to extend the term of the sole liberty of representing dramatic pieces given by that act to the full time by this act provided for the continuance of copyright*;" and it then enacts, that "the sole liberty of representing or performing, or causing or permitting to be represented or performed, any dramatic piece or musical composition, shall endure and be the property of the author thereof, and his assigns, for the term in this act provided for the duration of copyright in books, viz. during the author's life and for seven years after his decease, if the life and the term of seven years together make forty-two years, and if not, then for forty-two years from the first publication. The construction of the two acts together, will be aided by inquiring what term, in the act 3 Wm. IV. is referred to by the words in the preamble of the last act, "the term of the sole liberty," &c. which is to be extended. No other term is provided in the former act, than that for the performance of *published* plays. The sole right to perform *unpublished* plays is confirmed to the author without limitation of time. If, therefore, the preamble refers to the term before provided for published plays, and confines the general words of the enacting clause to the same reference, the sole right to perform unpublished plays is not reduced from a perpetuity to a term of forty-two years, but remains untouched.

Assuming this to be so, the law now stands thus:

1. The author or assignee of a dramatic or musical composition, unprinted and unpublished, has a sole and perpetual right to its performance.

2. The author or assignee of a dramatic or musical composition printed and published within ten years before the passing of the 3 and 4 Wm. IV. c. 15, (10th June, 1833,) or printed and published after the passing of that act, has the sole right of performance for the author's life, and seven years after his death, and if that time expire before forty-two years from the time of first performance, then for such forty-two years.[1]

3. *Engravings.* The 8 Geo. II. c. 13, vested a copyright in historical and other prints for the term of fourteen years, to commence from the day of the first publication. By the 7 Geo. III. c. 38, § 1, the benefits of the former act were extended to the prints of any portrait, conversation, landscape, or architecture, map, chart or plan, or any other prints whatsoever, whether taken from the artist's own original designs, or from any picture, drawing, model, or sculpture, either ancient or modern ; and the term of enjoying the right was in all cases enlarged from fourteen to twenty-eight years.

Maps, charts and plans are now, by the 5 and 6 Vict. c. 45, § 2, regarded as "books," and are consequently entitled to the same period of copyright.

4. *Sculpture.* In the subjects of sculpture, by the

[1] Burke on Copyright, p. 42.

54 Geo. III. c. 56, § 1, a term of fourteen years copyright is vested in the person who made or caused to be made the original sculpture, model, copy or cast; and, by the fifth section, an additional term of fourteen years is also given, if such person be living at the end of the first term, and have not divested himself of the copyright by sale or otherwise.[1]

2. Duration of Copyright in the United States.

By the act of congress of 3d February, 1831, § 1, books, maps, charts, musical compositions, prints, cuts and engravings, have a term of copyright of twenty-eight years from the time of recording the title thereof.[2]

If, at the expiration of the first term of twenty-eight years, the author, inventor, designer, engraver, or any of them, where the work had been originally composed and made by more than one person, be still living, and a citizen or citizens of the United States, or resident therein, or being dead, shall have left a widow, or child, or children, either or all then living, the same exclusive right shall be continued to such author, designer, or engraver, or if dead then to such widow and child, or children, for the further term of fourteen years: *Provided*, that the title of the work so secured shall be a second time recorded, and all the other regulations of the act in relation to

[1] See Appendix, p. 38. [2] See Appendix, p. 93.

original copyrights be complied with in respect to such renewed copyright, and that within six months before the expiration of the first term.[1] The act further requires that a copy of the record of renewal be published in one or more newspapers printed in the United States, within two months from the date of such renewal, for the space of four weeks.[2]

[1] See Appendix, p. 93.

[2] § 3.

CHAPTER VIII.

TRANSMISSION OF COPYRIGHT, AND OTHER INCIDENTS OF LITERARY PROPERTY.

THE law of England and that of America recognize, as we have seen, the exclusive right of an author over his own productions existing in manuscript.[1] This right is independent of the property in the paper itself, and consists in the exclusive authority to print and publish the literary contents. No question has ever been successfully made of the existence of this species of property, whatever disputes have arisen, from time to time, as to the effect upon it of publication and sale.

Literary property, in unpublished writings, has always been a well-settled right at common law.[2]

The nature of this property has been defined as "an incorporeal right in the nature of a faculty, and having reference to a future time for reaping the profits."[3] Lord Mansfield described it as "a nincor-

[1] Ante, Chap. II.

[2] Millar *v.* Taylor, 4 Burr. 2398. Donaldson *v.* Becket, Ibid. 2408. Duke of Queensbury *v.* Shebbeare, 2 Eden's Ch. R. 329. Macklin *v.* Richardson, Amb. 694. Southey *v.* Sherwood, 2 Meriv. 434. Wheaton *v.* Peters, 8 Peters S. C. R. 591, 661. 2 Story's Eq. Jurisp. § 943.

[3] 1 Bell's Com. 68.

poreal right to print a set of intellectual ideas or modes of thinking, communicated in a set of words and sentences and modes of expression. It is equally detached from the manuscript, or any other physical existence whatsoever."[1]

This species of property has long been, and is at the present day treated as an inheritable right. The copy in Lord Clarendon's History,[2] the manuscripts of a Conveyancer,[3] the Letters of Lord Chesterfield,[4] and the Writings of Washington,[5] were severally held to have passed to personal representatives,

[1] 4 Burr. 2396. His Lordship there said, "It has all along been expressly admitted, 'that, by the common law, an author is entitled to the copy of his own work until it has been once printed and published by his authority;' and 'that the four cases in chancery, cited for that purpose, are agreeable to the common law; and the relief was properly given, in consequence of the legal right.'

"The property in the copy thus abridged, is equally an incoporeal right to print a set of intellectual ideas or modes of thinking, communicated in a set of words and sentences and modes of expression. It is equally detached from the manuscript, or any other physical existence whatsoever.

"The property thus abridged is equally incapable of being violated by a crime indictable. In like manner, it can only be violated by another's printing without the author's consent; which is a civil injury.

"The only remedy is the same; by an action upon the case, for damages, or a bill in equity for a specific relief.

"No action of detinue, trover, or trespass *quare vi et armis*, can lie; because the copy thus abridged is equally a property in notion, and has no corporeal tangible substance.

"No disposition, no transfer of paper upon which the composition is written, marked, or impressed, (though it gives the power to print and publish,) can be construed a conveyance of the copy, without the author's express consent 'to print and publish;' much less, against his will.

"The property of the copy, thus narrowed, may equally go down from generation to generation, and possibly continue forever; though neither the author nor his representatives should have any manuscript whatsoever of the work, original, duplicate, or transcript."

[2] Duke of Queensbury *v.* Shebbeare, 2 Eden's C. R. 329.

[3] Webb *v.* Rose, cited 4 Burr. 2330.

[4] Thompson *v.* Stanhope, Amb. 737.

[5] Folsom *v.* Marsh, 2 Story's R. 100.

with the sole right of publication. Indeed, there seems to be no reason why the remark of Lord Mansfield is not strictly true, that the property in manuscript, being the incorporeal right to print a set of intellectual ideas, communicated in words and sentences, may go down from generation to generation, and possibly continue forever; though neither the author nor his representatives should have any manuscript copy whatever of the work, original, duplicate or transcript.[1]

It is also a right that adheres solely to the person entitled to exercise it, so long as he does not see fit to alienate it; and it cannot be seized by creditors, and does not pass to assignees under a bankruptcy.[2] Being detached from the manuscript, or any other physical existence, and being a mere incorporeal right to print, or to withhold from printing—a faculty, or right to exercise a choice—it would seem to be beyond the reach of execution, or the opera-

[1] See Millar *v.* Taylor, 4 Burr. 2397. The 5 and 6 Vict. c. 45, § 25, makes all copyright personal property, transmissible by bequest, or, in case of intestacy, subject to the same law of distribution as other personal property, and in Scotland it is to be deemed to be personal and movable estate.

[2] 1 Bell's Com. 68. See also 4 Burr. 2396, 2397. Mr. Godson says, "it is doubtful whether an unpublished manuscript can be taken in execution by creditors;" and cites 4 Burr. 2311, where the question is suggested by Lord Mansfield *arguendo*. Mr. Godson adds: "but the better opinion seems to incline against such a rule of law, because until the act of publication is accomplished, an author has an undoubted right to have full control over it," [his manuscript.] Godson on Patents and Copyright, 2d edition, p. 430. This seems to be merely stating the same proposition in a different form. But Lord Mansfield's exposition of the real basis of exclusive property before publication, shows that Mr. Godson touches the true grounds of the opinion, that such property does not pass under a commission of bankruptcy. See ante, p. 85, for the view taken by Mr. Bell, upon this point.

tion of the bankrupt laws. The manuscript itself may possibly be taken in execution; but the transfer of the manuscript does not alone carry with it a conveyance of the copy, that is, the authority to print and publish.[1] If the mere paper can be seized under execution, it must be taken subject to the sole right of the author over the intellectual ideas that are written upon it.

The author or proprietor of a manuscript may, by parol, at common law, license another to print and publish it; and such an authority may possibly be inferred from the acts of the parties.[2] But there must be a consent proved, and such consent cannot be inferred from possession of the manuscript alone, even if there be but a single copy of it in existence.[3] There are so many other purposes, which may account for the possession of a manuscript, without involving an authority to publish it, that mere possession would have a very slight tendency to prove that authority. The right to print and publish being a right detached from the manuscript, does not necessarily go along with it, and therefore its transfer must be proved by farther independent evidence. Whether the sole right to print forever the contents of an unpublished manuscript can, at common law, be conveyed by parol, so that the copyright will

[1] 4 Burr. 2396.

[2] Southey *v.* Sherwood, 2 Meriv. 434. Rundell *v.* Murray, Jacobs R. 311.

[3] Duke of Queensbury *v.* Shebbeare, 2 Eden's Ch. R. 329. Pope *v.* Curll, 2 Atk. 342. 2 Story's Eq. Jurisp. § 342. 4 Burr. 2396. Ante, p. 217, note 1.

vest in the person who may be thus authorized to publish, is a point admitting of great doubt. But it seems that under the statutes, in England, an assignment in writing has been held necessary to pass the copyright in an unpublished work. The 8 Anne, c. 19, § 1, declared that "the author *and his assignee or assigns* shall have the sole liberty of printing," and that "if any *other* bookseller, printer, or other person, &c. shall print, reprint, &c. *without the consent of the proprietor first had and obtained in writing, signed in the presence of two or more credible witnesses, he shall forfeit,*" &c. Upon this statute, Lord Macclesfield, C. is said to have held, that the author might grant the right of the copy to a subsequent publisher, after it had been once published by the person to whom he had originally delivered the manuscript, the bare delivery amounting only to a license to print the first edition.[1] In a more modern case, Lord Ellenborough said, that "the statute having required that the consent of the proprietor, in order to authorize the printing or reprinting of a book by any other person, shall be in writing, the conclusion from it seemed irresistible that the assignment must also be in writing; for if the license, which is the lesser thing, must be in writing, *a fortiori* the assignment, which is the greater thing, must also be." The plaintiff, who claimed as an assignee, was therefore nonsuited.[2] This decision, whether correct or

[1] Viner's Abr. 278.

[2] Power *v.* Walker, 3 M. & S. 7. It must be owned that this reasoning is not satisfactory. The stat-

not, has been since followed, and the settled construction of this and the subsequent act 54 Geo. III. c. 156, is, that a parol assignment is not sufficient to give to the assignee the privileges conferred by the legislature upon the author.[1]

The act 5 and 6 Vict. c. 45, § 15, declares, that "if *any* person shall, in any part of the British dominions, print or cause to be printed, either for sale or exportation, any book in which there shall be subsisting copyright, *without the consent in writing of the proprietors*, &c. he shall be liable," &c. This evinces a clearer intention, that all transfers of copyright shall be in writing, than appeared from the former acts; and the provisions of the 13th section, which provide a mode of transfer by a memorandum to be made in the books of the stationers' company, to be of the same force and effect as if *made by deed*, show the understanding of parliament as to the previously existing law.

The question recurs, then, what does the party acquire, as against the author and the public, at

ute does not require that the license to any other person than *the author* shall be in writing, but it declares that no other person than the author *and his assignee* shall print without a license in writing. The question turns upon the force of the word *assignee*, and the general intention of the act. See also S. C. 4 Campb. 8.

[1] Clementi *v.* Walker, 2 B. & C. 861. Power *v.* Walker, 3 Maule & Selw. 9. Barnett *v.* Glassop, 1 Bing. N. C. 633. In Latour *v.* Eland, 2 Starkie's N. P. C. 382, it was held, that a publication for six years, by a person (not the composer) of music, was not sufficient in itself to prove that the copyright had been transferred; and that the receipt of the proprietor for the price of the copyright would not bar the action. But where a copyright in music was not asserted against violation for *fifteen years*, the court of chancery refused an injunction until the right should be established at law. Platt *v.* Button, 19 Ves. 447.

common law, who receives a manuscript from the author, under a parol license to publish it, no assignment in writing being made of the copyright? In the first place, it seems to be admitted that an author may dedicate his work to the public, and that such a dedication may be inferred from long silence, from the absence of any conveyance of the property, from long acquiescence in its publication by various persons, and other circumstances.[1] In the second place, an author may, by unequivocal acts of a like nature, dedicate his work to an individual. Thus, where the plaintiff gave her manuscript to a publisher, with a parol license to publish it at his own risk and expense, and disclaimed any intention to receive any emolument from it, and the defendant published it for fourteen years (the first term under the statute then in force) and continued to publish and sell it afterwards, and the plaintiff then applied for an injunction to restrain its farther publication by the defendant; Lord Eldon refused the injunction, upon the ground that the defendant had been licensed to publish without any limitation of time.[2]

In this case, the question was left undecided, whether the right to publish did not remain in the plaintiff concurrently with the defendant, or whether the defendant had acquired any right as against the public. The defendant declined an offer made by

[1] 4 Burr. 2245, 2346. Platt *v.* Button, 19 Ves. 447. Folsom *v.* Marsh, 2 Story's R. 109. Rundell *v.* Murray, Jacobs R. 311, 316.

[2] Rundell *v.* Murray, Jacobs R. 311.

the court to try his title to the copyright, and his counsel expressly disclaimed any such title, admitting that there was no legal assignment of it.[1] The case therefore proceeds upon the effect of a parol license to publish, and admits that such a license conveys no copyright to the *exclusion* of the author.

Under such circumstances, the rights acquired by a publisher under a parol license depend upon the fact of there being or not being a limitation in point of time, in the license itself. If there is no limitation as to time, the inference is admissible that the author gave a concurrent authority to publish indefinitely. But the inference does not go beyond a concurrent authority. There can be no presumption that the author intended to convey the copyright, for the law requires that to be in writing ; and there have been cases where such a presumption has been rejected.[2] These cases show that the author retains the copyright, where there has been no assignment in writing, and may defend it by action or injunction against his licensee, where the license was not indefinite in point of time.[3] But it seems that a conveyance of the copyright may be proved by the defendant's admissions that he has conveyed it, although he does not refer to the mode of the conveyance.[4]

[1] Rundell *v.* Murray, Jacobs R. 312, 316.

[2] Storace *v.* Longman, 2 Campb. 27, n. Latour *v.* Bland, 2 Starkie's N. P. C. 382. Power *v.* Walker, 4 Campb. 8.

[3] Ibid.

[4] Power *v.* Walker, 4 Campb. 9, note.

As a mere licensee, therefore, a publisher under a parol license can maintain no action at law against a third person, because he has no legal title.[1] But according to the modern doctrine, he may, if he have a clear equitable title, maintain a bill for an injunction against any other person than the author, or his assignee.[2] And where the party claims as assignee of an assignee, he will not, in equity, be put to pro-

[1] Power *v.* Walker, 4 Campb. 9, n. There is a *dictum* of Lord Ellenborough, to the effect that the first publisher of a book, however he procured the copy, has such a property that he may bring an action at law against any person pirating it. Cary *v.* Kearsley, 4 Esp. N. P. C. 168, 169. Mr. Godson cites this case as authority for the same position. Godson on Patents and Copyright, 2d ed. p. 427. The book in question was Cary's Road Book. The defendant's counsel examined a witness, an officer of the post-office, to prove that the survey stated to have been made by the plaintiff was at the expense of the post-office, in order to show that the copyright belonged to the post-office and not to the plaintiff. Lord Ellenborough said, "I do not know that that will protect the defendant; at law, the first publisher, *even though he has abused his trust, by procuring the copy*, has a right to it, and to an action against a person who publishes it without authority from him. It may be a ground in equity, as between the person entitled and the person who first published it; but it does not destroy the right of the latter to sue a person pirating that right." I do not understand this to be law, as broadly stated. All copyright depends on title derived from the author; and unless there has been a transmission of title from him, the publisher can maintain no action for piracy, though, under some circumstances, he may obtain an injunction.

[2] Mawman *v.* Tegg, 2 Russ. 385. Sweet *v.* Shaw, 3 Jurist, 217. 2 Story's Eq. Jurisp. § 935. The impolicy of suffering literary works to be published under parol agreements, and the fatality of the supposition, that a copyright can be conveyed without writing, were strongly illustrated in the case of some of Mr. Moore's Irish Melodies. Mr. Moore sold his work to W. Power, of Dublin, who agreed verbally with J. Power, of London, his brother, that he (J. Power) should have the sole publication and sale of it in England; J. Power brought an action on the 8 Anne, c. 19, against one Walker for pirating the words of two of the songs, and was nonsuited for want of a legal title, being a mere licensee. Mr. Moore, the author, then brought an action in his own name against the same defendant, for the same piracy, and was nonsuited, because he had been heard by some of the witnesses to say, that he had parted with all his interest in the copyright to W. Power. See 4 Campb. 8, 9, n. But see Nicol *v.* Stocdale, 3 Swanst. 687.

duce the original assignment to his assignor, but the proof of want of title will be thrown on the defendants.[1]

An equitable title, which will support a bill for an injunction, occurs, where the legal right has not been vested, but from the dealings between the actual owner and the party bringing the bill, such party has acquired a limited equitable right in the copyright, to the extent of being entitled to be one of the publishers, or the sole publisher of the work, for a given or an indefinite time. But it is necessary that the party should have a real interest in the work, and not be a mere agent to sell it. Thus, where a publisher was employed by the board of admiralty, under direction of the crown, to publish a work, consisting of a narrative of a voyage undertaken by persons employed for that purpose by the crown, but the profits were to be at the disposal of the lords of the admiralty, it was held, that the publisher had not such an interest in the work as would enable him to sustain an injunction against another person for republishing it.[2] But where it was agreed, in writing, between an author and a publisher, (after reciting that the author had prepared a tenth edition of his work, and the publisher was desirous of *purchasing the same*,) that a certain printer should print a given number of copies, and the publisher should pay to the author for *the said tenth edition* a certain

[1] Morris *v.* Kelley, 1 Jac. & W. 481.

[2] Nicol *v.* Stockdale, 3 Swanst. 687.

sum, and that the work should be sold to the public for a given price, it was held that the publisher was not a mere licensee to sell a given number of copies, but that being bound by the agreement to sell, and the author being bound to abstain from doing anything which would interfere with the sale, the publisher had a limited equitable interest in the copyright, to the extent of being entitled to be the sole publisher, until the number of copies fixed by the terms of the agreement should be exhausted.[1]

It is not settled in England, whether a conveyance of copyright must be by deed, as well as in writing. The cases which have held that a transfer in writing is necessary, did not decide whether a writing, not being a deed, would be sufficient.[2] In a more recent case, Lord Ch. J. Tindal expressed an opinion that nothing short of a deed would answer; but the pleadings did not admit of the question being raised.[3] The act 5 and 6 Vict. c. 45, s. 13, which makes an assignment by entry in the register as valid *as if it had been made by deed*, has been supposed to show the understanding of parliament, that the usual and necessary mode of transfer of copyright is by deed.[4]

The preceding observations may aid us in determining the effect of the contracts which ordinarily

[1] Sweet *v.* Cater et al. 5 Jur. 68, cited Drewry on Injunctions, p. 211. See also Mawman *v.* Tegg, 2 Russ. 392. Sweet *v.* Shaw, 17 Law J. 216.

[2] Power *v.* Walker, 4 Campb. 8. Clementi *v.* Walker, 2 B. & C. 861.

[3] De Pinna *v.* Polhill, 8 Car. & P. p. 78.

[4] See Appendix, p. 70.

take place between the writers of articles for magazines, and other periodical works, and the proprietors of such works. Does the mere transmission of a manuscript essay or article to the conductor of a magazine, for publication, coupled with the receipt of such compensation as may be paid for it, carry with it the whole title of the copyright, so as to exclude the author from reprinting it in any other form thereafter? There is, doubtless, an implied contract on the part of the writer, not to reprint his essay at such a time, or in such a manner, as to deprive the party who has purchased the liberty of printing it, of the benefit of being the sole publisher thereof, for a reasonable length of time, which must depend on the circumstances of the case. Hence, the writer could not, without a breach of his implied contract, print his essay in another periodical, published simultaneously with the work for which he had originally written it. But where the law requires a written assignment of copyright, and no such assignment has been made, and there is no stipulation on the part of the writer never to re-print his essay, it would seem that the right to republish it, after a reasonable time, must remain with him at common law. But whether the projector and proprietor of a work, in which different persons have written parts, at his request, and have been paid for the same as contributors, without having made a legal assignment of their copyrights, is to be deemed the author and proprietor of the work, so as to entitle him to protection as against the public, is a different question. This point came before Sir John Leach, V. C., and he was of opinion that such a projector and proprietor was to be deemed the author and proprietor within the intendment of the statute of Anne, for the purposes of protection in a court of equity.[1]

Perhaps the provisions of the recent English statute on this subject may be regarded as, in part, declaratory of the previously existing law. Those provisions are made retrospective; manifesting thereby an intention to apply, by statute, to previously existing rights, principles understood to be already in existence, upon which the contracts might be presumed to have been made. The statute declares, in substance, that where essays, articles, &c. have been or shall be written for publication in, or as part of any encyclopedia, review, magazine, periodical work, or work published in a series of books in parts, or any book whatsoever, on the terms that the copyright therein shall belong to the proprietor, pro-

[1] Barfield *v.* Nicholson, 2 Law Journ. 90, 102. In this case, the vice chancellor said, "I am of opinion, that, under that statute [8 Anne, c. 19] the person who forms the plan, and who embarks in the speculation of a work, and who employs various persons to compose different parts of it, adapted to their own peculiar acquirements — that he, the person who so forms the plan and scheme of the work, and pays different artists of his own selection, who, upon certain conditions, contribute to it, is the author and proprietor of the work, if not within the literal expression, at least, within the equitable meaning of the statute of Anne, which, being a remedial law, is to be construed liberally." S. C. 2 Sim. & Stu. 1. As to the property in a review, and the right to prevent the publication of works handed out to the public under false colors, as continuations of a former established work, see Hogg *v.* Kirby, 8 Ves. 215.

jector, publisher or conductor of the work, and paid for by such proprietor, &c. the copyright thereof shall be the property of such proprietor, &c. who shall enjoy the same rights as if he were the actual author thereof, and shall have such term of copyright therein as is given by the act to the authors of books; except that in the case of essays, articles, &c. forming part of, or first published in reviews, magazines, or other periodical works of a like nature, after the term of twenty-eight years from the first publication thereof respectively, the right of publishing the same in a separate form shall revert to the author for the remainder of the term given by the act, provided, that during the twenty-eight years, the proprietor of the review, magazine, &c. shall not publish any such essay, article, &c. separately or singly, without the consent of the author or his assigns previously obtained; and provided also, that these enactments shall not affect the rights of any such author, who, by any contract, express or implied, may have reserved, or shall reserve to himself the right of separate publication; but that every author, so reserving the right of separate publication, shall have the copyright in his composition, when published, in a separate form, according to the act, without prejudice to the right of the proprietor of the review, magazine, &c.[1]

There have been several decisions in England,

[1] Act 5 & 6 Vict. c. 45, § 18. See Appendix, p. 73.

upon contracts between authors and publishers, which may illustrate the subject at present under consideration. Where an author agreed, in writing, to supply a bookseller with the manuscript of a work to be printed by the latter, the profits to be equally divided between them, Lord Ellenborough held that an action could be maintained for damages for refusing to supply the manuscript.[1] But where an author was engaged for a certain sum, to write an article, to appear among others in a work called "The Juvenile Library," and before he had completed his article, and before any portion of it was published, the work in which it was to appear was discontinued, Lord C. J. Tindall held, that the publishers were not entitled to claim the completion of the article, in order that it might be published in a separate form for general readers, but were bound to pay the author a reasonable sum for the part which he had prepared.[2] The contract in this case does not appear to have been in writing.

Where an author sells the copyright of a work published under his own name, and covenants with the purchaser not to publish any other work to prejudice the sale of it; it seems, that another pub-

[1] Gale *v.* Leckie, 2 Stark. N. P. C. 107. But if the author be justly apprehensive that the work, when published, will subject him to punishment, it seems that he may refuse to deliver the manuscripts. *Ib.* A contract with the proprietors of a theatre, not to write pieces for any other theatre, is lawful, as a similar restraint of a performer would be; not resembling a covenant restraining trade generally. Morris *v.* Colman, 18 Ves. 437.

[2] Planché *v.* Colburn, 5 C. & P. 58.

lisher, who has no notice of this covenant, may be restrained from publishing a work subsequently purchased by him from the same author, and published under his name, on the same subject, but under a different title, and though there be no piracy of the first book.[1]

But in an action by several plaintiffs, for piracy of copyright, it appeared that the defendant, the author, had published the work in question pursuant to the conditions of a *cognovit* given by him to one of the plaintiffs and another person, in an action for not performing an agreement to write the work in question; and it was held that this was a sufficient defence.[2]

Although the interest in a manuscript does not pass to assignees under a commission of bankruptcy, yet the copyright of a printed book does so pass; and it seems that it is not necessary that there should be any instrument in writing between the bankrupt and his assignees.[3]

The provisions of the act 5 and 6 Vict. c. 45, with regard to the assignment of copyright, apply to dramatic and musical compositions, as well as books. The assignment of the copyright of a play was formerly held to have carried with it the sole right of representation also, which was secured to the author

[1] Barfield *v.* Nicholson, 2 Sim. & Stu. 1. 2 Law Journal, 90.

[2] Sweet et al. *v.* Archbold, 10 Bing. R. 133.

[3] Mawman *v.* Tegg, 2 Russ. R. 385, 392. Keene *v.* Harris, cited 17 Ves. 338. Longman *v.* Tripp, 2 New R. 67.

by the 3 Wm. IV. c. 15.[1] But in order to obviate the effect of this decision, it is now provided, that no assignment of the copyright of any book consisting of or containing a dramatic piece or musical composition, shall be holden to convey to the assignee the right of representing or performing such dramatic piece or musical composition, unless an entry in the registry book shall be made of such assignment; wherein shall be expressed the intention of the parties, that such right should pass by the assignment.[2]

As to prints and engravings, it being enacted by the 8 Geo. II. c. 13, § 1, that before a print can be copied with impunity, the consent of the proprietor must be given in writing, signed in the presence of two witnesses, it is manifestly necessary to a valid assignment, in England, that it should be in writing.

The fourth section of the 54 Geo. III. c. 56, provides, that "no person who may purchase the right or property of a new and original sculpture or other matter above mentioned of its proprietor, by deed in writing, signed by such proprietor in the presence of and attested by two witnesses, shall be subject to any action for copying, casting, or vending the same." The assignment of copyright in sculpture must therefore be by deed signed in the presence of two witnesses, and attested by them.

In the United States, the act 30th June, 1834, § 1, provides, that all deeds or instruments in writing,

[1] Cumberland *v.* Planché, 1 Ad. & Ellis, 580.

[2] Act 5 & 6 Vict. c. 45, § 22.

for the transfer or assignment of copyrights, being proved or acknowledged in such manner as deeds for the conveyance of land are required by law to be proved or acknowledged in the same state or district, shall and may be recorded in the office where the original copyright is deposited and recorded; and every such deed or instrument that shall in any time hereafter be made and executed, and which shall not be proved or acknowledged and recorded as aforesaid, within sixty days after its execution, shall be judged fraudulent and void against any subsequent purchaser or mortgagee for valuable consideration without notice.[1]

This statute seems to recognize the doctrine, that transfers or copyright must be in writing, but it does not expressly declare that they shall be so. It applies to all kinds of literary property which can, in this country, be the subjects of copyright.

As to what passes by a general assignment of copyright, it is to be observed, that, after the publication of a book, the exclusive right to print and reprint it, or the estate of copyright, as it may be called, becomes a right for such term only as is provided by statute. In the United States, as was formerly the case in England, the statutes secure a resulting or contingent term to the author, in case he shall be living at the time of the expiration of the first term; and if the author be not living at the

[1] Act of Congress, 30th June, 1834, § 1. See Appendix, p. 100.

expiration of the first term, the second term goes to his widow, child, or children, if living.[1] By a general assignment of copyright, it is clear that the whole of the author's interest for the first term, passes to his assignee; but whether the resulting or second term passes, so as to exclude the author and his representatives, and to enable the assignee to secure such term by complying with the directions of the statute concerning the renewal of the copyright, is a question of some difficulty. In England, upon the statute 8 Anne, c. 19, which gave a second term of fourteen years to the author, if living, at the end of the first term, it was held that a general assignment of all the author's "interest" in a copyright conveyed the contingent as well as the present interest.[2]

In the United States, in a case where a publisher agreed with an author, that the latter should prepare a certain book for the press, and the publisher engaged to pay the author a certain sum "for the copyright of the said book," it was held, that the resulting term, under the statute, did not pass to the publisher, and that the word "copyright" embraced only the term then capable of being secured, which at the time of the contract constituted the copyright of the book.[3]

[1] Act Feb. 3d, 1831, § 1, 2.

[2] Carnan *v.* Bowles, 2 Bro. C. R. 80, and Rennet *v.* Thompson, there cited. Godson, p. 429, 2d edit. In Rundell *v.* Murray, Jacobs R. 315, Lord Eldon said, "I conceive that an author will not be taken to have assigned his contingent right in case of his surviving the fourteen years, unless the assignment is so expressed as to purport to pass it."

[3] Per Woodbury, J. in Pierpont *v.* Fowle, Circuit of the U. States, at Boston, May Term, 1847. See 1 Woodbury's R.

In like manner, the question may arise, whether a general assignment of copyright, by the author, will deprive his representatives of the additional term of fourteen years, given by the act of congress of 3d February, 1831, § 2; or whether the author himself has any power over this additional term, so far as the interests of his representatives are concerned. The statute provides that the author, if living at the expiration of the first term of twenty-eight years, shall have a further term of fourteen years, on making a new entry for that purpose. This contingent interest the author may undoubtedly assign. But if the author is not living at the end of the first term, the additional term vests in his widow and child, or children, living at the time. It is not easy to see how the author can dispose of this interest. It is not created for him, but for his family; it vests only in case of his death, and the policy of the statute, it seems to me, has removed it from his control.[1]

[1] See Appendix, p. 93.

CHAPTER IX.

INFRINGEMENT OF COPYRIGHT.

HAVING considered the nature and duration of that species of property which is protected under the denomination of copyright, we have now to treat of its violation, in the various forms of which the law has taken cognizance, and for which it has provided a remedy. It is obvious, that this species of property must be exposed to a great variety of injuries, some of which, from their subtle and ingenious character, may elude the meshes of the law. But the principles on which this kind of property depends, and the doctrines which are already well established in English and American jurisprudence, will be found hereafter, when fully carried out, to extend an adequate and just protection to literature, even if such protection is not now administered with all the success that could be desired. In endeavoring to trace the just scope of these principles and doctrines, we must bear in mind that while the primary object of the law of copyright is protection to the product of all literary labor, the interests of knowledge demand a reasonable freedom in the use of all antecedent literature. To administer the law in such a manner as not to curtail the fair use of existing materials, in any department of letters, is one of the great tasks of jurisprudence. It proposes to itself, first, the vindication of rights acquired by genius, discovery, invention, and labor, in the productions of the mind; secondly, the acknowledgment upon motives of public policy, of the right to a fair use by any writer of all that has been recorded by previous authors. The discovery and application of the rules which are to determine what such a fair use is, in a given case, is one of the most difficult of legal problems. Questions of this nature have justly been said to belong to the metaphysics of the law. But the law would ill deserve the name of a science, if its professors were unable to discharge the duties which the interests of society impose upon them, however subtle the distinctions may be with which they have to deal. It is the boast of the law, through which it claims rank among the sciences, that it is able to regulate the rights of men by principles; and this ought to be no less true of it, when it deals with subjects of a metaphysical character, than when it adjudicates controversies of the most simple nature.

The examination heretofore made into the nature of this property, has shown, that while the public enjoys the right of reading the intellectual contents of a book, to the author belongs the exclusive right to take all the profits of publication which the book can, in any form, produce. His exclusive right includes the whole book and every part of it. Hence it follows, that this right may be invaded in several ways; 1. By reprinting the whole work, verbatim; 2. By reprinting, verbatim, a part of it, either with or without acknowledgment of the source from which the extract or passage is taken; 3. By imitating the whole or a part, or by reproducing the whole or a part with colorable alterations and disguises, intended to give to it the character of a new work; 4. By reproducing the whole or a part under an abridged form.

With regard to each of these forms of infringement, it is to be observed, that the question of intention does not enter directly into the determination of the question of piracy. The exclusive privilege, which the law secures to authors, may be equally violated, whether the work complained of was written with or without the *animus furandi* — the intention to take what belongs to another, and thereby to do an injury. A party may mistake his own rights, or the rights of the author whose book he makes use of in the compilation of his own. The fact of his having made such a mistake, or the degree of good faith with which he has acted, cannot settle a question which depends upon other elements.[1]

To decide the question of piracy upon the motives

[1] Emerson *v.* Davies, 3 Story's R. 768. Folsom *v.* Marsh, 2 Story's R. 100.

of the party charged with the infringement, would reduce the exclusive right secured to authors by the law to a much lower scale of value and efficiency than the law intends to give to it. The most direct and palpable piracies would escape correction, where the party charged could make it appear that he had acted innocently. The privilege of authors would be rendered of no value whatever, where the existence of the right admitted of a reasonable doubt before adjudication; since the defendant would only have to show that such a doubt existed, and then to claim the benefit of that doubt in establishing his innocent intention.

It is necessary, therefore, in every inquiry whether a piracy has been committed, to look at the complex character of the question. It involves, first, an inquiry into the existence of the exclusive right claimed by the author whose book is supposed to have been infringed; and, secondly, the determination of the question whether this right has been infringed by what has been done by the party charged with an infringement.

The elements by which the first of these questions is to be determined, have been already pointed out. The second question forms the appropriate subject of discussion in the present chapter. Before considering particular forms and cases of piracy, the general doctrines, on which the solution of this question depends, may be here cursorily examined.

The statutes which secure the exclusive rights of

authors, do not define, in any terms, what shall constitute an infringement of copyright. It is left to the tribunals to decide, in each case, upon the circumstances of the case, whether a violation of the right has been committed. On the one hand, the courts must regard the existence of the exclusive right, when established or admitted; and on the other, the principle of public policy, which admits of some use of all antecedent literature. This last consideration, however, will not sanction direct and palpable injuries to the author, in whom the law has vested the sole right to take the profits of his own book and of every part of it. It becomes, therefore, a most material inquiry, in all cases, to ascertain whether the author has sustained or is likely to sustain any injury by the publication of which he complains; and perhaps it will be found that this is the test by which the question of infringement ought to be determined, in nearly all doubtful and difficult cases.

I am not aware of any recorded decision, or of any principle of law, which would deny redress to an author who should prove a direct injury, upon the ground that the writer who had caused it had made a justifiable use of his work. It is easy to imagine cases, where the use which a subsequent writer makes of a previous publication is apparently within the limits of the general right of selection, or citation, or tacit adoption; but if an injury can be proved to be the effect, I know of no rule of law, by which, consistently with the strict right of the previous author, such use can be pronounced to be admissible. The question, whether very trifling injuries will be redressed by one class of the public tribunals, is entirely aside from the strict right to redress from some tribunal, which depends upon no considerations of judicial convenience, or limits of jurisdiction. Notwithstanding some *dicta* in a few cases, and the general principle, (which cannot be established at a fixed line,) by which what is called the fair use of a previous publication is obscurely hinted at, I apprehend that the doctrine of our law is and must be, that where an injury is caused, an infringement is, in point of strict right, made out.

1. Piracy, by reprinting the whole work *verbatim*.

In cases of this kind, there can ordinarily be no question to be determined, except the existence of the copyright. The object with which the original work is thus taken, and the form in which it is used, are immaterial. It is equally a violation, whether the whole of a smaller work is inserted in a larger one, or whether it is reprinted by itself, with notes or additions, if the reprint works an injury to the proprietor.[1]

[1] There are some very doubtful *dicta* of Lord Ellenborough, on this subject. In the case of Cary *v.* Kearsly, 4 Esp. N. P. C. 168, 170. Erskine put this case: "Suppose a man took Paley's Philosophy, and copied a whole essay, with observations and notes, or additions at the

2. Piracy by reprinting any part of a work, *verbatim.*

This class of cases involves the inquiry — What use can lawfully be made of a previous publication, protected by copyright, in the way of quotation?

end of it, would that be piracy?" His lordship is reported to have answered, "That would depend on the facts of whether the publication of that essay was to convey to the public the notes and observations fairly, or only to color the publication of the original essay, and make that a pretext for pirating it; if the latter, it could not be sustained. That part of the work of one author is found in another, is not of itself piracy, or sufficient to support an action; a man may fairly adopt the work of another; he may so make use of another's labors for the promotion of science and the benefit of the public; but having done so, the question will be, 'Was the matter so taken used fairly with that view, and without what I may term the *animus furandi?*" — The motives of public benefit and advancement of the interests of science are dangerous grounds on which to allow the taking of another's property; although these great objects are to be so far kept in view, as to justify a fair use of previous publications, that is, a use which does no injury. But whether any use, which works a direct injury, can be justified, is the *crux argumenti.* We may suppose a perfectly honest and praiseworthy intention to refute a book, believed to be erroneous, by means of commentary; and for this purpose the whole text of the work is republished. What tendency has the intention of the commentator to prove that the original author's copyright has not been infringed? That question has but two elements: first, whether the work is under the protection of copyright; second, whether anything has been done to render the exclusive privilege less valuable to the proprietor. If both these questions are answered affirmatively, the object or purpose with which the injury was done cannot palliate the responsibility.

There is a similar *dictum* of Lord Erskine's, in Matthewson *v.* Stockdale, 12 Ves. 275, where he said, "I admit no man can monopolize such subjects as the English Channel, the Island of St. Domingo, [charts] or the events of the world; and every man may take what is useful from the original work; improve, add, and *give to the public the whole, comprising the original work,* with the additions and improvements; and in such a case there is no invasion of any right." This is extravagant; but it has been equalled by a *dictum* of Sir L. Shadwell, V. C. in a recent case, where, however, the point was not involved. "Any person may copy and publish the whole of a literary composition, *provided he writes notes upon it, so as to present it to the public, connected with matter of his own.*" Martin *v.* Wright, 6 Simons, 298. Mr. Justice Story has laid down the doctrine, that if the work of the defendant substantially includes the essential parts of the plaintiff's, *so as to supersede it,* it is a violation of the plaintiff's copyright, although the plan and objects of the defendant's book may be different from those of

By quotation, as here used, I mean the transfer of sentences, or passages, or paragraphs, *literatim*, whether with or without acknowledgment of the source from which they are taken.

The first circumstance to which we have to attend, in this inquiry, is, whether the use of matter by quotation, in a given case, tends to, or does, in fact, injure the sale of the book from which the extract is taken. The original author of the extract has the exclusive right to publish and sell it; and it is therefore a very material inquiry, to ascertain how far he is injured, or is likely to be injured, by its publication by another person.

It will be apparent, on reflection, that the quantity of matter taken cannot be decisive of this question. The most material and valuable part of a book, or other publication, may be embraced in a few paragraphs or even sentences, which contain all that is in fact original with the author. If a person, who had made a discovery in science, should choose to enunciate it in a work, of which, by securing the copyright, he intended to reap the profits, and should introduce the statement of his discovery into a general treatise on the branch of science to which it belonged, the matter of his treatise at large might be far from being original, while the portion of the

the plaintiff's. Emerson *v.* Davies, 3 Story's R. 768, 797. See also Mawman *v.* Tegg, 2 Russ. 385; Campbell *v.* Scott, 11 Simons, 31. In France, the same principles are applied. Any republication, either by inserting a smaller in a larger work, or with the addition of notes or commentaries, is there treated as a piracy. Renouard, tom. ii. pp. 15, 16, 19, 20. Merlin, Questions de Droit, tit. Contrefaçon, § iv.

work, containing the description of his discovery, would be purely and eminently novel. The republication of this part of the book would be a taking of that which constituted its chief value, and yet the proportion which it bore to the rest of the work might, in respect to quantity, be very inconsiderable.

Quantity, therefore, is of itself no test, by which to determine whether a quotation amounts to a piracy; and it has accordingly been disregarded in some cases. Thus, where it was suggested by counsel, that the quantity taken by the defendant from the plaintiff's book would be an unfair quantity, even if the source had been acknowledged, Lord Cottenham, C. said, "When it comes to a question of quantity, it must be very vague. One writer might take all the vital part of another's book, though it might be a small proportion of the book in quantity. It is not only quantity, but value that is always looked to."[1]

This doctrine is not to be considered as affected by those decisions, in which courts of equity have declined to interfere, on account of the minuteness of the injury occasioned by a short extract. Applications for injunctions have been refused, where the value of the extract and the amount of injury have been so minute and trifling, as to induce the court not to interfere, and so to restrain the practice of occupying its time by applications in which it would

[1] Bramhall *v.* Halcombe, 3 Mylne & Cr. 737, 738.

be difficult to take an account of the alleged injury.[1] But even in such cases, the infringement might be apparent, and the remedy at the hands of a jury remains.[2] There is, therefore, no material qualification of the general doctrine, that mere quantity does not determine the question of infringement. Be the quantity large or small, if the extract furnishes a substitute for the book from which it is taken, so as to work an appreciable injury, it is so far an actionable violation of the copyright.

The license of what is called fair quotation cannot, I apprehend, be said to furnish any different standard of determination, in cases of quotations or extracts. This license it is very difficult to define.[3] On the one hand, there is a class of publications,

[1] Bell *v.* Whitehead, 17 Law Journ. 142. Whittingham *v.* Wooler, 2 Swanst. 428. Tonson *v.* Walker, 3 Swanst. 672.

[2] Ibid.

[3] In Wilkins *v.* Aikin, 17 Ves. 422, 424, Lord Eldon said, "There is no doubt that a man cannot, under the pretence of quotation, publish the whole or a part of another's book, though he may use, what in all cases it is very difficult to define, fair quotation." This case suggests the *quære*, whether the copying of a map, as an illustration, in a fair history of all the maps of a county, would be restrained. Lord Eldon said, "Suppose a publication, professing to be an account of the improvement of maps of the county of Middlesex; compiling the history of all the maps of it ever published; pointing out the peculiarities belonging to them, and giving copies of them all; as well those the copyright of which have expired, as those of which it was subsisting; it is not easy to say with certainty what would be the decision upon such a case. If it was a fair history of the maps of the county, which had been published, and the publication of the individual work was merely an illustration of that history, that is one way of stating it; *but if a jury could perceive the object to make a profit by publishing the map of another man*, that would require a different consideration." Perhaps this is only another form of stating that the question would be, whether the owner of the map is injured by the use made of it. But if his lordship intended to say, that the question would depend on the intention of the party to do an injury, it seems to me that other authorities do not uphold his doctrine, and that it is not consistent with principle.

the object of which is to give extracts from other works, for the purposes of criticism; and the notion, that the insertion of such extracts tends to increase the sale of the works from which they are taken, if fairly made, has been judicially recognized, and is admitted to be practically true.[1] Any amount of extracts, which the purpose of illustrating fair criticism requires, may be made in such works, with this limitation, that the review or critical notice shall not furnish a substitute for the book; or, in other terms, shall not communicate the same knowledge with the original work. This was the distinction adopted by Lord Ellenborough, when he had occasion to use an illustration drawn from the practice of reviewing.[2]

[1] Bell *v.* Whitehead, 17 Law Journ. 142.

[2] Roworth *v.* Wilkes, 1 Campb. 94, 98. In this case the quantity taken from the plaintiff's book and inserted in an encyclopedia, amounted to seventy-five pages out of one hundred and eighteen. Lord Ellenborough said, in instructing the jury, "The question is, whether the defendant's publication would serve as a substitute for the plaintiff's? A review will not in general serve as a substitute for the book reviewed; and even there, if so much is extracted that it communicates the same knowledge with the original work, it is an actionable violation of literary property. The intention to pirate is not necessary in an action of this sort; it is enough that the publication complained of is in substance a copy, whereby a work vested in another is prejudiced." By substitute is not to be understood a substitute for the whole book, but a substitute *quoad hoc*. See the remarks of Sir L. Shadwell, V. C. in Sweet *v.* Shaw, Jurist, vol. i. p. 212. See also Macklin *v.* Richardson, Ambl. 694. Whittingham *v.* Wooler, 2 Swanst. 428. The case of Dodsley *v.* Kinnersley, Ambl. 403, which seems to look the same way, is a very defective report, and the decision, as stated, seems to me quite wrong, upon this point. The defendant printed, in a magazine, part of the narrative of Dr. Johnson's Rasselas, leaving out the reflections. Upon filing the bill, the Lord Keeper Henley refused an injunction, "doubting whether it was such a book as the stat. 2 Anne intended to protect?" The ground of this learned doubt is not stated. When the cause came on to be heard before Sir Thomas Clarke, M. R., two booksellers deposed that the sale of the book was prejudiced by its being printed in the magazine. This was answered

On the other hand, instances occur, in which extracts from other books are used with or without acknowledgment, not for purposes of criticism; and other instances, in books which are not established journals of criticism, but in which criticism is made the ostensible purpose for which extracts are made.

With regard to the first of these classes, the acknowledgment or concealment of the fact of quotation can have no other bearing than to determine whether it was or was not made with a fraudulent intention. The presence or the absence of such intention will not conclusively determine whether an injury has been done. The legitimate influence of the proof of intention is merely to assist the court, among other circumstances, in determining whether the party has transcended the limits of fair quotation. But if he has, with the fairest intentions, published extracts of such a character as to injure the work from which they are taken, his intentions are wholly immaterial to the issue.

One of the most marked cases of this class occurred in relation to the writings of Washington. The plaintiffs were the proprietors of a large work, containing the letters and other writings of Washington, with a life. The defendants published a smaller

by evidence of a usage of printing extracts of new books in magazines, without asking leave of the authors, and that the plaintiffs had themselves printed extracts in the Annual Register and in a newspaper. An injunction was thereupon refused; but that it would be granted at the present day, under the like circumstances, there can be little doubt.

work, containing a new and original life; but with copious extracts from the letters and papers contained in the plaintiffs' work. Mr. Justice Story granted an injunction as to these extracts, admitting at the same time, that the defendants might have acted under a mistake as to the plaintiffs' rights.[1]

[1] Folsom *v.* Marsh, 2 Story's R. 100, 115. In this case the learned judge said, "The question, then, is, whether this is a justifiable use of the original materials, such as the law recognizes as no infringement of the copyright of the plaintiffs. It is said, that the defendant has selected only such materials as suited his own limited purpose as a biographer. That is, doubtless, true; and he has produced an exceedingly valuable book. But that is no answer to the difficulty. It is certainly not necessary, to constitute an invasion of copyright, that the whole of a work should be copied, or even a large portion of it, in form or in substance. If so much is taken, that the value of the original is sensibly diminished, or the labors of the original author are substantially to an injurious extent appropriated by another, that is sufficient, in point of law, to constitute a piracy *pro tanto*. The entirety of the copyright is the property of the author; and it is no defence, that another person has appropriated a part, and not the whole, of any property. Neither does it necessarily depend upon the quantity taken, whether it is an infringement of the copyright, or not. It is often affected by other considerations, the value of the materials taken, and the importance of it to the sale of the original work. Lord Cottenham, in the recent cases of Bramhall *v.* Halcombe, (3 Mylne & Craig, 737, 738,) and Saunders *v.* Smith, (3 Mylne & Craig, 711, 736, 737,) adverting to this point, said: 'When it comes to a question of quantity, it must be very vague. One writer might take all the vital part of another's book, though it might be but a small proportion of the book in quantity. It is not only quantity, but value, that is always looked to. It is useless to refer to any particular cases, as to quantity.' In short, we must often, in deciding questions of this sort, look to the nature and objects of the selections made, the quantity and value of the materials used, and the degree in which the use may prejudice the sale, or diminish the profits, or supersede the objects of the original work. Many mixed ingredients enter into the discussion of such questions. In some cases, a considerable portion of the materials of the original work may be fused, if I may use such an expression, into another work, so as to be undistinguishable in the mass of the latter, which has other professed and obvious objects, and cannot fairly be treated as a piracy; or they may be inserted as a sort of distinct and mosaic work, into the general texture of the second work, and constitute the peculiar excellence thereof, and then it may be a clear piracy. If a person should, under color of publishing 'Elegant Extracts' of poetry, include all the best pieces at large of a favorite poet, whose volume was secured by

In the case of Lewis *v.* Fullerton, an attempt was made to justify the taking of por ons of the plaintiff's work, under a fair use of a former publication; but an injunction was granted, the court being satisfied that the defendant, in the compilation of his book, had habitually made use of all that suited his purpose in the plaintiff's work.[1]

a copyright, it would be difficult to say, why it was not an invasion of that right, since it might constitute the entire value of the volume.

"In the present case, I have no doubt whatever, that there is an invasion of the plaintiffs' copyright; I do not say designedly, or from bad intentions; on the contrary, I entertain no doubt, that it was deemed a perfectly lawful and justifiable use of the plaintiffs' work. But if the defendants may take three hundred and nineteen letters, included in the plaintiffs' copyright, and exclusively belonging to them, there is no reason why another bookseller may not take other five hundred letters, and a third, one thousand letters, and so on, and thereby the plaintiffs copyright be totally destroyed. Besides; every one must see, that the work of the defendants is mainly founded upon these letters, constituting more than one third of their work, and imparting to it its greatest, nay, its essential value. Without those letters, in its present form, the work must fall to the ground. It is not a case, where abbreviated or select passages are taken from particular letters; but the entire letters are taken, and those of most interest and value to the public, as illustrating the life, the acts, and the character of Washington. It seems to me, therefore, that it is a clear invasion of the right of property of the plaintiffs, if the copying of parts of a work, not constituting a major part, can ever be a violation thereof; as upon principle and authority, I have no doubt it may be. If it had been the case of a fair and *bona fide* abridgment of the work of the plaintiffs, it might have admitted of a very different consideration." See also Mawman *v.* Tegg, 2 Russ. 383. Sweet *v.* Shaw, Am. Jurist, vol. i. p. 212.

[1] Lewis *v.* Fullerton, 2 Beavan's R. 6, 8. In this case, Lord Langdale, M. R. said, "Any man is entitled to write and publish a topographical dictionary, and to avail himself of the labors of all former writers whose works are not subject to copyright, and of all public sources of information; but whilst all are entitled to resort to common sources of information, none are entitled to save themselves trouble and expense by availing themselves, for their own profit, of other men's works still subject to copyright and entitled to protection; and the question is, whether Mr. Bell did or did not, for the compilation of the work in which he was engaged, avail himself of the plaintiff's work unlawfully, and in violation of the plaintiff's copyright. For the purpose of ascertaining this, I have read a very considerable number of articles in both works; the trouble of comparing them has been greatly dimin-

The question has also arisen, whether it is lawful to publish verbatim cases from the Law Reports, upon certain subjects, or a selection of such cases, with annotations. Lord Cottenham, upon the book entitled "Smith's Leading Cases," assuming, but not deciding, the legal question of an infringement, was obliged to refuse an injunction, upon the ground of acquiescence on the part of the plaintiff.[1] But in

ished by the exhibits which have been prepared on both sides; and the result of the examination appears to me to show that Mr. Bell, in the compilation of his gazetteer, has extensively, and as far as my examination has gone, it would not be too much to say, habitually, made use of all that suited his purpose in the plaintiff's work; it is evident, that in a large proportion of the defendant's work, no other labor has been applied than in copying the plaintiff's work, and arranging the matter in the form which best suited the purpose of the compiler. Mr. Bell has evidently thought himself under no restraint, and probably did not think that the plaintiffs were entitled to any copyright; and if that which he did could be considered as lawful, it is plain no protection whatever could be given to any work in the nature of a gazetteer, dictionary, road-book, calendar, map or any other work, the subject-matter of which is open to common observation and inquiry; and that every man who had bestowed any amount of labor or expense in collecting and arranging the information requisite for the production of such a work, might immediately on its publication, be deprived of the fruit of his industry and ability. Having gone carefully through all the articles commented upon in the argument, and several others, I am of opinion that the defendant's work is, to a very considerable extent, a piracy of the plaintiff's copyright."

[1] Saunders *v.* Smith, 3 M. & Cr. 711. 728. In regard to the legal right, his lordship said, "In this case, I find the publication complained of to be of a character which, whether it be or be not an infringement of the copyright of the plaintiffs, is a course of proceeding which has been pretty largely admitted, and pretty generally adopted. Several cases occurred to me, and several were mentioned to me at the bar, in which a gentleman at the bar, desirous of publishing a work upon a particular subject, has collected the cases upon that subject, and has taken those cases, generally speaking, verbatim, from reports which are covered by copyright. No instance has been represented to me in which those entitled to the copyright have interfered; no judgment, therefore, has been pronounced upon that subject. I am not stating whether the owner of the copyright is entitled to interfere in such a case, or whether that use of published reports is or is not to be permitted. That is a question of legal right, upon which I find, at present, no reason for coming to an adjudication." Mr. Justice Story, referring to this case, said, "Much

a similar case, Sir L. Shadwell, V. C. granted an injunction upon the ground of injury to the plaintiff, where eleven cases only had been copied *verbatim ;* but a considerable number of what were called abridged cases were, in truth, copies of the plaintiff's volumes, with slight alterations.[1]

The same principle is to be applied to books, which, under the ostensible purpose of criticism or illustration, give extracts from other publications ; although it is to be admitted that fair criticism may be illustrated by fair quotation. Thus, where the defendant published a book, giving specimens of Modern English Poetry, with criticisms and biographical notices, and inserted therein entire poems and extracts from poems written by Mr. Campbell, which were under the protection of copyright, an injunction was granted in his favor against the publication.[2] In this case the *animus furandi* was held to be implied by law, from the taking.[3]

must in such cases depend upon the nature of the work, the value and extent of the copies, and the degree in which the original authors may be injured thereby." Folsom *v.* Marsh, 2 Story's R. 118.

[1] Sweet *v.* Shaw, The Jurist, vol. i. p. 212 ; S. C. 17 Law J. 216. This subject came under consideration in the case of Wheaton *v.* Peters, 8 Peters S. C. R. 591, in relation to the Reports of Cases in the supreme court of the United States; but the court held that there could be no copyright in the opinions of the judges of that court, which are published under an act of congress. But it was not doubted, it seems, that the reporter had copyright in his marginal notes and in the arguments of counsel, as prepared and arranged in his work. See Gray *v.* Russell, 1 Story's R. 11, 21.

[2] Campbell *v.* Scott, 11 Simons, 31.

[3] Ibid. I must here express my dissent from the doctrines laid down by Mr. Godson on the subject of quotations. In his work on Patents and Copyrights, p. 477, Mr. Godson says, "In judging of a quotation, whether it is fair and candid, or whether the person who quotes it has been swayed by the *animus furandi;* the quantity taken, and the manner in which it is adopted, of course

Upon the whole, the doctrine of the law with regard to quotations may be thus stated. To forbid to subsequent writers the citation of passages from the works of their predecessors, under all circumstances, would be a great obstacle to the progress of science and knowledge. If the extract is acknowledged, the acknowledgment shows that the party did not intend to pass as his own what belongs to another, and thus a presumption arises that he did not make use of the passage for the purpose of turning it to his own pecuniary account. Still, there must be a limit even to the citation of passages which are accompanied by an acknowledgment of the source from which they are taken; and there is no more definite and consistent limit than the point where an injury may be perceived, which varies of course in each

must be considered. If the work complained of is in substance a copy, then it is not necessary to show the intention to pirate; for the greater part of the matter of the book having been purloined, the intention is apparent, and other proof is superfluous. A piracy has undoubtedly been committed. But if only a small portion of the work be quoted, then it becomes necessary to prove that it was done *animo furandi;* with the intention of depriving the author of his just reward, by giving his work to the public in a cheaper form. And then the mode of doing it becomes a subject for inquiry. For it is not sufficient to constitute a piracy, that part of one author's book is found in that of another, unless it be nearly the whole, or so much as will show (being a question of fact for the jury) that it was done with a bad intent, and that the matter which accompanies it has been colorably introduced." It is certainly necessary, in determining whether the *animus furandi* exists, to look at the quantity taken and the manner in which it was taken. But the more recent authorities, as well as sound principle, do not look at the intention, whether the quantity be large or small. If an injury is caused, there is no occasion to prove the intention directly, or to establish it by inference from the circumstances. If part of one author's book is found in that of another, the question will be, what effect is it to have? not whether it was taken with a bad intent.

case, and is not by our law supposed to be capable of a distinct announcement by a positive rule.[1]

3. Piracy by imitation, or by reproducing with colorable alterations and disguises assuming the appearance of a new work.

This is, by far, the most frequent form in which the copyright of authors is infringed. Copying is not confined to literal repetition, but includes also the various modes in which the matter of any publication may be adopted, imitated, or transferred, with more or less colorable alterations to disguise the piracy. The main question in all such cases is, whether the author of the work, alleged to be a piracy, has resorted to the original sources, alike open to him and to all writers, or whether he has adopted and used the matter or plan of the work with the infringement of which he is charged, without resorting to the other sources from which he had a right to borrow. We have seen, in a former chapter, what is the just extent of an author's right in his own work. It is there laid down, that no writer

[1] In some countries, however, an arbitrary limit has been fixed by legislation. In Russia, quotations are permitted, provided the quantity taken does not exceed one-third of the book from which they are taken; and provided that the writer's own text is twice as large as the passages taken by him from another work. Renouard, tom. 1, p. 207. The Prussian code excepts from the penalties of piracy "the literal citation of *isolated passages* of a work already printed, and the reproduction of isolated articles, poems, &c. in works of literary history, or in collections for the use of schools." Upon this text, M. Renouard observes that we may conclude from the exceptions introduced into the law, that more important extracts would be deemed piratical. (Tom. 2, p. 17-18.)

can acquire an exclusive title to a subject, but that the results and products of his own intellectual labor, however common the subject, and however numerous and public the sources from which he has taken his materials, exclusively belong to him. In some cases, these results and products will appear in the new forms and combinations given to old materials, and in other cases they will consist merely in the collection and arrangement of information open to any one to collect, but collected perhaps by the particular writer for the first time. In all cases, the inquiry must start with assuming the general principle, that every writer is at liberty to treat of any subject whatever, whether it has been previously written upon by others or not; and then it resolves itself into the question, whether he has made any, and if any, whether he has made a lawful use of the particular work which he is alleged to have infringed.[1]

Comparison of the two works is, of course, the test to which the question should be brought. Among the proofs of piracy, upon which the courts have been much in the habit of relying, is the occurrence of the same inaccuracies in the two books; and when the question is, whether the defendant, in preparing his book, had before him and copied or imitated the book

[1] Longman *v.* Winchester, 16 Ves. 269. Mathewson *v.* Stockdale, 12 Ves. 270. Cary *v.* Faden, 5 Ves. 24. Tonson v. Walker, 3 Swanst. 672. Carnan *v.* Bowles, 2 Bro. Ch. R. 80. Mawman *v.* Tegg, 2 Russ. 385, 393. Roworth *v.* Wilkes, 1 Campb. 94. Sayre *v.* Moore, 1 East, 361, 362. Trusler *v.* Murray, 162, n. Cary *v.* Longman, 1 East, 360, Wilkins *v.* Aikin, 16 Ves. 422. Hogg *v.* Kirby, 8 Ves. 215. Cary *v.* Kearsley, 4 Esp. 169. 170. Gray *v.* Russell, 1 Story, 11. Emerson *v.* Davies, 3 Story, 768.

of the plaintiff, it is manifest that this kind of evidence is the strongest proof, short of direct evidence, of which the fact is capable. Thus, where the question was, whether, in a vast proportion of the work of the defendants, any other labor had been applied than copying the plaintiffs' work, Lord Eldon said, that from the identity of the inaccuracies, it was impossible to deny that the one was copied from the other *verbatim et literatim.*[1] So too, where the question was, how much of the plaintiff's book had been copied by the defendant, his lordship carried the force of the evidence from identity of inaccuracies so far, as to lay down the principle, that when a considerable number of passages are proved to have been copied by the copying of the blunders in them, other passages, which are the same with passages in the original book, must be presumed, *prima facie*, to be likewise copied, though no blunders occur in them.[2] But this kind of proof is often wanting; and where it is not found, it is necessary to determine by other results of the comparison, whether an unlawful use has been made of the plaintiffs' book. In many cases, the occurrence of passages identically the same, or but slightly varied, but not having the ear-mark of inaccuracies, has been held conclusive proof of piracy, even in that class of works in which, from the nature of the subject, there must be strong

[1] Longman *v.* Winchester, 16 Ves. 269.

[2] Mawman *v.* Tegg, 2 Russ. 385, 393. See also Cary *v.* Kearsly, 4 Esp. 169, 170.

resemblances between any two books in which it is treated, such as dictionaries, encyclopedias, calendars, road-books, and the like.[1] But where the resemblance does not amount to identity of parallel passages, the question becomes, in substance, this — whether there be such similitude and conformity between the two books, that the person who wrote the one must have used the other, as a model, and must have copied or imitated it ?[2] In these cases, the piracy is to be detected, through what have been called colorable alteration and servile imitation. The doctrines which have been laid down, with reference to this class of cases, require here a careful examination.

What degree of resemblance will authorize the inference that one book is a copy of another, notwithstanding the diversities that may be found in them, is a question of great nicety, which must depend on the circumstances of each case. In a case where the defendant had compiled into one large map four charts belonging to the plaintiff, and the

[1] Mathewson *v.* Stockdale, 12 Ves. 270. Carnan *v.* Bowles, 2 Bro. Ch. R. 80. Cary *v.* Longman, 1 East, 360. Mawman *v.* Tegg, 2 Russ. 385, 393. Gray *v.* Russell, 1 Story, 11.

[2] In a case concerning prints, Lord Ellenborough said to the jury, "It is still to be considered, whether there be such a similitude and conformity between the prints, that the person who executed the one set must have used the others as a model. In that case, he is a copyist of the main design. But if the similitude can be supposed to have arisen from accident, or necessarily from the nature of the subject, or from the artist having sketched designs merely from reading the letter-press of the plaintiff's work, the defendant is not answerable. It is remarkable, however, that he has given no evidence to explain the similitude, or to repel the presumption which that necessarily causes." Roworth *v.* Wilkes, 1 Campb. 94.

fact of his having so done was to be ascertained; Lord Mansfield said, "The act that secures copyright to authors, guards against the piracy of the words and sentiments; but it does not prohibit writing on the same subject. As in the case of histories and dictionaries: In the first, a man may give a relation of the same facts, and in the same order of time; in the latter, an interpretation is given of the identical same words. In all these cases, the question of fact to come before a jury is, whether the alteration be colorable or not? There must be such a similitude as to make it probable and reasonable to suppose that one is a transcript of the other, and nothing more than a transcript. So, in the case of prints, no doubt different men may take engravings from the same picture. The same principle holds with regard to charts, whoever has it in his intention to publish a chart, may take advantage of all prior publications. There is no monopoly of the subject here, any more than in the other instances; but upon any question of this nature, the jury will decide whether it be a servile imitation or not."[1]

So, also, Lord Kenyon, in an action for pirating a book of chronology, said, "The main question here is, whether in substance the work is a copy and imitation of the other; for undoubtedly in a chronological work the same facts must be related."[2]

[1] Sayre *v.* Moore, 1 East, 361, 362, n.

[2] Trusler *v.* Murray, 1 East, 363, n. See also, for applications

Mr. Justice Story, in a case where the same question arose, held that the resemblances in the parts and pages which correspond, must be so close, full, uniform and striking, as fairly to lead to the conclusion that the one book is a substantial copy of the other, or mainly borrowed from it: in short, that there is a substantial identity between them.[1] The

of the same doctrine. Cary *v.* Longman, 1 East, 358. Mathewson *v.* Stockdale, 12 Ves. 270. Longman *v.* Winchester, 16 Ves. 269. Wilkins *v.* Aiken, 17 Ves. 422.

[1] Emerson *v.* Davies, 3 Story's R. 768. In this case the court said, "The case, therefore, comes back at last to the naked consideration, whether the book of Davies, in the parts complained of, has been copied substantially from that of Emerson, or not. It is not sufficient to show, that it may have been suggested by Emerson's, or that some parts and pages of it have resemblances, in method and details and illustrations, to Emerson's. It must be further shown, that the resemblances in those parts and pages are so close, so full, so uniform, so striking, as fairly to lead to the conclusion that the one is a substantial copy of the other, or mainly borrowed from it. In short, that there is substantial identity between them. A copy is one thing, an imitation or resemblance another. There are many imitations of Homer in the Æneid; but no one would say that the one was a copy from the other. There may be a strong likeness without an identity; and as was aptly said by the learned counsel for the plaintiff in the close of his argument, *Facies non omnibus una, nec diversa tamen, sed qualem debet esse sororum.* The question is, therefore, in many cases, a very nice one, what degree of imitation constitutes an infringement of the copyright in a particular work. It is very clear that any use of materials, whether they are figures or drawings, or other things which are well-known and in common use, is not the subject of a copyright, unless there be some new arrangement thereof. Still, even here, it may not always follow, that any person has a right to copy the figures, drawings, or other things, made by another, availing himself solely of his skill and industry, without any resort to such common source." And after commenting on the cases of Barfield *v.* Nicholson, (2 Sim. & Stu. 1.) and the other authorities cited in the last preceding note, the learned judge said, "So that, I think, it may be laid down as the clear result of the authorities in cases of this nature, that the true test of piracy or not is to ascertain whether the defendant has, in fact, used the plan, arrangements, and illustrations of the plaintiff, as the model of his own book, with colorable alterations and variations only to disguise the use thereof; or whether his work is the result of his own labor, skill, and use of common materials and common sources of knowledge, open to all

question therefore, comes to this, in almost all such cases, whether the defendant has, in substance copied from the plaintiff's work, with merely colorable alterations and devices, to disguise the copying, or whether the resemblances are merely accidental, and naturally or necessarily grew out of the subject, without any use of the plaintiff's work. If the court can see proof that the defendant had the work of the plaintiff before him, and used it as a model for his own, in copying and imitating it, without drawing from common sources or common materials, it will hold the resemblances to be not accidental, and not necessary, notwithstanding the alterations and disguises which may have been introduced.[1]

Many persons seem to labor under the mistake of supposing that books of the character of compilations may be used with impunity; and that, generally, where the materials made use of by an author can be traced to other sources, his copyright cannot prevent the use of those materials by others. The whole distinction, in such cases, which is entirely overlooked by those who set up this kind of defence, is this; that every subsequent writer has a right to resort to the common sources for the same learning,

men, and the resemblances are either accidental or arising from the nature of the subject. In other words, whether the defendant's book is *quoad hoc*, a servile or evasive imitation of the plaintiff's work, or a *bona fide* original compilation from other common or independent sources."

[1] Ibid. It is not necessary, to amount to piracy, that the one work should be a copy of the other, and not an imitation. There may be a close imitation, so close as to be a mere evasion of the copyright, without being an exact and literal copy. *Ibid.*

and to make use of it at his pleasure; but if he takes it from one whose book is protected by copyright, who has collected and arranged it in a form and method peculiar to himself, and gives it out to the world in that form, without resorting to the original sources, he is guilty of piracy.[1] Thus, if a person prepares notes to an old work, the materials of which are selected from various authors who have written at different periods, but are collected and embodied by him for the first time, it is piracy to

[1] "There is no foundation in law," says Mr. Justice Story, "for the argument, that because the same sources of information are open to all persons, and by the exercise of their own industry and talents and skill, they could, from all these sources, have produced a similar work, one party may at second hand, without any exercise of industry, talents, or skill, borrow from another all the materials, which have been accumulated and combined together by him. Take the case of a map of a county, or of a state, or an empire; it is plain, that in proportion to the accuracy of every such map, must be its similarity to, or even its identity with, every other. Now, suppose a person has bestowed his time and skill and attention, and made a large series of topographical surveys in order to perfect such a map, and has thereby produced one far excelling every existing map of the same sort It is clear, that notwithstanding this production, he cannot supersede the right of any other person to use the same means by similar surveys and labors to accomplish the same end. But it is just as clear, that he has no right, without any such surveys and labors, to sit down and copy the whole of the map already produced by the skill and labors of the first party, and thus to rob him of all the fruit of his industry, skill, and expenditures. It would be a downright piracy."

"Neither is it of any consequence in what form the works of another author are used; whether it be by a simple reprint or by incorporating the whole or a large portion thereof in some larger work. Thus, for example, if in one of the large Encyclopædias of the present day, the whole or a large portion of a scientific treatise of another author, as, for example, one of Dr. Lardner's or Sir John Herschel's, or Mrs. Somerville's treatises, should be incorporated, it would be just as much a piracy upon the copyright, as if it were published in a single volume." Gray *v.* Russell, 1 Story's R. 11, 18. See also, Emerson *v.* Davies, 3 Story's R. 768. Barfield *v.* Nicholson, 2 Sim. & Stu. 6. Wyatt *v.* Barnard, 3 V. & B. 77. Matthewson *v.* Stockdale, 2 Ves. 270. Wilkins *v.* Aiken, 17 Ves. 422. Merlin, Rep. de Jurisp. tit. Contrefaçon, vol. 3, p. 701, *et seq.*

transcribe them, and it is no defence to show that any other person might have made a similar selection and compilation.[1] In such cases, if the same matter is found expressed in the same phraseology, or the same materials are found arranged in the same form and method, in two books, a violent presumption arises that the author of the later copied from the earlier book, and did not resort to the common sources. This presumption will approach more or less near to being conclusive, according to the identity of the two works.[2]

Another and more difficult question may arise, where an author has directly made use of the work of a previous writer, with the *bona fide* intention of adding to and improving the information which the wants of the public may require, upon the particular subject. This question occurs most frequently in relation to all that class of works devoted to statistical or other information. There are *dicta* of English judges, which seem to recognize the right of using previous publications of this kind, with real improvements and additions;[3] and there is one case, at Nisi Prius, where a verdict is reported to have been found upon this principle, under the direction of Lord Mansfield. It was a case of charts; and his lordship instructed the jury, that i. .hey found the defendant,

[1] Gray *v.* Russell, 1 Story's R. 11.

[2] Ibid. Emerson *v.* Davies, 3 Story's R. See also, ante, Chap. II.

[3] The most important of these *dicta* have been examined, ante, in connection with the subject of quotation.

although he used the plaintiff's chart, had been correcting errors, and not servilely copying, they should find a verdict for the defendant; but that if it was a mere servile imitation, they should find for the plaintiff.[1]

[1] Sayre *v.* Moore, at Guildhall, 1785. Reported 1 East, 361, n. *b.* It is manifest that the verdict was carried upon the strong testimony of the witnesses for the defendant, and, as I conceive, against principle. The following is the report, but the source from which it was derived is not stated. "The charts which had been copied were four in number, which Moore had made into one large map. It appeared in evidence that the defendant had taken the body of his publication from the work of the plaintiffs, but that he had made many alterations and improvements thereupon. It was also proved that the plaintiffs had originally been at a great expense in procuring materials for these maps. Delarochett, an eminent geographer and engraver, had been employed by the plaintiffs in the engraving of them. He said that the present charts of the plaintiffs were such an improvement on those before in use, as made an original work. Besides their having been laid down from all the charts and maps extant, they were improved by many manuscript journals and printed books and manuscript relations of travellers: he had no doubt the materials must have cost the plaintiffs between 3000*l.* and 4000*l.*, and that the defendant's chart was taken from these of the plaintiffs, with a few alterations. In answer to a question from the court, whether the defendant had pirated from the drawings and papers, or from the engravings, he answered, from the engravings. — Winterfelt, an engraver, said he was actually employed by the defendant to take a draft of the Gulf Passage (in the West Indies) from the plaintiffs' map.

"Many witnesses were called on behalf of the defendant, amongst others a Mr. Stephenson and Admiral Campbell. Mr. Stephenson said he had carefully examined the two publications; that there were very important differences between them, much in favor of the defendant's. That the plaintiffs' maps were founded upon no principle; neither upon the principle of the Mercator, nor the plain chart, but upon a corruption of both. That near the equator the plain chart would do very well, but that as you go further from the equator, there you must have recourse to the Mercator. That there were very material errors in the plaintiffs' maps. That they were in many places defective in pointing out the latitude and longitude, which is extremely essential in navigating. That most of these, as well as errors in the soundings, were corrected by the defendant. Admiral Campbell observed, that there were only two kinds of charts, one called a plain chart, which was now very little used; the other, which is the best, called the Mercator, and which is very accurate in the degrees of latitude and longitude. That this distinction was very necessary in the higher latitudes, but in places near the equator it made little or no difference. That the plaintiffs' maps were upon no principle recognized

The doctrine which this case, if correctly reported, explicitly sanctions, is, that where a work, though protected by statute, is erroneous, any person may make a direct use of it, copying the whole, provided he corrects the errors, without resorting to the original sources of information, or without making a new survey, in the case of maps or charts. This doctrine may be very convenient in some of its aspects ; but it admits of great doubt, whether it is consistent with the rights of original authors. The question is not, whether the author of the improve-

among seamen, and no rules of navigation could be applied to them ; and they were therefore entirely useless.

"Lord Mansfield, C. J. The rule of decision in this case is a matter of great consequence to the country. In deciding it, we must take care to guard against two extremes, equally prejudicial ; the one, that men of ability, who have employed their time for the service of the community, may not be deprived of their just merits, and the reward of their ingenuity and labor ; the other, that the world may not be deprived of improvements, nor the progress of the arts be retarded. The act that secures copyright to authors guards against the piracy of the words and sentiments ; but it does not prohibit writing on the same subject. As in the case of histories and dictionaries. In the first, a man may give a relation of the same facts, and in the same order of time ; in the latter an interpretation is given of the identical same words. In all these cases the question of fact to come before a jury is, whether the alteration be colorable or not? there must be such a similitude as to make it probable and reasonable to suppose that one is a transcript of the other, and nothing more than a transcript. So in the case of prints, no doubt different men may take engravings from the same picture. The same principle holds with regard to charts. Whoever has it in his intention to publish a chart, may take advantage of all prior publications. There is no monopoly of the subject here, any more than in the other instances, but upon any question of this nature the jury will decide whether it be a servile imitation or not. If an erroneous chart be made, God forbid it should not be corrected even in a small degree, if it thereby become more serviceable and useful for the purposes to which it is applied. But here you are told, that there are various and very material alterations. This chart of the plaintiffs' is upon a wrong principle, inapplicable to navigation. The defendant therefore has been correcting errors, and not servilely copying. If you think so, you will find for the defendant; if you think it is a mere servile imitation, and pirated from the other, you will find for the plaintiffs." — Verdict for defendant.

ment and additions to an old work has a copyright in the additions and improvements. Of this, there can be no doubt.[1] But the question is, whether a work, at the time being under the protection of the statute, can be taken as the *subject* of an improvement.[2]

It is quite clear, that every part of the original work is under the protection of the law. Where the defendant takes a part of the original work, without altering it, he takes what requires no improvement, by directly copying it. Why should the addition of valuable original matter of his own give him a right to do that which he cannot do, where his alterations and additions are merely colorable? In the one case, he seeks to disguise the fact of having copied from the plaintiff; in the other, he does not conceal the copying, but says he has added valuable original matter of his own. In both cases, the question must recur, whether he has taken and used what belonged to another? The general doctrine of the law is, that "none are entitled to save themselves trouble and expense, by availing themselves, for their own profit, of other men's works, still entitled to the protection of copyright;"[3] and the modern course, in courts of

[1] Cary *v.* Longman, 1 East, 358. Mason *v.* Murray, cited S. C.

[2] In the analogous case of patent rights, the subject of an existing and valid patent cannot be taken as the superstructure of an improvement. If the improvement cannot be used without the subject of an existing grant, the inventor of the improvement must wait until that grant has expired. But he may take out a patent for the improvement by itself, and sell it. Godson on Patents, p. 62, 2d edit.

[3] Per Lord Langdale, M. R. in Lewis *v.* Fullerton, 2 Beav. 6.

equity, is, to grant an injunction as to parts of a work pirated, although it contains much that is original.[1]

4. Piracy, by reproducing the whole or a part of a book, under an abridged form.

We have now to consider under what circumstances an ABRIDGMENT will constitute a violation of copyright. It has already been intimated, that the general doctrine of the English law on the subject of Abridgments needs revision. I propose here to examine the authorities, and to suggest some reasons why the doctrine which they seem to sanction cannot be carried out, consistently with the established rights of literary property.

The earliest case, in which there is a distinct recognition of abridgments, is Gyles *v.* Wilcox, in which the book charged to have been infringed was Sir Matthew Hale's Pleas of the Crown. In this case a distinction was taken between abridgments "fairly made," and works "colorably shortened." The doctrine was recognized, that a real and fair abridgment may with propriety be called a new book, because the invention, learning and judgment of the maker are shown in it. But the book in question was held not to be a fair abridgment, but merely "colorably shortened," by leaving out cer-

[1] Ibid. Mawman *v.* Tegg, 2 Russ. 385. Folsom *v.* Marsh, 2 Story, 100.

tain passages and translating Latin and French quotations.[1]

The next was a case relating to no less a book than Dr. Johnson's Rasselas. The defendant printed part of the narrative in a magazine, leaving out the reflections; and justified upon the ground of a fair abridgment, among other points of defence. Sir Thomas Clarke, M. R. said, that, "no certain line can be drawn, to distinguish a fair abridgment; but every case must depend on its own circumstances." It appeared that a small quantity only had been abstracted, and the plaintiffs had themselves printed a part of the work in a magazine; a circumstance upon which the court chiefly relied, as showing that they could not be prejudiced by what the defendants had done. The learned judge, however, seems to have recognized the doctrine of fair abridgments, inasmuch as he said that if he were to hold this to be elusory, he must hold every abridgment to be so; and he seems to have considered, that when a fair

[1] Gyles *v.* Wilcox, 2 Atkyns, 141, 143. Lord Hardwicke said, "Where books are colorably shortened only, they are undoubtedly within the meaning of the act of parliament, and are a mere evasion of the statute, and cannot be called an abridgment. But this must not be carried so far as to restrain persons from making a real and fair abridgment, for abridgments may with great propriety be called a new ook, because not only the paper nd print, but the invention, learning nd judgment of the author is shown in them, and in many cases are extremely useful. Though in some instances prejudicial, by mistaking and curtailing the sense of the author. If I should extend the rule so far as to restrain all abridgments, it would be of mischievous consequence, for the books of the learned, *les Journels des Scavans*, and several others that might be mentioned, would be brought within the meaning of the act of parliament." See also the case of Read *v.* Hodges, referred to in Tonson *v.* Walker, 3 Swanston, 672, 679.

abridgment is made, the question of injury to the original author cannot be considered.[1]

In the next case, we find for the first time an effort to define a true and proper abridgment. The book in question was an abridgment of Hawksworth's Voyages. The rule was laid down by Lord Chancellor Apsley, assisted by Sir William Blackstone; and it seems to have been adjudged, that where the understanding is employed in retrenching unnecessary and uninteresting circumstances, which rather deaden the narration, it is not an act of plagiarism upon the original work, nor against any property of the author in it, but an allowable and meritorious work.[2]

A few years afterwards, Sir Thomas Sewell, M. R. in a case of an abridgment of a biography, said that if it was a fair *bona fide* abridgment of the larger work, several cases in the court of chancery had de-

[1] Dodsley *v.* Kinnersley, Ambl. 403. The report is very imperfect.

[2] Anon. Lofft's R. 775. "On a bill praying an injunction against an edition by Mr. Newbery of an abridgment of Dr. Hawkesworth's Voyages, the Lord Chancellor was of opinion that this abridgment of the work was not any violation of the author's property whereon to ground an injunction. That to constitute a true and proper abridgment of a work, the whole must be preserved in its sense: and then the act of abridgment is an act of understanding, employed in carrying a large work into a smaller compass, and rendering it less expensive and more convenient both to the time and use of the reader. Which made an abridgment in the nature of a new and a meritorious work.

"That this had been done by Mr. Newbery, whose edition might be read in the fourth part of the time, and all the substance preserved, and conveyed in language as good or better than in the original, and in a more agreeable and useful manner. That he had consulted Mr. Justice Blackstone, whose knowledge and skill in his profession was universally known, and who as an author himself had done honor to his country. That they had spent some hours together, and were agreed that an abridgment, where the understanding is employed in retrenching unnecessary and uninteresting circumstances, which rather deaden cided that an injunction should not be granted ; and he referred to the case of Hawkesworth's Voyages. But it being shown that passages were taken *verbatim* from the original work, he granted an injunction, until answer and further order.[1]

In a subsequent case, an attempt was made to justify a selection of cases from the Term Reports, upon the ground of a fair abridgment; but it appeared that the cases had been arranged under heads and titles, instead of chronologically, and in this way had been copied *verbatim*. An injunction was accordingly granted.[2]

The foregoing are all the English authorities on this subject, and they show that for a considerable length of time the notion has prevailed, that what is called a *bona fide* abridgment may be made, without violating the right of property of the original author.[3]

the narrative, is not an act of plagiarism upon the original work, nor against any property of the author in it, but an allowable and meritorious work. And that this abridgment of Mr. Newbery's falls within these reasons and descriptions. Therefore the bill praying an injunction ought to be dismissed."

[1] Bell *v.* Walker, 1 Bro. Ch. R. 451.

[2] Butterworth *v.* Robinson, 5 Ves. 709.

[3] Among text-writers, Mr. Godson has laid down a doctrine too broad to be subscribed to, if we are to continue any protection to literature.

"Nearly upon the same principles, by which it is shown that there cannot be a monopoly of a general subject, it appears that *books themselves* for certain purposes, besides the mere act of reading them, may be used by the public. They are, in fact, general subjects — data — which may afford opportunites for other persons besides the authors to exercise their ingenuity. They may be taken as the groundwork of other literary labors. Thus a copyright may exist in *abridgments* or *translations* of works. Also in the *notes and additions* printed in a new edition of a book, over which the right of the author has expired. For one man may compose a work, for instance in the Latin language, another abridge it, a third translate it, and a fourth write annotations

In America, the subject has been only incidentally discussed. The authorities referred to in the note below, will fully justify an examination of the question *de novo*.[1]

upon it; and every one of them will acquire a copyright in the product of his own ingenuity and labor.

"Many valuable works are so voluminous that abridgments of them are extremely useful. To make them, some judgment must be exercised, and some labor employed; and therefore the authors of them ought certainly to be encouraged. In general, an abridgment tends to the advantage of the author, if the composition be good; and may serve the end of an advertisement. The inquiry, whether the work is prejudiced by the manner of making the abridgment, cannot be entertained." Godson, page 344.

[1] Mr. Justice Story, in Gray *v.* Russell, 1 Story's R. 19, 21, said, "In some cases, indeed, it may be a very nice question, what amounts to a piracy of a work, or not. Thus if large extracts are made therefrom in a review, it might be a question, whether those extracts were designed *bona fide* for the mere purpose of criticism, or were designed to supersede the original work under the pretence of a review, by giving its substance in a fugitive form. The same difficulty may arise in relation to an abridgment of an original work. The question, in such a case, must be compounded of various considerations; whether it be a *bona fide* abridgment, or only an evasion by the omission of some unimportant parts; whether it will, in its present form, prejudice or supersede the original work; whether it will be adapted to the same class of readers; and many other considerations of the same sort, which may enter as elements, in ascertaining whether there had been a piracy or not. Although the doctrine is often laid down in the books, that an abridgment is not a piracy of the original copyright; yet this proposition must be received with many qualifications. In many cases, the question may naturally turn upon the point, not so much of the quantity as of the value of the selected materials. As was significantly said on another occasion, *Non numerantur, ponderantur*. The quintessence of a work may be piratically extracted, so as to leave a mere *caput mortuum*, by the selection of all the important passages in a comparatively moderate space. In the recent case of Bramwell *v.* Halcomb. (3 Mylne & Craig, 737,) it was held, that the question, whether one author has made a piratical use of another's work, does not necessarily depend upon the quantity of that work, which he has quoted or introduced into his own book. On that occasion, Lord Cottenham said, 'When it comes to a question of quantity, it must be very vague. One writer might take all the vital part of another's book, though it might be but a small proportion of the book in quantity. It is not only quantity, but value, which is looked to. It is useless to look to any particular cases about quantity.' The same subject was a good deal considered by the same learned judge in Saunders *v.* Smith, (3 Mylne & Craig R. 711, 728, 729,) with reference to copyright in Reports; and how far another person was at

The definition of an abridgment given in the case decided by Lord Chancellor Apsley, has certainly come down to us with some weight of authority, from the circumstance that he was assisted by Sir

liberty to extract the substance of such reports, or to publish select cases therefrom, even with notes appended. In the case of Wheaton *v.* Peters, (8 Peters's R. 591,) the same subject was considered very much at large. It was not doubted by the court, that Mr. Peters's Condensed Reports would have been an infringement of Mr. Wheaton's copyright, (supposing that copyright properly secured under the act,) if the opinions of the court had been, or could be, the proper subject of the private copyright by Mr. Wheaton. But it was held that the opinions of the court, being published under the authority of congress, were not the proper subject of private copyright. But it was as little doubted by the court, that Mr. Wheaton had a copyright in his own marginal notes, and in the arguments of counsel as prepared and arranged in his work. The cause went back to the circuit court for the purpose of further inquiries as to the fact, whether the requisites of the act of congress had been complied with or not by Mr. Wheaton. This would have been wholly useless and nugatory, unless Mr. Wheaton's marginal notes and abstracts of arguments could have been the subject of a copyright (for that was all the work which could be the subject of copyright;) so that if Mr. Peters had violated that right, Mr. Wheaton was entitled to redress."

In 2 Story's Eq. Jurisp. § 939, the learned author says, " But what constitutes a *bona fide* case of extracts, or a *bona fide* abridgment, or a *bona fide* use of common materials, is often a matter of most embarrassing inquiry. The true question, in all cases of this sort, is, (it has been said,) whether there has been a legitimate use of the copyright publication, in the fair exercise of a mental operation, deserving the character of a new work. If there has been, although it may be prejudicial to the original author, it is not an invasion of his legal rights. If there has not been, then it is treated as a mere colorable curtailment of the original work, and a fraudulent evasion of the copyright. But this is another mode of stating the difficulty, rather than a test, affording a clear criterion to discriminate between the cases."

Mr. Chancellor Kent, referring to the case of Dodsley *v.* Kinnersley, says, "This latitudinary right of abridgment is liable to abuse, and to trench upon the copyright of the author. The question as to a *bona fide* abridgment may turn not so much upon the quantity as the value of the selected materials." 2 Kent's Com. 382, note.

Lord Campbell, in his Life of Lord Hardwicke, referring to the case of Gyles *v.* Wilcox, says; "I must own that I much question another rule he laid down with respect to literary property, although it has not yet been upset. . . I confess I do not understand why an abridgment tending to injure the reputation and lessen the profits of the author, should not be considered an invasion of his property." Campbell's Lives of the Chancellors, v. 56.

William Blackstone, brief as the report of the case is. It is also to be admitted, that the result to which those learned persons came, is in accordance with the doctrine which had been previously recognized by Lord Hardwicke, and which seems, so far as the reported cases show, to have been tacitly received into the English law.[1]

There can be no doubt that the definition of an abridgment, given in the anonymous case in Lofft, is correct, in a critical sense. That the understanding must be employed in the act of "carrying a larger work into a smaller compass, and rendering it less expensive, and more convenient both to the time and use of the reader," and that when this is done, the person who does it exhibits, according to Lord Hardwicke, his own "invention, learning, and judgment," is obvious. But whether this can be done with any work really original and actually under the protection of copyright — whether the property of the original author can be taken, and the taking be justified, by any amount of learning, judgment, or invention, shown in the act by him who thus appropriates the property of another — is the great question which seems to be assumed, and not satisfactorily solved by these authorities. There are many modes in which the wrongful taker of another's property may exhibit vast talent and ingenuity, and even genius, both in the act of taking, and in the use

[1] There has been no instance in which the doctrine has been directly resisted and examined with reference to principle.

which he makes of it; so that he may really be said to have incorporated with it both his own labor and his own intellectual energy. But the question of original title is still apt inconveniently to recur in such cases. In like manner, invention, learning, and judgment are often shown in the appropriation of the literary labors of others; but the courts have not hesitated, on this account, to ascertain what part of a book, laboring under suspicion, was taken from the complainant; and if the title of the latter is made out, to grant redress, even to the destruction of all that the piratical author can call his own.[1] In the case of a colorable curtailment of the original work, there may be the exercise of a mental operation, as well as in a professed abridgment; and if the original author is injured by the latter, as well as by the former, it seems to be a very unsatisfactory answer in either case, to say, that his book has been made, by a mental operation, to wear the appearance of a new work. In both cases, the true inquiry is — Has anything been taken which belongs to another? In either case, the form under which the original matter reappears should be treated as a disguise; and the extent of the transformation shows only the extent to which the disguise has been carried, as long as anything remains which the original author can show to be justly and exclusively his own.

[1] See the cases of Gray *v.* Russell, 1 Story's R. 11. Emerson *v.* Davies, 3 Story's R. 768. Bramwell *v.* Halcomb, 3 M. & Cr. 737. Lewis *v.* Fullerton, 2 Beavan's R. 6. Mawman *v.* Tegg, 2 Russ. 385, 390.

It is necessary, therefore, in this inquiry, to look, not to the origin of the right of literary property, for the right is to be assumed, but to what that right includes. When the author of a book, of whatever kind, possessing the legal attributes of originality, has secured his copyright according to the prevailing law of his country, he has secured the exclusive right to print and publish his own book.[1] In the jurisprudence with which we are co cerned, this right includes the whole book and every part of it ; for we have seen, that there may be a piratical taking of extracts and passages, and that the quantity thus taken may be immaterial.[2] It includes also, or may include, the style, or language, and expression ; the learning, the facts, or the narrative ; the sentiment and ideas, as far as their identity can be traced ; and the form, arrangement and combination which the author has given to his materials. These are, or may be, all distinct objects of the right of property ; and in every work of originality, likely to be abridged, or capable of being abridged, they are all important objects of that right. However imperfectly the subject may have been regarded in former times, it is now, I think, to be regarded as settled, that whatever is metaphysically part or parcel of the intellectual contents of a book, if in a just sense original, is protected and included under the right of property vested by law in the author ;

[1] As to the legal standard of originality, see ante Ch. V.

[2] Ante.

and it is very material to observe, that the arrangement, the method, the plan, the course of reasoning, or course of narrative, the exhibition of the subject, or the learning of the book, may be, according to its character, as much objects of the right of property, as the language and the ideas.[1]

What then does the maker of an abridgment print, publish and sell, after he has made it? He has been employed, according to the definition above quoted, "in retrenching unnecessary and uninteresting circumstances, which rather deaden the narration;" that is to say, he has rejected what *in his judgment* are redundancies. Does this make him the author or proprietor of what remains? If the work be a history, did he, the person abridging it, compile the materials into their present shape, and describe the course of events, and embody the whole of what constitutes the intellectual contents of the book, or are these things the product of another's labor, research and faculty of writing? If it be a fictitious narrative, whose genius created the characters, and animated them with the sentiments which they utter, and invented the pleasing incidents of their mock existences, and wove the whole into the novel or

[1] Of course I do not mean to give any encouragement to the idea that a man may appropriate to himself learning that is open to every one, or that any exclusive property can be acquired in a subject. The position of the text is that of the authorities, that no subsequent writer can avail himself even of the learning and information collected by the original author, by copying from him without resorting to the common sources. See the cases of Gray *v.* Russell, 1 Story, 11; Emerson *v.* Davies, 3 Story, 768.

the poem; which exists as an intellectual whole, after as well as before the process by which "the unnecessary and uninteresting circumstances" are "retrenched?" Or if it be a work of science, or a treatise in any branch of knowledge, whose are the ideas, the course of reasoning and illustration, the plan and analysis of the subject, and the collection and arrangement of materials which constitute the identity of the book?[1] These questions can have but one answer; and if the abridgment, in any given case, consists solely in the reduction of the bulk of the volume, by the rejection of redundancies, it is a mere republication of a connected series of extracts, in a different juxtaposition from the original author's, to which the party had no title whatever. On the other hand, if the abridgment not only rejects redundancies, but also clothes the sentiments and ideas which may be left, in different phraseology, then it falls under the predicament of a colorable alteration, which cannot escape the censure of justice.

When we consider the incorporeal nature of lite-

[1] Take the very case of Dr. Johnson's Rasselas, and endeavor to apply to it Lord Apsley's rule, bearing in mind that the author and his assigns, during the existence of the copyright, had the sole right to reap the profits of the publication of the whole and every part of it. The moral reflections are left out, the narrative goes into the Gentleman's Magazine. Whose genius produced that stately and immortal fiction? Who described and created the characters of Imlac, and the Princess, and the Prince of Abyssinia, and placed them in the Happy Valley, and sent them forth in a series of gentle trials and pleasing and sad perplexities, in the world beyond its walls? Who wrote that narrative? Not, certainly, the Grub street hack, who was employed to "leave out the reflections." What he took and his employers published, was the literary property of another, the profits of which the law had not vested in them.

rary property, it will be apparent that no writer can make and publish an abridgment, without taking to himself profits of literary matter which belong to another. It has been stated, in a fo mer chapter, that literary property is an exclusive right to print a written composition, and to take the profits thereof after publication. The mere definition of an abridgment shows that the writer makes use of a composition of which he is not the author; for whatever he may have rejected as redundant, he does actually print, publish and sell, in an abbreviated form — and in a form abbreviated by the rejection of parts — a certain amount of literary matter, the profits of which exclusively belong to another. Moreover, the very form in which this matter is reproduced, of necessity tends to the injury of the true proprietor. The real object of most abridgments is to undersell the original work. Cases are often met with, it is true, for which the apology is urged, that they are not designed to supersede the originals, and are not likely in fact to do so. But they are made to be sold; and if sold, it is at least as consistent with principle and analogy, to presume that the sale is injurious to the original author, as to presume that it is not.

The argument that a purchaser would not have purchased the original, if the abridgment had not been thrown in his way, rests merely upon conjecture in most cases. The fact is not capable of proof by evidence, but can only be arrived at through the opinions of third persons. In the analogous cases of piracy by colorable alterations and disguises, the law does not stop to inquire whether the purchaser of the piratical publication would have bought the genuine work. It presumes damage, to just the extent of the number of copies sold, and decrees the whole profits to the true proprietor. It also stops the piratical publication; thereby declaring that the true proprietor shall not be exposed to the probability and hazard of injury. In no case, after proof of piracy, has it been permitted to the defendant to show by evidence that his publication is not likely to injure the plaintiff, and therefore that he ought to be allowed to go on.[1]

[1] In the cases of extracts and quotations, where the amount taken is small, the question of injury may be an element in determining whether the court will treat the extract as a piracy; but even there, as we have seen, if the extract may serve *quoad hoc* as a substitute for the original book, it is to be treated as a piracy; and in a case of this kind, Lord Cottenham said, that the plaintiff was the person best able to judge of the question of injury himself, and that if the court clearly saw that anything had been done which tends to an injury, it being done against a legal right, the court would stop the defendant's publication. (Campbell *v.* Scott, 11 Simons, 31.) But in cases of piracy by copying, imitation and colorable alteration, the defence is wholly unavailable, that the piratical publication is designed for a class of readers who would not have purchased the genuine work, and it is rarely made. (See Folsom *v.* Marsh, 2 Story's R. 100; Mawman *v.* Tegg, 2 Russ. R. 385; Campbell *v.* Scott, *ut supra.*) The jurisdiction of courts of equity, in cases of this kind, is founded upon the fact that the actual damages cannot be traced, and therefore in order to make the legal right effectual, the publication which violates it is prohibited altogether. (Wilkins *v.* Aiken, 17 Ves. 424.) In France, under the law of July 19th, 1793, the publisher of a piratical book is condemned to pay to the true proprietor a sum equivalent to the price of 3000 copies of the original edition. In other countries, there is a similar fixed standard of damages. In Belgium, the number of copies is 300. Merlin Rep. de Jurisp. Tit. Contrefaçon, tom. 3, p. 717, 718. In Prussia, the court is required to fix the indemnity, according to the circumstances, at a sum equal to the sales of from 50 to 1000 copies of the lawful edition, where the proprietor cannot prove that he has suffered greater damages. Renouard, Droits D'Auteurs, tom. 1, p. 271. In all these countries, these

It is also to be considered, that the publication of an abridgment not only tends to injure the sale of the copies which the true proprietor has already published, but it also interferes with his use of his copyright, and with his power of disposing of it. His property in the original work includes the right to publish it in any form which he may see fit to adopt. He may choose to. publish an abridgment himself; and his right to do so is perfect, since he is absolutely the proprietor of the matter embraced in his original work. His copyright must be held to have secured to him the right to avail himself of the profits to be reaped from all classes of readers, both those who would purchase his production in a cheap and condensed form, and those who would purchase it in its more extended and costly shape. To construe his right upon any narrower terms, would confine him to the paper and print which he may have selected for the first issue of his work, and would deprive him of the profits on a cheaper form of publication. If, therefore, he sees fit to publish his own work in a condensed form, as well as in its original and more elaborate shape, his right is clearly broad enough to give him the power to do so, and to take the profits of both forms of publication.[1]

penalties are in addition to the penalty of confiscation; and they proceed upon the presumption of damage, in all cases.

[1] "Un examen détaillé des droits divers dont l'ensemble constitue le domaine privé conferé par les priviléges d'auteur, concluira à recounaitre que tous ces droits peuvent etre ramenés à un droit unique, celui d'exploiter seul les produits vénaux que l'ouvrage est susceptible de procurer." Renouard, tom. 2, p. 10.

There are very few works, capable of being usefully abridged, of which the right to publish an abridgment is not a valuable part of the copyright. If, during the existence of the copyright, the work is abridged by a stranger, the copyright is shorn of an incident, the loss of which may greatly affect its value as property. In this sense, therefore, an abridgment, without leave of the proprietor, seems to be a direct usurpation of his rights. The law can never presume that the author or proprietor will not avail himself of his right to publish his own abridgment. The correct presumption is, that the owner of any property reserves to himself every right inherent in it, which he has not waived or ceded in some of the forms known to the law; and in regard to literary property, publication alone is not a dedication to the public of any right attached or incident to the property itself.

These considerations are not a little fortified by the argument arising from the fitness of leaving the reputation of an author under his own care, or under the care of those to whom he sees fit to entrust it. An unlimited right to make abridgments deprives the author, while living, and his representatives after his decease, of their just control over his reputation, and consigns his works to reproduction in forms to which his assent is not asked and cannot be presumed, for no other purpose than the accommodation of the avarice of individuals and a fancied advantage to the public. Lord Mansfield did not disdain to resort to the argument of fitness, with regard to the reputation of an author, in support of his right over his own productions. He held it to be one of the foundations of literary property.[1]

In short, the publication of a mere and professed abridgment, is an invasion of the rights of an author, in several ways. It pledges and compromises his reputation and responsibility, to the same extent as the republication of the original work. It makes use of his work to raise a competition which must always be dangerous, by bringing it in a contracted form within the reach of a larger number of purchasers; and it creates a direct obstacle to the exercise of his right of giving the work to the public himself, under the form of an abridgment.[2]

I cannot but think, therefore, that the result to which English and American jurisprudence ought to come, upon this question, is, that an abridgment, in which the text, the plan, the ideas, arguments, narrative and discussion of an original author are reproduced, in a condensed form, is a violation of his right of property.[3]

This position seems to be sustained by the doctrine of a recent decision in England; although some of the remarks which fell from the court apparently recognize the right of making an abridgment of some

[1] Millar *v.* Taylor, 4 Burr. ——. See his observations, cited ante p. 84.

[2] See Renouard, Droits D'Auteurs, tom. 2, p. 30 et seq.

[3] Such an abridgment falls under the class of piracies which the French jurists call "partially identical"—*Contrefaçon partielle identique.*" Renouard, tom. 2, p. 30.

kind, in the case of a *book*, as distinguishable from an abridgment or adaptation of *music*. When examined, however, the reasoning of Lord Lyndhurst on this point, taken in connection with the point decided in the cause, will be found to give a different view of the general doctrine of abridgments, from that which has loosely prevailed in England for above a century.

The defendant in this case had published portions of an opera, (which was under the protection of a copyright,) consisting of entire airs, and other portions consisting of whole bars, united with other bars of his own composition, the whole being arranged and adapted for dancing, in the forms of quadrilles and waltzes, and being described on the title-page as having been taken from the opera in question.[1] The defence involved most of the doctrines usually advanced in defence of abridgments. It was contended that the object of the defendant's publication

[1] "In support of the plaintiff's case, the affidavit of Mr. Rodwell, an experienced musician, was read. With reference to the 57th set of quadrilles published by the defendant, he deposed that the second quadrille was so completely similar to an air of the opera called 'Gentille Muscovite,' that it was nearly note for note the same, even to the accompaniments; that the melody of the fourth quadrille was like another air of the opera, with some variations in certain bars, which he specified; and that the melody of the fifth quadrille was contained in certain bars of the overture, which he specified. With reference to the 58th set, he said that the first quadrille was founded on, though much varied from, an air of the opera called 'Le pauvre Ivan.' He mentioned the several bars in which alterations had been made, and stated that in one instance there had been a change of key. He made similar statements with respect to the other quadrilles and the waltzes; observing, however, that in one of the waltzes there were sixteen bars which were not in the original air. He concluded his affidavit by saying, that although in several instances the music of the quadrilles in question was slightly varied from the airs of the opera, yet such variation was not more than is always found to be necessary when the music of an opera is arranged in the form of quadrilles." 1 Younge & Coll. 290.

was different from that of the plaintiff's; that the defendant had adapted and arranged the music which he had taken from the plaintiff's opera, for dancing, to which it was not adapted in the original work; that such arrangement and adaptation involved much labor, musical knowledge, and skill; that the defendant had only taken certain airs and melodies, whereas the plaintiff's copyright embraced the entire opera, which consists not merely of certain airs and melodies, but of the whole score.[1]

The court applied to this case the principle which I have endeavored to keep in view in the preceding observations. The air, or melody, in music, is the invention of the author; it may be the subject of piracy, because in taking it, the taker appropriates what another, and not he, has invented; and a piracy is committed if so much is taken as constitutes the meritorious part of the invention, whether it be the whole invention or the whole of a distinct part of the invention. Upon the ground that the defendant had taken consecutive bars, forming the entire air or melody, an injunction was granted.[2]

[1] In music, the form called the score is when the work contains the whole of the music to be used by all the performers collectively with their several instruments.

[2] D'Almaine *v.* Boosey, 1 Y. & Coll. 288, 300, in the Exchequer, in Equity. Lord Lyndhurst, L. C. B. said, "It is admitted that the defendant has published portions of the opera containing the melodious parts of it; that he has also published entire airs; and that in one of his waltzes he has introduced seventeen bars in succession, containing the whole of the original air, although he adds fifteen other bars which are not to be found in it. Now it is said that this is not a piracy, first, because the whole of each air has not been taken; and, secondly, because what the plaintiff purchased was the entire opera; and the opera consists, not merely of certain airs

Lord Lyndhurst, in his judgment on this occasion, did not refer to any particular works, or class of

and melodies, but of the whole score. But, in the first place, piracy may be of part of an air as well as of the whole; and, in the second place, admitting that the opera consists of the whole score, yet if the plaintiffs were entitled to the whole, *a fortiori* they were entitled to publish the melodies which form a part. Again, it is said, that the present publication is adapted for dancing only, and that some degree of art is needed for the purpose of so adapting it; and that but a small part of the merit belongs to the original composer. That is a nice question. It is a nice question, what shall be deemed such a modification of an original work as shall absorb the merit of the original in the new composition. No doubt such a modification may be allowed in some cases; as in that of an abridgment or a digest. Such publications are in their nature original. Their compiler intends to make of them a new use; not that which the author proposed to make. Digests are of great use to practical men, though not so, comparatively speaking, to students. The same may be said of an abridgment of any study; but it must be a *bona fide* abridgment, because if it contains many chapters of the original work, or such as made that work salable, the maker of the abridgment commits a piracy. Now it will be said that one author may treat the same subject very differently from another who wrote before him. That observation is true in many cases. A man may write upon morals in a manner quite distinct from that of others who preceded him; but the subject of music is to be regarded upon very different principles. It is the air or melody which is the invention of the author, and which may in such case be the subject of piracy; and you commit a piracy if, by taking not a single bar, but several, you incorporate in the new work that in which the whole meritorious part of the invention consists. I remember in a case of copyright, at *nisi prius*, a question arising as to how many bars were necessary for the constitution of a subject or phrase. Sir George Smart, who was a witness in the case, said, that a mere bar did not constitute a phrase, though three or four bars might do so. Now it appears to me that if you take from the composition of an author all those bars consecutively which form the entire air or melody, without any material alteration, it is a piracy; though, on the other hand, you might take them in a different order or broken by the intersection of others, like words, in such a manner as should not be a piracy. It must depend on whether the air taken is substantially the same with the original. Now the most unlettered in music can distinguish one song from another, and the mere adaptation of the air, either by changing it to a dance or by transferring it from one instrument to another, does not, even to common apprehensions, alter the original subject. The ear tells you that it is the same. The original air requires the aid of genius for its construction, but a mere mechanic in music can make the adaptation or accompaniment. Substantially, the piracy is, where the appropriated music, though adapted to a different purpose from that of the original, may still be recognized by the ear. The adding variations makes no difference in the principle."

works, presenting instances of what he would consider *bona fide* and allowable abridgments. Whether he had reference, as would seem, to such works as are called abridgments in the law,[1] or to a more numerous class, in which some one existing work is reproduced under a merely condensed form, it is clear, that the principle upon which he decided the cause before him brings the doctrine in relation to abridgments, within far more restricted limits than had previously been assigned to it. The broad doctrine of the case of Gyles *v.* Wilcox, and the still broader doctrine in the anonymous case in Lofft's Reports, would have justified the use which the defendant made of the plaintiff's music, but for the single qualification which Lord Lyndhurst has introduced. He admits the general right to use, in the way of abridgment or digest, what a previous writer has created; but if a considerable portion of that which constitutes *per se* the invention of the author, is taken, although it be adapted to a different purpose, a piracy is committed. The distinction which he makes between music and a literary composition seems to be merely that an air or melody in music is the pure

[1] During the argument, upon the case of Gyles *v.* Wilcox being cited by the defendant's counsel, in support of the doctrine that an adaptation of an original work to new purposes is not a piracy, his lordship made the following remarks: "I think that if the original air is published, though with adaptations and harmonies, or for different instruments, it is a piracy, and an action will lie. This is not like the case of an abridgment of a book. The purpose of abridgments is very distinct from that of the works from which they are taken. No one can doubt that Viner's Abridgment and Comyn's Digest are original works." Ibid. p. 296.

invention of the author, and there is no ground of a common subject for a subsequent composer to fall back upon; whereas, in literature, although the particular composition is original, and exclusively the fruit of the author's mind, the subject is common to all men, and may admit of distinctions between the modes of treating it, which music will not admit of. In literature, therefore, some weight is to be given to the circumstance that the purpose to which a subsequent writer adapts the materials which he finds in an original author, is of itself new. But, according to his lordship, even in literature, if material parts of what constitutes the subject of an author's property be taken, although with a new adaptation, a piracy is committed.

If this be so, then it is highly important to inquire how far the supposed right to make what is called a *bona fide* abridgment is affected by the doctrine laid down by Mr. Justice Story, that an original author may have copyright in the plan of his book.

In the case in which this doctrine was laid down, the plaintiff was the author of an arithmetic constructed upon a peculiar plan. He claimed, as his own invention, the plan of the lessons, which consisted in the peculiar arrangement of a set of tables, with a gradation of examples placed in a particular manner, to teach and illustrate the combinations of numbers; and this plan and arrangement he alleged had been borrowed and imitated by the defendant. The defence consisted in showing, that the materials and some of the modes of illustration used by the plaintiff could be found in other books; but the court held, that this was entirely immaterial, if the materials and modes of illustration had never been before united in one combination, in the manner in which the plaintiff had united and connected them; and declared, that no person had a right to borrow the same plan and arrangement and illustrations, and servilely to copy them into another work.[1] What-

[1] Emerson *v.* Davies, 3 Story's R. 768, 783. This subject of copyright in the plan or method of a book is so evanescent and metaphysical, that it is nearly impossible to state with precision the abstract doctrine of the law in regard to it, if indeed the law upon this point may yet be considered as developed or settled. Before the case of Emerson *v.* Davies was in print, a master's report was made, in the same court, in another case, by Charles Sumner, Esq. containing the following able discussion upon the question, whether there can be copyright in a mere plan, independent of materials: "And the first question that arises is the general question, whether the plan, combination, or arrangement of a book, independent of the materials and language, is susceptible of copyright. Important as this question may seem to be, it does not appear to be illustrated by the light of decided cases. The case of Hogg *v.* Kirby, 8 Ves. 215, has been thought to exclude the conclusion that the plan of a book was the subject of copyright; but the injunction granted in this case seems not to have been founded on copyright, but on the power of the court to restrain a party from carrying on a trade, or from publishing a work, under a fraudulent representation that such trade or work was that of the plaintiff. (See Ibid. note, Sumner's edition.) The case of Cary v. Faden, 5 Ves. 23, recognizes a copyright in a road-book; but it was in the plan in combination with the materials. The case of Gray *v.* Russell, 1 Story, says that a work may be the subject of copyright, although the materials which compose it may be found in the works of other authors antecedently printed, provided the plan, the arrangement, and the combination of those materials be original; but even this case does not decide the distinct question whether a plan, independent of the materials to which it is applied, and on which it is wrought, is a subject of copyright.

"In the absence of any governing authority, the question must be regarded in the light of principle. It cannot be disguised that the plan of a book is often a peculiar part of its merits. Some authors receive high commendation merely for the arrangement of their subject, descending even to such particulars as the division into chapters and sections; and again even into the further division of paragraphs. This is applicable to historical compositions as well as to scientific and philoever may be the case, where a subsequent writer, taking only the plan or method of a previous author, uses different materials and illustrations, and adapts them to some plan, it is obvious that a real abridgment of a scientific treatise, for example, must borrow both the plan and method, and the literary matter, in the same combination and arrangement, from the original work; otherwise it is not an abridgment, and is to be judged upon different rules. It

sophic productions. It would be difficult, however, if not impossible, to hold a subsequent writer amenable to any other tribunal than that of criticism, who should write another work on the same subject in language of his own, but cast in the same chapters and sections. Indeed, the law in such a case as I am now supposing, seems to be clearly settled in the matter of abridgments. An honest abridgment is admitted to be no violation of the copyright of the work abridged; but the very idea of an abridgment implies the preservation of the original plan, arrangement and combination, abridged, or reduced to a smaller scale. Indeed, it will cease to be an abridgment exclusively, if it does not preserve these features; as a miniature would fail to be a portrait, if the original proportions and traits of the countenance are not represented. In making an abridgment of Mr. Irving's Life of Columbus, or Mr. Bancroft's History of the United States, the natural and inevitable course would be to follow their plan, to walk by their light, to keep firm hold of the thread which they have provided in their narratives; to adopt their mode of developing the subject; to rely upon their divisions; to lean upon all the landmarks which they have set up; in short, to abridge their works, by preserving, as far as possible, the original peculiarities in a smaller compass. Perhaps no class of works are subjected to abridgments more than dictionaries, nor has any person questioned the lawfulness of such abridgments; but they cannot fail to preserve the plan, arrangement, and combination of the original dictionary. Take, for instance, the recent extensive and most important dictionary of the English language, by Richardson, which is on a plan entirely new, I believe, as applied to the English language. Can it be doubted that an abridgment of this work might be made, reducing its two quartos to a single octavo, in which its peculiar plan should be preserved? Nor does it seem to me that it can be doubted that another dictionary, of another language, or even of the English language, may be made on Richardson's plan, which shall not be an abridgment, but shall be founded on fresh labor and fresh materials." See Law Reporter, (Boston) vol. x. pp. 155–156, note. Webb and Gray *v.* Powers and Bagley, S. C. 1 Woodbury's R.

seems to me, that when an author takes a scientific subject, however common it may be to all other writers, and upon a peculiar plan and with a distinct classification, produces a treatise novel in its method of teaching and exhibiting the subject, he has a right of property in what may be called, (by a not happy illustration,) the skeleton of his book, which is necessarily invaded by a condensed reproduction of the same treatise. This is what takes place in the making of a real abridgment.

To these views should be added the support derived from the laws of several of the continental nations.

In France, the question seems to be one of construction ; but there can be little doubt that the text of the law of 1793, which secures to authors the exclusive right of selling their works, and of ceding the proprietorship, in whole or in part, will authorize the conclusion that an abridgment is an injury to the proprietorship.[1] This opinion is maintained by M. Renouard, whose work on the Rights of Authors I have so often cited.[2]

In Belgium, abridgments are expressly included, by the text of the law, among the rights of authors, which are forbidden to be violated.[3]

[1] "Les auteurs en tout genre, les compositeurs de musique, les peintres et dessinateurs qui feront graver des tableaux ou dessins, jouiront durant leur vie entiere du droit exclusif de vendre, fair vendre, distribuer leurs ouvrages dans le territrire de la république et d'en céder la propriété en tout et en partie." Decret du 19 Juillet, 1793, art. 1.

[2] Tom. ii. p. 29–34.

[3] "Le droit de copie ou le droit de copier au moyen de l'impression est, pour ce qui coucerne les ouvrages originaux, soit productions littéraires ou productions des arts,

The Prussian law, (the most elaborate code on the subject of literary property in the world,) besides declaring that the exclusive rights of an author include the right of multiplying his work, already published, "in whole or in part," enumerates what shall not be considered infringements of this right, and does not place abridgments among the exceptions.[1] It seems to be highly probable, therefore, that in Prussia, the license of abridging another man's work is wholly unknown.

In Russia there are similar enactments to those of the Prussian code, and among the enumerated offences, it is declared that an edition of a dictionary in which the greater part of the definitions, explanations and examples is actually copied from a work of

soumis au droit exclusivement reservé à leurs auteurs et à leurs ayant-cause, de rendre publics par la voie de l' impression, de vendre, ou de faire vendre ces ouvrages, en tout ou en partie, par abrégé ou sur une échelle reduite, en une ou plusieurs langues, ornés ou non ornés de gravures et autres accessoires de l'art." Law of the 25th Jan. 1817, cited Renouard, tom. i. p. 249.

[1] "§ 1. Le droit de faire imprimer de nouveau ou de faire multiplier par un procédé mécanique quelconque tout ou partie d'un écrit déjà publié, appartient exclusivement à son auteur, ou à ceux qui tirent leurs droits de lui. § 2 Toute multiplication nouvelle, si elle a lieu sans l'approbation de l'ayant-droit exclusif, se nomme contrefaçon et est défendue. § 3. Est réputée contrefaçon, et est, par conséquent, également défendue l'impression faite sans l'approbation de l'auteur ou de ses ayant-droit: *a*. De manuscrits de tout genre ; *b*. De sermons prononcés ou de cours professés oralement, et écrits par un des auditeurs, soit que la publication ait eu lieu sous le véritable nom de l'auteur, soit qu'elle ait été faite sans son nom. Cette approbation est même nécessaire au possesseur legal d'un manuscrit ou de sa copie (*lettre a*) ou de sermons ou cours écrits (*lettre b*). § 4. Ne sont point considérées comme contrefaçons : 1. La citation littérale de passages isolés d'un ouvrage déjà imprimé, 2. La reproduction d'articles isolés, de poésies. etc, dans les ouvrages ayant pour objet la critique ou l'histoire littéraire, ou dans des recueils à l'usage des écoles ; 3. La publication de traductions d'ouvrages déjà imprimés." Law of the 11th June, 1837. Renouard, tom. i. p. 269.

the same kind, enjoying the protection of copyright, shall be deemed a piracy.[1]

A translation from a work not under the protection of copyright in the country where the translation is made, of course infringes no one's rights; but it is a very interesting and important question, whether a translation be not an infringement, where the orignal is protected.

[1] "Est également réputé contrefacteur: 1° quiconque, sous le titre de seconde ou troisième, etc. édition, imprime un ouvrage déjà publié, sans observer les conditions ci-dessus indiquées; 2° quiconque, ayant réimprimé à l'étranger un ouvrage publié en Russie, ou avec la permission de la censure russe, même en y ajoutant une traduction, vendrait en Russie des exemplaires de cette réimpression sans le consentement par écrit de l'éditeur légitime; 3° quiconque, sans le consentement de l'auteur, imprime un discours ou toute autre composition prononcée ou lue en public; 4° le journaliste qui, à titre d'analyse, ou sous tout autre prétexte, réimprime constamment et en entier de petits articles pris dans d'autres publications, lors même que ces articles ne formeraient pas une feuille d'impression; mais une réimpression accidentelle d'un article détaché ayant moins d'une feuille d'impression, comme aussi la réimpression de nouvelles politiques, de littérature, de sciences ou d'arts, avec indication des sources, n'est pas interdite. L'insertion, dans les chrestomaties et autres livres scolaires, d'articles ou extraits quelconques d'autres auteurs, n'est pas réputée contrefaçon, encore que ces emprunts, répartis dans les diverses parties du livre, formassent un contenu de plus d'une feuille d'impression. Les citations ne sont pas réputées contrefaçon, pourvu: 1° qu'elles ne dépassent pas le tiers du livre dont elles sont tirées, si se livre est de plus d'une feuille d'impression; 2° que le propre texte de l'auteur dépasse deux fois les citations prises par lui dans un autre ouvrage. La traduction d'un ouvrage déjà traduit n'est envisagée comme contrefaçon que lorsqu'on y a copié mot à mot et de suite deux tiers d'une traduction jouissant encore du droit de propriété exclusive. Est aussi réputée contrefaçon l'édition d'un dictionnaire dans lequel la majeure partie des définitions, explications et exemples, est textuellement copiée d'un autre ouvrage du même genre, jouissant encore du droit de propriété exclusive. Il en est de même de la publication des cartes géographiques, des tableaux historiques; des tables de logarithmes, des indicateurs et autres ouvrages de ce genre, consistant en chiffres ou noms propres, lorsqu'ils ont été copiés mot à mot, ou avec des changemens insignifians, sur d'autres ouvrages." 1 Renouard, p. 287, 288.

The principles upon which translations have been held to be original works, entitled to the protection of the law, have been referred to in a previous part of this treatise.[1] But the admitted right to make use of the work of a foreign author, who is not in a situation to claim the benefit of the law of copyright, has no tendency to establish such a right in cases where the original work is actually under protection, as would be the case where the original and the translation are both first published in the same country. The cases which have treated translations, made from foreign works, as original, and therefore fit subjects of copyright, have but little bearing upon the question now under consideration; they merely tend to show that the act of translation, by giving a new dress to the work, incorporates with it the pains and labor and learning of the translator.[2] This being conceded, it still remains a question, admitting of much doubt, whether a work, under the protection of the statute, if printed in a foreign or a dead language, can be thus taken as the subject of a translator's labor, so that by merely incorporating with the matter of the book the fruit of his own industry, he can entirely absorb the rights of the original author.

Upon principle, I can have no doubt that this cannot be done. The arguments derived from the fact that a translation brings the work within the reach

[1] Ante, p. 186, et seq.

[2] Burnett *v.* Chetwood, 2 Meriv. 443, n. Wyatt *v.* Barnard, 3 V. & B. 77.

of a greater number of readers, and from the incorporation of new labor with old material, or the clothing of the old sentiments and ideas in a new dress, are the principal suggestions that can be made in favor of such a license. Both of them, however, imply that the party is dealing with a book that has become *publici juris*, or as the French jurists express it, has entered into the *public domain*. If the book be under the private dominion of the author, or his assigns, the fact that a republication brings it within the reach of a greater number of readers, does not palliate an infringement of the copyright. If a republication could have this effect in any case, the argument would be as good, in the case of every piratical and literal republication on a cheaper paper than that of the original, as it is in the case of a reproduction under the new dress of a vernacular tongue. The law does not look to see what class of readers, or what numbers of readers are addressed by a piratical publication. It inquires whether the complaining author was exclusively entitled to take the profits of the book which he has published, and if it finds that such a right was well vested in him, it protects him under every form in which that literary composition can be reproduced.

Does then the mere act of giving to a literary composition the new dress of another language, add to the case an element, which ought to take it out of the rule by which reproduction in other forms is prohibited? The property of the original author embraces something more than the words in which his sentiments are conveyed. It includes the ideas and sentiments themselves, the plan of the work, and the mode of treating and exhibiting the subject. In such cases, his right may be invaded, in whatever form his own property may be reproduced. The new language in which his composition is clothed by translation affords only a different medium of communicating that in which he has an exclusive property; and to attribute to such a new medium the effect of entire originality, is to declare that a change of dress alone annihilates the most important subject of his right of property. It reduces his right to the narrow limits of an exclusive privilege of publishing in that idiom alone in which he first publishes. But we do not find that his privilege is thus circumscribed; because a mere change of phraseology is not held to justify the adoption of matter that is under the protection of the law.[1]

Literary property may also be invaded by the publication of a work purporting, in its title or other-

[1] In France, this is an open question, as I conceive it to be both in England and America. M. Pardessus denies the right of translation of works published in France *Cours de Droit Commercial, 2d Partie, titre* 1, Nos. 164, 167. M. Renouard supports it, tom. ii. pp. 36–41. In England the question has not been directly adjudged, although Mr. Godson (page 347) cites the case of Burnett *v.* Chetwood, 2 Meriv. 441, n. in support of the position, that a translation of a book, written in the Latin language by a British subject, is a work to be protected. I have shown (ante, p. 189, n.) that this case was disposed of on other grounds. The British international copyright act provides that foreign books which may by treaty become privileged in England, shall still be subject to being translated. In Prussia a translation cannot be made of a native work, which the author has published in a dead language. Law of 1837. Renouard, tom. i. p. 269.

wise, to be what it is not. If a party puts forth a work in fact represented to the public to be the work of another, which is actually under the protection of copyright, so as to intercept the profits which would otherwise accrue to the proprietor of the latter, such a proprietor may obtain the aid of a court of equity to prevent the injury thus occasioned or threatened.[1] This offence has not been treated strictly as a piracy, where no part of the body of the genuine work has been copied or imitated. But he who carries his work into the world as that of another person, may do the same injury as if he actually published that of another person; and if the consequences are or are likely to be the same, the remedy ought to be coextensive with the injury.[2]

But, in England, the jurisdiction exercised by courts of equity, to prevent the use of the title of an established work, is exerted in the same manner and upon the same principles as in the cases of the good-will of trades.[3] The doctrine that the title of a book or periodical is part of the work, capable of being infringed like the body of the publication, and that the infringement is to be redressed as a piracy, has not been expressly affirmed.[4] The result that is

[1] Hogg *v.* Kirby, 8 Ves. 215.

[2] Ibid.

[3] The ground of the decision, in Hogg *v.* Kirby, was, that the defendant represented his publication to be a continuation of that of the plaintiff. See Crutwell *v.* Lye, 17 Ves. 335, 342, where Lord Eldon refers to and comments on the case of Hogg *v.* Kirby. See also Keene *v.* Harris, cited in Crutwell *v.* Lye, where the trustee of a newspaper published another newspaper under the same title, and it was held a breach of trust. See also ante, p. 166, and the authorities there cited.

[4] Spottiswood *v.* Clarke, 2 Phillips's Ch. R. 154, presents a case

reached through the branch of equity jurisdiction relating to the good-will of a trade or employment, is perhaps, in most cases, as beneficial to the interests of literature as any other form of redress. But there may be cases in which this branch of the jurisdiction would not give an adequate remedy. Perhaps it would be necessary, in order to make a case for interference on the ground of a violated trade, to show that the work brought in periodical returns ; or that the conduct of the defendant interfered with an established course of profits, regularly flowing from the publication of the plaintiff.[1] But in the case of a newly published work, the profits are not ascertained, and no regularity or established course of profits can be proved ; at the same time it is perfectly clear that the proprietor of the work is by law exclusively entitled to the profits, whatever they are likely to be, and on this ground a distinct branch of equity jurisdiction makes his legal right effectual. It is therefore necessary to inquire, whether the title of a book should not, as part of the work, be deemed to be under the protection of the copyright, so as to make the copying or imitating it a piracy, to be redressed as such.

The solution of this question will probably be found to depend upon the rules and principles which determine the question of infringement, in cases

of colorable imitation of the title of an Almanac. The injunction was sought for on the ground that defendant represented his almanac to be the same as that printed and sold by the plaintiff.

[1] See 2 Story's Eq. Jurisp. § 951.

where any distinct portion of a work under the protection of a copyright is improperly used. It must depend on the existence of an exclusive property in the part thus taken, and on the fact of injury to the exclusive right of the party complaining. Thus, if the titles of two books are identically the same, and the books are dissimilar in all other respects, the question will arise, whether the title of the earlier publication is descriptive of its individuality, and is of a character appropriate to the setting forth that book to the public. If it be such a title, and if the effect of its adoption be to mislead the public in their purchases, then both the elements of a piracy concur, and there seems to be no reason why it should not be regarded as an infringement of the copyright. But if the title be merely a generic description of the subject, or a description consecrated by usage to works of the particular class to which the book belongs, and there is nothing to cause a confusion between the two works, there is no reason for judicial interference, either on the ground of copyright or of good-will in trade.[1]

[1] Instances of the second class would be, "A Dictionary of the English Language;" "A History of England;" "A Treatise on the Law of Patents;" "Biographie Universelle," &c. &c. But such titles as "The Dictionary of the French Academy," — "Dictionnaire de l'Académie Francaise;" "History of the Conquest of Mexico, with a preliminary view of the Ancient Mexican Civilization, and the Life of the Conqueror Hernando Cortes," are each descriptive of the particular work, peculiar and appropriate to its individuality; and if by adopting such a title an injury is caused to the work to which it belongs, the proprietor of that work should be entitled to redress, under the principles of a consistent and effectual jurisprudence. See Spottiswood *v.* Clarke, 2 Phillips Ch. R. 154.

There may, indeed, be a third class of cases, where the title is not descriptive of an individual publication, and is *ab ante* open to any one to adopt, but by long use and possession has come to be the received designation of a particular work. In such cases, the title has become appropriated to the party who has thus used it, and whose profits may be intercepted by its adoption by another. These cases, however, can rarely arise in any other than the class of periodical publications; and in the actual state of our jurisprudence, perhaps redress for such injuries must be sought in that jurisdiction which protects trades, by bringing the case within the principles regulating that branch of the law.[1]

If a periodical work, that has long worn a particular title, changes it for another, the adoption of the old title by a new periodical, after the lapse of a reasonable time, would ordinarily not be such an interference as the courts of justice should notice.[2]

This subject of titles has been much discussed in France, where an ample protection vindicates the just rights of literary property. The remedy is sometimes administered in damages for an unlawful interception of profits, as in cases of trade; and

[1] To cases of this description belong that of "The Bath Chronicle," (cited under the name of Keene *v.* Harris, 8 Ves. 215.) "Le Constitutionnel," which came before the Tribunal of Commerce at Paris, in 1832; (Renouard, tom. 2, p. 125,) and Hogg *v.* Kirby, 8 Ves. 215, the case of a magazine.

[2] *The Cour Royale* at Paris in 1834 sanctioned the publication of a journal under the title of *Gazette de Sante*, which another journal had formerly worn, but which it had for seven months abandoned for the title *Gazette Medicale de Paris*. Renouard, tom. 2, p. 128.

sometimes under the law of copyright, as for a piratical infringement, according to the circumstances.[1] The rules established by the adjudged cases are the following. 1. That a title intended to mark the individuality of a work, and to set it forth to the public, cannot be used, even for a work of entirely different contents; and that it is a usurpation, when such a title is taken, though it may be used with slight modifications, if there is any chance of confusion, so that the one work is likely to be mistaken for the other. 2. That a title which does not mark the individuality of the work, and the use of which by another book is not likely to do injury to the work which had first adopted it, does not give a right of exclusive possession, 3. That the title of a journal belongs to it, as long as it is worn, through the whole period of its existence; and the longer this period

[1] In a case concerning the Dictionary of the French Academy — *Dictionnaire de l'Academie Francaise* — M. Merlin argued before the Court of Cassation, that the title of the Dictionary of the French Academy is an essential part of the dictionary itself; that to usurp it is to usurp a part of the work; that the law treats the usurpation of part of a literary work as an infringement (*contre façon*,) and punishes it in a peculiar manner: — that if, under the title of *Theatre de Racine*, a printer were to publish the plays of Bradon, and if Racine were living, and in the enjoyment of all his rights of property, it would be impossible to say that the printer had not committed a piracy, (*vol litteraire*) and ought not to be visited with the penalties enacted for that offence. The court adopted this reasoning, and held that the object of the law of 1793 (the copyright law) was to secure to authors, their heirs and assigns, the exclusive right to print, sell and distribute their own works, and consequently to prohibit the printing and distribution of every work, which, by an invasion, more or less extensive, could interfere with this exclusive right; and that the adoption of such a title as that in question was an offence against the law of 1793, inasmuch as it tended directly to injure the proprietors of the genuine work. Merlin, Questions de Droit, *Propriete Litteraire*, § 1.

has existed, the more importance is acquired to the title, and the more it becomes a distinguishing part of the property.[1]

The use of the name alone of another person is a wrong that will be prevented by the interference of a court of equity, but not as an infringement of copyright. Lord Eldon granted an injunction to restrain the publication of certain poems under the name of Lord Byron, who was abroad, upon an affidavit of his agent making it highly probable that it was not a genuine work, and on the refusal of the defendant to swear that in his belief Lord Byron was the author.[2]

The usurpation of an author's name is morally a more reprehensible proceeding than the usurpation of a title. But if it is not accompanied by the reproduction of anything which the imputed author has actually written, it cannot be treated as a piracy.[3] But if the adoption of matter really written by an author accompanies the fraudulent use of his name, the whole publication ought to be restrained at once as a piracy, aggravated by the fraud attempted upon the title-page.[4] It has previously been stated, that a

[1] Renouard, tom 2, p. 118-128. Merlin, Questions de Droit, *Propriété Litteraire*, § 1. Repertoire de Jurisprudence, v. *Livre*.

[2] Lord Byron *v.* Johnson, 2 Meriv. 29.

[3] This species of fraud has frequently been checked in France, but as a fraud of a special nature, and not as the offence denominated *contrefaçon*, unless there has also been a copying of genuine matter. Renouard, tom. ii. pp. 128–130.

[4] A bookseller in Paris, in 1828, published a spurious edition of the works of Cardinal Maury, in which he had copied the notes of his nephew, (who had edited the genuine edition,) under the following title: *Nouvelle édition publiée sur les manuscrits autographes de l'auteur, par* LOUIS SIFFREIN MAURY *son neveu.* The fraud of holding out the name of M. Maury, as the editor of this edition, was justly considered as an element in the infringement of co-

work which thus usurps the name of a person who is not the author, cannot enjoy the protection of a copyright.[1]

As to what constitutes infringement, in the case of dramatic and musical compositions, it has been well settled that representation of a published play is not a violation of the copyright in the book itself.[2] But it seems that where a play is unpublished, and the copyright has been assigned by the author to a particular theatre, an injunction will be granted against its performance at any other theatre.[3] This implies that there is a common law right of performance, in the case of an unpublished play, capable of being assigned by the author, and existing previously to the statute of 3 Wm. IV. c. 15; and such a right is recognized in the first section of that act, which confirms the right of representation, where the author had consented to or authorized it previously to the passing of the act, to the person to whom he had given such consent or authority.

The second section of this act inflicts a penalty upon the unauthorized representation of any dramatic or musical composition, *or any part thereof*. What

pyright, which consisted in the reproduction of the genuine notes. Renouard, tom. ii. pp. 109, 130.

[1] Ante, p. 166.

[2] Coleman *v.* Walthen, 5 T. R. 245; Murray *v.* Elliston, 5 B. & Ald. 657. So, too, the representation of an unpublished play, under the sanction of the author, is not a publication by him, and an injunction will be granted to prevent the acting or publishing such a play, by persons who have taken it down from the mouths of the authorized performers. Macklin *v.* Richardson, Ambl. 694.

[3] Morris *v.* Kelley, 1 Jac. & W. 481. It does not distinctly appear, that the play in question had not been published, but the case implies that it had not been.

amounts to a representation of a part of a dramatic or musical composition has been held to be a question of fact for the jury, and not a question of law, in an action founded on this statute; and where the jury found the unauthorized singing of three songs of an opera to be such a representation, the court of common pleas refused to disturb the verdict, being of opinion that the statute intended to prohibit the performance altogether.[1]

The extent to which music may be used, by adaptation for a different kind of performance than that for which it was originally composed and published, came under consideration in a recent case, already referred to in the discussion on literary abridgments.[2] The doctrine was laid down, that a piracy is committed, where the appropriated music, though adapted to a different purpose from that of the original, may still be recognized by the ear; and that the adding variations makes no difference in the principle.[3]

The rules which determine when the copyright of a print or engraving is infringed, are entirely analogous to those applied to literary compositions. There may be an exact reproduction, or an imitation of the main design, with alterations merely colorable. When the design is the original production of the artist — the fruit of his own imagination — no other

[1] Planché *v.* Braham, 16 Law Jour. 25.

[2] Ante, pp. 280, 281.

[3] D'Almaine *v.* Boosey, 1 Y. & Coll. Excheq. R. 288, 302.

person can publish it, because there is no common source to resort to; and where there is a common source, as where the subject of the engraving is an object in nature or a work of art, that common source, and not the original print, may be resorted to.[1] The question therefore will be in both cases, whether the defendant has copied or unlawfully imitated the plaintiff's print. A copy has been said to be that which comes so near to the original, as to give every person the idea created by the original.[2] So, too, if there be such a similitude and conformity between the two prints, that the person who executed the one must have used the other as a model, he will be deemed a copyist of the main design.[3]

But when the original design of an artist is taken from a print and appropriated and used in another form and by another vehicle than by a reprint, and without a sale, a very nice question arises, whether the statutes have given any remedy. The 17 Geo. III. c. 57, enacted, that "if any engraver, etcher, print-seller, or *other person* shall, within the time, &c. engrave, etch, work, or cause or procure to be engraved, etched, or worked in *mezzotinto or chiaro oscuro*, or *otherwise or in any other manner copy* in the whole or in part, by varying, adding to or diminishing from

[1] Blackwall *v.* Harper, 2 Atk. 92. Wilkins *v.* Aiken, 17 Ves. 422. De Berenger *v.* Wheble, 2 Starkie N. P. C. 548.

[2] West *v.* Francis, 5 B. & Ald. 737, per Bayley J. Under the 17 Geo. III. c. 57, § 1, a person who sells a piratical print is liable to an action, whether he knew it to be pirated or not. *Ibid.*

[3] Roworth *v.* Wilkes, 1 Campb. 94.

the main design, or shall print, reprint or import for sale, or cause or procure to be printed, reprinted or imported for sale, or shall publish, sell or otherwise dispose of any copy or copies of any historical print or prints of any portrait, conversation, landscape or architecture, map, chart or plan, or any other print or prints whatsoever, which hath or have been or shall be engraved, etched, drawn or designed in any part of Great Britain, without the consent of the proprietor, &c., such proprietor shall and may, by a special action upon the case to be brought, &c., recover such damages as a jury on the trial of such action or on the execution of a writ of inquiry thereon, shall give or assess, together with double costs of suit."[1]

Mr. Martin, a celebrated artist, painted from sketches, which he had designed, a picture called *Belshazzar's Feast*, which he subsequently sold. A few years afterwards, he engraved and published, from the sketches, a print of the same name, having previously done all necessary acts for securing to himself the copyright of the print. The defendant, having purchased one of the prints, had it copied on canvass, in colors, on a very large scale, and with dioramic effect; and he publicly exhibited the dioramic copy, for money, and described it, in advertisements as "Mr. Martin's Grand Picture of Belshazzar's Feast, painted with dioramic effect." The

[1] See Appendix, p. 24.

sale of the plaintiff's print having been injured, as he alleged, by the exhibition, a bill was filed, praying that the defendant might be restrained from further exhibiting the dioramic copy, and from representing to the public that it was the production of the plaintiff; and that the defendant might account for and pay to the plaintiff the profits he had made by the exhibition.

Sir L. Shadwell, V. C. refused to grant the injunction, until the right had been established at law, thinking that the statute, 17 Geo. III. c. 57, was not intended to apply to a case where there was no intention to print, publish or sell, but only to exhibit in a certain manner; that exhibiting for profit is in no way analogous to selling a copy of a print; and that the copy exhibited being in oils and of different dimensions from the plaintiff's print, and being exhibited in a fixed place and in a given manner, made a case which the statute did not contemplate.[1]

[1] Martin *v.* Wright, 6 Simons R. 297. His Honor observed, that if Mr. Martin had exhibited his picture as a diorama, he might have been entitled to an injunction. With great deference, I venture to suggest, that the act of 17 Geo. III. c. 57, is much more broad in its terms than the 8 Geo. II. c. 13. The words of the latter are, "shall engrave etch or work as aforesaid, or in any other manner copy *and* sell or cause to be engraved etched or copied *and* sold in the whole or in part, by varying adding to or diminishing from the main design," &c. This provision is clearly directed against the offence of copying *and* selling. But the words of the more recent act are, "otherwise or in any other manner copy in the whole or in part by varying adding to or diminishing from the main design," seem to stand disjunctively in the contest, and to create a separate offence from that of selling, which is prohibited in the clause immediately following. If so, then the mere copying of a print, in *mezzotinto*, *chiaro oscuro*, or otherwise or in any other manner," gives the proprietor a right of action, without any sale, and he may show his damages to have accrued from exhibi-

In the United States, the statute of 1831 provides, that if any person shall engrave, etch, or work, sell, or copy, or cause to be engraved, etched, worked or sold, or copied, either on the whole, or by varying, adding to, or diminishing the main design of a print, cut or engraving, map, chart, or musical composition, with intent to evade the law, or shall print or import for sale, or cause to be printed or imported for sale, any such map, chart, &c. without the consent of the proprietor of the copyright, first obtained in writing, signed in the presence of two credible witnesses, or knowing the same to be so printed or imported without such consent, shall publish, sell, or expose to sale, or in any manner dispose of any such map, chart, &c. without such consent, then such offender shall forfeit, &c.

tion, or injury to his reputation, or interception of profits. The preamble of the act 17 Geo. III. c. 57, declares, that the motive for further provisions is that "the former acts have not effectually answered the purposes for which they were intended," and that "it is necessary for the encouragement of artists and for securing to them the property of and in their works, and for the advancement and improvement of the aforesaid arts that such further provisions should be made as are hereinafter mentioned and contained. If copying alone is not made a new substantive ground of action; the statute has added nothing but an action on the case, in the place of penalties. Yet it has manifestly described the causes of action in different terms from the former acts. See the remarks of Bailey J. in West *v.* Francis, 5 B. & Ald. 741. S. C. 1 Dowl. & R. 400.

CHAPTER X.

OF THE REMEDY FOR AN INFRINGEMENT OF COPYRIGHT.

LITERARY property is protected by several remedies, which differ widely from each other in point of efficiency, as well as in form.

1. Common Law and Statute Remedies.

The question whether there is any common law remedy for the protection of this species of property — which, since the year 1774, has been held, as to printed books, to depend entirely upon statute — was decided by Lord Kenyon in the affirmative. He held that the statute having vested the right in the author, for a given period, the common law remedy attaches to the right, notwithstanding the statute gave an action for penalties to any common informer. The penalties were not provided as a remedy to the party aggrieved; and consequently the common law remedy attaches, no other being specifically provided.[1]

[1] Beckford *v.* Hood, 7 T. R. 620. In this case it was also held, that an entry at Stationers' Hall was not necessary to enable the party to sue at common law for damages, but only to bring his action for the penalty. See ante, p. 194, as to the law in the United States.

This decision was upon the statute 8 Anne, c. 19. Subsequently, the act 54 Geo. III. c. 156, gave a special action on the case to the proprietor of a book, against any person for printing, reprinting, importing or publishing or exposing it to sale, by which he may recover such damages as the jury may see fit to assess.

The act 5 & 6 Vict. c. 45, § 15, provides, that if any person, in any part of the British dominions, shall print, or cause to be printed, either for sale or exportation, any book in which there shall be subsisting copyright, without the consent in writing of the proprietor thereof, or shall import for sale or hire any such book so having been unlawfully printed from parts beyond the sea, or, knowing such book to have been so unlawfully printed or imported, shall sell, publish, or expose to sale or hire, or cause to be sold published or exposed to sale or hire, or shall have in his possession for sale or hire, any such book so unlawfully printed or imported, without such consent as aforesaid, such offender shall be liable to a special action on the case at the suit of the proprietor of the copyright.

The 17th section of the same statute enacts, "that after the passing of this act, it shall not be lawful for any person, not the proprietor of the copyright or some one authorized by him, to import into the united kingdom, or other parts of the British dominions for sale or hire, any printed book, first composed or written, or printed and published, in the united kingdom, wherein there is copyright, and re-printed in any country or place out of the British dominions; and if any person, not the proprietor or party authorized by him, shall import or bring, or cause to be imported or brought, for sale or hire, any such printed book into the British dominions, contrary to this act; or shall knowingly sell, publish, or expose to sale, or let to hire, or have in his possession for sale or hire, any such book; then, every such book shall be forfeited, and be seized and destroyed by any officer of the customs or excise; and every person so offending shall, on due conviction before two magistrates of the county or place where such book is found, forfeit the sum of ten pounds, and double the value of every such book so unlawfully imported, sold, published, or exposed to sale, or let to hire, or had in possession for sale or hire; five pounds of this penalty are to go to the officer of customs or excise making the seizure, and the remainder to the proprietor of the copyright."[1]

Pursuant to the 23d section of the same act, "all copies of any book having copyright, and entered in the registry book, which have been unlawfully printed or imported, without the previous written consent of the registered proprietor of the copyright, shall

[1] 5 & 6 Vict. c. 45, § 17. A subsequent act, 5 & 6 Vict. c. 47, § 23, a statute relating to the customs, absolutely prohibits the importation of foreign reprints of works having copyright, where the proprietor of the copyright or his agent has given notice in writing to the commissioners of the customs, that such copyright subsists, and when it will expire.

be deemed the property of such registered proprietor; and after demand in writing he will be entitled to sue for and recover such printed copies, or damages for their detention, in an action of detinue, from any party detaining them, or to sue for and recover damages for their conversion in an action of trover."[1]

The 16th section of the 5 & 6 Vict. c. 45, enacts, that after the passing of that act, in any action brought within the British dominions against a person for printing a pirated book for sale, hire, or exportation, or for importing, selling, publishing, or exposing it to sale or hire, or causing it to be imported, sold, published, or exposed to sale or hire, the defendant, on pleading to the action, shall give to the plaintiff a notice in writing of any objections on which he means to rely on the trial of the action. If the nature of the defence be, that the plaintiff in the action is not the author or first publisher of the book in which by the action he claims copyright, or that he is not the proprietor of the copyright, or that some other person than the plaintiff is the author or first publisher or proprietor of the copyright, then the defendant must specify in his notice the name of the person he alleges to have been the author, first publisher, or proprietor of the copyright, together with the title of the book, and the time and place of its first publication; otherwise the defendant at the trial will not be

[1] 5 & 6 Vict. c. 45, § 23. See post, p. 76.

allowed to give any evidence that the plaintiff is not the author, first publisher, or proprietor of the copyright. At the trial also no other objection will be allowed to be made on behalf of the defendant than the objections stated in his notice, nor can it then be urged that any other person is the author, first publisher, or proprietor, of the copyright, than the person specified in the defendant's notice; nor can any other book be given in evidence in support of the defence than the one substantially corresponding in title, time, and place of publication with the title, time, and place specified in the notice.

The 26th section enacts, that if any action or suit be commenced or brought against any person for doing or causing to be done anything in pursuance of this act, the defendant may plead the general issue, and give the special matter in evidence; and if upon such action a verdict be given for the defendant, or the plaintiff become nonsuited, or discontinue his action, then the defendant shall have and recover his full costs, for which he shall have the same remedy as a defendant has by law in any case.

The 26th section of the same statute enacts, that all actions, suits, bills, indictments, or informations for any offence committed against this act shall be commenced within twelve calendar months after the committing of the offence, or the same shall be void and of none effect; provided, that such limitation shall not extend to any actions, suits, or proceedings commenced under this act in respect of copies of books required to be delivered to the British Museum and the four other libraries.

The 21st section of the 5 & 6 Vict. c. 45, gives to the proprietors of the right of dramatic or musical representation or performance during the term of their interest, all the remedies provided by the 3 W. IV. c. 15. By the 3 W. IV. c. 15, § 2, it is enacted, that if any person, during the continuance of the exclusive right of representing a dramatic piece, cause to be represented, without the author's or proprietor's previous written consent, such production at any place of dramatic entertainment within the British dominions, every such offender shall, for each representation, be liable to the payment of not less than 40*s.*, or of the full amount of the advantage arising from the representation, or of the loss sustained by the plaintiff, whichever shall be the greater damage. These penalties are recoverable by the author or proprietor, together with double costs of suit in any court having jurisdiction in such cases, in that part of the British dominions where the offence is committed. Pursuant to the 24th section of the 5 & 6 Vict. c. 45, the right to recover these penalties is not prejudiced by an omission to register on the part of the proprietor of the sole liberty of representing a dramatic piece.

The 3d section of the 3 W. IV. c. 15, provides that all actions or proceedings for any offence or injury against that act shall be commenced within twelve calendar months from the committing of the offence, or else the same shall be void and of no effect.

By the 8 Geo. II. c. 13, any person pirating a print or engraving is made liable to forfeit the plate on which such print shall be copied, and every sheet whereon such print shall be copied or printed to the proprietor of the original, who is forthwith to destroy the same; and the offender is further to forfeit five shillings for every print found in his custody, one moiety to the king, and the other to any person who shall sue for the same. And by the 17 Geo. III. c. 57, extended to Ireland by the 6 & 7 W. IV. c. 59, persons pirating such prints are made liable to an action on the case for damages at the suit of the proprietor, together with double costs.

The 3d section of the 54 Geo. III. c. 56, enacts that if any person, within the term of copyright, make or import, or cause to be made, imported, exposed to sale, or otherwise disposed of, a pirated copy or pirated cast of any original sculpture or other matter abovementioned, whether such pirated copy or cast be produced by moulding, copying, or other means of imitation, to the detriment, damage, or loss of the proprietor, then such proprietor or his assignee may, by special action on the case, recover against a person so offending such damages as a jury may assess at the time, together with double costs of suit.

Pursuant to the fifth section of the same act, all actions for piracy of sculpture must be brought within six calendar months after the discovery of the offence.

In the United States, the statute of 1831 provides penalties to be recovered by action of debt, one moiety to the use of the proprietor of the copyright, and the other moiety to the use of the United States.[1] No action on the case for damages is provided by statute; but there can be no doubt that here, as well as in England, such an action lies at common law.

The statute also inflicts a forfeiture of the pirated copies of the book, in addition to the other penalties;[2] and for a false representation that a book has been entered for copyright according to the requirements of the statute, it inflicts a forfeiture of one hundred dollars, to be recovered by action of debt, one moiety to the use of the person who shall sue for the same, and one moiety to the use of the United States.[3]

The 10th section provides, that if any person or persons shall be sued or prosecuted, for any matter, act, or thing done under or by virtue of this act, he or they may plead the general issue, and give the special matter in evidence.[4]

The 13th section limits the right of action to two years after the cause of action shall have arisen.[5]

The penalties for violating the copyright of maps,

[1] The penalties are fifty cents for every sheet in the party's possession, printed or printing, published, imported or exposed to sale. Act of Cong. 3d February, 1831, § 6. See Appendix, p. 95.

[2] Ibid.

[3] Ibid. § 11.

[4] Ibid. § 10.

[5] Ibid. § 13.

charts, musical compositions, engravings, cuts or prints, are, the forfeiture of the plate or plates, and of one dollar for every sheet found in the possession of the party, printed or published, or exposed to sale, the one moiety to the true proprietor, and the other moiety to the use of the United States.[1]

The printing or publishing any manuscript whatever, without the consent of the author or legal proprietor first obtained, (if such author or proprietor be a citizen of the United States or resident therein,) renders the party liable to suffer and pay to the author or proprietor all damages occasioned by such injury, to be recovered by a special action on the case founded upon the statute, in any court having cognizance thereof; and the several courts of the United States empowered to grant injunctions to prevent the violation of the rights of authors and inventors, are empowered to grant injunctions in like manner, according to the principles of equity, to restrain such publications of manuscripts.[2]

2. Remedies in Equity.

The jurisdiction of courts of equity, in cases of copyright, is exercised by injunction, and extends, incidentally, to the taking an account of the damages occasioned by the piratical publication.

The ground upon which a court of equity exercises its jurisdiction, is, that damages do not give adequate

[1] § 7.

[2] § 9. See post, pp. 329, 330, et seq.

relief; and that the sale of copies by the defendant is in each instance not only taking away the profit upon the individual work, which the plaintiff probably would have sold, but that it may injure him to an incalculable extent, which no inquiry for the purpose of damages can ascertain. A court of equity therefore acts with a view to make the legal right effectual, by preventing the publication altogether.[1]

In general, when proceedings are instituted to obtain the interference of a court of equity, it is necessary for the plaintiff to show a *prima facie* legal title. If the author of the book is himself the plaintiff, he alleges in his bill, or in an affidavit accompanying it, his title by authorship; and, in the United States, it is necessary to offer proof that he has complied with the statute directions for securing his right, though in England it is not necessary to relief in equity that the book should have been entered at stationers' hall.[2] It is not, however, indispensable to relief, that the party should have a strictly legal title. It is sufficient that he has a clear equitable title. Formerly, courts of equity would not interfere, by way of injunction, to protect copyrights or patents, until the title had been established at law. But the present course is to exercise jurisdiction, in all cases where there is a clear color of title, founded on long possession, and assertion of right.[3]

[1] Hogg *v.* Kirby, 8 Ves. 215, 225. Wilkins *v.* Aiken, 17 Ves. 422, 424. Lawrence *v.* Smith, Jacobs R. 471. 2 Story's Eq. Jurisp. § 930, 933.

[2] Rundell *v.* Murray, Jacobs R. 314.

[3] 2 Story's Eq. Jurisp. § 935. Mawman *v.* Tegg, 2 Russ. 385.

But if the plaintiff claims as assignee of the author's title, he must, by affidavit or otherwise, show that his title came by written assignment.[1] He must make a particular title; it is not enough to say that he has acquired the copyright, but he must trace his title to the author or his assignee, who alone have title under the statute.[2] But if the plaintiff claims as assignee of an assignee, it seems that he will not be put to prove the original assignment to his assignor, but the proof of want of title will be thrown on the defendant;[3] and the court will interfere at the suit of plaintiffs who have a good equitable title, even though it should not be quite clear that their legal title is complete.[4]

Where a fair doubt appears as to the plaintiff's legal right, the court directs it to be tried at law, making in the interim the best provision it can, for the benefit of both parties.[5] An injunction should be granted and maintained, in the interim, if the defendant's publication is prejudicial to the plaintiff, although the plaintiff's right admits of a fair doubt; and an action should be brought forthwith to try it.[6] But in cases of works, the whole value of which arises from a temporary demand, the court acts upon the opposite principle, and if there is a doubt as to

[1] Morris *v.* Kelley, 1 Jac. & W. 481.

[2] Gilliver *v.* Snaggs, 2 Eq. Abr. 522. 4 Viner's Abr. 278, A. 4.

[3] Morris *v.* Kelley, 1 Jac. & W. 481.

[4] Mawman *v.* Tegg, 2 Russ. 385.

[5] Wilkins *v.* Aiken, 17 Ves. 422. Bramhall *v.* Holcomb, 3 M. & Cr. 737.

[6] Ibid. Universities of Oxford and Cambridge *v.* Richardson, 6 Ves. 689, 707.

the legal right, does not grant the injunction before a trial at law, where it would work an irremediable injury to the defendant.[1]

[1] Spottiswoode *v.* Clarke, 2 Phillips's Ch. R. 154. In this case the lord chancellor laid down the principles which ought to govern the discretion of the court, as follows: "I have often expressed my opinion that unless a case of this kind, depending upon a legal right, is very clear, it is the duty of the court to take care that the right be ascertained before it exercises its jurisdiction by injunction. The first question to be determined is as to the legal right, and if the court doubts about that, it may commit great injustice by interfering until that question has been decided.

"One objection to that course is, that it compels future litigation, for it orders the plaintiff to bring an action; whereas, by adopting the alternative course — suspending the injunction, with liberty to the plaintiff to bring an action — it enables him to pause a little, and consider whether it is worth his while to embark in such a course of litigation as will be necessary to establish the right on which he insists. A second objection is, that the court, in granting the injunction, is expressing a strong opinion upon the legal question, before that question is discussed in the proper tribunal. It is much better, if the legal right is to be litigated, that this court should abstain from expressing any opinion upon it in the mean time.

"But the greatest of all objections is, that the court runs the risk of doing the greatest injustice in case its opinion upon the legal right should turn out to be erroneous. Here is a publication, which, if not issued this month, will lose a great part of its sale for the ensuing year. If you restrain the party from selling immediately, you probably make it impossible for him to sell at all. You take property out of his pocket and give it to nobody. In such a case, if the plaintiff is right, the court has some means, at least, of indemnifying him, by making the defendant keep an account; whereas, if the defendant be right, and he be restrained, it is utterly impossible to give him compensation for the loss he will have sustained. And the effect of the order in that event will be to commit a great and irremediable injury. Unless, therefore, the court is quite clear as to what are the legal rights of the parties, it is much the safest course to abstain from exercising its jurisdiction till the legal right has been determined.

"In the course of the argument cases of trade-marks were referred to; but trade-marks have nothing to do with this case. Take a piece of steel: the mark of the manufacturer from which it comes is the only indication to the eye of the customer of the quality of the article; so it is of blacking, or any other article of manufacture, the particular quality of which is not discernible by the eye. But these cases are quite different from the present case, in which, if you are deceived at all, it is not by the eye. The size, the color, the engravings are all different in the two works, so that no one who sees the two could mistake the one for the other. At the same time I must say, that there is in the descriptions given of the two works a very remarkable coincidence of ideas in the plaintiff and defendant, if the

It seems to have been Lord Eldon's practice, not to grant an injunction before trial, where the doubt as to the plaintiff's legal right arose from the character of the work. In one case, having, from inspection of the book, a doubt whether it would be held entitled to protection at law, because it impugned the doctrine of the immortality of the soul, he refused to assist such a doubtful right by injunction.[1] So, also, in Mr. Southey's case, he acted upon the same doctrine, without considering it necessary to determine positively whether the work was innocent or not, although the author had never published it, and wished to restrain its publication altogether, having changed his opinions.[2]

Even in cases where the plaintiff can only have an injunction, and from any cause it should be impossible to take an account, the plaintiff is entitled to the injunction.[3] So, too, where the injury is only threatened, the party has a right to the injunction, to prevent that mischief, if the circumstances warrant it, though no account is required to be taken.[4]

two wrappers be supposed to have been designed independently of each other. It is difficult to believe that that was pure accident; though if any fraud was intended, it certainly was a very clumsy one.

"I am not, however, so satisfied that this is a case in which the plaintiff has a legal right against the defendant as to justify me in restraining the latter from the sale of his work, until that right has been established in the proper tribunal. Therefore the injunction must be dissolved, the defendant keeping an account, and the plaintiff to be at liberty to bring an action."

1 Lawrence *v.* Smith, Jacobs R. 471.

2 Southey *v.* Sherwood, 2 Meriv. 435.

3 Universities of Oxford and Cambridge *v.* Richardson, 6 Ves. 689, 707.

4 Ibid.

But wherever an injunction is granted, the plaintiff is entitled to go on and take the account, as incidental relief, in addition to the relief by injunction.[1]

It has also been suggested, by Lord Eldon, that in some cases it may be proper to direct an issue of *quantum damnificatus*, where the plaintiff can show that the profits handed over to him by the defendant are not a satisfaction for the injury done to him.[2]

The court will not interfere by injunction in the first instance, where the plaintiff has for a long time acquiesced in the violation of his rights, but will leave him to an action at law;[3] and where the con-

[1] Grierson *v.* Eyre, 9 Ves. 341. Universities of Oxford and Cambridge *v.* Richardson, 6 Ves. 705, 706. Baily *v.* Taylor, 1 Russ. & M. 73. Sheriff *v.* Coates, 1 Russ. & M. 159. 2 Story's Eq. Jurisp. § 933. Eden on Injunctions, ch. xii. p. 261, ch. xiii. p. 364.

[2] Mawman *v.* Tegg, 2 Russ. 385, 400. The following are his lordship's observations: "Another way of ascertaining the facts of the case is to send it to a jury; and, in either of those ways of disposing of it, the court will order the defendant to keep an account of the profits in the mean time. But one difficulty in all these cases is, that though keeping an account of the profits may prevent the defendant from deriving any profit, as he may ultimately be obliged to account to the plaintiff for all his gains, yet if the work which the defendant is publishing in the meantime, really affects the sale of the work which the plaintiff seeks to protect, the consequence is, that the rendering the profits of the former work to the complaining party may not be a satisfaction to him for what he might have been enabled to have made of his own work, if it had been the only one published; for he would argue, that the profits of the defendant, as compared with the profits which he, the plaintiff, has been improperly prevented from making, could only be in the proportion of eight shillings, the price of a copy of the one book, to one guinea, the price of a copy of the other. If the principle, upon which the court acts, is, that satisfaction is to be made to the plaintiff, I cannot see, though I never knew it done, why, if a party succeeds at law in proving the piracy, the court should not give him leave to go on to ascertain, if he can, his damages at law; or if, after applying the profits which are handed over to him by the defendants, he can show that they were not a satisfaction for the injury done to him, I cannot see why the court might not in such a case direct an issue to try what further damnification the plaintiff had sustained."

[3] Platt *v.* Button, 19 Ves. 447. Rundell *v.* Murray, Jacobs R. 314.

duct of the plaintiff has been such as to induce the defendant to believe that the publication of the latter would not be objected to, the court will not interfere by injunction, until after a trial at law.[1]

Where there is a dispute as to the construction of an agreement between the parties, the court will not grant an injunction, until the effect of the agreement has been established at law.[2]

Where the plaintiff states circumstances which are not denied, showing that he is entitled to an equitable copyright in a work, the court, in directing an action to be brought by him, to determine the question of piracy, will direct the defendant, for the purposes of the action, to admit a legal copyright in the plaintiff.[3]

In exercising its jurisdiction, the court has first to decide whether there ought to be an injunction; and if there is to be an injunction, it has next to determine, whether the injunction shall be against the whole work, or only against a part of it. The extent to which the injunction ought to go, must in each case depend on the particular circumstances of that case.[4]

The manner in which the injunction is to issue, and the extent to which it is to be applied to the

But if the delay in making application to the court can be accounted for, the plaintiff will lose none of his rights. Mawman v. Tegg, 2 Russ. 393.

[1] Saunders v. Smith, 3 M. & Cr. 711.

[2] Walcott v. Walker, 7 Ves. 1. Lowndes v. Duncombe, 1 Law Jour. 51.

[3] Sweet v. Shaw, 17 Law Journ. 216.

[4] Mawman v. Tegg, 2 Russ. 393.

work of the defendant, may cause some embarrassment, where a part only of the defendant's book has been borrowed from that of the plaintiff. The general principle upon which the court proceeds in the exercise of its jurisdiction, is, that in order to amount to an infringement, so that an injunction ought to be granted, it is not necessary that there should be a complete copy or imitation throughout; but only that there should be an important and valuable portion, which operates injuriously to the copyright of the plaintiff.[1] Wherever it appears by sufficient evidence that a copyright exists, and that piracy has been committed to an extent which is likely to be seriously prejudicial to the plaintiff, an injunction ought to be granted, the extent of which must depend on the amount of the piracy proved, and the nature of the work.[2]

[1] Emerson *v.* Davies, 3 Story's R. 768, 795; Wilkins *v.* Aiken, 17 Ves. 422; Bramhall *v.* Holcomb, 3 M. & Cr. 737; Campbell *v.* Scott, 11 Simons, 31; Mawman *v.* Tegg, 2 Russ. 385, 397, 400. In Campbell *v* Scott, Lord Cottenham said, "If the court clearly sees that there has been anything done which tends to an injury, I cannot but think that the safest rule is to follow the legal right and grant the injunction." Sir J. Leach, V. C., directed an injunction, to "restrain the publication of any works or work in which the matter of the plaintiff's publication, or any part thereof, was verbally or substantially introduced." See Pinnock *v.* Rose, cited 2 Bro. Ch. R. 85, n.

[2] Lewis *v.* Fullerton, 2 Beavan, 6. Lord Langdale, M. R., in this case, said, "I conceive that when it has been ascertained that the defendant has in any degree violated the right of the plaintiff, the nature and extent of the order to be made must depend on the circumstances of the cases, and the amount and extent of the evidence adduced. The piracy proved may be so inconsiderable, and so little likely to injure the plaintiff, that the court may decline to interfere at all, and may leave the plaintiff to his remedy at law; or the piracy proved may be extensive in a greater or less degree, such as to leave it extremely doubtful whether the parts not examined are in any degree piratical, or such as to make it more or less probable that they have been composed in the same manner, collected from the like sources as the parts which have been examined, and are in an equal degree liable to the charge of piracy.

Notwithstanding the effect of an injunction against parts of a book may be to destroy it altogether, if

"The hardship of restraining, or doing that which is equivalent to restraining the whole of a work, when part of it consists of original matter, has always been urged in cases of this nature, and the answer which is given by Lord Eldon, in the case to which I have already referred, seems conclusive: 'If the parts which have been copied cannot be separated from those which are original without destroying the use and value of the original matter, he who has made an improper use of that which did not belong to him must suffer the consequences of so doing; if a man mixes what belongs to him with what belongs to me, and the mixture be forbidden by the law, he must again separate them, and he must bear all the mischief and loss which the separation may occasion. If an individual chooses in any work to mix my literary matter with his own, he must be restrained from publishing the literary matter which belongs to me; and if the other parts of the work cannot be separated, and if by that means the injunction which restrained the publication of my literary matter prevents also the publication of his own literary matter, he has only himself to blame.'

"In cases of this nature, it must be observed, that nothing but an injunction can sufficiently protect the injured party. In the same case Lord Eldon has observed that, 'though keeping an account of the profits may prevent the defendant from deriving any profit, as he may ultimately be obliged to account to the plaintiff for all his gains, yet if the work which the defendant is publishing in the meantime really affects the sale of the work which the plaintiff seeks to protect, the consequence is, that the rendering the profits of the former work to the complaining party, may not be a satisfaction to him, for what he might have been enabled to have made of his own work, if it had been the only one published; for he would argue, that the profits of the defendant, as compared with the profits which he, the plaintiff, has been improperly prevented from making, could only be in the proportion of the price of a copy of the one book to the price of a copy of the other.' On the whole, for the reasons thus stated, it appears to me, that an injunction ought to be granted, whenever it appears, by sufficient evidence, that a copyright exists, and that piracy has been committed to an extent which is likely to be seriously prejudicial to the plaintiff; and that the extent of the injunction must depend on the amount of proof and the nature of the work. The plaintiffs in the present case ask for an injunction, to restrain the defendant from publishing the whole or any part of the defendant's gazetteer. As it appears from the evidence that there are parts of the defendant's gazetteer which are not borrowed from the plaintiff's work, I cannot grant an injunction in those terms; and it becomes a question, whether an injunction should be granted in general terms against such parts as have been pirated, or whether means should be taken to ascertain what particular parts have been pirated, in order that the publication of those particular parts may be restrained. Now it appears to me, not, it must be admitted, by absolute proof and demonstration, for the two works have not been examined in every part, but upon proof and demonstrathe piracy is proved, these consequences will not avert the injunction, even if the other parts of the book be wholly original.[1]

tion as to part, and as to the rest by strong inference and presumption, arising from the proof given as to those parts to which the proof applies, and from the nature of the work and the circumstances under which it is proved to have been composed, that if the parts pirated were taken away, though some articles would remain in their entirety, yet the greater number would be left in a state so imperfect and incomplete, that the defendant's work would lose its distinctive and useful character as a gazetteer.

"If the defendant were desirous to avail himself, as he has an undoubted right to do, of any original matter of his own, or of any matter which he has fairly taken from other sources, he would, I think, be under the necessity of recomposing his work, for the purpose of separating that which appears to me to have been improperly taken from the plaintiff's work. Lord Eldon says, (2 Russ. 399,) 'In the cases which have come before me, my language has been, that there must be an injunction against such part as has been pirated, but in those cases the part of the work which was affected with the character of piracy was so very considerable, that if it were taken away, there would have been nothing left to publish except a few broken sentences;' and it was because the evidence before him did not enable him to approach sufficiently to that result, that he made the particular order which he did in that case.

"But in this case, having availed myself of the evidence which has been so industriously collected during the long time that this motion was pending, and having read with great care all the affidavits laid before me, and more particularly the affidavits of Mr. Holliday and Mr. Cunningham, I think that I have reasons on which I ought judicially to act, for considering, that the parts of the works which have been examined and compared, afford fair indications of the nature and character of those parts of the works which have not yet been examined and compared; and it appearing to me, under these circumstances, that if the parts affected with the character of piracy were taken away, there would be left, I cannot say nothing but a few broken sentences, but there would be left an imperfect work, which could not, to any useful extent, serve the purposes of a gazetteer, I think that I ought to grant an injunction, to restrain the publication of the parts which are pirated, without waiting till all the parts which have been pirated can be distinctly specified; and therefore the order which I shall make will be: Let the defendant, his agents, servants and workmen be restrained from further printing, publishing, selling or otherwise disposing of any copy or copies of a book called 'A New and Comprehensive Gazetteer,' &c., containing any articles or article, passages or passage, copied, taken or colorably altered from a book called 'The Topographical Dictionary of England,' published by the plaintiffs."

[1] In Mawman *v.* Tegg, 2 Russ. 390, Lord Eldon said, "As to the hard consequences which would follow from granting an injunction,

The court, however, seldom grants an injunction against the whole of a work, without having first ascertained, either by inspection or by reference to a master, the quantity of matter pirated. Where the extracts are trifling, the court will not interfere.[1] But in order to ascertain how the injunction is to be applied, the quantity of matter pirated by the defendant ought to be ascertained.[2] Where, however, a considerable portion of the defendant's publication has thus proved to be pirated, the court will grant an injunction to restrain the publication of the parts which are pirated, without waiting till all the parts pirated can be ascertained.[3]

In a later case, the alleged piracy consisted in taking from a periodical work devoted to reports of cases in the courts of law. It was objected that the plaintiff did not specifically point out what were the articles in which he claimed copyright, but the court held that was not necessary, as in voluminous works

when a very large proportion of the work is unquestionably original, I can only say, that, if the parts, which have been copied, cannot be separated from those which are original, without destroying the use and value of the original matter, he who has made an improper use of that which did not belong to him must suffer the consequences of so doing. If a man mixes what belongs to him with what belongs to me, and the mixture be forbidden by the law, he must again separate them, and he must bear all the mischief and loss which the separation may occasion. If an individual chooses in any work to mix my literary matter with his own, he must be restrained from publishing the literary matter which belongs to me; and if the parts of the work cannot be separated. and if by that means the injunction, which restrained the publication of my literary matter, prevents also the publication of his own literary matter, he has only himself to blame." See also Emerson *v.* Davies, 3 Story's R. 768, 795, 796; Folsom *v.* Marsh, 2 Story's R. 100, 119.

[1] Bell *v.* Whitehead, 17 Law J. 141.

[2] Mawman *v.* Tegg, 2 Russ. 398.

[3] Lewis *v.* Fullerton, 17 Law J. 291; S. C. 2 Beavan, 6.

the practice is to point out some specific acts of piracy, as evidence of infringement, and then, if the injunction is granted at all, it is granted generally.[1]

In general, if the court sees strong ground for supposing that the defendant's work is a violation of the plaintiff's copyright, the course is, to grant an injunction *ex parte*, until answer or further order. Then, in order to ascertain the fact of piracy or no piracy, it is referred to a master to examine into the originality of the new book,[2] or the court takes upon itself the inspection of both works.[3] Where the works are long and of a complex character, containing original matter mixed with much that is common property, they will be referred to a master ;[4] but where they are of a class affording facility for the detection of piracy by immediate inspection, the court will examine them.[5]

This is the practice in the courts of the United States, as well as in England.[6]

When the master reports that the two books are in parts different and in parts the same, an injunction will be granted against those parts of the defendant's book, which are similar to parts of the

[1] Sweet *v.* Mangham, 9 Law J. 323 ; 4 Jurist, 479.

[2] Carnan *v.* Bowles, 2 Bro. C. R. 80 ; 1 Cox, 283 ; Bell *v.* Walker, 1 Br. C. R. 451 ; —— *v.* Leadbetter, 4 Ves. 681.

[3] Butterworth *v.* Robinson, 5 Ves. 709.

[4] —— *v.* Leadbetter, 4 Ves. 681.

[5] Butterworth *v.* Robinson, 5 Ves. 709 ; Whittingham *v.* Wooler, 2 Swanst. 431.

[6] Gray *v.* Russell, 1 Story's R. 11 ; Folsom *v.* Marsh, 2 Story's R. 100 ; Emerson *v.* Davies, 3 Story's R. 768.

plaintiff's.[1] But where the master reported that the books were not the same, but that one was a description of roads by letter press, and the other a description as to the greater part by maps, and as to the remainder by letter press, but that the roads were in substance the same, the court referred it back to the master, to inquire whether the defendant's was a *new and original* work.[2]

Courts of equity do not redress, by the summary process of injunction, injuries of a very trifling character, but leave the party to his remedy at law. Thus, where the defendant had, in two numbers of a periodical work of theatrical criticism, inserted detached extracts, to the extent of six or seven pages, from a farce, the property of the plaintiff's, containing forty pages, interspersed with criticisms, a bill for a perpetual injunction and an account of the profits of the numbers, which amounted to not £3, was dismissed with costs.[3] So too, where the defendant had copied from the plaintiff's work, certain tables of calculations, and it was in evidence that the tables might be calculated anew in a very short time and at an expense of about £7 10s., which would have given him a complete title to publish them, an injunction was refused.[4]

1 Carnan *v.* Bowles, 2 Bro. Ch. R. 80.

2 Ibid.

3 Whittingham *v.* Wooler, 2 Swanst. 428. There was also, in this case, the additional circumstance, that the defendant had probably not transcended the limits of fair quotation for the purposes of criticism. See also Webb *v.* Powers, 10 Law Rep. 152; S. C. 1 Woodbury's R.

4 Baily *v.* Taylor, 1 Russ. & M. 73. In this case the bill was filed

But where an injunction was granted on filing the bill, and afterwards the cause was brought to a hearing, and it was contended that on account of the trifling character of the injury, the defendant ought not to pay costs, it was held, that the defendant ought to have tendered the costs after the injunction was granted, and having refused to do so, he must pay the costs of the suit.[1]

In most cases, the bill seeks an account of the books printed, and of the profits thereof, from the person who has pirated from the plaintiff's work, as well as an injunction. If the cause is brought to a hearing, and a perpetual injunction is decreed, the plaintiff will have a right to have the account decreed as incidental, in addition to the other relief by injunction, unless the amount would be very trifling.[2]

But in order to obtain an account, it is necessary that the plaintiff should entitle himself to an injunction, since the account is a relief strictly incidental to the injunction.[3] The account is in practice gen-

after the defendant's work had been published ten years.

[1] Fradella *v.* Weller, 2 Russ. & M. 247. In this case, it was held not to be necessary, though usual, to produce the pirated prints, or any of them, where the fact of the prints being a piracy was proved, and not denied by the answer. As to the recovery of costs, where the plaintiff has been compelled to bring the cause to a hearing, notwithstanding the defendant's submission, see Kelly *v.* Hooper, 1 Y. & Col. Ch. R. 197.

[2] Hogg *v.* Kirby, 8 Ves. 323–325. Universities of Oxford and Cambridge *v.* Richardson, 6 Ves. 705, 706. Bailey *v.* Taylor, 1 Russ & M. 73. Sheriff *v.* Coates, 1 Russ. & M. 159. Kelly *v.* Hooper, 1 Y. & Col. Ch. R. 197. 2 Story's Eq. Jurisp. § 933. Mitford's Eq. Pl. by Jeremy, 138. Eden on Injunctions, ch. 12, p. 261; ch. 13, p. 364.

[3] Baily *v.* Taylor, 1 Russ. & M. 73.

erally waived; but where it is not, the court grants it, upon principles which have been thus stated by Sir J. Wigram, V. C. "It is true, that the court does not, by an account, accurately measure the damage sustained by the proprietor of an expensive work from the invasion of his copyright by the publication of a cheaper book. It is impossible to know how many copies of the dearer book are excluded from sale by the interposition of the cheaper one. The court, by the account, as the nearest approximation which it can make to justice, takes from the wrong-doer all the profits he has made by his piracy, and gives them to the party who has been wronged. In doing this the court may often give the injured party more, in fact, than he is entitled to, for *non constat* that a single additional copy of the more expensive book would have been sold, if the injury by the sale of the cheaper book had not been committed. The court of equity, however, does not give anything beyond the account."[1]

The delivery up of copies of the unlawful publication is supposed to depend entirely upon statute. However it might have been regarded in England, if the common law right of authors had not been abrogated by the decision in Donaldson *v.* Beckett, it has been held, that there is now no common law right in the author or proprietor of a book which is pirated, to the delivery up of the copies of the illegal work;

[1] Colburn *v.* Simms, 2 Hare, 560.

and therefore if such relief is given in equity, it must be under the provisions of some statute.[1]

The act 54 Geo. III. c. 156, § 4, does not authorize the delivery up of the copies of a pirated book, unless the genuine work had been duly registered as well as composed at the time the act is done to which the penalty and forfeiture would attach.[2] The same requisite is contained in the 5 & 6 Vict. c. 45, § 23.[3]

The jurisdiction of the courts of the United States, in cases of copyright depends upon a statute passed February 15, 1819, by which it is enacted, "That

[1] Colburn *v.* Simms, 2 Hare, 554. In this case, Sir J. Wigram, V. C. said, "There would be great difficulty in applying to this subject the principles of the common law, which in certain cases give to the owner of an original material the right of seizing it, in whatever shape it may be found, if he can prove it it to be his own; or which relate to what is termed confusion of goods, by which, if one man voluntarily mixes his property with that of another, so that the two becomes inseparable, the entirety is held to belong to him whose property has been invaded. It may be true, that, if one writes or prints upon the paper of another, the writing or printing becomes his to whom the paper belongs, but it does not necessarily follow that the converse of that proposition would be true, — that one who writes or prints upon his own paper the composition of another, has thereby so mixed his property with the property of the author whose work he has copied, that he has lost his original title to the material which he has so employed. There might indeed have been some countenance for such a principle before the judgment of the house of lords, in the case of Donaldson *v.* Beckett, had confined the exclusive right of authors within the limits prescribed by the statute, and thereby negatived the existence of that absolute common law right in their works which had been previously supposed to exist, and which the decision of the court of king's bench, in the case of Millar *v.* Taylor, had tended to affirm. I think, therefore, the case for the plaintiff on this point must be placed on another ground, and that his right to a decree of this court for the delivery up of the copies, if that right exists, must be found within the provisions of the statutes, and not upon any common law right independent of them."

[2] Ibid.

[3] See Appendix, p. 76.

the circuit courts of the United States shall have original cognizance, as well in equity as at law, of all actions, suits, controversies and cases, arising under any law of the United States, granting or confirming to authors or inventors, the exclusive right to their respective writings, inventions, and discoveries; and upon any bill in equity, filed by any party aggrieved in any such cases, shall have authority to grant injunctions, according to the course and principles of courts of equity, to prevent the violation of the rights of any authors or inventors, secured to them by any laws of the United States, on such terms and conditions as the said courts may deem fit and reasonable: Provided, however, That from all judgments and decrees of any circuit courts, rendered in the premises, a writ of error or appeal, as the case may require, shall lie to the supreme court of the United States, in the same manner and under the same circumstances, as is now provided by law in other judgments and decrees of such circuit courts."[1]

The jurisdiction conferred by this act is ample. It embraces all cases, both at law and in equity, arising under the laws which protect patents and copyrights, without regard to the citizenship of the parties, or the amount in controversy. The act of 1831, which gives a special action on the case for damages, for the unlawful printing or publishing of any manuscript, makes such damages recoverable in any court

[1] Act of Congress, February 15, 1819, ch. xix. 3 U. S. Statutes at large, p. 481.

having cognizance thereof; and also empowers the courts of the United States, which are authorized to grant injunctions to prevent the violation of the rights of authors and inventors, to grant injunctions in like manner, according to the principles of equity, to restrain such publication of manuscripts.[1]

The circuit courts of the United States, therefore, may entertain actions at law, to recover damages for the unlawful publication of any printed book, under the protection of copyright, or of any manuscript whatever; and may also entertain bills in equity for injunctions to restrain and prevent such publications; although both the parties are citizens of the same state, and although the value in controversy may not exceed five hundred dollars.

[1] Act of Congress, February 3, 1831, § 9.

APPENDIX.

BRITISH STATUTES.

8 Anne, c. 19. — An Act for the Encouragement of Learning, by vesting the Copies of printed Books in the Authors or Purchasers of such Copies, during the Times therein mentioned.

8 Anne, c. 19.

See the case of Miller *v.* Taylor, in 4 Bur. 2303 to 2418.

"WHEREAS printers booksellers and other persons have of late frequently taken the liberty of printing reprinting and publishing or causing to be printed reprinted and published books and other writings without the consent of the authors or proprietors of such books and writings to their very great detriment and too often to the ruin of them and their families:" For preventing therefore such practices for the future and for the encouragement of learned men to compose and write useful books; May it please your Majesty that it may be enacted; and be it enacted by the Queen's most excellent Majesty, by and with the advice and consent of the Lords Spiritual and Temporal and Commons in this present Parliament assembled, and by the authority of the same, That from and after the tenth day of *April* one thousand seven hundred and ten the author of any book or books already printed who hath not transferred to any other the copy or copies of such book or books share or shares thereof, or the bookseller or booksellers printer or printers or other person or persons who hath or have purchased or acquired the copy or copies of any book or books in order to print or reprint the same shall have the sole right

After 10 April 1710, the authors of books already printed, who have not transferred their rights, and the booksellers, &c. who have purchased

8 Anne, c. 19.

copies, shall have the sole right of printing them for the term of 21 years.

And the authors of books not printed to have the sole right of printing for fourteen years.

and liberty of printing such book and books for the term of one-and-twenty years to commence from the said tenth day of *April* and no longer; and that the author of any book or books already composed and not printed and published or that shall hereafter be composed and his assignee or assigns shall have the sole liberty of printing and reprinting such book and books for the term of fourteen years to commence from the day of the first publishing the same and no longer; and that if any other bookseller printer or other person whatsoever from and after the tenth day of *April* one thousand seven hundred and ten, within the times granted and limited by this Act as aforesaid, shall print reprint or import or cause to be printed reprinted or imported any such book or books without the consent of the proprietor or proprietors thereof first had and obtained in writing signed in the presence of two or more credible witnesses; or knowing the same to be so printed or reprinted without the consent of the proprietors, shall sell publish or expose to sale or cause to be sold published or exposed to sale any such book or books without such consent first had and obtained as aforesaid: then such offender or offenders shall forfeit such book or books and all and every sheet or sheets being part of such book or books to the proprietor or proprietors of the copy thereof who shall forthwith damask and make waste paper of them; and further, that every such offender or offenders shall forfeit one penny for every sheet which shall be found in his her or their custody either printed or printing published or exposed to sale contrary to the true intent and meaning of this Act; the one moiety thereof to the Queen's most excellent Majesty her heirs and successors, and the other moiety thereof to any person or persons that shall sue for the same, to be recovered in any of her Majesty's courts of record at *Westminster* by action of debt bill plaint or information in which no wager of law essoign privilege or protection or more than one imparlance shall be allowed.

Punishment of bookseller, &c. printing without consent of the proprietor.

II. "And whereas many persons may through ignorance offend against this Act, unless some provision be made whereby the property in every such book as is intended by this Act to be secured to the proprietor or proprietors thereof may be ascertained, as likewise the consent of such proprietor or proprietors for the printing or reprinting of such book or books may from time to time be known;" Be it therefore further enacted by the authority aforesaid, That nothing in this Act contained shall be construed to extend to subject any bookseller printer or other person whatsoever to the forfeitures or penalties therein mentioned for or by reason of the printing or reprinting of any book or books without such consent as aforesaid, unless the title to the copy of such book or books hereafter published shall, before such publication, be entered in the register book of the Company of Stationers in such manner as hath been usual, which register book shall at all times be kept at the hall of the said company, and unless such consent of the proprietor or proprietors be in like manner entered as aforesaid, for every of which several entries six pence shall be paid and no more; which said register-book may at all seasonable and convenient times be resorted to and inspected by any bookseller printer or other person for the purposes before mentioned without any fee or reward; and the clerk of the said Company of Stationers shall when and as often as thereunto required give a certificate under his hand of such entry or entries and for every such certificate may take a fee not exceeding six pence.

Copies of books to be entered before publication in the register book of the Company of Stationers; which may be inspected at any time without fee.

III. Provided nevertheless, That if the clerk of the said Company of Stationers for the time being shall refuse or neglect to register or make such entry or entries or to give such certificate, being thereunto required by the author or proprietor of such copy or copies in the presence of two or more credible witnesses, that then such person and persons so refusing, notice being first duly given of such refusal by an advertisement in the *Gazette*, shall have the like benefit as if such entry or entries certificate or certificates had been duly made and given; and that the clerks so refusing shall for any such offence forfeit to the proprietor of such copy or copies the

Penalty of the clerk refusing so to do.

8 Anne, c. 19.

sum of twenty pounds, to be recovered in any of her Majesty's courts of record at *Westminster* by action of debt bill plaint or information, in which no wager of law essoign privilege or protection or more than one imparlance shall be allowed.

After 25 March, the Archbishop of Canterbury, &c. to settle the prices of books, upon complaint made that they are unreasonable.

IV. Provided nevertheless and it is hereby further enacted by the authority aforesaid, That if any bookseller or booksellers printer or printers shall after the said five-and-twentieth day of *March* one thousand seven hundred and ten set a price upon or sell or expose to sale any book or books at such a price or rate as shall be conceived by any person or persons to be too high and unreasonable; it shall and may be lawful for any person or persons to make complaint thereof to the Lord Archbishop of *Canterbury* for the time being the Lord Chancellor or Lord Keeper of the great seal of *Great Britain* for the time being the Lord Bishop of *London* for the time being the Lord Chief Justice of the court of *Queen's Bench* the Lord Chief Justice of the court of *Common Pleas* the Lord Chief Baron of the court of *Exchequer* for the time being the Vice-Chancellors of the two universities for the time being in that part of *Great Britain* called *England* the Lord President of the sessions for the time being the Lord Justice General for the time being the Lord Chief Baron of the *Exchequer* for the time being the Rector of the college of *Edinburgh* for the time being in that part of *Great Britain* called *Scotland*; who or any one of them shall and have hereby full power and authority from time to time to send for summon or call before him or them such bookseller or booksellers printer or printers and to examine and inquire of the reason of the dearness and enhancement of the price or value of such book or books by him or them so sold or exposed to sale; and if upon such inquiry and examination it shall be found that the price of such book or books is enhanced or any wise too high or unreasonable, then and in such case the said Archbishop of *Canterbury* Lord Chancellor or Lord Keeper Bishop of *London* two Chief Justices Chief Baron Vice-Chancellors of the universities in that part of *Great*

Britain called *England* and the said Lord President of the sessions Lord Justice General Lord Chief Baron and Rector of the College of *Edinburgh* in that part of *Great Britain* called *Scotland*, or any one or more of them so inquiring and examining have hereby full power and authority to reform and redress the same and to limit and settle the price of every such printed book and books from time to time according to the best of their judgments and as to them shall seem just and reasonable; and in case of alteration of the rate or price from what was set or demanded by such bookseller or booksellers printer or printers to award and order such bookseller and booksellers printer and printers to pay all the costs and charges that the person or persons so complaining shall be put unto by reason of such complaint and of the causing such rate or price to be so limited and settled; all which shall be done by the said Archbishop of *Canterbury* Lord Chanceller or Lord Keeper Bishop of *London* two Chief Justices Chief Baron Vice-Chancellors of the two universities in that part of *Great Britain* called *England* and the said Lord President of the sessions Lord Justice General Lord Chief Baron and Rector of the college of *Edinburgh* in that part of *Great Britain* called *Scotland* or any one of them by writing under their hands and seals, and thereof public notice shall be forthwith given by the said bookseller or booksellers printer or printers by an advertisement in the *Gazette*; and if any bookseller or booksellers printer or printers shall after such settlement made of the said rate and price sell or expose to sale any book or books at a higher or greater price than what shall have been so limited and settled as aforesaid, then and in every such case such bookseller and booksellers printer and printers shall forfeit the sum of five pounds for every such book so by him her or them sold or exposed to sale; one moiety thereof to the Queen's most excellent Majesty her heirs and successors, and the other moiety to any person or persons that shall sue for the same, to be recovered with costs of suit in any of her Majesty's courts of record

8 Anne, c. 19.

and if altered from the price the bookseller set, may order him to pay costs to the party complaining.

Penalty on booksellers selling at higher rates.

This clause repealed by 15 Geo. II. c. 36.

8 Anne, c. 19.

at *Westminster* by action of debt bill plaint or information, in which no wager of law essoign privilege or protection or more than one imparlance shall be allowed.

After 10 April, nine copies of each book shall be delivered to the warehouse keeper of the company of Stationers, for the use of the university libraries, &c.

V. Provided always and it is hereby enacted, That nine copies of each book or books upon the best paper that from and after the said tenth day of *April* one thousand seven hundred and ten shall be printed and published as aforesaid or reprinted and published with additions shall by the printer and printers thereof be delivered to the warehouse-keeper of the said Company of Stationers for the time being at the hall of the said company before such publication made, for the use of the royal library the libraries of the universities of *Oxford* and *Cambridge* the libraries of the four universities in *Scotland* the library of *Sion College* in *London* and the library commonly called the library belonging to the Faculty of Advocates at *Edinburgh* respectively; which said warehouse-keeper is hereby required within ten days after demand by the keepers of the respective libraries or any person or persons by them or any of them authorized to demand the said copy to deliver the same for the use of the aforesaid libraries; and if any proprietor bookseller or printer or the warehouse-keeper of the said Company of Stationers shall not observe the direction of this Act therein, that then he and they so making default in not delivering the said printed copies as aforesaid shall forfeit, besides the value of the said printed copies, the sum of five pounds for every copy not so delivered as also the value of the said printed copy not so delivered; the same to be recovered by the Queen's Majesty her heirs and successors and by the chancellor masters and scholars of any of the said universities and by the president and fellows of *Sion College* and the said Faculty of Advocates at *Edinburgh*, with their full costs respectively.

Warehouse keeper to deliver the books ten days after demand.

Penalty of proprietor, &c. not observing the directions of this act.

Penalties in Scotland, how recoverable.

VI. Provided always and be it further enacted, That if any person or persons incur the penalties contained in this Act in that part of *Great Britain* called *Scotland* they shall be recoverable by any action before the court of session there.

8 Anne, c. 19.

VII. Provided, That nothing in this Act contained do extend or shall be construed to extend to prohibit the importation vending or selling of any books in *Greek Latin* or any other foreign language printed beyond the seas; anything in this Act contained to the contrary notwithstanding.

This act not to hinder the importation, &c. of books in Greek, &c. printed beyond sea, &c.

VIII. And be it further enacted by the authority aforesaid, That if any action or suit shall be commenced or brought against any person or persons watsoever for doing or causing to be done any thing in pursuance of this Act, the defendants in such action may plead the general issue and give the special matter in evidence; and if upon such action a verdict be given for the defendant or the plaintiff become nonsuited or discontinue his action, then the defendant shall have and recover his full costs for which he shall have the same remedy as a defendant in any case by law hath.

General issue.

IX. Provided, That nothing in this Act contained shall extend or be construed to extend either to prejudice or confirm any right that the said universities or any of them or any person or persons have or claim to have to the printing or reprinting any book or copy already printed or hereafter to be printed.

This act not to prejudice the right of the universities.

X. Provided nevertheless, That all actions suits bills indictments or informations for any offence that shall be committed against this Act shall be brought sued and commenced within three months next after such offence committed or else the same shall be void and of none effect.

Actions for offences against this act to be brought in three months.

XI. Provided always, That after the expiration of the said term of fourteen years the sole right of printing or disposing of copies shall return to the authors thereof, if they are then living, for another term of fourteen years.

After the fourteen years, the right of printing, &c. to return to the author for other fourteen years.

8 George II. c. 13. — An Act for the Encouragement of the Arts of Designing, Engraving and Etching Historical and other Prints, by vesting the Properties thereof in the Inventors and Engravers, during the time therein mentioned.

8 Geo. II. c. 13.

Preamble. See 3 Wills. 60.

"WHEREAS divers persons have by their own genius industry pains and expense invented and engraved or worked in *mezzotinto* or *chiaro oscuro* sets of historical and other prints in hopes to have reaped the sole benefit of their labors: And whereas printsellers and other persons have of late, without the consent of the inventors designers and proprietors of such prints, frequently taken the liberty of copying engraving and publishing or causing to be copied engraved and published base copies of such works designs and prints to the very great prejudice and detriment of the inventors designers and proprietors thereof;" For remedy thereof, and for preventing such practices for the future, may it please your Majesty that it may be enacted; and be it enacted by the King's most excellent Majesty, by and with the advice and consent of the Lords Spiritual and Temporal and Commons in this present Parliament assembled, and by the authority of the same, that from and after the twenty-fourth day of *June* which shall be in the year of our Lord one thousand seven hundred and thirty-five every person who shall invent and design engrave etch or work in *mezzotinto* or *chiaro oscuro*, or from his own works and inventions shall cause to be designed and engraved etched or worked in *mezzotinto* or *chiaro oscuro* any historical or other print or prints shalt have the sole right and liberty of printing and reprinting the same for the term of fourteen years to commence from the day of the first publishing thereof, which shall be truly engraved with the name of the proprietor on each plate, and printed on every such print or prints; and that if any printseller or other person whatsoever, from and after the said twenty-fourth day of *June* one thousand seven hundred and thirty-five within the

Property of prints vested in the inventor for fourteen years.

Proprietor's name to be affixed to each print.

8 Geo. II. c. 13.

time limited by this Act shall engrave etch or work as aforesaid or in any other manner copy and sell or cause to be engraved etched or copied and sold in the whole or in part by varying adding to or diminishing from the main design, or shall print reprint or import for sale or cause to be printed reprinted or imported for sale any such print or prints or any parts thereof without the consent of the proprietor or proprietors thereof first had and obtained in writing signed by him or them respectively in the presence of two or more credible witnesses, or knowing the same to be so printed or reprinted without the consent of the proprietor or proprietors shall publish sell or expose to sale or otherwise or in any other manner dispose of or cause to be published sold or exposed to sale or otherwise or in any other manner disposed of any such print or prints without such consent first had and obtained as aforesaid, then such offender or offenders shall forfeit the plate or plates on which such print or prints are or shall be copied, and all and every sheet or sheets (being part of or whereon such print or prints are or shall be so copied or printed) to the proprietor or proprietors of such original print or prints, who shall forthwith destroy and damask the same; and further that every such offender or offenders shall forfeit five shillings for every print which shall be found in his her or their custody either printed or published and exposed to sale or otherwise disposed of contrary to the true intent and meaning of this Act; the one moiety thereof to the King's most excellent Majesty his heirs and successors and the other moiety thereof to any person or persons that shall sue for the same, to be recovered in any of his Majesty's courts of record at *Westminster* by action of debt bill plaint or information, in which no wager of law essoign privilege or protection or more than one imparlance shall be allowed.

Penalty on print sellers or others pirating the same.

II. Provided nevertheless, That it shall and may be lawful for any person or persons who shall hereafter purchase any plate or plates for printing from the original proprietors thereof to print and reprint from the said

Not to extend to purchasers of plates from the original proprietors.

8 Geo. II. c. 13. plates without incurring any of the penalties in this Act mentioned.

Limitation of actions. III. And be it further enacted by the authority aforesaid, That if any action or suit shall be commenced or brought against any person or persons whatsoever for doing or causing to be done any thing in pursuance of this Act, the same shall be brought within the space of three months after so doing; and the defendant or defendants in such action or suit shall or may plead the general issue and give the special matter in evidence; and if upon such action or suit a verdict shall be given for the defendant or defendants, or if the plaintiff or plaintiffs become nonsuited or discontinue his her or their action or actions, then the defendant or defendants shall have and recover full costs, for the recovery whereof he shall have the same remedy as any other defendant or defendants in any other case hath or have by law.

General issue.

IV. Provided always and be it further enacted by the authority aforesaid, That if any action or suit shall be commenced or brought against any person or persons for any offence committed against this Act, the same shall be brought within the space of three months after the discovery of every such offence and not afterwards; any thing in this Act contained to the contrary notwithstanding.

Clause relating to J. Pine. V. " And whereas *John Pine* of *London* engraver doth propose to engrave and publish a set of prints copied from several pieces of tapestry in the House of Lords and his Majesty's wardrobe and other drawings relating to the *Spanish* invasion in the year of our Lord one thousand five hundred and eighty-eight;" Be it further enacted by the authority aforesaid, That the said *John Pine* shall be entitled to the benefit of this Act to all intents and purposes whatsoever in the same manner as if the said *John Pine* had been the inventor and designer of the said prints.

Public act. VI. And be it further enacted by the authority aforesaid, That this Act shall be deemed adjudged and taken to be a public Act, and be judicially taken notice of as such by all judges justices and other persons whatsoever without specially pleading the same.

12 Geo. II. c. 36. — An Act for prohibiting the Importation of Books reprinted abroad, and first composed or written and printed in *Great Britain;* and for repealing so much of an Act made in the eighth year of the reign of her late Majesty Queen *Anne*, as empowers the limiting the prices of Books.

12 G. II. c. 36.

Preamble.

"Whereas the duties payable upon paper imported into this kingdom to be made use of in printing greatly exceed the duties payable upon the importation of printed books whereby foreigners and others are encouraged to bring in great numbers of books originally printed and published in this kingdom and reprinted abroad, to the diminution of his Majesty's revenue and the discouragement of the trade and manufacture of this kingdom;" For the preventing thereof for the future, May it please your most excellent Majesty that it may be enacted; and be it enacted by the King's most excellent Majesty, by and with the advice and consent of the Lords Spiritual and Temporal and Commons in this present Parliament assembled, and by the authority of the same, that from and after the twenty-ninth day of *September* one thousand seven hundred and thirty-nine it shall not be lawful for any person or persons whatsoever to import or bring into this kingdom for sale any book or books first composed or written and printed and published in this kingdom and reprinted in any other place or country whatsoever; and if any person or persons shall import or bring into this kingdom for sale any printed book or books so first composed or written and printed in this kingdom and reprinted in any other place or country as aforesaid; or knowing the same to be so reprinted or imported contrary to the true intent and meaning of this Act shall sell publish or expose to sale any such book or books; then every such person or persons so doing or offending shall forfeit the said book or books and all and every sheet or sheets thereof; and the same shall be forthwith damasked and made waste paper; and further that every such offender or offenders

12 G. II. c. 36.

shall forfeit the sum of five pounds and double the value of every book which he or they shall so import or bring into this kingdom or shall knowingly sell publish or expose to sale or cause to be sold published or exposed to sale contrary to the true intent and meaning of this Act; the one moiety thereof to the King's most excellent Majesty his heirs and successors and the other moiety to any person or persons that shall sue for the same; to be recovered with costs of suit in any of his Majesty's courts of record at *Westminster* by action of debt bill plaint or information, in which no wager of law essoign or protection or more than one imparlance shall be allowed; and if the offence be committed in *Scotland* to be recovered before the Court of Session there by summary action: Provided that this Act shall not extend to any book that has not been printed or reprinted in this kingdom within twenty years before the same shall be imported.

II. Provided always, That nothing in this Act contained shall extend to prevent or hinder the importation of any book first composed or written and printed in this kingdom which shall or may be reprinted abroad and inserted among other books or tracts to be sold therewith in any collection where the greatest part of such collection shall have been first composed or written and printed abroad; any thing in this Act contained to the contrary notwithstanding.

Clause in 8 Anne, c. 19, repealed.

III. And be it further enacted by the authority aforesaid, That so much of an Act made in the eighth year of the reign of her late Majesty Queen *Anne*, intituled *An Act for the Encouragement of Learning, by vesting the Copies of printed Books in the Authors or Purchasers of such Copies during the times therein mentioned*, whereby it is provided and enacted, That if any bookseller or booksellers printer or printers shall after the said five and twentieth day of *March* one thousand seven hundred and ten set a price upon or sell or expose to sale any book or books at such a price or rate as shall be conceived by any person or persons to be high and unreasonable; it shall and may be lawful for any person or persons to make complaint thereof to the Lord Archbishop of *Canterbury* for the time being the Lord Chancellor or Lord Keeper of the great seal of *Great Britain* for the time being the Lord Bishop of *London* for the time being the Lord Chief Justice of the Court of *Queen's Bench* the Lord Chief Justice of the Court of *Common Pleas* the Lord Chief Baron of the Court of *Exchequer* for the time being the Vice-Chancellors of the two Universities for the time being in that part of *Great Britain* called *England* the Lord President of the Sessions for the time being the Lord Justice General for the time being the Lord Chief Baron of the *Exchequer* for the time being the Rector of the college of *Edinburgh* for the time being in that part of *Great Britain* called *Scotland*, who or any one of them shall and have hereby full power and authority from time to time to send for summon or call before him or them such bookseller or booksellers printer or printers and to examine and inquire of the reason of the dearness and enhancement of the price of value of such book or books by him or them so sold or exposed to sale; and if upon such inquiry and examination it shall be found that the price of such book or books is enhanced or anyways too high or unreasonable, then and in such case the said Archbishop of *Canterbury* Lord Chancellor or Lord Keeper Bishop of *London* two Chief Justiccs Chief Baron Vice-Chancellors of the Universities in that part of *Great Britain* called *England* and the said Lord President of the Sessions Lord Justice General Lord Chief Baron and Rector of the College of *Edinburgh* in that part of *Great Britain* called *Scotland*, or any one or more of them so inquiring and examining, have hereby full power and authority to reform and redress the same and to limit and settle the price of every such printed book and books from time to time according to the best of their judgments and as to them shall seem just and reasonable; and in case of alteration of the rate or price from what was set or demanded by such bookseller or booksellers printer or printers to award and order such bookseller and booksellers printer and printers to pay all the costs

12 G. II. c. 36.

12 G. II. c. 36.

and charges that the person or persons so complaining shall be put unto by reason of such complaint and of the causing such rate or price to be so limited and settled; all which shall be done by the said Archbishop of *Canterbury* Lord Chancellor or Lord Keeper Bishop of *London* two Chief Justices Chief Baron Vice Chancellors of the two Universities in that part of *Great Britain* called *England* and the said Lord President of the Sessions Lord Justice General Lord Chief Baron and Rector of the college of *Edinburgh* in that part of *Great Britain* called *Scotland*, or any one of them, by writing under their hands and seals, and thereof public notice shall be forthwith given by the said bookseller or booksellers printer or printers by an advertisement in the *Gazette*; and if any bookseller or booksellers printer or printers shall after such settlement made of the said rate and price sell or expose to sale any book or books at a higher or greater price than what shall have been so limited and settled as aforesaid, then and in every such case such bookseller or booksellers printer or printers shall forfeit the sum of five pounds for every such book so by him her or them sold or exposed to sale, one moiety thereof to the Queen's most excellent Majesty her heirs and successors, and the other moiety to any person or persons that shall sue for the same, to be recovered with costs of suit in any of her Majesty's courts of record at *Westminster* by action of debt bill plaint or information, in which no wager of law essoign privilege or protection or more than one imparlance shall be allowed; and every part of the said clause shall be and the same is hereby repealed.

Further continued by 27 G. II. c. 18, and 33 G. II. c. 16.

IV. And be it further enacted, That this Act (except so much thereof as repeals the before-mentioned clause in the said Act of the eighth year of the reign of the late Queen *Anne* relating to the prices of books) shall continue and be in force from the said twenty-ninth day of *September* one thousand seven hundred and thirty-nine for and during the space of seven years, and from thence to the end of the then next session of Parliament and no longer.

7 Geo. III. c. 38. — An Act to amend and render more effectual an Act made in the Eighth Year of the Reign of King *George* the Second, for Encouragement of the Arts of Designing, Engraving and Etching Historical and other Prints; and for vesting in and securing to *Jane Hogarth*, Widow, the Property in certain Prints.

" WHEREAS an Act of Parliament passed in the eighth year of the reign of his late Majesty King *George* the Second, intituled *An Act for the Encouragement of the Arts of Designing, Engraving, and Etching Historical and other Prints, by vesting the Properties thereof in the Inventors and Engravers during the time therein mentioned* has been found ineffectual for the Purposes thereby intended;" Be it enacted by the King's most excellent Majesty, by and with the advice and consent of the Lords Spiritual and Temporal and Commons in this present Parliament assembled, and by the authority of the same, That from and after the first day of *January* one thousand seven hundred and sixty-seven all and every person and persons who shall invent or design engrave etch or work in *mezzotinto* or *chiaro oscuro*, or from his own work design or invention shall cause or procure to be designed engraved etched or worked in *mezzotinto* or *chiaro oscuro* any historical print or prints, or any print or prints of any portrait conversation landscape or architectural map chart or plan or any other print or prints whatsoever, shall have and are hereby declared to have the benefit and protection of the said Act and this Act under the restrictions and limitations hereinafter mentioned.

[Margin: 7 G. III. c. 38. — 8 Geo. II. c. 13. — Original inventors, &c. of prints, &c. intitled to the benefit of recited and present act, &c.]

II. And be it further enacted by the authority aforesaid, That from and after the said first day of *January* one thousand seven hundred and sixty-seven all and every person and persons who shall engrave etch or work in *mezzotinto* or *chiaro oscuro*, or caused to be engraved etched or worked any print taken from any picture drawing model or sculpture either ancient or modern, shall

7 G. III. c. 38.

have and are hereby declared to have the benefit and protection of the said Act and this Act for the time hereinafter mentioned in like manner as if such print had been graved or drawn from the original design of such graver etcher or draftsman, and if any person shall engrave print and publish or import for sale any copy of any such print contrary to the true intent and meaning of this and the said former Act, every such person shall be liable to the penalties contained in the said Act, to be recovered as therein and hereinafter is mentioned.

"The sole right of printing and reprinting the late *W. Hogarth's* prints vested in his widow and executrix for twenty years. Penalty of copying, &c. any of them before expiration of the term; such copies excepted as were made and exposed to sale after the term of fourteen years for which the said works were first licensed, &c."

V. And be it further enacted by the authority aforesaid, That all and every the penalties and penalty inflicted by the said Act and extended and meant to be extended to the several cases comprised in this Act shall and may be sued for and recovered in like manner and under the like restrictions and limitations as in and by the said Act is declared and appointed; and the plaintiff or common informer in every such action (in case such plaintiff or common informer shall recover any of the penalties incurred by this or the said former Act) shall recover the same together with his full costs of suit.

VI. Provided also, That the party prosecuting shall commence his prosecution within the space of six calendar months after the offence committed.

The right intended vested in the proprietors for 28 years.

VII. And be it further enacted by the authority aforesaid, that the sole right and liberty of printing and reprinting intended to be secured and protected by the said former Act and this Act shall be extended continued and be vested in the respective proprietors for the space of twenty-eight years, to commence from the day of the first publishing of any of the works respectively hereinbefore and in the said former Act mentioned.

VIII. And be it further enacted by the authority aforesaid, That if any action or suit shall be commenced or brought against any person or persons whatsoever for doing or causing to be done any thing in pursuance of this Act, the same shall be brought within the space of six calendar months after the fact committed; and the defendant or defendants in any of such action or suit shall or may plead the general issue and give the special matter in evidence; and if upon such action or suit a verdict shall be given for the defendant or defendants, or if the plaintiff or plaintiffs become non-suited or discontinue his her or their action or actions, then the defendant or defendants shall have and recover full costs; for the recovery whereof he shall have the same remedy as any other defendant or defendants in any other case hath or have by law.

7 G. III. c. 38.

Limitation of actions.

General issue.

Full costs.

15 George III. c. 53. — An Act for enabling the two Universities in *England*, the four Universities in *Scotland*, and the several Colleges of *Eton*, *Westminster*, and *Winchester*, to hold in perpetuity their Copyright in Books, given or bequeathed to the said Universities and Colleges for the Advancement of useful Learning and other purposes of Education: and for amending so much of an Act of the Eighth Year of the Reign of Queen *Anne*, as relates to the Delivery of Books to the Warehouse-keeper of the Stationers' Company, for the Use of the several Libraries therein mentioned.

15 G. III. c. 53. "WHEREAS authors have heretofore bequeathed or given and may hereafter bequeath or give the copies of books composed by them to or in trust for one of the two universities in that part of *Great Britain* called *England*, or to or in trust for some of the colleges or houses of learning within the same, or to or in trust for the four universities in *Scotland*, or to or in trust for the several colleges of *Eton Westminster* and *Winchester*, and in and by their several wills or other instruments of donation have directed or may direct that the profits arising from the printing and reprinting such books shall be applied or appropriated as a fund for the advancement of learning and other beneficial purposes of education within the said universities and colleges aforesaid: And whereas such useful purposes will frequently be frustrated unless the sole printing and reprinting of such books, the copies of which have been or shall be so bequeathed or given as aforesaid, be preserved and secured to the said universities colleges and houses of learning respectively in perpetuity:" May it therefore please your Majesty that it may be enacted; and be it enacted by the King's most excellent Majesty, by and with the advice and consent of the Lords Spiritual and Temporal and Commons in this pre-

15 G. III. c. 53.

sent Parliament assembled, and by the authority of the same, That the said universities and colleges respectively shall at their respective presses have for ever the sole liberty of printing and reprinting all such books as shall at any time hereafter have been or (having not been heretofore published or assigned) shall at any time hereafter be bequeathed or otherwise given by the author or authors of the same respectively or the representatives of such author or authors to or in trust for the said universities, or to or in trust for any college or house of learning within the same, or to or in trust for the said four universities in *Scotland*, or to or in trust for the said colleges of *Eton Westminster* and *Winchester* or any of them for the purposes aforesaid, unless the same shall have been bequeathed or given or shall hereafter be bequeathed or given for any term of years or other limited term; any law or usage to the contrary hereof in any wise notwithstanding.

Universities, &c. to have for ever the sole right of printing, &c.

II. And it is hereby further enacted, That if any bookseller printer or other person whatsoever from and after the twenty-fourth day of *June* one thousand seven hundred and seventy-five shall print reprint or import or cause to be printed reprinted or imported any such book or books; or knowing the same to be so printed or reprinted shall sell publish or expose to sale or cause to be sold published or exposed to sale any such book or books; then such offender or offenders shall forfeit such book or books and all and every sheet or sheets being part of such book or books to the university college or house of learning respectively to whom the copy of such book or books shall have been bequeathed or given as aforesaid, who shall forthwith damask and make waste paper of them; and further that such offender or offenders shall forfeit one penny for every sheet which shall be found in his her or their custody either printed or printing published or exposed to sale contrary to the true intent and meaning of this Act; one moiety thereof to the King's most excellent Majesty his heirs and successors, and the other moiety thereof to any person or persons who shall sue for the same; to be recovered in any of his Majesty's courts of

Persons printing or selling such books shall forfeit the same, and also 1*d*. for every sheet;

one moiety to his Majesty and the other to the prosecutor.

15 G. III. c. 53. record at *Westminster* or in the Court of Sessions in *Scotland* by action of debt bill plaint or information, in which no wager of law essoign privilege or protection or more than one imparlance shall be allowed.

III. Provided nevertheless, That nothing in this Act shall extend to grant any exclusive right otherwise than so long as the books or copies belonging to the said universities or colleges are printed only at their own printing presses within the said universities or colleges respectively and for their sole benefit and advantage; and that if any university or college shall delegate grant lease or sell their copy rights or exclusive rights of printing the books hereby granted or any part thereof, or shall allow permit or authorize any person or persons or bodies corporate to print or reprint the same, that then the privileges hereby granted are to become void and of no effect in the same manner as if this Act had not been made; but the said universities and colleges as aforesaid shall nevertheless have a right to sell such copies so bequeathed or given as aforesaid in like manner as any author or authors now may do under the provisions of the statute of the eighth year of her Majesty Queen *Anne*.

No person subject to penalties unless entered before, &c.

IV. "And whereas many persons may through ignorance offend against this Act unless some provision be made whereby the property of every such book as is intended by this Act to be secured to the said universities colleges and houses of learning within the same and to the said universities in *Scotland* and to the respective colleges of *Eton Westminster* and *Winchester* may be ascertained and known;" Be it therefore enacted by the authority aforesaid, That nothing in this Act contained shall be construed to extend to subject any bookseller printer or other person whatsoever to the forfeitures or penalties herein mentioned for or by reason of the printing or reprinting importing or exposing to sale any book or books unless the title to the copy of such book or books which has or have been already bequeathed or given to any of the said universities or colleges aforesaid be entered in the register book of the Company of Stationers kept

15 G. III. c. 53.

for that purpose in such manner as hath been usual on or before the twenty-fourth day of *June* one thousand seven hundred and seventy-five; and of all and every such book or books as may or shall hereafter be bequeathed or given as aforesaid be entered in such register within the space of two months after any such bequest or gift shall have come to the knowledge of the vice-chancellors of the said universities or heads of houses and colleges of learning or of the principal of any of the said four universities respectively; for every of which entries so to be made as aforesaid the sum of six pence shall be paid and no more; which said register book shall and may at all seasonable and convenient times be referred to and inspected by any bookseller printer or other person without any fee or reward; and the clerk of the said Company of Stationers shall when and as often as thereunto required give a certificate under his hand of such entry or entries, and for every such certificate may take a fee not exceeding six pence.

Books must be entered within two months after bequest.

V. And be it further enacted, That if the clerk of the said Company of Stationers for the time being shall refuse or neglect to register or make such entry or entries or to give such certificate, being thereunto required by the agent of either of the said universities or colleges aforesaid lawfully authorized for that purpose, then either of the said universities or colleges aforesaid, being the proprietor of such copyright or copyrights as aforesaid (notice being first given of such refusal by advertisement in the *Gazette*) shall have the like benefit as if such entry or entries certificate or certificates had been duly made and given; and the clerk so refusing shall for every such offence forfeit twenty pounds to the proprietor or proprietors of every such copyright; to be recovered in any of his Majesty's courts of record at *Westminster* or in the court of Session in *Scotland* by action of debt bill plaint or information, in which no wager of law essoign privilege protection or more than one imparlance shall be allowed.

If clerk neglect to make entry, &c. proprietor to have like benefit, &c.

15 G. III, c. 53.

8 Anne, c. 19.

VI. "And whereas in and by an Act of Parliament made in the eighth year of the reign of her late Majesty Queen *Anne*, intituled *An Act for the Encouragement of Learning by vesting the Copies of printed Books in the Authors or Purchasers of such Copies during the times therein mentioned*, it is enacted, That nine copies of each book or books upon the best paper that from and after the tenth day of *April* one thousand seven hundred and ten should be printed and published as therein mentioned, or reprinted and published with additions, shall by the printer or printers thereof be delivered to the warehouse-keeper of the said Company of Stationers for the time being at the hall of the said Company before such publication made, for the use of the royal library the libraries of the universities of *Oxford* and *Cambridge* the libraries of the four universities in *Scotland* the library of *Sion College* in *London* and the library commonly called *The Library belonging to the Faculty of Advocates in* Edinburgh respectively; which such warehouse-keeper was thereby required within ten days after demand by the keepers of the respective libraries, or any person or persons by them or any of them authorized to demand the said copy, to deliver the same for the use of the aforesaid libraries; and if any proprietor bookseller or printer or the said warehouse-keeper of the said Company of Stationers should not observe the direction of the said Act therein, that then he and they so making default in not delivering the said printed copies as aforesaid should forfeit as therein mentioned: And whereas the said provision has not proved effectual but the same hath been eluded by the entry only of the title to a single volume or of some part of such book or books so printed and published or reprinted and republished as aforesaid;" Be it enacted by the authority aforesaid, That no person or persons whatsoever shall be subject to the penalties in the said Act mentioned for or by reason of the printing or reprinting importing or exposing to sale any book or books without the consent mentioned in the said Act, unless the title to the copy of the whole of such book and

No person subject to penalties in the said act unless the title to the copy of the whole be entered, &c.

every volume thereof be entered in manner directed by the said Act in the register book of the Company of Stationers, and unless nine such copies of the whole of such book or books and every volume thereof printed and published or reprinted or republished as therein mentioned shall be actually delivered to the warehouse-keeper of the said Company as therein directed for the several uses of the several libraries in the said Act mentioned.

15 G. III. c. 53.

Limitation of actions.

VII. And be it further enacted by the authority aforesaid, That if any action or suit shall be commenced or brought against any person or persons whatsoever for doing or causing to be done any thing in pursuance of this Act, the defendants in such action may plead the general issue and give the special matter in evidence; and if upon such action a verdict, or if the same shall be brought in the Court of Session in *Scotland* a judgment be given for the defendant, or the plaintiff become nonsuited and discontinue his action, then the defendant shall have and recover his full costs, for which he shall have the same remedy as a defendant in any case by law hath.

General issue.

Public act.

VIII. And be it further enacted by the authority aforesaid, That this Act shall be adjudged deemed and taken to be a public Act; and shall be judicially taken notice of as such by all judges justices and other persons whatsoever without specially pleading the same.

17 George III. c. 57.—An Act for more effectually securing the Property of Prints to Inventors and Engravers, by enabling them to sue for and recover Penalties in certain Cases.

17 G. III. c. 57.

8 Geo. II. 7 Geo. III.

"Whereas an Act of Parliament passed in the eighth year of the reign of his late Majesty King *George* the Second, intituled *An Act for the Encouragement of the Arts of Designing, Engraving, and Etching Historical and other Prints, by vesting the Properties thereof in the Inventors and Engravers during the time therein mentioned:* And whereas by an Act of Parliament passed in the seventh year of the reign of his present Majesty, *for amending and rendering more effectual* the aforesaid Act, and for other purposes therein mentioned, it was (among other things) enacted, That from and after the first day of *January* one thousand seven hundred and sixty-seven all and every person or persons who should engrave etch or work in *mezzotinto* or *chiaro oscuro*, or cause to be engraved etched or worked any print taken from any picture drawing model or sculpture either ancient or modern, should have and were thereby declared to have the benefit and protection of the said former Act and that Act for the term therein-after mentioned, in like manner as if such print had been graved or drawn from the original design of such graver etcher or draughtsman: And whereas the said acts have not effectually answered the purposes for which they were intended, and it is necessary for the encouragement of artists and for securing to them the property of and in their works and for the advancement and improvement of the aforesaid arts that such further provisions should be made as are herein-after mentioned and contained;" May it therefore please your Majesty that it may be enacted; and be it enacted by the King's most excellent Majesty, by and with the advice and consent of the Lords Spiritual and Temporal and Commons in this present Parliament assembled, and by the authority of the

If any engraver, &c. shall engrave, &c. any print without the consent of the proprietor, he shall be liable to damages and double costs.

same, That from and after the twenty-fourth day of *June* one thousand seven hundred and seventy-seven if any engraver etcher printseller or other person shall within the time limited by the aforesaid Acts, or either of them, engrave etch or work or cause or procure to be engraved etched or worked in *mezzotinto* or *chiaro oscuro*, or otherwise or in any other manner copy in the whole or in part by varying adding to or diminishing from the main design, or shall print reprint or import for sale or cause or procure to be printed reprinted or imported for sale, or shall publish sell or otherwise dispose of or cause or procure to be published sold or otherwise disposed of any copy or copies of any historical print or prints or any print or prints of any portrait conversation landscape or architecture map chart or plan, or any other print or prints whatsoever which hath or have been or shall be engraved etched drawn or designed in any part of *Great Britain* without the express consent of the proprietor or proprietors thereof first had and obtained in writing signed by him or her or them respectively with his her or their own hand or hands in the presence of and attested by two or more credible witnesses, then every such proprietor or proprietors shall and may, by and in a special action upon the case to be brought against the person or persons so offending recover such damages as a jury on the trial of such action or on the execution of a writ of inquiry thereon shall give or assess together with double costs of suit. 17 G. III. c. 57.

38 George III. c. 71. — An Act for encouraging the Art of making new Models and Casts of Busts, and other things therein mentioned. — [21*st June* 1798.]

38 G. III. c. 71.

"WHEREAS divers persons have by their own genius industry pains and expence improved and brought the art of making new models and casts of busts and of statues of human figures and of animals to great perfection, in hopes to have reaped the sole benefit of their labours; but divers persons have (without the consent of the proprietors thereof) copied and made moulds from the said models and casts and sold base copies and casts of such new models and casts to the great prejudice and detriment of the original proprietors and to the discouragement of the art of making such new models and casts as aforesaid:" For remedy whereof and for preventing such practices for the future, may it please your Majesty that it may be enacted; and be it enacted by the King's most excellent Majesty, by and with the advice and consent of the Lords Spiritual and Temporal and Commons in this present Parliament assembled, and by the authority of the same, That from and after the passing of this Act every person who shall make or cause to be made any new model or copy or cast made from such new model of any bust or any part of the human figure or any statue of the human figure or the head of any animal or any part of any animal or the statue of any animal; or shall make or cause to be made any new model copy or cast from such new model in alto or basso relievo or any work in which the representation of any human figure or figures or the representation of any animal or animals shall be introduced, or shall make or cause to be made any new cast from nature of any part or parts of the human figure or of any part or parts of any animal, shall have the sole right and property in every such new model copy or cast, and also in every such new model copy or cast in alto or basso relievo or any work as aforesaid, and also in every such

The sole right and property of making models or casts shall be vested in the original proprietor for 14 years.

new cast from nature as aforesaid, for and during the term of fourteen years from the time of first publishing the same: Provided always, That every person who shall make or cause to be made any such new model copy or cast or any such new model copy or cast in alto or basso relievo or any work as aforesaid, or any new cast from nature as aforesaid, shall cause his or her name to be put thereon with the date of the publication before the same shall be published and exposed to sale. 38 G. III. c. 71.

II. And be it further enacted, That if any person shall within the said term of fourteen years make or cause to be made any copy or cast of any such new model copy or cast or any such model copy or cast in alto or basso relievo or any such work as aforesaid, or any such new cast from nature as aforesaid, either by adding to or diminishing from any such new model copy or cast or adding to or diminishing from any such new model copy or cast in alto or basso relievo or any such work as aforesaid, or adding to or diminishing from any such new cast from nature or shall cause or procure the same to be done, or shall import any copy or cast of such new model copy or cast, or copy or cast of such new model copy or cast in alto or basso relievo or any such work as aforesaid, or any copy or cast of any such new cast from nature as aforesaid for sale, or shall sell or otherwise dispose of or cause or procure to be sold or exposed to sale or otherwise disposed of any copy or cast of any such new model copy or cast, or any copy or cast of such new model copy or cast in alto or basso relievo or any such work as aforesaid, or any copy or cast of any such new cast from nature as aforesaid without the express consent of the proprietor or proprietors thereof first had and obtained in writing signed by him her or them respectively with his her or their hand or hands in the presence of and attested by two or more credible witnesses, then and in all or any of the cases aforesaid every proprietor or proprietors of any such original model copy or cast and every proprietor or proprietors of any such original model or copy or cast in alto or basso relievo or any such work as aforesaid,

Person making copies of any model or cast without the written consent of the proprietor, may be prosecuted for damages, by a special action on the case.

38 G. III. c. 71.

or the proprietor or proprietors of any such new cast from nature as aforesaid respectively, shall and may by and in a special action upon the case to be brought against the person or persons so offending recover such damages as a jury on the trial of such action or on the execution of a writ of enquiry thereon shall give or assess together with full cost of suit.

Except such persons who shall purchase the same of the original proprietor.

III. Provided nevertheless, That no person who shall hereafter purchase the right either in any such model copy or cast or in any such model copy or cast in alto or basso relievo or any such work as aforesaid or any such new cast from nature of the original proprietor or proprietors thereof shall be subject to any action for vending or selling any cast or copy from the same; any thing contained in this Act to the contrary hereof notwithstanding.

Limitation of actions.

IV. Provided also, That all actions to be brought as aforesaid against any person or persons for any offence committed against this Act shall be commenced within six callendar months next after the discovery of every such offence and not afterwards.

41 George III. c. 107. — An Act for the further Encouragement of Learning, in the United Kingdom of *Great Britain* and *Ireland*, by securing the Copies and Copyright of printed Books to the Authors of such Books, or their Assigns for the Time herein mentioned. — [*2d July* 1801.]

41 G. III. c. 107.

"Whereas it is expedient that further protection should be afforded to the authors of books and the purchasers of the copies and copyright of the same in the United Kingdom of *Great Britain* and *Ireland*;" May it therefore please your Majesty that it may be enacted; and be it enacted by the King's most excellent Majesty, by and with the advice and consent of the Lords Spiritual and Temporal and Commons in this present Parliament assembled, and by the authority of the same, That the author of any book or books already composed and not printed or published and the author of any book or books which shall hereafter be composed and the assignee or assigns of such authors respectively shall have the sole liberty of printing and reprinting of such book and books for the term of fourteen years, to commence from the day of first publishing the same and no longer; and that if any other bookseller printer or other person whosoever in any part of the said United Kingdom or in part of the *British* dominions in *Europe* shall from and after the passing of this Act print reprint or import or shall cause to be printed reprinted or imported any such book or books without the consent of the proprietor or proprietors of the copyright of and in such book or books first had and obtained in writing, signed in the presence of two or more credible witnesses, or knowing the same to be so printed reprinted or imported without such consent of such proprietor or proprietors shall sell publish or expose to sale or cause to be sold published or exposed

Authors of books already composed, and not printed or published, and of books to be hereafter composed, and their assigns shall have the sole right of printing them for fourteen years:

Booksellers, &c. in any part of the United Kingdom, or British European dominions, who shall print, reprint, or import, &c. any such book without consent of the proprietor, shall be liable to an action for damages, and shall also forfeit the books to the proprietor, and 3*d*. per sheet. Half to the King, and half to the informer.

41 G. III. c. 107. to sale, or shall have in his her or their possession for sale any such book or books without such consent first had and obtained as aforesaid, then such offender or offenders shall be liable to a special action on the case at the suit of the proprietor or proprietors of the copyright of such book or books so unlawfully printed reprinted or imported or published or exposed to sale, or being in the possession of such offender or offenders for sale as aforesaid contrary to the true intent and meaning of this Act; and every such proprietor and proprietors shall and may by and in such special action upon the case to be so brought against such offender or offenders in any court of record in that part of the said United Kingdom or of the *British* dominions in *Europe* in which the offence shall be committed, recover such damages as the jury on the trial of such action or on the execution of a writ of enquiry thereon shall give or assess together with double costs of suit; in which action no wager of law essoign privilege or protection nor more than one imparlance shall be allowed; and all and every such offender or offenders shall also forfeit such book or books and all and every sheet and sheets being part of such book or books, and shall deliver the same to the proprietor or proprietors of the copyright of such book or books upon order of any court of record in which any action or suit in law or equity shall be commenced or prosecuted by such proprietor or proprietors, to be made on motion or petition to the said court; and the said proprietor or proprietors shall forthwith damask or make waste paper of the said book or books and sheet or sheets respectively; and all and every such offender or offenders shall also forfeit the sum of three pence for every sheet which shall be found in his or their custody, either printed or printing or published or exposed to sale contrary to the true intent and meaning of this Act, the one moiety thereof to the King's most excellent Majesty his heirs and successors, and the other moiety thereof to any person or persons who shall sue for the same in any such court of record by action of debt bill plaint or information, in which no wager of

law essoign privilege or protection nor more than one imparlance shall be allowed: Provided always, That after the expiration of the said term of fourteen years the right of printing or disposing of copies shall return to the authors thereof, if they are then living, for another term of fourteen years.

41 G. III. c. 107.

Authors have a second 14 years' term, if living.

II. Provided also and be it further enacted, That nothing in this Act contained shall extend or be construed to extend to any book or books heretofore composed and printed or published in any part of the said United Kingdom, nor to exempt or indemnify any person or persons whomsoever from or against any penalties or actions to which he she or they shall or may have become or shall or may be hereafter liable for or on account of the unlawful printing reprinting or importing such book or books, or the selling, publishing or exposing the same to sale or the having the same in his or their possession for sale contrary to the laws and statutes in force respecting the same at the time of the passing an Act in the session of Parliament of the thirty-ninth and fortieth years of the reign of his present Majesty, intituled *An Act for the Union of* Great Britain *and* Ireland.

Act shall not extend to books already published, nor indemnify against penalties under former acts in force at the union of Great Britain and Ireland.

39 & 40 G. III. 67.

III. "And whereas authors have heretofore bequeathed given or assigned and may hereafter bequeath give or assign the copies or copyrights of and in books composed by them to or in trust for the college of the Holy Trinity of *Dublin;* and in and by their several wills or other instruments have directed or may direct that the profits arising from the printing or reprinting such books shall be applied or appropriated as a fund for the advancement of learning and other beneficial purposes of education within the college aforesaid: And whereas such useful purposes will frequently be frustrated unless the sole right of printing and reprinting of such books, the copies of which shall have been or shall be so bequeathed given or assigned as aforesaid, be preserved and secured to the said college in perpetuity:" Be it therefore further enacted, That the said college shall at their own printing press within the said college have for ever the sole liberty

Trinity College, Dublin, shall for ever have the sole right of printing books given or bequeathed to them, unless they are given, &c. for a limited time only.

41 G. III. c. 107.

of printing and reprinting all such books as shall at any time hereafter have been or (not having been heretofore published or assigned) shall at any time hereafter be bequeathed or otherwise given or assigned by the author or authors of the same respectively, or the representatives of such author or authors to or in trust for the said college for the purposes aforesaid, unless the same shall have been bequeathed given or assigned or shall hereafter be bequeathed given or assigned for any term of years or any other limited term; any law or usage to the contrary thereof in any wise notwithstanding; and that if any printer bookseller or other person whosoever shall from and after the passing of this Act unlawfully print reprint or import or cause to be printed reprinted or imported, or knowing the same to be so unlawfully printed reprinted or imported, shall sell publish or expose to sale or cause to be sold published or exposed to sale, or have in his or their possession for sale any such last-mentioned book or books, such offender or offenders shall be subject and liable to the like actions penalties and forfeitures as are herein-before mentioned and contained with respect to offenders against the copyrights of authors and their assigns: Provided nevertheless, That nothing in this Act shall extend to grant any exclusive right to the said college of the Holy Trinity of *Dublin* otherwise than so long as the books or copies belonging to the said college are and shall be printed only at the printing press of the said college within the said college and for the sole benefit and advantage of the said college; and that if the said college shall delegate grant lease or sell the copyrights or exclusive rights of printing the books hereby granted or any part thereof, or shall allow permit or authorize any person or persons or bodies coporate to print or reprint the same, then the privilege hereby granted shall become void and of no effect in the same manner as if this Act had not been made; but the said college shall nevertheless have a right to sell such copies so bequeathed or given as aforesaid in like manner as any author or authors can or may lawfully do under

Penalty on persons printing such books the same as under § 1.

To extend only to books printed at the college press.

But the college may sell their copyrights.

41 G. III. c. 107.

the provisions of this Act or any other Act now in force.

Booksellers, &c. shall not be liable to the penalty of 3*d.* per sheet,

IV. Provided also and be it further enacted. That no bookseller printer or other person whosoever shall be liable to the said penalty of three pence *per* sheet for or by reason of the printing reprinting importing or selling of any such book or books or the having the same in his or their custody for sale without the consent of the proprietor or proprietors of the copyright thereof as aforesaid, unless before the time of the publication of such book or books by the proprietor or proprietors thereof (other than the said college) the right and title of such proprietor or proprietors shall be duly entered in the register book of the Company of Stationers in *London* in such manner as hath been usually heretofore done by the proprietors of copies and copyrights in *Great Britain;* nor if the consent of such proprietor or proprietors for the printing reprinting importing or selling such book or books shall be in like manner entered; nor unless the right and title of the said college to the copyright of such book or books as has or have been already bequeathed given or assigned to the said college be entered in the said register book before the twenty-ninth day of *September* one thousand eight hundred and one, and of all and every such book or books as may or shall hereafter be bequeathed given or assigned as aforesaid be entered in the said register book within the space of two months after any such bequest gift or assignment shall have come to the knowledge of the provost of the said college; for every of which several entries six pence shall be paid and no more; which said register book shall at all times be kept at the hall of the said Company and shall and may at all seasonable and convenient times be resorted to and inspected by any bookseller printer or other person for the purposes before mentioned without any fee or reward; and the clerk of the said Company of Stationers shall when and as often as thereto required give a certificate

unless the title to the copyright be entered by the proprietor, &c. at Stationers' Hall, London; nor of the consent of the proprietor be so entered.

Clerk of the company shall give certificates of entries, and make a half-yearly list of the books so entered for the use of Trinity College.

41 G. III. c. 107. under his hand of such entry or entries and for every such certificate may take a fee not exceeding sixpence; and the said clerk shall also without fee or reward within fifteen days next after the thirty-first day of *December* and the thirtieth day of *June* in each and every year make or cause to be made for the use of the said college a list of the titles of all such books, the copyright to which shall have been so entered in the course of the half year immediately preceding the said thirty-first day of *December* and the thirtieth day of *June* respectively, and shall upon demand deliver the said lists or cause the same to be delivered to any person or persons duly authorized to receive the same for and on behalf of the said college.

If the clerk refuses to make entries, &c.

V. Provided also and be it further enacted, That if the clerk of the said Company of Stationers for the time being shall refuse or neglect to register or make such entry or entries or to give such certificate or certificates being thereupon respectively required by the author or authors proprietor or proprietors of such copies or copyrights, or by the person or persons to whom such consent shall be given or by some person on his or their behalf in the presence of two or more credible witnesses, then such party or parties so refused, notice being first duly given by advertisement in the *London Gazette*, shall have the like benefit as if such entry or entries certificate or certificates had been duly made and given; and the clerk so refusing shall for any such offence forfeit to the author or proprietor of such copy or copies or to the person or persons to whom such consent shall be given the sum of twenty pounds; or if the said clerk shall refuse or neglect to make the list aforesaid or to deliver the same to any person duly authorized to demand the same on behalf of the said college the said clerk shall also forfeit to the said college the like sum of twenty pounds; which said respective penalties shall and may be recovered in any of his Majesty's courts of record in the said United Kingdom by action of debt bill plaint or information, in which no wager of law essoign

Parties may give notice in the London Gazette, and the clerk shall forfeit 20*l*.

or protection nor more than one imparlance shall be allowed.

41 G. III. c. 107.

Two additional copies of books entered at Stationers' Hall, shall be delivered there for the use of the libraries of Trinity College, and the King's Inns, Dublin.

VI. Provided also and be it further enacted, That from and after the passing of this Act, in addition to the nine copies now required by law to be delivered to the warehouse-keeper of the said Company of Stationers of each and every book and books which shall be entered in the register book of the said Company, one other copy shall be in like manner delivered for the use of the library of the said college of the Holy Trinity of *Dublin*, and also one other copy for the use of the library of the society of the King's Inns *Dublin*, by the printer or printers of all and every such book and books as shall hereafter be printed and published and the title to the copyright whereof shall be entered in the said register book of the said Company; and that the said college and the said society shall have the like remedies for enforcing the delivery of the said copies; and that all proprietors booksellers and printers and the warehouse-keeper of the said Company shall be liable to the like penalties for making default in delivering the said copies for the use of the said college and the said society as are now in force with respect to the delivering or making default in delivering the nine copies now required by law to be delivered in manner aforesaid.

No person shall import into any part of the United Kingdom for sale any book first composed, &c. within the United Kingdom, and reprinted elsewhere.

VII. And be it further enacted, That from and after the passing of this Act it shall not be lawful for any person or person whomsoever to import or bring into any part of the United Kingdom of *Great Britain* and *Ireland* for sale any printed book or books first composed written or printed and published in any part of the said United Kingdom and reprinted in any other country or place whatsoever; and if any person or persons shall import or bring or cause to be imported or brought for sale any such printed book or books into any part of the said United Kingdom contrary to the true intent and meaning of this Act, or shall knowingly sell publish or expose to sale or have in his or their possession for sale any such book or books, then every such book or books shall be

41 G. III. c. 107.

Penalty on importing, selling, or keeping for sale any such books, forfeiture thereof, and also 10l. and double the value.

forfeited and shall and may be seized by any officer or officers of Customs or Excise and the same shall be forthwith made waste paper; and all and every person and persons so offending, being duly convicted thereof, shall also for every such offence forfeit the sum of ten pounds and double the value of each and every copy of such book or books which he she or they shall so import or bring or cause to be imported or brought into any part of the said United Kingdom, or shall knowingly sell publish or expose to sale or shall cause to be sold published or exposed to sale, or shall have in his or their possession for sale contrary to the true intent and meaning of this Act; and the commissioners of Customs in *England Scotland* and *Ireland* respectively (in case the same shall be seized by any officer or officers of Customs), and the commissioners of Excise in *England Scotland* and *Ireland* respectively (in case the same shall be seized by any officer or officers of Excise) shall also reward the officer or officers who shall seize any books which shall be so made waste paper of with such sum or sums of money as they the said respective commissioners shall think fit, not exceeding the value of such books; such reward respectively to be paid by the said respective commissioners out of any money in their hands respectively arising from the duties of Customs and Excise: Provided, that no person or persons shall be liable to any of the last-mentioned penalties or forfeitures for or by reason or means of the importation of any book or books which has not been printed or reprinted in some part of the said United Kingdom within twenty years next before the same shall be imported, or of any book or books reprinted abroad and inserted among other books or tracts to be sold therewith in any collection where the greatest part of such collection shall have been first composed or written abroad.

Books may be seized by officers of customs or excise, who shall be rewarded.

Exceptions as to books not having been printed in the United Kingdom for 20 years, &c.

General issue.

VIII. And be it further enacted, That if any action or suit shall be commenced or brought against any person or persons whomsoever for doing or causing to be done any thing in pursuance of this Act, the defendants in such action may plead the general issue and give the special matter in evidence; and if upon such action a verdict shall be given for the defendant, or the plaintiff become non-suited or discontinue his action, then the defendant shall have and recover his full costs, for which he shall have the same remedy as a defendant in any case by law hath; and that all actions suits bills indictments or informations for any offence that shall be committed against this Act shall be brought sued and commenced within six months next after such offence committed, or else the same shall be void and of none effect.

41 G. III. c. 107.

Limitation of actions under this act six months.

d

54 Geo. III. c. 56. — An Act to amend and render more effectual an Act of his present Majesty, for encouraging the Art of making new Models and Casts of Busts, and other Things therein mentioned; and for giving further Encouragement to such Arts. — [18*th May* 1814.]

54 G. III. c. 56.

38 Geo. III. c. 1, § 1.

"WHEREAS by an Act passed in the thirty-eighth year of the reign of his present Majesty, intituled, *An Act for encouraging the Art of making new Models and Casts of Busts, and other Things therein mentioned;* the sole right and property thereof were vested in the original proprietors for a time therein specified: And whereas the provisions of the said Act having been found ineffectual for the purposes thereby intended, it is expedient to amend the same and to make other provisions and regulations for the encouragement of artists and to secure to them the profits of and in their works and for the advancement of the said arts:" May it therefore please your Majesty that it may be enacted; and be it enacted by the King's most excellent Majesty, by and with the advice and consent of the Lords Spiritual and Temporal and Commons in this present Parliament assembled, and by the authority of the same, That from and after the passing of this Act every person or persons who shall make or cause to be made any new and original sculpture or model or copy or cast of the human figure or human figures or of any bust or busts, or of any part or parts of the human figure clothed in drapery or otherwise, or of any animal or animals or of any part or parts of any animal combined with the human figure or otherwise, or of any subject being matter of invention in sculpture or of any alto or basso-relievo representing any of the matters or things herein-before mentioned, or any cast from nature of the human figure or of any part or parts of the human figure, or of any cast from nature of any animal or of any part or parts of any animal, or of any such subject containing or representing any of the matters and things herein-before men-

Sole right and property of all new and original sculpture, models, copies and casts, vested in proprietors for 14 years.

54 G. III. c. 56.

tioned, whether separate or combined, shall have the sole right and property of all and in every such new and original sculpture model copy and cast of the human figure and human figures and of all and in every such bust or busts and of all and in every such part or parts of the human figure clothed in drapery or otherwise, and of all and in every such new and original sculpture model copy and cast representing any animal or animals, and of all and in every such work representing any part or parts of any animal combined with the human figure or otherwise, and of all and in every such new and original sculpture model copy and cast of any subject being matter of invention in sculpture, and of all and in every such new and original sculpture model copy and cast in alto or basso-relievo representing any of the matters or things herein-before mentioned and of every such cast from nature, for the term of fourteen years from first putting forth or publishing the same; provided, in all and every case, the proprietor or proprietors do cause his her or their name or names with the date to be put on all and every such new and original sculpture model copy or cast and on every such cast from nature before the same shall be put forth or published.*

* Name and date affixed.

Works published under Act, vested in proprietors for 14 years.

II. And be it further enacted, That the sole right and property of all works which have been put forth or published under the protection of the said recited Act shall be extended continued to and vested in the respective proprietors thereof for the term of fourteen years to commence from the date when such last-mentioned works respectively were put forth or published.

Putting forth pirated copies or pirated casts prosecuted.

III. And be it further enacted, That if any person or persons shall within such term of fourteen years make or import or cause to be made or imported or exposed to sale or otherwise disposed of any pirated copy or pirated cast of any such new and original sculpture or model or copy or cast of the human figure or human figures or of any such bust or busts, or of any such part or parts of the human human figure clothed in drapery or otherwise, or of any such work of any animal or animals or of any

54 G. III. c. 56.

such part or parts of any animal or animals combined with the human figure or otherwise, or of any such subject being matter of invention in sculpture, or of any such alto or basso-relievo representing any of the matters or things herein-before mentioned, or of any such cast from nature as aforesaid, whether such pirated copy or pirated cast be produced by moulding or copying from or imitating in any way any of the matters or things put forth or published under the protection of this Act, or of any works which have been put forth or published under the protection of the said recited Act, the right and property whereof is and are secured extended and protected by this Act in any of the cases as aforesaid, to the detriment damage or loss of the original or respective proprietor or proprietors of any such works so pirated; then and in all such cases the said proprietor or proprietors or their assignee or assignees shall and may, by and in a special action upon the case to be brought against the person or persons so offending, receive such damages as a jury on a trial of such action shall give or assess together with double costs of suit.

Damages. Double costs.

Purchasers of copyright secured in the same.

IV. Provided nevertheless, That no person or persons who shall or may hereafter purchase the right or property of any new and original sculpture or model or copy or cast, or of any cast from nature or of any of the matters and things published under or protected by virtue of this Act, of the proprietor or proprietors expressed in a deed in writing signed by him her or them respectively with his her or their own hand or hands in the presence of and attested by two or more credible witnesses, shall be subject to any action for copying or casting or vending the same; any thing contained in this Act to the contrary notwithstanding.

Limitation of actions.

V. Provided always and be it further enacted, That all actions to be brought as aforesaid against any person or persons for any offence committed against this Act shall be commenced within six calendar months next after the discovery of every such offence and not afterwards.

VI. Provided always and be it further enacted, That from and immediately after the expiration of the said term of fourteen years the sole right of making and disposing of such new and original sculpture or model or copy or cast of any of the matters or things herein-before mentioned shall return to the person or persons who originally made or caused to be made the same, if he or they shall be then living, for the further term of fourteen years, excepting in the case or cases where such person or persons shall by sale or otherwise have divested himself herself or themselves of such right of making or disposing of any new and original sculpture or model or copy or cast of any of the matters or things herein-before mentioned previous to the passing of this Act.

54 G. III. c. 56.

Additional term of 14 years, in case maker of original sculpture, &c. shall be living.

54 George III. c. 156. — An Act to amend the several Acts for the Encouragement of Learning, by securing the Copies and Copyright of printed Books to the Authors of such Books, or their Assigns.—[29*th July* 1814.]

54 G. III. c. 156. 8 Anne, c. 19, § 5. " Whereas by an Act made in the eighth year of the reign of her late Majesty Queen *Anne*, intituled *An Act for the Encouragement of Learning, by vesting the Copies of printed Books in the Authors or Purchasers of such Copies during the times therein mentioned*, it was among other things provided and enacted, That nine copies of each book or books upon the best paper that from and after the said tenth day of *April* one thousand seven hundred and ten should be printed and published as in the said Act mentioned, or reprinted and published with additions, should by the printer and printers thereof be delivered to the warehouse-keeper of the Company of Stationers for the time being at the hall of the said Company before such publication made for the use of the royal library, the libraries of the universities of *Oxford* and *Cambridge*, the libraries of the four universities in *Scotland* the library of *Sion College* in *London*, and library of the Faculty of Advocates at *Edinburgh;* which said warehouse-keeper is by the said Act required to deliver such copies for the use of the said libraries; and that if any proprietor bookseller or printer or the said warehouse-keeper should not observe the directions of the said Act therein, that then he or they so making default in not delivering the said printed copies should forfeit besides the value of the said printed copies the sum of five pounds for every copy not so delivered: And whereas by an Act made in the forty-first year of the reign of his present Majesty, intituled *An Act for the further Encouragement of Learning in the United Kingdom of* Great Britain *and* Ireland, *by securing the Copies and Copyright of printed Books to the Authors of such Books or their assigns for the time herein mentioned*, it is amongst other

41 G. III. (U. K.) c. 107, § 6.

things provided and enacted, That in addition to the nine copies required by law to be delivered to the warehouse-keeper of the said Company of Stationers of each and every book and books which shall be entered in the register books of the said company two other copies shall in like manner be delivered for the use of the library of the college of the *Holy Trinity* and the library of the society of the *King's Inns* in *Dublin* by the printer and printers of all and every such book and books as should thereafter be printed and published and the title of the copyright whereof should be entered in the said register book of the said Company: And whereas it is expedient that copies of books hereafter printed or published should be delivered to the libraries herein-after mentioned with the modifications that shall be provided by this Act;" May it therefore please your Majesty that it may be enacted; and be it enacted by the King's most excellent Majesty, by and with the advice and consent of the Lords Spiritual and Temporal and Commons in this present Parliament assembled, and by the authority of the same, That so much of the said several recited Acts of the eighth year of Queen *Anne* and of the forty-first year of his present Majesty as requires that any copy or copies of any book or books which shall be printed or published, or reprinted and published with additions, shall be delivered by the printer or printers thereof to the warehouse-keeper of the said Company of Stationers for the use of any of the libraries in the said Act mentioned and as requires the delivery of the said copies by the said warehouse-keeper for the use of the said libraries, and as imposes any penalty on such printer or warehouse-keeper for not delivering the said copies shall be and the same is hereby repealed.

54 G. III. c. 156.

repealed.

II. And be it further enacted, That eleven printed copies of the whole of every book and of every volume thereof upon the paper upon which the largest number or impression of such book shall be printed for sale, together with all maps and prints belonging thereto, which from and after the passing of this Act shall be printed and

Eleven printed copies delivered on demand within 12 months after publication, for use of public libraries.

54 G. III. c. 156.

published on demand thereof being made in writing to or left at the place of abode of the publisher or publishers thereof at any time within twelve months next after the publication thereof under the hand of the warehouse-keeper of the Company of Stationers or the librarian or other person thereto authorized by the persons or body politic and corporate proprietors or managers of the libraries following, *videlicet* the *British Museum Sion College* the *Bodleian Library* at *Oxford* the *Public Library* at *Cambridge* the library of the *Faculty of Advocates* at *Edinburgh*, the libraries of the four universities of *Scotland Trinity College Library* and the *King's Inns Library* at *Dublin*, or so many of such eleven copies as shall be respectively demanded on behalf of such libraries respectively, shall be delivered by the publisher or publishers thereof respectively within one month after demand made thereof in writing as aforesaid to the warehouse-keeper of the said Company of Stationers for the time being; which copies the said warehouse-keeper shall and he is hereby required to receive at the hall of the said Company for the use of the library for which such demand shall be made within such twelve months as aforesaid; and the said warehouse-keeper is hereby required within one month after any such book or volume shall be so delivered to him as aforesaid to deliver the same for the use of such library: and if any publisher or the warehouse-keeper of the said Company of Stationers shall not observe the directions of this Act therein, that then he and they so making default in not delivering or receiving the said eleven printed copies as aforesaid shall forfeit besides the value of the said printed copies the sum of five pounds for each copy not so delivered or received together with the full costs of suit; the same to be recovered by the person or persons or body politic or corporate proprietors or managers of the library for the use whereof such copy or copies ought to have been delivered or received; for which penalties and value such person or persons body politic or corporate is or are now hereby authorized to sue by action of debt or other

Publishers, &c. neglecting.

Penalty.

54 G. III. c. 156.

proper action in any court of record in the United Kingdom.

No copies of second, &c. edition, without addition or alteration, demanded.

III. Provided always and be it further enacted, That no such printed copy or copies shall be demanded by or delivered to or for the use of any of the libraries hereinbefore mentioned of the second edition or of any subsequent edition of any book or books so demanded and delivered as aforesaid, unless the same shall contain additions or alterations: and in case any edition after the first of any book so demanded and delivered as aforesaid shall contain any addition or alteration no printed copy or copies thereof shall be demanded or delivered as aforesaid, if a printed copy of such additions or alterations only printed in an uniform manner with the former edition of such book be delivered to each of the libraries aforesaid, for whose use a copy of the former edition shall have been demanded and delivered as aforesaid: Provided also, that the copy of every book that shall be demanded by the *British Museum* shall be delivered of the best paper on which such work shall be printed.

Additions printed and delivered separate.

Proviso for British Museum.

8 Anne, c. 19, § 1. 41 G. III. (U. K.) c. 107, § 1.

Instead of copyright for 14 years and contingently for 14 more, authors, &c. shall have 28 years' copyright in works, and for residue of life.

IV. "And whereas by the said recited Acts of the eighth year of Queen *Anne* and the forty-first year of his present Majesty's reign it is enacted that the author of any book or books and the assignee or assigns of such author respectively, should have the sole liberty of printing and reprinting such book or books for the term of fourteen years, to commence from the day of first publishing the same and no longer; and it was provided, that after the expiration of the said term of fourteen years, the right of printing or disposing of copies should return to the authors thereof, if they were then living, for another term of fourteen years: And whereas it will afford further encouragement to literature if the duration of such copyright were extended in manner herein-after mentioned;" Be it further enacted, That from and after the passing of this Act the author of any book or books composed and not printed and published, or which shall hereafter be composed and be printed and published and his assignee or assigns shall have the sole liberty of printing and

54 G. III. c. 156.

reprinting such book or books for the full term of twenty-eight years to commence from the day of first publishing the same, and also if the author shall be living at the end of that period for the residue of his natural life; and that if any bookseller or printer or other person whatsoever in any part of the United Kingdom of *Great Britain* and *Ireland* in the Isles of *Man Jersey* or *Guernsey* or in any other part of the *British* dominions shall from and after the passing of this Act, within the terms and times granted and limited by this Act as aforesaid, print reprint or import or shall cause to be printed reprinted or imported any such book or books without the consent of the author or authors or other proprietor or proprietors of the copyright of and in such book and books first had and obtained in writing; or knowing the same to be so printed reprinted or imported without such consent of such author or authors or other proprietor or proprietors, shall sell, publish or expose to sale or cause to be sold published or exposed to sale or shall have in his or their possession for sale any such book or books without such consent first had and obtained as aforesaid, then such offender or offenders shall be liable to a special action on the case at the suit of the author or authors or other proprietor or proprietors of the copyright of such book or books so unlawfully printed reprinted or imported or published or exposed to sale or being in the possession of such offender or offenders for sale as aforesaid contrary to the true intent and meaning of this Act: and every such author or authors or other proprietor or proprietors shall and may by and in such special action upon the case to be so brought against such offender or offenders in any court of record in that part of the said United Kingdom or of the *British* dominions in which the offence shall be committed, recover such damages as the jury on the trial of such action or on the execution of a writ of enquiry thereon, shall give give or assess together with double costs of suit; in which action no wager of law essoign privilege or protection nor more than one imparlance shall be allowed; and all and every such offender and

Booksellers, &c. in any part of United Kingdom, or British dominions, who shall print, &c. any book, without consent of proprietor, liable to action for damages.

Penalty.

54 G. III. c. 156.

offenders shall also forfeit such book or books and all and every sheet being part of such book or books, and shall deliver the same to the author or authors or other proprietor or proprietors of the copyright of such book or books upon order of any court of record in which any action or suit in law or equity shall be commenced or prosecuted by such author or authors or other proprietor or proprietors to be made on motion or petition to the said court; and the said author or authors or other proprietor or proprietors shall forthwith damask or make waste paper of the said book or books and sheet or sheets; and all and every such offender or offenders shall also forfeit the sum of three pence for every sheet thereof either printed or printing or published or exposed to sale contrary to the true intent and meaning of this Act; the one moiety thereof to the King's most excellent Majesty his heirs and successors, and the other moiety thereof to any person or persons who shall sue for the same, in any such court of record by action of debt bill plaint or information, in which no wager of law essoign privilege or protection nor more than one imparlance shall be allowed: Provided always, that in *Scotland* such offender or offenders shall be liable to an action of damages in the court of session in *Scotland*, which shall and may be brought and prosecuted in the same manner in which any other action of damages to the like amount may be brought and prosecuted there; and in any such action where damages shall be awarded double costs of suit or expenses of process shall be allowed.

Penalty.

Offenders in Scotland.

V. And in order to ascertain what books shall be from time to time published, Be it enacted, That the publisher or publishers of any and every book demandable under this Act, which shall be published at any time after the passing of this Act, shall within one calendar month after the day on which any such book or books respectively shall be first sold published advertised or offered for sale within the bills of mortality, or within three calendar months if the said book shall be sold published or advertised in any other part of the United Kingdom enter the

Within what time title of books entered at Stationers' Hall.

54 G. III. c. 156.

title to the copy of every such book and the name or names and place of abode of the publisher or publishers thereof in the register book of the Company of Stationers in *London*, in such manner as hath been usual with respect to books the title whereof hath heretofore been entered in such register book, and deliver one copy on the best paper as aforesaid for the use of the *British Museum*; which register book shall at all times be kept at the hall of the said Company; for every of which several entries the sum of two shillings shall be paid and no more; which said register book may at all seasonable and convenient times be resorted to and inspected by any person; for which inspection the sum of one shilling shall be paid to the warehouse-keeper of the said Company of Stationers, and such warehouse-keeper shall when and as often as thereto required, give a certificate under his hand of every or any such entry, and for every such certificate the sum of one shilling shall be paid; and in case such entry of the title of any such book or books shall not be duly made by the publisher or publishers of any such book or books within the said calendar month or three months as the case may be, then the publisher or publishers of such book or books shall forfeit the sum of five pounds together with eleven times the price at which such book shall be sold or advertised, to be recovered together with full cost of suit by the person or persons body politic or corporate authorized to sue and who shall first sue for the same in any court of record in the United Kingdom by action of debt bill plaint or information, in which no wager of law essoign privilege or protection nor more than one imparlance shall be allowed: Provided always, That in the case of magazines reviews or other periodical publications, it shall be sufficient to make such entry in the register book of the said Company within one month next after the publication of the first number or volume of such magazine review or other periodical publication: Provided always, That no failure in making any such entry shall in any manner affect any copyright, but shall only subject the person making default to the penalty aforesaid under this Act.

Copy for British Museum.

Inspection of register-book.

Certificate.

Title of book not entered.

Penalty.

Proviso for Magazines, &c.

Proviso.

54 G. III. c. 156.

VI. And be it further enacted, That the said warehouse-keeper of the Company of Stationers shall from time to time and at all times, without any greater interval than three months, transmit to the librarian or other person authorized on behalf of the libraries before mentioned correct lists of all books entered in the books of the said Company and not contained in former lists; and that on being required so to do by the said librarians or other authorized person or either of them, he shall call on the publisher or publishers of such books for as many of the said copies as may have been demanded of them.

Warehouse keeper of Stationers' Hall to transmit to librarians lists of books entered; and call on publisher for copies.

VII. Provided always and be it further enacted, That if any publisher shall be desirous of delivering the copy of such book or volume as aforesaid as shall be demanded on behalf of any of the said libraries at such library, it shall and may be lawful for him to deliver the same at such library to the librarian or other person authorized to receive the same (who is hereby required to receive and to give a receipt in writing for the same): and such delivery shall to all intents and purposes of this Act be as equivalent to a delivery to the said warehouse-keeper.

Publishers to deliver books at library.

What deemed delivery.

VIII. And whereas it is reasonable that authors of books already published and who are now living should also have the benefit of the extension of copyright; Be it further enacted, That if the author of any book or books which shall not have been published fourteen years at the time of passing this Act shall be living at the said time, and if such author shall afterwards die before the expiration of the said fourteen years, then the personal representative of the said author and the assignees or assigns of such personal representative shall have the sole right of printing and publishing the said book or books for the further term of fourteen years after the expiration of the first fourteen years: Provided that nothing in this Act contained shall affect the right of the assignee or assigns of such author to sell any copies of the said book or books which shall have been printed by such assignee or assigns within the first fourteen years or the terms of any contract between such author and such assignee or assigns.

Authors of books published, now living, to have benefit of extension of copyright.

Proviso.

54 G. III. c. 156.

Authors living at end of 28 years sole right of publication for life.

IX. And be it also further enacted, That if the author of any book or books which have been already published shall be living at the end of twenty-eight years after the first publication of the said book or books, he or she shall for the remainder of his or her life have the sole right of printing and publishing the same: Provided that this shall not affect the right of the assignee or assigns of such author to sell any copies of the said book or books which shall have been printed by such assignee or assigns within the said twenty-eight years or the terms of any contract between such author and such assignee or assigns.

Limitation of actions.

X. Provided nevertheless and be it further enacted, That all actions suits bills indictments or informations for any offence that shall be committed against this Act shall be brought sued and commenced within twelve months next after such offence committed, or else the same shall be void and of no effect.

3 Will. IV. c. 15.—An Act to amend the Laws relating to Dramatic and Literary Property.—[10*th June* 1833.]

3 W. IV. c. 15.

54 Geo. III. c. 156.

Whereas by an Act passed in the fifty-fourth year of the reign of his late Majesty King George the Third, intituled "An Act to amend the several Acts for the Encouragement of Learning, by securing the Copies and Copyright of Printed Books to the Authors of such Books, or their Assigns," it was amongst other things provided and enacted, that from and after the passing of the said act the author of any book or books composed, and not printed or published, or which should thereafter be composed and printed and published, and his assignee or assigns, should have the sole liberty of printing and reprinting such book or books for the full term of twenty-eight years, to commence from the day of first publishing the same, and also, if the author should be living at the end of that period, for the residue of his natural life: and whereas it is expedient to extend the provisions of the said act; be it therefore enacted by the King's most excellent Majesty, by and with the advice and consent of the lords spiritual and temporal, and commons, in this present parliament assembled, and by the authority of the same, That from and after the passing of this act the author of any tragedy, comedy, play, opera, farce, or any other dramatic piece or entertainment, composed, and not printed and published by the author thereof or his assignee, or which hereafter shall be composed, and not printed or published by the author thereof or his assignee, or the assignee of such author, shall have as his own property the sole liberty of representing, or causing to be represented, at any place or places of dramatic entertainment whatsoever, in any part of the United Kingdom of Great Britain and Ireland, in the isles of Man, Jersey, and Guernsey, or in any part of the British dominions, any such production as aforesaid, not printed and published by the author thereof or his assignee, and shall be deemed and taken to be the

The author of any dramatic piece shall have as his property the sole liberty of representing it, or causing it to be represented, at any place of dramatic entertainment.

3 W. IV. c. 15.

proprietor thereof; and that the author of any such production, printed and published within ten years before the passing of this act by the author thereof or his assignee, or which shall hereafter be so printed and published, or the assignee of such author, shall, from the time of passing this act, or from the time of such publication respectively, until the end of twenty-eight years from the day of such first publication of the same, and also, if the author or authors, or the survivor of the authors, shall be living at the end of that period, during the residue of his natural life, have as his own property the sole liberty of representing, or causing to be represented, the same at any such place of dramatic entertainment as aforesaid, and shall be deemed and taken to be the proprietor thereof: provided nevertheless, that nothing in this act contained shall prejudice, alter, or affect the right or authority of any person to represent or cause to be represented, at any place or places of dramatic entertainment whatsoever, any such production as aforesaid, in all cases in which the author thereof or his assignee shall, previously to the passing of this act, have given his consent to or authorized such representation, but that such sole liberty of the author or his assignee shall be subject to such right or authority.

Proviso as to cases where, previous to the passing of this act, a consent has been given.

Penalty on persons performing pieces contrary to this act.

II. And be it further enacted, That if any person shall, during the continuance of such sole liberty as aforesaid, contrary to the intent of this act, or right of the author or his assignee, represent, or cause to be represented, without the consent in writing of the author or other proprietor first had and obtained, at any place of dramatic entertainment within the limits aforesaid, any such production as aforesaid, or any part thereof, every such offender shall be liable for each and every such representation to the payment of an amount not less than forty shillings, or to the full amount of the benefit or advantage arising from such representation, or the injury or loss sustained by the plaintiff therefrom, whichever shall be the greater damages, to the author or other proprietor of such production so represented contrary to the true intent and meaning of this act, to be recovered, together with double costs of suit, by such author or other proprietors, in any court having jurisdiction in such cases in that part of the said United Kingdom or of the British dominions in which the offence shall be committed; and in every such proceeding where the sole liberty of such author or his assignee as aforesaid shall be subject to such right or authority as aforesaid, it shall be sufficient for the plaintiff to state that he has such sole liberty, without stating the same to be subject to such right or authority, or otherwise mentioning the same.

Limitation of actions.

III. Provided nevertheless, and be it further enacted, That all actions or proceedings for any offence or injury that shall be committed against this act shall be brought, sued, and commenced within twelve calendar months next after such offence committed, or else the same shall be void and of no effect.

Explanation of words.

IV. And be it further enacted, That whenever authors, persons, offenders, or others are spoken of in this act in the singular number or in the masculine gender, the same shall extend to any number of persons and to either sex.

e*

5 & 6 W. IV. — An Act for preventing the Publication of Lectures without Consent. — [*9th September* 1835.]

5 & 6 Will. IV.

Authors of lectures, or their assigns, to have the sole right of publishing them.

Penalty on other persons publishing, &c. lectures without leave.

WHEREAS printers, publishers, and other persons have frequently taken the liberty of printing and publishing lectures delivered upon divers subjects, without the consent of the authors of such lectures, or the persons delivering the same in public, to the great detriment of such authors and lecturers: Be it enacted, &c., That from and after the first day of September one thousand eight hundred and thirty-five the author of any lecture or lectures, or the person to whom he hath sold or otherwise conveyed the copy thereof, in order to deliver the same in any school, seminary, institution, or other place, or for any other purpose, shall have the sole right and liberty of printing and publishing such lecture or lectures; and that if any person shall, by taking down the same in short hand or otherwise in writing, or in any other way, obtain or make a copy of such lecture or lectures, and shall print or lithograph or otherwise copy and publish the same, or cause the same to be printed, lithographed, or otherwise copied and published, without leave of the author thereof, or of the person to whom the author thereof hath sold or otherwise conveyed the same, and every person who, knowing the same to have been printed or copied and published without such consent, shall sell, publish or expose to sale, or cause to be sold, published, or exposed to sale any such lecture or lectures, shall forfeit such printed or otherwise copied lecture or lectures, or parts thereof, together with one penny for every sheet thereof which shall be found in his custody, either printed, lithographed, or copied, or printing, lithographing or copying, published or exposed to sale, contrary to the true intent and meaning of this act, the one moiety thereof to his Majesty, his heirs or successors, and the other moiety thereof to any person who shall sue for the same, to be recovered in any of his Majesty's courts of record in

Westminster by action of debt, bill, plaint, or information, in which no wager of law, essoign, privilege, or protection, or more than one imparlance, shall be allowed.

5 & 6 Will. IV.

II. That any printer or publisher of any newspaper who shall, without such leave as aforesaid, print and publish in such newspaper any lecture or lectures, shall be deemed and taken to be a person printing and publishing without leave within the provisions of this act, and liable to the aforesaid forfeitures and penalties in respect of such printing and publishing.

Penalty on printers or publishers of newspapers, publishing lectures without leave.

III. That no person allowed for certain fee and reward, or otherwise, to attend and be present at any lecture delivered in any place, shall be deemed and taken to be licensed or to have leave to print, copy, and publish such lectures only because of having leave to attend such lecture or lectures.

Persons having leave to attend lectures not on that account licensed to publish them.

IV. Provided always, That nothing in this act shall extend to prohibit any person from printing, copying, and publishing any lecture or lectures which have or shall have been printed and published with leave of the authors thereof or their assignees, and whereof the time hath or shall have expired within which the sole right to print and publish the same is given by an act passed in the eighth year of the reign of queen Anne, intituled *An Act for the Encouragement of Learning, by vesting the Copies of Printed Books in the Authors or Purchasers of such Copies during the Times therein mentioned*, and by another passed in the fifty-fourth year of the reign of king George the third, intituled *An Act to amend the several Acts for the Encouragement of Learning, by securing the Copies and Copyright of printed Books to the Authors of such Books, or their Assigns*, or to any lectures which have been printed or published before the passing of this act.

Act not to prohibit the publishing of lectures after the expiration of the copyright

8 Anne, c. 19.

54 G. III. c. 156.

V. Provided further, That nothing in this act shall extend to any lecture or lectures, or the printing, copying, or publishing any lecture or lectures, or parts thereof, of the delivering of which notice in writing shall not have been given to two justices living within five miles from

Act not to extend to lectures delivered in unlicensed places, &c.

5 & 6 Will. IV. the place where such lecture or lectures shall be delivered two days at the least before delivering the same, or to any lecture or lectures delivered in any university or public school or college, or on any public foundation, or by any individual in virtue of or according to any gift, endowment, or foundation; and that the law relating thereto shall remain the same as if this act had not been passed.

1 & 2 Vict. c. 59. — An Act for securing to Authors, in certain Cases, the Benefit of International Copyright. — [31*st July* 1838.]

1 & 2 Vict. c. 59.

Her Majesty, by order in council, may direct that authors of books first published in foreign countries, and their assigns, shall have a copyright in such books within her Majesty's dominions.

WHEREAS it is desirable to afford protection within her Majesty's dominions to the authors of books first published in foreign countries, and their assigns, in cases where protection shall be afforded in such foreign countries to the authors of books first published in her Majesty's dominions, and their assigns; be it therefore enacted by the Queen's most excellent Majesty, by and with the advice and consent of the lords spiritual and temporal, and commons, in this present parliament assembled, and by the authority of the same, That it shall be lawful for her Majesty, by any order of her Majesty in council, to direct that the authors of books which shall, after a future time to be specified in such order in council, be published in any foreign country to be specified in such order in council, and their executors, administrators, and assigns, shall have the sole liberty of printing and reprinting such books within the United Kingdom of Great Britain and Ireland, and every other part of the British dominions, for such term as her Majesty shall by such order in council direct, not exceeding the term which authors being British subjects are now by law entitled to in respect of books first published within the United Kingdom; provided that no such author or his assigns shall be entitled to the benefit of this act unless, within a time to be in that behalf prescribed by such order in council, the title to the copy of every such book, and the name and place of abode of the author thereof, and the time and place of the first publication thereof in such foreign country, shall be entered in the register book of the Company of Stationers in London; and unless, within a time to be also prescribed by such order in council, one printed copy of the whole of such book and of every volume thereof, upon the best paper upon which the largest number or impressions of such book shall have been printed for sale, together with

Title of book to be entered at Stationers' Hall, and one copy delivered to the warehouse keeper.

1 & 2 Vict. c. 59.

all maps and prints relating thereto, shall be delivered to the warehouse-keeper of the Company of Stationers at the hall of the said company.

In case of books published anonymously, the name of the publisher to be sufficient.

II. Provided always, and be it enacted, That if a book be published anonymously it shall be sufficient to insert in the entry thereof in such register book the name and place of abode of the first publisher thereof, instead of the name and place of abode of the author thereof, together with a declaration that such entry is made either on behalf of the author or on behalf of such first publisher, as the case may require.

Wrongful first publication may be amended by court of chancery.

III. And be it enacted, That every such entry shall be *prima facie* proof of a rightful first publication; but if there be a wrongful first publication, and any party have availed himself thereof to obtain an entry of a spurious work, the author or his first publisher may apply by petition or on motion to the Court of Chancery to order such entry to be amended; but no such order shall be made unless it be proved to the satisfaction of the said court, first with respect to a wrongful publication in a country to which the author or first publisher does not belong, and in regard to which there does not subsist with this country any treaty of international copyright, that the party making the application was the author or first publisher, as the case requires; second, with respect to a wrongful first publication either in the country where a rightful first publication has taken place, or in regard to which there subsists with this country a treaty of international copyright, that a court of competent jurisdiction in any such country where such wrongful first publication has taken place has given judgment in favor of the right of the party claiming to be the author or first publisher.

Register book to be kept at Stationers' Hall, and to be open to inspection.

IV. And be it enacted, That such register book shall at all times be kept at the hall of the said company, and for every such entry the sum of two shillings, and no more, shall be paid, and the same register book may at all seasonable and convenient times be inspected by any person on payment of the sum of one shilling, and no more, to the warehouse keeper of the said Company of

1 & 2 Vict. c. 59.

Stationers; and such warehouse keeper shall, when and as often as thereto required, give a certificate under his hand of every or any such entry and delivery, and of the time of making the same respectively, and for every such certificate the sum of one shilling shall be paid; and such certificate, upon proof of the handwriting of the person signing the same, and that such person was in fact the warehouse keeper of the said company, shall without further proof be admitted in all courts as evidence of such entry and delivery, and of the time of making the same respectively.

Certificate by warehouse keeper.

V. And be it enacted, That the said warehouse keeper shall receive at the hall of the said company every book or volume so to be delivered as aforesaid, and within one calendar month after receiving such book or volume shall deposit the same in the library of the British Museum.

Warehouse keeper to deposit books in the British Museum.

VI. Provided always, and be it enacted, that it shall not be requisite to deliver to the warehouse keeper of the said Stationers' Company any printed copy of the second or of any subsequent edition of any book or books so delivered as aforesaid, unless the same shall contain additions or alterations; and in case any edition after the first of any book so delivered as aforesaid shall contain any addition or alteration, it shall not be requisite to deliver any printed copies thereof, if one printed copy of such additions or alterations only, printed in an uniform manner with the former edition of such book, be, within a time in that behalf to be prescribed by any such order in council as aforesaid, delivered to the warehouse keeper of the said Company of Stationers.

Second or subsequent editions.

VII. And be it enacted, That the respective terms to be specified by such orders in council respectively for the continuance of the privilege to be granted to the authors of books to be first published in foreign countries, and their respective assigns, may be different for books first published in different foreign countries, and that the times to be prescribed for the entry of the titles to the copies of such books, and the delivery to the said warehouse keeper of the aforesaid copy, may be different for

Orders in council may specify different periods for different foreign countries, &c.

1 & 2 Vict. c. 59.

different foreign countries and for different classes of books.

Booksellers, &c. who shall print, &c. any book to which order in council may extend, without consent of proprietor, liable to penalties.

VIII. And be it enacted, That if any bookseller or printer, or other person whatsoever, in any part of the United Kingdom of Great Britain and Ireland, or in any other part of the British dominions, shall, within the term to be limited by any such order in council, print, reprint, or import for sale, or cause to be printed, reprinted, or imported for sale, any book to which such order in council shall extend, without the consent of the author or other proprietor of the copyright of and in such book first had and obtained in writing, or, knowing the same to be so printed, reprinted, or imported for sale without such consent of such author or other proprietor, shall sell, publish, or expose to sale, or cause to be sold, published, or exposed to sale, or have in his possession for sale, any such book without such consent first had and obtained as aforesaid, then every such offender shall be liable to a special action on the case, at the suit of the author or other proprietor of the copyright of and in such book so unlawfully printed, reprinted, imported, or published or exposed to sale, or being in the possession of such offender for sale as aforesaid, contrary to the true intent and meaning of this act; and every such author or other proprietor shall and may, by and in such special action on the case to be so brought against such offender in any court of record in that part of the said United Kingdom or of the British dominions in which the offence shall be committed, recover such damages as the jury on the trial of such action or on the execution of a writ of inquiry thereon shall give or assess, together with double costs of suit, in which action no privilege or protection shall be allowed; and every such offender shall also forfeit such book, and every sheet being part of such book, and shall upon order of any court of record in which any action at law or suit in equity shall be commenced or prosecuted by such author or other proprietor, to be made on motion or petition to the said court, deliver the same to the author or other proprietor of the copyright of such book, or to his

1 & 2 Vict. c. 59.

attorney or agent to be thereto lawfully authorized, and he shall forthwith damask or make waste paper of the same; and every such offender shall also forfeit the sum of threepence for every sheet thereof, either printed or printing, or published or exposed to sale contrary to the true intent and meaning of this act; the one moiety thereof to her Majesty, and the other moiety thereof to any person who shall sue for the same in any such court of record by action of debt, bill, plaint, or information, in which no privilege or protection shall be allowed: provided always, that in Scotland such offender shall be liable to an action of damages in the court of Session in Scotland, which shall and may be brought and prosecuted in the same manner in which any other action of damages to the like amount may be brought and prosecuted there, and in any such action where damages shall be awarded double costs of suit or expenses of process shall be allowed.

No order in council to have any effect unless it states that reciprocal protection is secured.

IX. Provided always, and be it enacted, That no such order in council shall have any effect unless it shall be therein stated, as the ground for issuing the same, that due protection for the benefit of the authors of printed books first published in the dominions of her Majesty, and their assigns, has been secured by the foreign power in whose dominions the books to which such order in council shall relate shall be first published.

Orders in council may be revoked.

X. And be it enacted, That it shall be lawful for her Majesty, by an order in council, from time to time to revoke or alter any order in council previously made under the authority of this act, but nevertheless without prejudice to any rights acquired previously to such revocation or alteration.

Orders in council to be published in Gazette, and to have same effect as this act.

XI. And be it enacted, That every order in council to be made under the authority of this act shall, as soon as may be after the making thereof by her Majesty in council, be published in the London Gazette, and from the time of such publication shall have the same effect as if every part thereof were included in this act.

Orders in council to be laid before parliament.

XII. And be it enacted, That a copy of every order of her Majesty in council made under this act shall be laid

1 & 2 Vict. c. 59.

before both houses of parliament within six weeks after issuing the same if parliament be then sitting, and if not, then within six weeks after the commencement of the then next session of parliament.

Translations of books first published abroad.

XIII. Provided always, and be it enacted, that nothing in this act contained shall be construed to prevent the printing, publication, or sale of any translation of any book, the author whereof and his assigns may be entitled to the benefit of this act.

Foreign authors not entitled to copyright except under this act.

XIV. And be it enacted, That the author of any book to be after the passing of this act first published out of her Majesty's dominions, or his assigns, shall have no copyright therein within her Majesty's dominions otherwise than such (if any) as he may become entitled to under this act.

Limitation of actions.

XV. Provided nevertheless, and be it enacted, that all actions, suits, bills, indictments, or informations for any offence that shall be committed against this act shall be brought, sued, and commenced within twelve months next after such offence committed, and not afterwards.

Interpretation clause.

XVI. And be it enacted, That in the construction of this act the word "book" shall be construed to include "volume," "pamphlet," "sheet of letter-press," "sheet of music," "map," "chart," or "plan"; and the words "printing" and "reprinting" shall include engraving and any other method of multiplying copies; and the expression "her Majesty" shall include the heirs and successors of her Majesty; and the expressions "order of her Majesty in council" and "order in council" shall respectively mean order of her Majesty, acting by and with the advice of her Majesty's most honourable privy council; and in describing any persons or things any word importing the plural number shall mean also one person or thing, and any word importing the singular number shall include several persons or things, and any word importing the masculine shall include also the feminine gender; unless in any of such cases there shall be something in the subject or context repugnant to such construction.

XVII. And be it enacted, That this act may be amended or repealed by any act to be passed in this present session of parliament.

1 & 2 Vict. c. 59.

Act may be amended.

5 & 6 Vict. c. 45.—An Act to amend the Law of Copyright.—[1st *July*, 1842.]

5 & 6 Vict. c. 45.

Whereas it is expedient to amend the law relating to copyright, and to afford greater encouragement to the production of literary works of lasting benefit to the world; be it enacted by the Queen's most excellent Majesty, by and with the advice and consent of the lords spiritual and temporal, and commons, in this present parliament assembled, and by the authority of the same, That from the passing of this act, an act passed in the eighth year of the reign of her Majesty Queen Anne, intituled "An Act for the Encouragement of Learning, by vesting the copies of printed books in the authors or purchasers of such copies during the times therein mentioned;" and also an Act passed in the forty-first year of the reign of his Majesty King George the Third, intituled "An Act for the further Encouragement of Learning in the United Kingdom of Great Britain and Ireland, by securing the copies and copyright of printed books to the authors of such books, or their assigns, for the time therein mentioned;" and also an act passed in the fifty-fourth year of the reign of his Majesty King George the Third, intituled "An Act to amend the several Acts for the Encouragement of Learning, by securing the copies and copyright of printed books to the authors of such books, or their assigns," be and the same are hereby repealed, except so far as the continuance of either of them may be necessary for carrying on or giving effect to any proceedings at law or in equity pending at the time of passing this act, or for enforcing any cause of action or suit, or any right or contract, then subsisting.

Repeal of former acts; 8 Anne, c. 19. 41 G. III. c. 107. 54 Geo. III. c. 156.

Interpretation of act.

II. And be it enacted, That in the construction of this act, the word "book" shall be construed to mean and include every volume, part or division of a volume, pamphlet, sheet of letter-press, sheet of music, map, chart, or plan separately published; that the words "dramatic piece" shall be construed to mean and include every tragedy, comedy, play, opera, farce, or other scenic, musical, or dramatic entertainment; that the word "copyright" shall be construed to mean the sole and exclusive liberty of printing or otherwise multiplying copies of any subject to which the said word is herein applied; that the words "personal representative" shall be construed to mean and include every executor, administrator, and next of kin entitled to administration; that the word "assigns" shall be construed to mean and include every person in whom the interest of an author in copyright shall be vested, whether derived from such author before or after the publication of any book, and whether acquired by sale, gift, bequest, or by operation of law, or otherwise; that the words "British dominions" shall be construed to mean and include all parts of the United Kingdom of Great Britain and Ireland, the islands of Jersey and Guernsey, all parts of the East and West Indies, and all the colonies, settlements, and possessions of the Crown which now are or hereafter may be acquired; and that whenever in this act, in describing any person, matter, or thing, the word importing the singular number or the masculine gender only is used, the same shall be understood to include and to be applied to several persons as well as one person, and females as well as males, and several matters or things as well as one matter or thing, respectively, unless there shall be something in the subject or context repugnant to such construction.

5 & 6 Vict. c. 45.

Endurance of term of copyright in any book hereafter to be published in the lifetime of the author:

III. And be it enacted, That the copyright in every book which shall after the passing of this act be published in the lifetime of its author shall endure for the natural life of such author, and for the further term of seven years, commencing at the time of his death, and shall be the property of such author and his assigns: provided always, that if the said term of seven years shall expire before the end of forty-two years from the first publication of such book, the copyright shall, in that case, endure for such period of forty-two years; and that the copyright in every book which shall be published after the death of its author shall endure for the term of forty-two years from

if published after the author's death

5 & 6 Vict. c. 45.

the first publication thereof, and shall be the property of the proprietor of the author's manuscript from which such book shall be first published, and his assigns.

In cases of subsisting copyright, the term to be extended, except when it shall belong to an assignee for other consideration than natural love and affection; in which case it shall cease at the expiration of the present term, unless its extension be agreed to between the proprietor and the author.

IV. And whereas it is just to extend the benefits of this act to authors of books published before the passing thereof, and in which copyright still subsists; be it enacted, That the copyright which at the time of the passing of this act shall subsist in any book theretofore published (except as hereinafter mentioned) shall be extended and endure for the full term provided by this act in cases of books thereafter published, and shall be the property of the person who at the time of passing of this act shall be the proprietor of such copyright: provided always, that in all cases in which such copyright shall belong in whole or in part to a publisher or other person who shall have acquired it for other consideration than that of natural love and affection, such copyright shall not be extended by this act, but shall endure for the term which shall subsist therein at the time of passing of this act, and no longer, unless the author of such book, if he shall be living, or the personal representative of such author, if he shall be dead, and the proprietor of such copyright, shall, before the expiration of such term, consent and agree to accept the benefits of this act in respect of such book, and shall cause a minute of such consent, in the form in that behalf given in the schedule to this act annexed, to be entered in the book of registry hereinafter directed to be kept, in which case such copyright shall endure for the full term by this act provided in cases of books to be published after the passing of this act, and shall be the property of such person or persons as in such minute shall be expressed.

Judicial committee of the privy council may license the republication of books which the proprietor refuses to republish after death of the author

V. And whereas it is expedient to provide against the suppression of books of importance to the public; be it enacted, That it shall be lawful for the Judicial Committee of her Majesty's Privy Council, on complaint made to them that the proprietor of the copyright in any book after the death of its author has refused to republish or

5 & 6 Vict. c. 45.

to allow the republication of the same, and that by reason of such refusal such book may be withheld from the public, to grant a licence to such complainant to publish such book, in such manner and subject to such conditions as they may think fit, and that it shall be lawful for such complainant to publish such book according to such licence.

Copies of books published after the passing of this act, and of all subsequent editions, to be delivered within certain times at the British Museum.

VI. And be it enacted, That a printed copy of the whole of every book which shall be published after the passing of this act, together with all maps, prints, or other engravings belonging thereto, finished and coloured in the same manner as the best copies of the same shall be published, and also of any second or subsequent edition which shall be so published with any additions or alterations, whether the same shall be in letter-press, or in the maps, prints, or other engravings belonging thereto, and whether the first edition of such book shall have been published before or after the passing of this act, and also of any second or subsequent edition of every book of which the first or some preceding edition shall not have been delivered for the use of the British Museum, bound, sewed, or stitched together, and upon the best paper on which the same shall be printed, shall, within one calendar month after the day on which any such book shall first be sold, published, or offered for sale within the bills of mortality, or within three calandar months if the same shall first be sold, published or offered for sale in any other part of the United Kingdom, or within twelve calendar months after the same shall first be sold, published, or offered for sale in any other part of the British dominions, be delivered, on behalf of the publisher thereof, at the British Museum.

Mode of delivering at the British Museum.

VII. And be it enacted, That every copy of any book which under the provisions of this act ought to be delivered as aforesaid shall be delivered at the British Museum between the hours of ten in the forenoon and four in the afternoon on any day except Sunday, Ash Wednesday, Good Friday, and Christmas Day, to one of the officers of the said Museum, or to some person authorized by the

5 & 6 Vict. c. 45.

trustees of the said Museum to receive the same; and such officer or other person receiving such copy is hereby required to give a receipt in writing for the same, and such delivery shall to all intents and purposes be deemed to be good and sufficient delivery under the provisions of this act.

A copy of every book to be delivered within a month after demand to the officer of the Stationers' Company, for the following libraries: the Bodleian at Oxford, the Public Library at Cambridge, the Faculty of Advocates at Edinburgh, and that of Trinity College, Dublin.

VIII. And be it enacted, That a copy of the whole of every book, and of any second or subsequent edition of of every book containing additions and alterations, together with all maps and prints belonging thereto, which after the passing of this act shall be published, shall, on demand thereof in writing, left at the place of abode of the publisher thereof at any time within twelve months next after the publication thereof, under the hand of the officer of the Company of Stationers, who shall from time to time be appointed by the said company for the purposes of this act, or under the hand of any other person thereto authorized by the persons or bodies politic and corporate, proprietors and managers of the libraries following, (*videlicet,*) the Bodleian Library at Oxford, the Public Library at Cambridge, the library of the Faculty of Advocates at Edinburgh, the library of the College of the Holy and Undivided Trinity of Queen Elizabeth near Dublin, be delivered upon the paper of which the largest number of copies of such book or edition shall be printed for sale, in the like condition as the copies prepared for sale by the publisher thereof respectively, within one month after demand made thereof in writing as aforesaid, to the said officer of the said Company of Stationers for the time being, which copies the said officer shall and he is hereby required to receive at the hall of the said company, for the use of the library for which such demand shall be made within such twelve months as aforesaid; and the said officer is hereby required to give a receipt in writing for the same, and within one month after any such book shall be so delivered to him as aforesaid to deliver the same for the use of such library.

IX. Provided also, and be it enacted, That if any publisher shall be desirous of delivering the copy of such

5 & 6 Vict. c. 45.

book as shall be demanded on behalf of any of the said libraries at such library, it shall be lawful for him to deliver the same at such library, free of expence, to such librarian or other person authorized to receive the same (who is hereby required in such case to receive and give a receipt in writing for the same,) and such delivery shall to all intents and purposes of this act be held as equivalent to a delivery to the said officer of the Stationers' Company.

Publishers may deliver the copies to the libraries, instead of at the Stationers' Company.

X. And be it enacted, That if any publisher of any such book, or of any second or subsequent edition of any such book, shall neglect to deliver the same, pursuant to this act, he shall for every such default forfeit, besides the value of such copy of such book or edition which he ought to have delivered, a sum not exceeding five pounds, to be recovered by the librarian or other officer (properly authorized) of the library for the use whereof such copy should have been delivered, in a summary way, on conviction before two justices of the peace for the county or place where the publisher making default shall reside, or by action of debt or other proceeding of the like nature, at the suit of such librarian or other officer, in any court of record in the United Kingdom; in which action, if the plaintiff shall obtain a verdict, he shall recover his costs reasonably incurred, to be taxed as between attorney and client.

Penalty for default in delivering copies for the use of the libraries.

XI. And be it enacted, That a book of registry, wherein may be registered, as hereinafter enacted, the proprietorship in the copyright of books, and assignments thereof, and in dramatic and musical pieces, whether in manuscript or otherwise, and licences affecting such copyright, shall be kept at the hall of the Stationers' Company by the officer appointed by the said company for the purposes of this act, and shall at all convenient times be open to the inspection of any person, on payment of one shilling for every entry which shall be searched for or inspected in the said book; and that such officer shall, whenever thereunto reasonably required, give a copy of any entry in such book, certified under his hand, and impressed with the

Book of registry to be kept at Stationers' Hall.

5 & 6 Vict. c. 45.

stamp of the said company, to be provided by them for that purpose, and which they are hereby required to provide, to any person requiring the same, on payment to him of the sum of five shillings; and such copies so certified and impressed shall be received in evidence in all courts, and in all summary proceedings, and shall be *prima facie* proof of the proprietorship or assignment of copyright or licence as therein expressed, but subject to be rebutted by other evidence, and in the case of dramatic or musical pieces shall be *prima facie* proof of the right of representation or performance, subject to be rebutted as aforesaid.

Making a false entry in the book of registry a misdemeanor.

XII. And be it enacted, That if any person shall wilfully make or cause to be made any false entry in the registry book of the Stationers' Company, or shall wilfully produce or cause to be tendered in evidence any paper falsely purporting to be a copy of any entry in the said book, he shall be guilty of an indictable misdemeanor, and shall be punished accordingly.

Entries of copyright may be made in the book of registry.

XIII. And be it enacted, That after the passing of this act it shall be lawful for the proprietor of copyright in any book heretofore published, or in any book hereafter to be published, to make entry in the registry book of the Stationers' Company of the title of such book, the time of the first publication thereof, the name and place of abode of the publisher thereof, and the name and place of abode of the proprietor of the copyright of the said book, or of any portion of such copyright, in the form in that behalf given in the schedule to this act annexed, upon payment of the sum of five shillings to the officer of the said company; and that it shall be lawful for every such registered proprietor to assign his interest, or any portion of his interest therein, by making entry in the said book of registry of such assignment, and of the name and place of abode of the assignee thereof, in the form given in that behalf in the said schedule, on payment of the like sum; and such assignment so entered shall be effectual in law to all intents and purposes whatsoever, without being subject to any stamp or duty, and shall be of the same force and effect as if such assignment had been made by deed.

5 & 6 Vict. c. 45.

Persons aggrieved by any entry in the book of registry may apply to a court of law in term, or judge in vacation, who may order such entry to be varied or expunged.

XIV. And be it enacted, That if any person shall deem himself aggrieved by any entry made under color of this act in the said book of registry, it shall be lawful for such person to apply by motion to the Court of Queen's Bench, Court of Common Pleas, or Court of Exchequer, in term time, or to apply by summons to any judge of either of such courts in vacation, for an order that such entry may be expunged or varied; and that upon any such application by motion or summons to either of the said courts, or to a judge as aforesaid, such court or judge shall make such order for expunging, varying, or confirming such entry, either with or without costs, as to such court or judge shall seem just; and the officer appointed by the Stationers' Company for the purposes of this act shall, on the production to him of any such order for expunging or varying any such entry, expunge or vary the same according to the requisitions of such order.

Remedy for the piracy of books by action on the case.

XV. And be it enacted, That if any person shall, in any part of the British dominions, after the passing of this act, print or cause to be printed, either for sale or exportation, any book in which there shall be subsisting copyright, without the consent in writing of the proprietor thereof, or shall import for sale or hire any such book so having been unlawfully printed from parts beyond the sea, or, knowing such book to have been so unlawfully printed or imported, shall sell, publish, or expose to sale or hire, or cause to be sold, published, or exposed to sale or hire, or shall have in his possession, for sale or hire, any such book so unlawfully printed or imported, without such consent as aforesaid, such offender shall be liable to a special action on the case at the suit of the proprietor of such copyright, to be brought in any court of record in that part of the British dominions in which the offence shall be committed: provided always, that in Scotland such offender shall be liable to an action in the Court of Session in Scotland, which shall and may be brought and prosecuted in the same manner in which any other action

5 & 6 Vict. c. 45.

of damages to the like amount may be brought and prosecuted there.

In actions for piracy the defendant to give notice of the objections to the plaintiff's title on which he means to rely.

XVI. And be it enacted, That after the passing of this act, in any action brought within the British dominions against any person for printing any such book for sale, hire, or exportation, or for importing, selling, publishing, or exposing to sale or hire, or causing to be imported, sold, published, or exposed to sale or hire, any such book, the defendant, on pleading thereto, shall give to the plaintiff a notice in writing of any objections on which he means to rely on the trial of such action; and if the nature of his defence be, that the plaintiff in such action was not the author or first publisher of the book in which he shall by such action claim copyright, or is not the proprietor of the copyright therein, or that some other person than the plaintiff was the author or first publisher of such book, or is the proprietor of the copyright therein, then the defendant shall specify in such notice the name of the person who he alleges to have been the author or first publisher of such book, or the proprietor of the copyright therein, together with the title of such book, and the time when and the place where such book was first published, otherwise the defendant in such action shall not at the trial or hearing of such action be allowed to give any evidence that the plaintiff in such action was not the author or first publisher of the book in which he claims such copyright as aforesaid, or that he was not the proprietor of the copyright therein; and at such trial or hearing no other objection shall be allowed to be made on behalf of such defendant than the objections stated in such notice, or that any other person was the author or first publisher of such book, or the proprietor of the copyright therein, than the person specified in such notice, or give in evidence in support of his defence any other book than one substantially corresponding in title, time, and place of publication with the title, time, and place specified in such notice.

No person except the proprie-

XVII. And be it enacted, That after the passing of this act it shall not be lawful for any person, not being

5 & 6 Vict. c. 45.

the proprietor of the copyright, or some person authorized by him, to import into any part of the United Kingdom, or into any other part of the British dominions, for sale or hire, any printed book first composed or written or printed and published in any part of the said United Kingdom, wherein there shall be copyright, and reprinted in any country or place whatsoever out of the British dominions; and if any person, not being such proprietor or person authorized as aforesaid, shall import or bring, or cause to be imported or brought, for sale or hire, any such printed book, into any part of the British dominions, contrary to the true intent and meaning of this act, or shall knowingly sell, publish, or expose to sale or let to hire, or have in his possession for sale or hire, any such book, then every such book shall be forfeited, and shall be seized by any officer of customs or excise, and the same shall be destroyed by such officer; and every person so offending, being duly convicted thereof before two justices of the peace for the county or place in which such book shall be found, shall also for every such offence forfeit the sum of ten pounds, and double the value of every copy of such book which he shall so import or cause to be imported into any part of the British dominions, or shall knowingly sell, publish, or expose to sale or let to hire, or shall cause to be sold, published, or exposed to sale or let to hire, or shall have in his possession for sale or hire, contrary to the true intent and meaning of this act, five pounds to the use of such officer of customs or excise, and the remainder of the penalty to the use of the proprietor of the copyright in such book.

tor, &c. shall import into the British dominions for sale or hire any book first composed, &c. within the United Kingdom, and reprinted elsewhere, under penalty of forfeiture thereof, and also of 10*l*. and double the value.

Books may be seized by officers of customs or excise.

XVIII. And be it enacted, That when any publisher or other person shall, before or at the time of the passing of this act, have projected, conducted, and carried on, or shall hereafter project, conduct and carry on, or be the proprietor of any encyclopædia, review, magazine, periodical work, or work published in a series of books or parts, or any book whatsoever, and shall have employed or shall employ any persons to compose the same, or any volumes, parts, essays, articles, or portions thereof, for

As to the copyright in encyclopædias, periodicals, and works published in a series, reviews, or magazines.

5 & 6 Vict. c. 45.

publication in or as part of the same, and such work, volumes, parts, essays, articles, or portions shall have been or shall hereafter be composed under such employment, on the terms that the copyright therein shall belong to such proprietor, projector, publisher, or conductor, and paid for by such proprietor, projector, publisher, or conductor, the copyright in every such encyclopædia, review, magazine, periodical work, and work published in a series of books or parts, and in every volume, part, essay, article, and portion so composed and paid for, shall be the property of such proprietor, projector, publisher, or other conductor, who shall enjoy the same rights as if he were the actual author thereof, and shall have such term of copyright therein as is given to the authors of books by this act; except only that in the case of essays, articles, or portions forming part of and first published in reviews, magazines, or other periodical works of a like nature, after the term of twenty-eight years from the first publication thereof respectively the right of publishing the same in a separate form shall revert to the author for the remainder of the term given by this act: provided always, that during the term of twenty-eight years the said proprietor, projector, publisher, or conductor shall not publish any such essay, article, or portion separately or singly without the consent previously obtained of the author thereof, or his assigns: provided also, that nothing herein contained shall alter or affect the right of any person who shall have been or who shall be so employed as aforesaid to publish any such his composition in a separate form, who by any contract, express or implied, may have reserved or may hereafter reserve to himself such right; but every author reserving, retaining, or having such right shall be entitled to the copyright in such composition when published in a separate form, according to this act, without prejudice to the right of such proprietor, projector, publisher, or conductor as aforesaid.

Proviso for authors who have reserved the right of publishing their articles in a separate form.

Proprietors of encyclopædias, periodicals,

XIX. And be it enacted, That the proprietor of the copyright in any encyclopædia, review, magazine, periodical work, or other work published in a series of books

5 & 6 Vict. c. 45.

or parts, shall be entitled to all the benefits of the registration a Stationers' Hall under this act, on entering in the said book of registry the title of such encyclopædia, review, periodical work, or other work published in a series of books or parts, the time of the first publication of the first volume, number, or part thereof, or of the first number or volume first published after the passing of this act in any such work which shall have been published heretofore, and the name and place of abode of the proprietor thereof, and of the publisher thereof, when such publisher shall not also be the proprietor thereof.

and works published in series, may enter at once at Stationers' Hall, and thereon have the benefit of the registration of the whole

XX. And whereas an act was passed in the third year of the reign of his late Majesty, to amend the law relating to dramatic literary property, and it is expedient to extend the term of the sole liberty of representing dramatic pieces given by that act to the full time by this act provided for the continuance of copyright: and whereas it is expedient to extend to musical compositions the benefits of that act, and also of this act; be it therefore enacted, That the provisions of the said act of his late Majesty, and of this act, shall apply to musical compositions, and that the sole liberty of representing or performing, or causing or permitting to be represented or performed, any dramatic piece or musical composition, shall endure and be the property of the author thereof, and his assigns, for the term in this act provided for the duration of copyright in books; and the provisions hereinbefore enacted in respect of the property of such copyright, and of registering the same, shall apply to the liberty of representing or performing any dramatic piece or musical composition, as if the same were herein expressly enacted and applied thereto, save and except that the first public representation or performance of any dramatic piece or musical composition shall be deemed equivalent, in the construction of this act, to the first publication of any book: provided always, that in case of any dramatic piece or musical composition in manuscript, it shall be sufficient for the person having the sole liberty of representing or performing, or causing to be represented or performed the

The provisions of 3 & 4 W. IV. c. 15, extended to musical compositions, and the term of copyright, as provided by this act, applied to the liberty of representing dramatic pieces and musical compositions.

5 & 6 Vict. c. 45.

same, to register only the title thereof, the name and place of abode of the author or composer thereof, the name and place of abode of the proprietor thereof, and the time and place of its first representation or performance.

Proprietors of right of dramatic representations shall have all the remedies given by 3 & 4 W. IV. c. 15.

XXI. And be it enacted, That the person who shall at any time have the sole liberty of representing such dramatic piece or musical composition shall have and enjoy the remedies given and provided in the said act of the third and fourth years of the reign of his late Majesty King William the Fourth, passed to amend the laws relating to dramatic literary property, during the whole of his interest therein, as fully as if the same were re-enacted in this act.

Assignment of copyright of a dramatic piece not to convey the right of representation.

XXII. And be it enacted, That no assignment of the copyright of any book consisting of or containing a dramatic piece or musical composition shall be holden to convey to the assignee the right of representing or performing such dramatic piece or musical composition, unless an entry in the said registry book shall be made of such assignment, wherein shall be expressed the intention of the parties that such right should pass by such assignment.

Books pirated shall become the property of the proprietor of the copyright, and may be recovered by action.

XXIII. And be it enacted, That all copies of any book wherein there shall be copyright, and of which entry shall have been made in the said registry book, and which shall have been unlawfully printed or imported without the consent of the registered proprietor of such copyright, in writing under his hand first obtained, shall be deemed to be the property of the proprietor of such copyright, and who shall be registered as such, and such registered proprietor shall, after demand thereof in writing, be entitled to sue for and recover the same, or damages for the detention thereof, in an action of detinue, from any party who shall detain the same, or to sue for and recover damages for the conversion thereof in an action of trover.

No proprietor of copyright commencing after this act shall sue or proceed for any infringement before making entry in the book of registry.

XXIV. And be it enacted, That no proprietor of copyright in any book which shall be first published after the passing of this act shall maintain any action or suit, at law or in equity, or any summary proceeding, in respect of any infringement of such copyright, unless he shall, before commencing such action, suit, or proceeding, have caused an entry to be made, in the book of registry of the Stationers' Company, of such book, pursuant to this act: provided always, that the omission to make such entry shall not affect the copyright in any book, but only the right to sue or proceed in respect of the infringement thereof as aforesaid: provided also, that nothing herein contained shall prejudice the remedies which the proprietor of the sole liberty of representing any dramatic piece shall have by virtue of the act passed in the third year of the reign of his late Majesty King William the Fourth, to amend the laws relating to dramatic literary property, or of this act, although no entry shall be made in the book of registry aforesaid.

5 & 6 Vict. c. 45.

Proviso for dramatic pieces.

XXV. And be it enacted, That all copyright shall be deemed personal property, and shall be transmissible by bequest, or, in case of intestacy, shall be subject to the same law of distribution as other personal property, and in Scotland shall be deemed to be personal and moveable estate.

Copyright shall be personal property.

XXVI. And be it enacted, That if any action or suit shall be commenced or brought against any person or persons whomsoever for doing or causing to be done any thing in pursuance of this act, the defendant or defendants in such action may plead the general issue, and give the special matter in evidence; and if upon such action a verdict shall be given for the defendant, or the plaintiff shall become nonsuited, or discontinue his action, then the defendant shall have and recover his full costs, for which he shall have the same remedy as a defendant in any case by law hath; and that all actions, suits, bills, indictments, or informations for any offence that shall be committed against this act shall be brought, sued, and commenced within twelve calendar months next after such offence committed, or else the same shall be void and of none effect: provided that such limitation of time shall

General issue.

Limitation of actions;

5 & 6 Vict. c. 45.

not to extend to actions, &c. in respect of the delivery of books.

not extend or be construed to extend to any actions, suits, or other proceedings which under the authority of this act shall or may be brought, sued, or commenced for or in respect of any copies of books to be delivered for the use of the British Museum, or of any one of the four libraries hereinbefore mentioned.

Saving the rights of the Universities, and the colleges of Eton, Westminster, and Winchester.

XXVII. Provided always, and be it enacted, That nothing in this act contained shall affect or alter the rights of the two universities of Oxford and Cambridge, the colleges or houses of learning within the same, the four universities in Scotland, the college of the Holy and Undivided Trinity of Queen Elizabeth near Dublin, and the several colleges of Eton, Westminster, and Winchester, in any copyrights heretofore and now vested or hereafter to be vested in such universities and colleges respectively, any thing to the contrary herein contained notwithstanding.

Saving all subsisting rights, contracts, and engagements.

XXVIII. Provided also, and be it enacted, That nothing in this act contained shall affect, alter, or vary any right subsisting at the time of passing of this act, except as herein expressly enacted; and all contracts, agreements, and obligations made and entered into before the passing of this act, and all remedies relating thereto, shall remain in full force, any thing herein contained to the contrary notwithstanding.

Extent of the act.

XXIX. And be it enacted, that this act shall extend to the United Kingdom of Great Britain and Ireland, and to every part of the British dominions.

Act may be amended this session.

XXX. And be it enacted, That this act may be amended or repealed by any act to be passed in the present session of parliament.

SCHEDULE *to which the preceding act refers.*

No. 1.

FORM OF MINUTE OF CONSENT TO BE ENTERED AT STATIONERS' HALL.

WE, the undersigned, A. B. of , the author of a certain book, intituled Y. Z. [or the personal representative of the author, *as the case may be*], and C. D. of , do hereby certify, that we have consented and agreed to accept the benefits of the act passed in the fifth year of the reign of her Majesty Queen Victoria, cap. , for the extension of the term of copyright therein provided by the said act, and hereby declare that such extended term of copyright therein is the property of the said A. B. or C. D.

Dated this day of , 18 .
Witness (Signed) A. B.
C. D.

To the Registering Officer appointed by the Stationers' Company.

No. 2.

FORM OF REQUIRING ENTRY OF PROPRIETORSHIP.

I, A. B., of , do hereby certify, that I am the proprietor of the copyright of a book, intituled Y. Z., and I hereby require you to make entry in the register book of the Stationers' Company of my proprietorship of such copyright, according to the particulars underwritten.

Title of Book.	Name of Publisher and Place of Publication.	Name and Place of Abode of the Proprietor of the Copyright.	Date of First Publication.
Y. Z.		A. B.	

Dated this day of , 18 .
Witness, C. D. (Signed) A. B.

No. 3.

ORIGINAL ENTRY OF PROPRIETORSHIP OF COPYRIGHT OF A BOOK.

Time of making the Entry.	Title of Book.	Name of the Publisher, and Place of Publication.	Name and Place of Abode of the Proprietor of the Copyright.	Date of First Publication.
	Y. Z.	A. B.	C. D.	

No. 4.

FORM OF CONCURRENCE OF THE PARTY ASSIGNING IN ANY BOOK PREVIOUSLY REGISTERED.

I, A. B., of being the assigner of the copyright of the book hereunder described, do hereby require you to make entry of the assignment of the copyright therein.

Title of Book.	Assigner of the Copyright.	Assignee of Copyright.
Y. Z.	A. B.	C. D.

Dated this day of , 18 .

(Signed) A. B.

No. 5.

FORM OF ENTRY OF ASSIGNMENT OF COPYRIGHT IN ANY BOOK PREVIOUSLY REGISTERED.

Date of Entry.	Title of Book.	Assigner of the Copyright.	Assignee of Copyright.
	[*Set out the title of the book, and refer to the page of the registry book in which the original entry of the copyright thereof is made.*]	A. B.	C. D.

6 & 7 Wm. IV. c. 59. — An Act to extend the Protection of Copyright in Prints and Engravings in Ireland.

6 & 7 Will. IV. c. 59.

17 G. III. c. 57.

"WHEREAS an act was passed in the seventeenth year of the reign of his late Majesty King *George* the third, intituled *An Act for more effectually securing the Property of Prints to Inventors and Engravers, by enabling them to sue for and recover Penalties in certain Cases:* and whereas it is desirable to extend the provisions of the said act to *Ireland;* be it therefore enacted by the King's most excellent Majesty, by and with the advice and consent of the Lords Spiritual and Temporal, and Commons, in this present Parliament assembled, and by the authority of the same, that from and after the passing of this act all the provisions contained in the said recited act of the seventeenth year of the reign of his late Majesty King *George* the third, and of all the other acts therein recited, shall be and the same are hereby extended to the united kingdom of *Great Britain* and *Ireland.*

Provisions of recited act extended to Ireland.

Penalty on engraving or publishing any print without consent of proprietor.

II. And be it further enacted, that from and after the passing of this act, if any engraver, etcher printseller, or other person shall, within the time limited by the aforesaid recited acts, engrave, etch, or publish, or cause to be engraved, etched, or published any engraving or print of any description whatever, either in whole or in part, which may have been or which shall hereafter be published in any part of *Great Britain* or *Ireland,* without the express consent of the proprietor or proprietors thereof first had and obtained in writing, signed by him, her, or them respectively, with his, her or their own hand or hands, in the presence of and attested by two or more credible witnesses, then every such proprietor shall and may, by and in a separate action upon the case, to be brought against the person offending in any Court of Law in *Great Britain* or *Ireland,* recover such damages as a jury on the trial of such action or on the execution of a writ of inquiry thereon shall give or assess, together with double costs of suit.

6 & 7 Wm. IV. c. 110. — An Act to repeal so much of an Act of the Fifty-fourth Year of King George the Third, respecting Copyrights, as requires the delivery of a copy of every published Book to the Library of Sion College, the Four Universities of Scotland, and of the King's Inns in Dublin.

6 & 7 Will. IV. c. 110.

54 G. III. c. 146.

WHEREAS by an act passed in the fifty-fourth year of the reign of his late Majesty King *George* the third, intituled *An Act to amend the several Acts for the encouragement of Learning by securing the Copies and Copyright of printed Books to the Authors of such Books or their Assigns*, it is amongst other things enacted, that eleven copies of every published book shall be gratuitously delivered to eleven public libraries named in the said act; and whereas the provisions of the said act have in certain respects operated to the injury of authors and publishers, and have in some cases checked or prevented the publication of works of great utility and importance, and it is therefore expedient that the said act should be amended: be it therefore enacted by the King's most excellent Majesty, by and with the advice and consent of the Lord's Spiritual and Temporal, and Commons, in this present Parliament assembled, and by the authority of the same, that so much of the said recited act as requires that a copy of every book which shall be printed and published shall be delivered in manner therein mentioned to the warehouse-keeper of the Company of Stationers for the use of the library of *Sion College*, the libraries of the four universities of *Scotland*, and the *King's Inns Library* at *Dublin*, shall be and the same is hereby repealed.

So much of recited act as requires the delivery of copies of books for the libraries herein mentioned repealed.

II. And be it further enacted, that it shall be lawful for the Lord High Treasurer or for the Commissioners of his Majesty's Treasury, or any three or more of them, from time to time to issue and pay out of the consolidated fund of the united kingdom of *Great Britain* and *Ireland*, to the person or persons or body politic or corporate, proprietors or managers of each of the aforesaid libra-

Compensation to be made to the said libraries out of consolidated fund.

6 & 7 Will. IV. c. 110.

ries, such an annual sum as may be equal in value to and a compensation for the loss which any such library may sustain by reason of the said act being repealed, so far as relates to such library; such annual compensation to be ascertained and determined according to the value of the books which may have been actually received by each such library, in such manner as the commissioners of his Majesty's treasury or any three or more of them shall direct, upon an average of the three years ending the thirtieth day of *June* one thousand eight hundred and thirty-six.

Application of the compensation.

III. And be it further enacted, that the person or persons or body politic or corporate, proprietors or managers of the library for the use whereof any such book would have been delivered, shall and they are hereby required to apply the annual compensation hereby authorized to be made in the purchase of books of literature, science, and the arts, for the use of and to be kept and preserved in such library; provided always, that it shall not be lawful for the said lord high treasurer or commissioners of his Majesty's treasury to direct the issue of any sum of money for such annual compensation until sufficient proof shall have been adduced before him or them of the application of the money last issued to the purpose aforesaid.

AMERICAN STATUTES.

I. An Act for the encouragement of learning, by securing the copies of maps, charts, and books, to the authors and proprietors of such copies, during the times therein mentioned.

Stat. May 31, 1790.

Repealed. Act of April 29, 1802, c. 36. Act of Feb. 15, 1819, c. 19. Act of Feb. 3, 1831, c. 16. June 30, 1834, c. 157.

Authors of maps, charts and books: and purchasers from them, to have the sole right of publication, &c. for 14 years; recording the title, &c.

SECTION 1. *Be it enacted by the Senate and House of Representatives of the United States of America in Congress assembled*, That from and after the passing of this act, the author and authors of any map, chart, book or books already printed within these United States, being a citizen or citizens thereof, or resident within the same, his or their executors, administrators or assigns, who hath or have not transferred to any other person the copyright of such map, chart, book or books, share or shares thereof; and any other person or persons, being a citizen or citizens of these United States, or residents therein, his or their executors, administrators or assigns, who hath or have purchased or legally acquired the copyright of any such map, chart, book or books, in order to print, reprint, publish or vend the same, shall have the sole right and liberty of printing, reprinting, publishing and vending such map, chart, book or books, for the term of fourteen years from the recording the title thereof in the clerk's office, as is herein after directed: And that the author and authors of any map, chart, book or books already made and composed, and not printed or published, or that shall hereafter be made and composed, being a citizen or citizens of these United States, or resident therein, and his or their executors, administrators or assigns, shall have the sole right and liberty of printing, reprinting, publishing and vending such map, chart, book or books,

Stat. May 31, 1790.

Also, if living at the end of that term, to have the further term of 14 years; recording the title, &c.

for the like term of fourteen years from the time of recording the title thereof in the clerk's office as aforesaid. And if, at the expiration of the said term, the author or authors, or any of them, be living, and a citizen or citizens of these United States, or resident therein, the same exclusive right shall be continued to him or them, his or their executors, administrators or assigns, for the further term of fourteen years: *Provided*, he or they shall cause the title thereof to be a second time recorded and published in the same manner as is herein after directed, and that within six months before the expiration of the first term of fourteen years aforesaid.

Other persons printing, &c. without consent of the author, how to be proceeded against and punished.

SEC. 2. *And be it further enacted*, That if any other person or persons, from and after the recording the title of any map, chart, book or books, and publishing the same as aforesaid, and within the times limited and granted by this act, shall print, reprint, publish, or import, or cause to be printed, reprinted, published, or imported from any foreign kingdom or state, any copy or copies of such map, chart, book or books, without the consent of the author or proprietor thereof, first had and obtained in writing, signed in the presence of two or more credible witnesses; or knowing the same to be so printed, reprinted, or imported, shall publish, sell, or expose to sale, or cause to be published, sold, or exposed to sale, any copy of such map, chart, book or books, without such consent first had and obtained in writing as aforesaid, then such offender or offenders shall forfeit all and every copy and copies of such map, chart, book or books, and all and every sheet and sheets, being part of the same, or either of them, to the author or proprietor of such map, chart, book or books, who shall forthwith destroy the same: And every such offender and offenders shall also forfeit and pay the sum of fifty cents for every sheet which shall be found in his or their possession, either printed or printing, published, imported or exposed to sale, contrary to the true intent and meaning of this act, the one moiety thereof to the author or proprietor of such map, chart, book or books who shall sue for the same, and the other moiety thereof to and for the use of the United States, to be recovered by action of debt in any court of record in the United States, wherein the same is cognizable. *Provided always*, That such action be commenced within one year after the cause of action shall arise, and not afterwards.

Stat. May 31, 1790.

1802, c. 36, sec. 3.

Conditions on which the benefit of this act shall be obtained.

SEC. 3. *And be it further enacted*, That no person shall be entitled to the benefit of this act, in cases where any map, chart, book or books, hath or have been already printed and published, unless he shall first deposit, and in all other cases, unless he shall before publication deposit a printed copy of the title of such map, chart, book or books, in the clerk's office of the district court where the author or proprietor shall reside: And the clerk of such court is hereby directed and required to record the same forthwith, in a book to be kept by him for that purpose, in the words following, (giving a copy thereof to the said author or proprietor, under the seal of the court, if he shall require the same.) "District of   to wit: *Be it remembered*, That on the   day of   in the   year of the independence of the United States of America, A. B. of the said district, hath deposited in this office the title of a map, chart, book or books, (as the case may be) the right whereof he claims as author or proprietor, (as the case may be) in the words following, to wit: [here insert the title] in conformity to the act of the Congress of the United States, intituled 'An act for the encouragement of learning, by securing the copies of maps, charts, and books, to the authors and proprietors of such copies, during the times therein mentioned.' C. D. clerk of the district of   ." For which the said clerk shall be entitled to receive sixty cents from the said author or proprietor, and sixty cents for every copy under seal actually given to such author or proprietor as aforesaid. And such author or proprietor shall, within two months from the date thereof, cause a copy of the said record to be published in one or more of the newspapers printed in the United States, for the space of four weeks.

1802, c. 36, sec. 1. 2.

Stat. May 31, 1790.

Authors to deliver a copy of their work to the Secretary of State.

SEC. 4. *And be it further enacted*, That the author or proprietor of any such map, chart, book or books, shall, within six months after the publishing thereof, deliver, or cause to be delivered to the Secretary of State a copy of the same, to be preserved in his office.

No prohibition against importing, reprinting, &c. of foreign writings or publications.

SEC. 5. *And be it further enacted*, That nothing in this act shall be construed to extend to prohibit the importation or vending, reprinting or publishing within the United States, of any map, chart, book or books, written, printed, or published by any person not a citizen of the United States, in foreign parts or places without the jurisdiction of the United States.

Penalty for publishing manuscripts without consent of the authors.

SEC. 6. *And be it further enacted*, That any person or persons who shall print or publish any manuscript, without the consent and approbation of the author or proprietor thereof, first had and obtained as aforesaid, (if such author or proprietor be a citizen of or resident in these United States) shall be liable to suffer and pay to the said author or proprietor all damages occasioned by such injury, to be recovered by a special action on the case founded upon this act, in any court having cognizance thereof.

Persons sued for any thing done under this act may give special matter in evidence.

SEC. 7. *And be it further enacted*, That if any person or persons shall be sued or prosecuted for any matter, act or thing done under or by virtue of this act, he or they may plead the general issue, and give the special matter in evidence.

Approved, May 31, 1790.

II. An Act supplementary to an act, intituled "An act for the encouragement of learning, by securing the copies of maps, charts, and books to the authors and proprietors of such copies during the times therein mentioned," and extending the benefits thereof to the arts of designing, engraving, and etching historical and other prints.

Stat. April 29, 1802.

[Repealed.] Additional requisites prescribed for persons claiming to be authors or proprietors of maps, charts, or books. 1790, c. 15.

Be it enacted by the Senate and House of Representatives of the United States of America in Congress assembled, That every person who shall, from and after the first day of January next, claim to be the author or proprietor of any maps, charts, book or books, and shall thereafter seek to obtain a copyright of the same agreeable to the rules prescribed by law, before he shall be entitled to the benefit of the act, entituled "An act for the encouragement of learning, by securing the copies of maps, charts, and books, to the authors and proprietors of such copies, during the time therein mentioned," he shall, in addition to the requisites enjoined in the third and fourth sections of said act, if a book or books, give information by causing the copy of the record, which, by said act he is required to publish in one or more of the newspapers, to be inserted at full length in the title-page or in the page immediately following the title of every such book or books; and if a map or chart, shall cause the following words to be impressed on the face thereof, viz: "*Entered according to act of Congress, the day of* 18 [here insert the date when the same was deposited in the office] *by A. B. of the state of* [here insert the author's or proprietor's name and the state in which he resides.]

Same rules prescribed with respect to persons who shall invent, and design, engrave, etch, or work historical or other prints.

Sec. 2. *And be it further enacted*, That from and after the first day of January next, every person being a citizen of the United States, or resident within the same, who shall invent and design, engrave, etch or work, or

Stat. April 29, 1802.

from his own works and inventions, shall cause to be designed and engraved, etched or worked, any historical or other print or prints, shall have the sole right and liberty of printing, re-printing, publishing and vending such print or prints, for the term of fourteen years from the recording the title thereof in the clerk's office, as prescribed by law for maps, charts, book or books: *Provided*, he shall perform all the requisites in relation to such print or prints, as are directed in relation to maps, charts, book or books, in the third and fourth sections of the act to which this is a supplement, and shall moreover cause the same entry to be duly engraved on such plate, with the name of the proprietor, and printed on every such print or prints as is herein before required to be made on maps or charts.

Penalties for engraving, etching or working, or copying and selling a print or prints, without the consent of the owner or owners, in writing. 4 Wash. C. C. R. 48.

Sec. 3. *And be it further enacted*, That if any printseller or other person whatsoever, from and after the said first day of January next, within the time limited by this act, shall engrave, etch or work, as aforesaid, or in any other manner copy or sell, or cause to be engraved, etched, copied or sold, in the whole or in part, by varying, adding to, or diminishing from the main design, or shall print, re-print, or import for sale, or cause to be printed, reprinted, or imported for sale, any such print or prints, or any parts thereof, without the consent of the proprietor or proprietors thereof, first had and obtained, in writing, signed by him or them respectively, in the presence of two or more eredible witnesses; or knowing the same to be so printed or re-printed, without the consent of tne proprietor or proprietors, shall publish, sell, or expose to sale or otherwise, or in any other manner dispose of any such print or prints, without such consent first had and obtained, as aforesaid, then such offender or offenders shall forfeit the plate or plates on which such print or prints are or shall be copied, and all and every sheet or sheets (being part of or whereon such print or prints are or shall be copied or printed) to the proprietor or proprietors of such original print or prints, who shall forthwith destroy the same; and further, that every such offender or offenders shall forfeit one dollar for every print which shall be found in his, her, or their custody; either printed, published, or exposed to sale, or otherwise disposed of, contrary to the true intent and meaning of this act, the one moiety thereof to any person who shall sue for the same, and the other moiety thereof to and for the use of the United States, to be recovered in any court having competent jurisdiction thereof.

Stat. April 29, 1802.

A moiety of the forfeiture to any one who shall sue for the same.

SEC. 4. *And be it further enacted*, That if any person or persons from and after the passing of this act, shall print or publish any map, chart, book or books, print or prints, who have not legally acquired the copyright of such map, chart, book or books, print or prints, and shall, contrary to the true intent and meaning of this act, insert therein or impress thereon that the same has been entered according to act of Congress, or words purporting the same, or purporting that the copyright thereof has been acquired; every person so offending shall forfeit and pay the sum of one hundred dollars, one moiety thereof to the person who shall sue for the same, and the other moiety thereof to and for the use of the United States, to be recovered by action of debt in any court of record in the United States, having cognizance thereof. *Provided always*, that in every case for forfeitures herein before given, the action be commenced within two years from the time the cause of action may have arisen.

Penalties for publishing maps, charts, books or prints, but in the way prescribed by law.

Limitation of action in cases of forfeiture.

Approved, April 29, 1802.

III. An Act to extend the jurisdiction of the circuit courts of the United States to cases arising under the law relating to patents.

Stat. Feb. 15, 1819.

The circuit courts to have original cognizance, in equity and at law, in controversies respecting the right to inventions and writings.

Act of Feb. 21, 1793, c. 11.

Act of May 31, 1790, c. 15.

Be it enacted by the Senate and House of Representatives of the United States of America, in Congress assembled, That the circuit courts of the United States shall have original cognizance, as well in equity as at law, of all actions, suits, controversies, and cases arising under any law of the United States, granting or confirming to authors or inventors the exclusive right to their respective writings, inventions, and discoveries: and upon any bill in equity, filed by any party aggrieved in any such cases, shall have authority to grant injunctions, according to the course and principles of courts of equity, to prevent the violation of the rights of any authors or inventors, secured to them by any laws of the United States, on such terms and conditions as the said courts may deem fit and reasonable:

Proviso.

Provided, however, That from all judgments and decrees of any circuit courts, rendered in the premises, a writ of error or appeal, as the case may require, shall lie to the Supreme Court of the United States, in the same manner, and under the same circumstances, as is now provided by law in other judgments and decrees of such circuit courts.

Approved, February 15, 1819.

An Act to amend the several acts respecting copy-rights.

Stat. Feb. 3, 1831.

Be it enacted by the Senate and House of Representatives of the United States of America, in Congress assembled, That from and after the passing of this act, any person or persons, being a citizen or citizens of the United States, or resident therein, who shall be the author or authors of any book or books, map, chart, or musical composition, which may be now made or composed, and not printed and published, or shall hereafter be made or composed, or who shall invent, design, etch, engrave, work, or cause to be engraved, etched, or worked from his own design, any print or engraving, and the executors, administrators, or legal assigns of such person or persons, shall have the sole right and liberty of printing, reprinting, publishing, and vending such book or books, map, chart, musical composition, print, cut, or engraving, in whole or in part, for the term of twenty-eight years from the time of recording the title thereof, in the manner hereinafter directed.

Authors of books, &c. and their executors, &c. to have sole right for twenty-eight years.

SEC. 2. *And be it further enacted*, That if, at the expiration of the aforesaid term of years, such author, inventor, designer, engraver, or any of them, where the work had been originally composed and made by more than one person, be still living, and a citizen or citizens of the United States, or resident therein, or being dead, shall have left a widow, or child, or children, either or all then living, the same exclusive right shall be continued to such author, designer, or engraver, or, if dead, then to such widow and child, or children, for the further term of fourteen years: *Provided*, That the title of the work so secured shall be a second time recorded, and all such other regulations as are herein required in regard to original copyrights, be complied with in respect to such renewed copyright, and that within six months before the expiration of the first term.

Renewal of privilege for fourteen years.

Conditions.

Stat. Feb. 3, 1831.

Publication of renewal.

Sec. 3. *And be it further enacted,* That in all cases of renewal of copyright under this act, such author or proprietor shall, within two months from the date of said renewal, cause a copy of the record thereof to be published in one or more of the newspapers printed in the United States, for the space of four weeks.

Copy of title to be deposited.

Sec. 4. *And be it further enacted,* That no person shall be entitled to the benefit of this act, unless he shall, before publication, deposit a printed copy of the title of such book, or books, map, chart, musical composition, print, cut, or engraving, in the clerk's office of the district court of the district wherein the author or proprietor shall reside, and the clerk of such court is hereby directed and required to record the same thereof forthwith, in a book to be kept for that purpose, in the words following (giving a copy of the title, under the seal of the court, to the said author or proprietor, whenever he shall require the same:) "District of to wit: Be it remembered, that on the day of anno domini, A. B., of the said district, hath deposited in this office the title of a book, (map, chart, or otherwise, as the case may be,) the title of which is in the words following, to wit: (here insert the title;) the right whereof he claims as author (or proprietor as the case may be;) in conformity with an act of Congress, entitled 'An act to amend the several acts respecting copyrights.' C. D. clerk of the district." For which record, the clerk shall be entitled to receive, from the person claiming such right as aforesaid, fifty cents; and the like sum for every copy, under seal, actually given to such person or his assigns. And the author or proprietor of any such book, map, chart, musical composition, print, cut, or engraving, shall, within three months from the publication of said book, map, chart, musical composition, print, cut, or engraving, deliver or cause to be delivered a copy of the same to the clerk of said district. And it shall be the duty of the clerk of each district court, at least once in every year, to transmit a certified list of all such records of copyright, including the titles so recorded, and the dates of

To be recorded.

Form of record.

Fee.

Copy of work to be deposited.

List of works and copies to be transmitted to the Secretary of State.

record, and also all the several copies of books or other works deposited in his office according to this act, to the Secretary of State, to be preserved in his office.

Stat. Feb. 3, 1831.

Notice of copyright to be printed, &c.

SEC. 5. *And be it further enacted*, That no person shall be entitled to the benefit of this act, unless he shall give information of copyright being secured, by causing to be inserted in the several copies of each and every edition published during the term secured on the title-page, or the page immediately following, if it be a book, or, if a map, chart, musical composition, print, cut, or engraving, by causing to be impressed on the face thereof, or if a volume of maps, charts, music, or engravings, upon the title or frontispiece thereof, the following words, viz: "Entered according to act of Congress, in the year , by A. B., in the clerk's office of the district court of ," (as the case may be.)

Infringement of copyright to books.

SEC. 6. *And be it further enacted*, That if any other person or persons, from and after the recording the title of any book or books, according to this act, shall, within the term or terms herein limited, print, publish, or import, or cause to be printed, published, or imported, any copy of such book, or books, without the consent of the person legally entitled to the copyright thereof, first had and obtained in writing, signed in presence of two or more credible witnesses, or shall, knowing the same to be so printed or imported, publish, sell, or expose to sale, or cause to be published, sold, or exposed to sale, any copy of such book without such consent in writing; then such offender shall forfeit every copy of such book to the person legally, at the time, entitled to the copyright thereof; and shall also forfeit and pay fifty cents for every such sheet which may be found in his possession, either printed, or printing, published, imported, or exposed to sale, contrary to the intent of this act, the one moiety thereof to such legal owner of the copyright as aforesaid, and the other to the use of the United States, to be recovered by action of debt in any court having competent jurisdiction thereof.

Penalty.

SEC. 7. *And be it further enacted*, That, if any person

Stat. Feb. 3, 1831.

Infringement of copyright to prints, maps, &c.

or persons, after the recording the title of any print, cut, or engraving, map, chart, or musical composition, according to the provisions of this act, shall, within the term or terms limited by this act, engrave, etch, or work, sell, or copy, or cause to be engraved, etched, worked, or sold, or copied, either on the whole, or by varying, adding to, or diminishing the main design with intent to evade the law; or shall print or import for sale, or cause to be printed, or imported for sale, any such map, chart, musical composition, print, cut or engraving, or any parts thereof, without the consent of the proprietor or proprietors of the copyright thereof, first obtained in writing, signed in the presence of two credible witnesses; or, knowing the same to be so printed or imported without such consent, shall publish, sell, or expose to sale, or in any manner dispose of any such map, chart, musical composition, engraving, cut, or print, without such consent, as aforesaid; then such offender or offenders shall forfeit the plate or plates on which such map, chart, musical composition, engraving, cut, or print, shall be copied, and also all and every sheet thereof so copied or printed as aforesaid, to the proprietor or proprietors of the copyright thereof; and shall further forfeit one dollar for every sheet of such map, chart, musical composition, print, cut, or engraving, which may be found in his or their possession, printed or published, or exposed to sale, contrary to the true intent and meaning of this act; the one moiety thereof to the proprietor or proprietors, and the other moiety to the use of the United States, to be recovered in any court having competent jurisdiction thereof.

Penalty.

Privilege restricted to citizens or residents.

Sec. 8. *And be it further enacted*, That nothing in this act shall be construed to extend to prohibit the importation or vending, printing, or publishing, of any map, chart, book, musical composition, print or engraving, written, composed, or made, by any person not being a citizen of the United States, nor resident within the jurisdiction thereof.

Sec. 9. *And be it further enacted*, That any person or

Stat. II. Feb. 3, 1831.

persons who shall print or publish any manuscript whatever without the consent of the author or legal proprietor first obtained as aforesaid, (if such author or proprietor be a citizen of the United States, or resident therein,) shall be liable to suffer and pay to the author or proprietor, all damages occasioned by such injury, to be recovered by a special action on the case founded upon this act, in any court having cognizance thereof; and the several courts of the United States empowered to grant injunctions to prevent the violation of the rights of authors and inventors, are hereby empowered to grant injunctions, in like manner, according to the principles of equity, to restrain such publication of any manuscript as aforesaid.

Publication of manuscripts without consent, &c. Remedy.

Injunction to prevent.

SEC. 10. *And be it further enacted*, That, if any person or persons shall be sued or prosecuted, for any matter, act, or thing done under or by virtue of this act, he or they may plead the general issue and give the special matter in evidence.

General issue, &c.

SEC. 11. *And be it further enacted*, That, if any person or persons, from and after the passing of this act, shall print or publish any book, map, chart, musical composition, print, cut, or engraving, not having legally acquired the copyright thereof, and shall insert or impress that the same hath been entered according to act of Congress, or words purporting the same, every person so offending shall forfeit and pay one hundred dollars: one moiety thereof to the person who shall sue for the same, and the other to the use of the United States, to be recovered by action of debt, in any court of record having cognizance thereof.

False entry of copyright.

Penalty.

SEC. 12. *And be it further enacted*, That, in all recoveries under this act, either for damages, forfeitures, or penalties, full costs shall be allowed thereon, any thing in any former act to the contrary notwithstanding.

Costs.

SEC. 13. *And be it further enacted*, That no action or prosecution shall be maintained, in any case of forfeiture or penalty under this act, unless the same shall have been

Limitation of action.

Stat. II. Feb. 3, 1831.

commenced within two years after the cause of action shall have arisen.

Repeal of act of May 31, 1790, c. 15.

Act of April 29, 1802, c. 36.

SEC. 14. *And be it further enacted*, That the "Act for the encouragement of learning, by securing the copies of maps, charts, and books, to the authors and proprietors of such copies during the times therein mentioned," passed May thirty-first, one thousand seven hundred and ninety, and the act supplementary thereto, passed April twenty-ninth, one thousand eight hundred and two, shall be, and the same are hereby, repealed: saving, always, such rights as may have been obtained in conformity to their provisions.

Provisions of this act for security of copy-rights, &c. to extend to existing copyrights.

SEC. 15. *And be it further enacted*, That all and several the provisions of this act, intended for the protection and security of copyrights, and providing remedies, penalties, and forfeitures, in case of violation thereof, shall be held and construed to extend to the benefit of the legal proprietor or proprietors of each and every copyright heretofore obtained, according to law, during the term thereof, in the same manner as if such copyright had been entered and secured according to the directions of this act.

Extension of existing copyrights,

SEC. 16. *And be it further enacted*, That, whenever a copyright has been heretofore obtained by an author or authors, inventor, designer, or engraver, of any book, map, chart, print, cut, or engraving, or by a proprietor of the same: if such author or authors, or either of them, such inventor, designer, or engraver, be living at the passage of this act, then such author or authors, or the survivor of them, such inventor, engraver, or designer, shall continue to have the same exclusive right to his book, chart, map, print, cut, or engraving, with the benefit of each and all the provisions of this act, for the security thereof, for such additional period of time as will, together with the time which shall have elapsed from the first entry of such copyright, make up the term of twenty-eight years, with the same right to his widow, child, or children, to renew the copyright, at the expiration thereof, as is above provided in relation to copyrights originally secured under this act. And if such author or authors, inventor, designer, or engraver, shall not be living at the passage of this act, then, his or their heirs, executors and administrators, shall be entitled to the like exclusive enjoyment of said copyright, with the benefit of each and all the provisions of this act for the security thereof, for the period of twenty-eight years from the first entry of said copyright, with the like privilege of renewal to the widow, child, or children, of author or authors, designer, inventor, or engraver, as is provided in relation to copyrights originally secured under this act: *Provided*, That this act shall not extend to any copyright heretofore secured, the term of which has already expired.

Stat. II. Feb. 3, 1831.

Proviso.

Approved, February 3, 1831.

An Act supplementary to the act to amend the several acts respecting copyrights.

Stat. 1. June 30, 1834.

Deeds of transfer to be recorded, &c.

Be it enacted by the Senate and House of Representatives of the United States of America in Congress assembled, That all deeds or instruments in writing for the t ansfer or assignment of copyrights, being proved or acknowledged in such manner as deeds for the conveyance of land are required by law to be proved or acknowledged in the same state or district, shall and may be recorded in the office where the original copyright is deposited and recorded; and every such deed or instrument that shall in any time hereafter be made and executed, and which shall not be proved or acknowledged and recorded as aforesaid, within sixty days after its execution, shall be judged fraudulent and void against any subsequent purchaser or mortgagee for valuable consideration without notice.

Fees of clerk of district court.

SEC. 2. *And be it further enacted*, That the clerk of the district court shall be entitled to such fees fcr performing the services herein authorized and required, as he is entitled to for performing like services under existing laws of the United States.

Approved, June 30, 1834.

An Act in addition to an act to promote the progress of the useful arts, and to repeal all acts and parts of acts heretofore made for that purpose.

SEC. 3. *Be it further enacted*, That any citizen or citizens, or alien or aliens, having resided one year in the United States and taken the oath of his or their intention to become a citizen or citizens, who by his, her, or their own industry, genius, efforts, and expense, may have invented or produced any new and original design for a manufacture, whether of metal or other material or materials, or any new and original design for the printing of woollen, silk, cotton, or other fabrics, or any new and original design for a bust, statue, or bas relief or composition in alto or basso relievo, or any new and original impression or ornament, or to be placed on any article of manufacture, the same being formed in marble or other material, or any new and useful pattern, or print, or picture, to be either worked into or worked on, or printed or painted or cast or otherwise fixed on, any article of manufacture, or any new and original shape or configuration of any article of manufacture not known or used by others, before his, her or their invention or production thereof, and prior to the time of his, her, or their application for a patent therefor, and who shall desire to obtain an exclusive property or right therein to make, and use, and sell and vend the same, or copies of the same, to others, by them to be made, used, and sold, may make application in writing to the commissioner of patents, expressing such desire, and the commissioner, on due proceedings had, may grant a patent therefor, as in the case now of application for a patent. *Provided*, That the fee in such cases which by the now existing laws would be required of the particular applicant shall be one half the sum, and that the duration of said patent shall be seven years, and that all the regulations and provisions which

Stat. II. Aug. 29, 1842.

Citizens, &c. may obtain a patent, how.

Proviso.

Stat. II. Aug. 29, 1842.

now apply to the obtaining or protection of patents not inconsistent with the provisions of this act, shall apply to applications under this section.

Oath may be taken before U. S. ministers, &c.

SEC. 4. *And be it further enacted*, That the oath required for applicants for patents may be taken, when the applicant is not, for the time being, residing in the United States, before any minister, plenipotentiary, chargé d'affaires, consul, or commercial agent holding commission under the government of the United States, or before any notary public of the foreign country in which such applicant may be.

Penalty for infringing the rights of a patentee, &c. by marking.

SEC. 5. *And be it further enacted*, That if any person or persons shall paint or print, or mould, cast, carve, or engrave, or stamp, upon anything made, used, or sold, by him, for the sole making or selling which he hath not or shall not have obtained letters patent, the name or any imitation of the name of any other person who hath or shall have obtained letters patent for the sole making and vending of such thing, without consent of such patentee, or his assigns or legal representatives; or if any person, upon any such thing not having been purchased, from the patentee, or some person who purchased it from or under such patentee, or not having the license or consent of such patentee, or his assigns or legal representatives, shall write, paint, print, mould, cast, carve, engrave, stamp, or otherwise make or affix the word "patent," or the words "letters patent," or the word "patentee," or any word or words of like kind, meaning, or import, with the view or intent of imitating or counterfeiting the stamp, mark, or other device of the patentee, or shall affix the same or any word, stamp, or device, of like import, on any unpatented article, for the purpose of deceiving the public, he, she, or they, so offending, shall be liable for such offence, to a penalty of not less than one hundred dollars, with costs, to be recovered by action in any of the circuit courts of the United States, or in any of the district courts of the United States, having the powers and jurisdiction of a circuit court; one half of which

How recoverable, &c.

penalty, as recovered, shall be paid to the patent fund, and the other half to any person or persons who shall sue for the same.

Stat. II. Aug. 29, 1842.

Sec. 6. *And be it further enacted*, That all patentees and assignees of patents hereafter granted, are hereby required to stamp, engrave, or cause to be stamped or engraved, on each article vended, or offered for sale, the date of the patent; and if any person or persons, patentees or assignees, shall neglect to do so, he, she, or they, shall be liable to the same penalty, to be recovered and disposed of in the manner specified in the foregoing fifth section of this act.

Patentees, &c. required to mark articles offered for sale.

Penalty for neglect.

Approved, August 29, 1842.

INDEX.

A.

D.

P.

Q.

R.

S.